Reasoning
and
Writing

Reasoning and Writing

KATHLEEN DEAN MOORE

Oregon State University

Macmillan Publishing Company

New York

Maxwell Macmillan Canada

Toronto

Editor: Maggie Barbieri
Production Supervisor: Kathy Riley-King/ Spectrum Publisher Services, Inc.
Production Manager: Linda Greenberg
Cover Designer: Thomas Mack
Cover Illustration: Marc Lincewicz

This book was set in Perpetua by Carlisle Communications Ltd. and was printed and bound by
R. R. Donnelley & Sons Company. The cover was printed by Phoenix Color Corp.

Macmillan Publishing Company
866 Third Avenue, New York, New York 10022

Macmillan Publishing Company is part of
the Maxwell Communication Group of Companies.

Maxwell Macmillan Canada, Inc.
1200 Eglinton Avenue East
Suite 200
Don Mills, Ontario M3C 3N1

Library of Congress Cataloging-in-Publication Data

Moore, Kathleen Dean.
        Reasoning and writing / Kathleen Dean Moore.
            p.   cm.
        Includes bibliographical references.
        ISBN 0-02-383325-4
        1. English language—Rhetoric.   2. Reasoning.   I. Title.
PE1408.M654   1993   92-20965
808′ .042 —dc20   CIP

Printing: 1 2 3 4 5 6 7   Year: 3 4 5 6 7 8 9

Excerpt from Modern Chemistry by Nicholas Tzimopoulos, copyright © 1990 by
Saunders College Publishing, reprinted by permission of the publisher.

To Frank,
with love and gratitude.

Preface

For fifteen years, my goal has been to teach students to do a better job of thinking. Sometimes, the task overwhelms me. Sometimes, I think the goal may be attainable. And, sometimes, I believe I succeed, that students come away from class changed—thinking more clearly and more effectively, energized and empowered by the ability to make ideas work for them.

This textbook was written to help professors succeed in their own efforts to empower their students by teaching them how to think critically and creatively. I wrote the book because I thought other professors would want a textbook that put together the pedagogical elements that have worked in my classrooms:

- A synthesis of reasoning and writing skills
- An adventuresome, active learning experience for students, with an abundance of activities and assignments that draw on students' interests and resources
- An applied, immediately useful approach to critical thinking
- Examples and explanations that include women and minorities in the intellectual venture
- A ready-made course, complete with clear explanations, class activities, homework assignments, and (in the Instructor's Manual and on computer disk) answer keys and exams

A Synthesis of Reasoning and Writing Skills

This textbook brings together the skills of reasoning and writing in hopes of improving both. It teaches critical thinking skills that improve student writing, and it uses writing exercises to improve students' critical thinking skills. Thus, it can be used as a complete textbook for a writing-intensive critical thinking class or as a supplementary textbook for an introductory composition class.

The traditional separation of reasoning and writing into different departments and different courses is one of the more preposterous results of the organization of the modern university. Critical thinking, a branch of logic, has traditionally been claimed and defended by philosophy departments. Writing, like all composition, has been the exclusive property of English departments. The resulting artificial fragmentation of learning has made it difficult for students to learn to think *or* write critically and effectively.

This book is part of a nationwide effort to bring reasoning and writing together. Realizing that clarity and elegance in writing depend utterly on clarity and elegance of thought, composition teachers are turning to critical thinking teachers for ways to improve their students' prose by improving their reasoning. Meanwhile, critical thinking teachers are turning to composition teachers for ideas about how to use writing assignments in their classes. This book should help both critical thinking and composition teachers.

An Active Learning Experience

The primary pedagogical presupposition of this text is that active participation by students is a necessary condition for learning. Writing and reasoning are activities—things people do. Whether they are done well or poorly depends in large part on practice. One can no more teach writing and reasoning through a series of lectures than one can teach bicycle riding through an illustrated lecture on the bicycle.

So, the heart of this text consists of hundreds of challenging, instructive, and rewarding exercises, opportunities for students to participate actively in their own education. There are "hands-on" exercises, writing-intensive assignments, examples, experiments, activities, essays, games, and projects, to be done individually and cooperatively, in pairs and in groups, at home and in class. The ideas in the book can be used in both small and large classes and can be evaluated efficiently.

A second pedagogical presupposition is that learning must begin where the students are. That is, the more connected the material is to the students' own experiences, the more readily will they integrate it into their lives. For this reason, the examples and activities are carefully chosen to interest students and to refer to their own experiences. They come from writers of various races, both sexes, and many eras. Many examples are from splendid writers, who set a high standard of clarity and beauty in prose.

Many examples are controversial. Because I believe that reasoning well is most important when emotions are most intense, I have not tried to avoid controversy. But I have tried hard to include a variety of points of view—to be, so to speak, impartially controversial.

An Applied Approach to Critical Thinking

This textbook is designed to help students acquire a set of immediately applicable and widely useful intellectual skills and values. The California State University System defined the goals of a critical thinking course this way:

> [I]nstruction in Critical Thinking is . . . designed to achieve an understanding of the relationship of language to logic, which should lead to the ability to (1) analyze, (2) criticize, and (3) advocate ideas, (4) to reason inductively and deductively, and (5) to reach factual or judgmental conclusions based on sound inferences drawn from unambiguous statements of knowledge or belief. (Executive Order 338)

This kind of understanding and these skills can immediately be put to work in the classroom, in the workplace, and in the wider marketplace of ideas, the domain of the citizen. Through its explanations and its exercises, this textbook shows students how to use critical thinking effectively and, at the same time, honorably. Just as the need for critical thinking skills never ends, the usefulness of *Reasoning and Writing* extends beyond a particular course. Many students may keep the text as a reference book, using it throughout college and after graduation.

Inclusive Examples and Exercises

For too long, logic was an exclusive domain, its textbooks cloaked in manly brown tweed, its examples making reference to a primarily Western world. This textbook invites all kinds of people into the intellectual undertaking. To this end, its language is inclusive; instead of using *he* to refer to both men and women, the text alternates between *he* and *she*. Students may be startled when a judge or murderer or professor is referred to as *she*, but recognizing one's presuppositions about gender is part of critical thinking. In addition, the examples in the textbook are drawn from a wide variety of cultures, and the exercises give students a chance to make the connection between their own lives and the world of critical thinking.

Even in its pedagogy, the textbook tries to make students welcome. Many, perhaps most, of the activities are designed to be done *cooperatively,* in small groups. Thus, the activities draw students into the social fabric, as well as the intellectual weave, of the course. Some of the activities draw on the special expertise of international or traditionally marginalized students, enriching the understanding of all the students in the class. Critical thinking skills are intellectual skills, but they are also social and political skills; the activities help make this connection and, in the process, help connect the students to each other.

A Ready-made Course

All the elements for a complete course are here. There are clear and complete *explanations* of standard critical thinking concepts and skills, following an agenda originally created by logician Irving Copi, and enriched and informed by concepts and skills of effective writing. The organization of the book is from simple to complex. The first part teaches students to recognize, analyze, and write arguments. The second part introduces students to a whole repertoire of argument forms, deductive and inductive. The third part invites the students to write clear and honorable arguments and effective refutations. Together, the parts form a semester-long course. Alternatively, any chapter can stand alone as a supplement to another course of study. Thus, composition teachers might, for example, use the sections on clear and honorable argumentation as a supplementary unit in their classes.

The book is full of *activities* that students can do in class; many of these are writing projects. Because the pedagogical techniques of writing-intensive courses are new to many of us, complete directions are included in every exercise, and the Instructor's Manual gives lots of advice to help professors make effective, efficient use of the activities and exercises.

There are homework *assignments* of all sorts, from the most traditional identification/analysis exercises to the most adventuresome. The Instructor's Manual includes answer keys to all the homework assignments. The Instructor's Manual also includes *exams* for each chapter, answer keys, study guides, and suggestions for efficient grading. All the assignments, exams, answer keys, and study guides are available on computer disk, so they can be easily adapted and duplicated for classroom use.

Welcome, colleagues, to *Reasoning and Writing.* I hope you have a good time.

....

Acknowledgments

In this book project, as in all my professional life, I have the great good fortune of being part of a community of scholars. I am grateful for the assistance and the richness of ideas that have come from all these people, working together and apart.

Many of the ideas presented here evolved in Oregon State University's critical thinking program, an undertaking that, at its peak, included 2,000 students a year, five professors, a secretary, and three clerks. To this team should go much of the credit for what is helpful and original in this book. So, I would like first to acknowledge my debt to my colleagues in the critical thinking program of the Philosophy Department: Jon Dorbolo, Flora Leibowitz, Lani Roberts, Michael Scanlan, and William Uzgalis. Thanks go also to the thousands of students who served as subjects in our pedagogical experiments. This book's approach grew from heated and repeated discussions and dramatic successes and failures, over many years of team teaching. I have tried to acknowledge individual authorship where I could. But I would like to thank my colleagues also for ideas and refinements that grew anonymously and collectively from the intellectual critical mass gathered at Oregon State University.

Professors Lisa Ede and Lex Runciman, of Oregon State University's Center for Writing and Learning, introduced me—and all the OSU community—to the concept and techniques of writing-intensive courses. Professor Ede was my mentor when I taught my first writing-intensive class; she was an inspired and supportive problem solver and source of ideas. Lex Runciman, Director of OSU's Writing-Intensive Curriculum, taught work-

xi

shops and sponsored speakers, providing many suggestions for how to use writing in every kind of class. The excitement and effectiveness of their ideas inspired this book.

Jon Dorbolo, Erin Moore, Frank Moore, Lex Runciman, and Michael Scanlan read first drafts of parts of the manuscript and made suggestions that were invariably helpful. Jon Dorbolo and Amy Gibson field-tested the manuscript with students at Oregon State and at Lewis and Clark College; they shared a wealth of ideas for improvements. Erin Moore wrote the Glossary. Lois Summers typed the final manuscript. Katy Rivers and Kari Dooley helped with research. I am grateful for the willingness of all these people to share those two most valuable commodities—time and expertise.

My family—Frank, Erin, and Jonathan—are my strength and my inspiration. Thank you, all of you, for being with me on this latest Grand Expedition.

K.D.M.

Contents

·······················

Table of Exercises

PART I

GIVING REASONS TO SUPPORT CLAIMS

SUMMARY OF PART ONE

To reason is to make a decision about what to believe or to do, on the basis of evidence about what is true or what is wise. To reason with someone is to try to influence a person's beliefs or behavior by giving the person good reasons for preferring one belief to another or for choosing one course of action over another. Thus, reasoning can be distinguished from other kinds of activities such as bullying or seducing or deceiving by its commitment to reasoned discourse and to a set of intellectual virtues that includes honesty, open-mindedness, flexibility, and objectivity.

The basic unit of reasoning is the argument. An argument is a claim put forward and defended with reasons. A deep understanding of an argument comes through analysis, the art of breaking an argument into its constituent parts in order to examine how the parts relate to one another.

Reasoning well is a skill that is closely connected to writing well. Skill in reasoning is a necessary condition for clear and effective writing. Writing often and thoughtfully is, in its turn, helpful in the development of reasoning skills. Part I introduces the concept of argument and the skills of logical analysis and puts them to work in the service of writing well.

CHAPTER 1

Understanding Arguments

To reason is to think in a particular way, to make a decision about what is true or what is wise, based on information. In addition, to reason is to speak or write in a particular way, to use evidence in an attempt to convince someone else about what is true or wise. Or, as Webster's Dictionary puts it:

> **reason** *v* **1:** To use one's powers of rational thought so as to arrive at conclusions based on evidence. **2:** To talk or write persuasively so as to influence, modify, or change another person's actions or opinions.[1]

• • • • • • • • • • • The Functions of Reasoning • • • • • • • • • • •

Developing strong reasoning skills and the determination to use those skills in appropriate ways is important to the development of trustworthy knowledge, reliable judgments, and effective and honorable persuasion.

Done well, reasoning has the power to transform belief into knowledge. What is the difference between believing something and knowing it? Suppose a murder has been committed in a small college town. The district attorney announces that she knows who did it—a drifter named Monroe. What is the D.A. claiming about herself? She is not saying that she simply has a hunch about the identity of the murderer. If she were convinced of the truth of her hunch but had no grounds for it, she would claim merely to believe that Monroe was the murderer. But what if she is right? What if Monroe is the murderer and the D.A. believes he is? Is knowledge the same as true belief? No, because, without any grounds for her belief, the D.A. may simply have made a lucky guess. The D.A. really knows that Monroe is the murderer only after she has collected very strong evidence, such as bullets, fingerprints, and confessions. The D.A. really knows that Monroe is the murderer only when she believes that he is, and he really is, and she has good reason to believe that he is. Thus, it is reasoning—building up evidence, facts, and reasons to support a claim—that transforms belief into knowledge.

Moreover, reasoning has the power to transform mere opinion into reasoned judgment. Suppose that Mr. Monroe confesses to the killing but says he should not be punished because he was under the insane delusion that the victim was trying to kill him with death rays. Some people in the community think the insanity plea is misguided, and others think it is morally correct: "I don't think we should jail him if he's insane; that's just what I think—always have, always will." This is merely an opinion if the claim is made but not defended. It becomes a reasoned judgment when the claim is supported by good reasons: "I don't think we should jail him if he's insane. In our society, we punish only people whom we can blame. And, if he really was insane, he couldn't help but kill the victim. You can't blame somebody for something they couldn't help but do." Again, it is reasoning—providing reasons to support a claim—that transforms mere opinion into reasoned judgment.

Finally, reasoning makes the difference between indoctrination and rational persuasion. Consider two attorneys. The prosecuting attorney tries to make the jury believe that Monroe is the killer but offers no reasons at all or only reasons that are irrelevant: "Look at Monroe. Doesn't he look like a killer? Don't you worry about the safety of your children? You should find Monroe guilty." The jury is being asked to accept a claim without evidence; this is indoctrination or propagandizing, a kind of intellectual bullying. The defense attorney, on the other hand, tries to make the jury believe that Monroe is not the killer by presenting them with evidence that builds a case for his innocence. Since it is based on reasons, this is rational persuasion. So, it is reasoning—using evidence to influence a person's opinions or actions—that transforms indoctrination into persuasion.

• •

1.1 THE STADIUM MURDER

Read the account below, and write your reaction. Write quickly. Don't plan, just write. If you need a way to start, begin with "Reading this makes me . . ." Finish that sentence, and continue writing until your instructor tells you to stop. Save this freewrite[2] for later.

JURY SELECTION SLATED FOR AUTZEN SNIPER CASE

By Dana Tims
Correspondent, *The Oregonian*

EUGENE—Jury selection is scheduled to get under way Thursday in a lawsuit filed by the wife of a former Olympic sprinter who was killed by a sniper's bullet two years ago near Autzen Stadium.

Sharon Brathwaite is seeking $1.75 million in damages from Anderson's Sporting Goods of Eugene stemming from allegations that inadequate security at the store allowed the theft of guns that were later used to kill Christopher Brathwaite.

Brathwaite, 36, a former two-time Olympic sprinter from Trinidad, died while jogging on a trail near Autzen Stadium, Nov. 12, 1984, as a result of a shot fired by Michael Evan Feher. Feher, who was 19 at the time, fired 67 bullets in and around the stadium during a 60-minute spree before killing himself shortly after 9:00 A.M. . . .

Brathwaite's lawsuit contends that the sporting goods store owner was negligent in failing to provide adequate security measures on the premises. . . .

Brathwaite's lawsuit claims the guns were not kept in locked cabinets and that the firing pins were left in the weapons. . . .[3]

· ·

· · · · · · · · · · · · · · **Reasoning and Writing** · · · · · · · · · · · · · · ·

Developing strong reasoning skills and the determination to use them is important also to clear and effective writing. Writing is externalized thought,[4] ideas put down on paper. It follows that the quality of the reasoning is directly reflected in the quality of the writing. With the possible exception of those who are divinely inspired, it is highly unlikely that a person who cannot think clearly will be able to write clearly. Conversely, knowing how to reason effectively makes it easier to write well. *Rem tene; verba sequentur,* said Cato the Elder: "Hold fast to the idea; the words will follow." Good reasoning improves writing; this much is no surprise.

What is not so widely recognized is the extent to which writing improves reasoning. In many different ways, people use writing to make the reasoning process easier and more effective. Read the following problem aloud to friends, and ask them to solve it; their reasoning process will, more than likely, involve a pencil.

> Everybody lies to somebody. If Carol lies at all, she lies to David. David does not lie to many people, and Carol is one of those to whom he does not lie. Does it follow that Carol lies to David?[5]

What are some of the ways writing makes it easier to solve this problem? The most straightforward service rendered by the pencil is to help the memory; only an unusual person could remember this list of statements without making some notes. Writing down ideas also helps to clarify abstract ideas and relationships because it puts abstractions in a form you can see and manipulate. Increasingly, writing is used throughout universities in the service of reasoning: to brainstorm ideas, to clarify questions, to organize ideas, to reinforce understanding, to try out a line of thought.[6]

But writing is not only an aid to reasoning; in one sense, writing *is* reasoning. When you use reasons to "influence, modify, or change another person's actions or opinions," you must make your reasoning public, often by writing it down. Interoffice memos, letters to the editor, position papers, and scientific articles, when they make a claim and defend it with reasons, are written forms of reasoning.

In this book, the skills of reasoning and writing come together. You will learn a set of reasoning strategies for using evidence reliably and persuasively in a variety of contexts, and you will learn how to use those strategies to write clear and effective argumentative prose.

•••••••••••••   Argument in Reasoning   •••••••••••••

The basic unit of reasoning is the *argument*. An argument is a claim or proposition put forward along with reasons or evidence supporting it.

When a person puts forward a *claim,* she makes an assertion that she expects to have taken seriously. The word *claim* comes from the Latin word *clamare,* meaning "to cry out, to call, to summon." Like a gold-mining claim or a claim check for suitcases at the airport, a claim clamors for recognition of a right, in this case, a right to attention and, ultimately, to assent.[7] "A meteorologist predicting rain for tomorrow, an injured workman alleging negligence on the part of his employer, . . . a doctor diagnosing measles, a businessman questioning the honesty of a client," in the words of logician Stephen Toulmin,[8] are all making claims. A claim says, "Here is what I believe and what you should believe also."

A claim is most often put forward in the form of a *proposition,* technically defined as a statement that can be either true or false. "It will rain tomorrow," "My employer was negligent in not monitoring levels of lead in the factory," "The child has measles" are all propositions (as opposed to questions, commands, and other sentences that are neither true nor false). Claims go by different labels in different contexts. In logic, a claim is called a *conclusion.* In debate, the claim is the *resolution.* In argumentative essays and positions papers, the claim is called the *thesis statement.*

Whether a claim merits the assent it clamors for depends on the reasons that support it. These reasons are the statements of fact or value that give grounds for believing that the claim is true. "A water-laden Pacific front is headed this way, and the temperature and air pressure are dropping" are reasons to believe "It will rain tomorrow." "The child has a fever and is covered with a red rash" is reason to believe "The child has measles." In logic, the statements of evidence that support the claim are called *premises.*

The relationship between reasons and a claim is what makes an argument out of a collection of statements. This is the *inference* (from the Latin *in-*, "in," + *ferre,* "to carry"), the supporting relationship between the evidence and the claim. The inference "carries" a person from a set of reasons to the claim they justify. Here is an argument containing an inference: "Since a water-laden Pacific front is headed this way and the temperature and air pressure are dropping, it is likely that it will rain tomorrow." Here is another: "The child probably has measles because she has a fever and is covered with a red rash."

In this context, *argument* has a technical meaning quite different from its ordinary use as a word signifying a quarrel, a verbal battle, or an unpleasant disagreement. In "The Argument Clinic," a sketch by British comedian Monty Python, the argument is about whether their discussion is an argument, and the disagreement rests on a confusion between the technical and everyday meanings of *argument.* Here is part of the dialogue:

Yes I did.
Didn't.
Yes I did.
Didn't.
Yes I did!!

Look, this isn't an argument.

Yes it is.

No it isn't, it's just contradiction.

No it isn't.

Yes it is.

It is not.

It is. You just contradicted me.

No I didn't.

Ooh, you did.

No, no, no, no, no.

You did, just then.

No, nonsense!

Oh, look, this is futile.

No it isn't.

I came here for a good argument.

No you didn't, you came here for a good *argument*.

Well, an argument's not the same as contradiction.

It can be.

No it can't. An argument is a connected series of statements to establish a definite proposition.

No it isn't.

Yes it is.[9]

* *

1.2 THE STADIUM MURDER AGAIN

Look back at the material you wrote about the stadium murder (Exercise 1.1). Did you make any claims? Did you provide reasons to support any of the claims? If so, you have the raw material for an argument. Write out the argument you might present to convince a classmate that your claim is correct.

If, on the other hand, you made some claims that were not supported by reasons, choose one of these claims. Ask yourself what reasons would support it. Then, write out an argument that supports your claim.

* *

4.   When the discussion ends, go back to your seat and write out the argument that you now think is strongest.

• •

How to Distinguish Arguments from
• • • • • • • • • • • • Other Sorts of Discourse • • • • • • • • • • • • •

It is easy to confuse arguments with other sorts of discourse. Yet it is important to distinguish them because arguments are held to standards quite different from standards for prose with other purposes. The best way to identify arguments is to focus on the purpose of the discourse and the nature of the audience.

Some kinds of prose—reports and descriptions, explanations, and expressions of emotion—look something like arguments but, in fact, have very different purposes. Other kinds of prose—unsupported claims, threats, seductions—have the same purpose as arguments but do not qualify as arguments because they do not use good reasons as a means of persuasion.

Nonarguments

Reports and Descriptions

The purpose of an argument is to bring reasons to bear to convince a person (possibly yourself) that a claim is true or that a course of action is wise. This distinguishes arguments from *reports* or *descriptions,* which have as their purpose the simple dissemination of information. This is a report:

> One summer I started off to visit for the first time the city of Los Angeles. I was riding with some friends from the University of New Mexico. On the way we stopped off briefly to roll an old tire into the Grand Canyon.[12]

Edward Abbey's recounting of these dismaying events makes no attempt to use one statement to support another; it simply tells what happened. It is directed to an audience that is perhaps ignorant but not skeptical; this audience needs information but no convincing.

1.5 PICTURES NEVER LIE

Write a paragraph in which you describe what you see in the photograph shown here. In class, compare your description to a classmate's. Find one aspect in which you disagree about what you see. Now, write a paragraph in which you try to convince your classmate that your description is the correct one. Understand that your first paragraph will be a description and the second an argument.

© Sebastiao Salgado/Magnum

Explanations

Considerations of audience and purpose serve to distinguish arguments from explanations, as well. An argument takes shape in an atmosphere of skepticism, with the purpose of convincing an audience of doubters that a claim is true. On the other hand, an explanation takes shape in an atmosphere of puzzlement, with the purpose of explaining a claim to an audience that already believes the claim is true. An argument answers the question, Is that claim really true? An explanation answers the question, Given that the claim is true, can you explain why that is so? This is an explanation:

> *A crop duster in Wyoming told me the life expectancy of a crop-duster pilot is five years. They fly too low. They hit buildings and power lines. They have no space to fly out of trouble, and no space to recover from a stall.*[13]

In this example, essayist Annie Dillard assumes that her audience believes her when she says that a crop duster's life expectancy is dismal. Her purpose is to explain *why* it is as they know it is. Had she wanted to convince readers *that* crop dusters' life expectancy is short, she would have cited statistics about mortality rates. For example, an argument supporting the conclusion that the life expectancy of a crop-duster pilot is five years might look something like this:

> Of the eight crop-duster pilots employed by AgriAir, Inc., between 1980 and 1990, one died in the first year of employment, three in the fourth year, three in the sixth year, and one in the ninth year. If one assumes that AgriAir employees are typical of crop-duster pilots in general, it follows that the average life expectancy of a crop-duster pilot is five years.

· ·

1.6 ARGUMENT AND EXPLANATION

For this exercise, each of you will need one three-by-five-inch index card. On one side of the card, write *either* an argument in support of one of the following claims *or* an explanation of one of the following claims. It's your choice. Go ahead and make up any data you may need to write an effective passage. On the other side of the card, write whether you have written an argument or an explanation.

Claims:

Someone hit Tom in the face last night.

It is raining today.

Lightning sometimes does strike twice in the same place.

Women are more likely than men to have dogs as pets.

Janie has a terrible cold.

The university does not schedule enough classes that meet during the evening.

Hundreds of refugees are fleeing Haiti.

There is less racism in the American South than in the North.

Your card is a sort of flash card that other students can use to practice distinguishing arguments from explanations. Pass your card to the student behind you, who will read what you have written, decide whether it is an argument or an explanation, and check her answer against the answer you have written on the back of the card. In the meantime, you will have received a card from the person in front of you. Read it, determine whether it is an argument or an explanation, and check your answer against the author's. By continuing to pass the cards back (and by "wrapping around" to the front of the classroom), you will have a chance to study many passages.

If you come across a passage that is not clearly an argument or an explanation or if you disagree with the author's identification, put a question mark on the back of that card. During discussion, your professor may want to show you how unclear passages can be improved by revision and by close attention to purpose and audience.

• •

Expressions of Emotion

Expressions of emotions are usually clearly distinguishable from arguments. A person expresses emotion in order to communicate information about his or her emotional state, not to influence another person's beliefs. Here is a passage from *The Journals of Lewis and Clark:*

> Ocian in view! *O! the joy. . . . Great joy in camp we are in* view *of the* Ocian, *this great Pacific Ocean which we been so long anxious to See.* [sic][14]

So far, so good: When a passage does not aim to change a person's mind or actions, it probably is not an argument. But there are some forms of discourse that do have the same purpose as an argument; they aim to influence a person's beliefs or actions, but they do so without recourse to reasons: by forcefully stating a claim without any supporting reasons, by threatening, or by seducing. These quasi arguments, or *argument surrogates,* are often very difficult to distinguish from real arguments. And, in fact, this difficulty is sometimes created deliberately, for if any discourse can be disguised as argument, it can benefit from the presumption of legitimacy that goes along with argumentation, without the trouble of including good reasons.

Argument Surrogates

Argument surrogates generally fall into three categories: unsupported claims, threats, and seduction.

Unsupported Claims

A list of claims forcefully made often looks like an argument. But close examination shows that there is no inference and no supporting relationship among the statements. Each statement stands alone, without evidence to show that it is true. Instead of a combination of reasons and claims, there are only claims, one after another. Here are two passages from a book about the one hundred most influential persons in history.[15] The first is not an argument. Although several claims are made, none of the claims give reason to believe any of the other claims.

> *Of humble origins, Muhammad founded and promulgated one of the world's great religions, and became an immensely effective political leader. Today, thirteen centuries after his death, his influence is still powerful and persuasive.*[16]

In contrast, the following passage *is* an argument, because the first sentence is a claim that is supported by the second. Moreover, the second sentence is a claim that is supported by the third.

> *Muhammad [was a more important person in history] than Jesus. . . . Muhammad played a far more important role in the development of Islam than Jesus did in the development of Christianity. Although Jesus was responsible for the main ethical and moral precepts of Christianity, St. Paul was the main developer of Christian theology . . . and the author of a large portion of the New Testament.*[17]

Threats

Another way to influence a person's beliefs and actions without troubling to come up with good reasons is by threats. These sometimes give the appearance of arguments, but close examination shows that the claims are not supported by reasons. Here is an example from a Nazi subscription-renewal notice:

> *Our paper certainly deserves the support of every German. We shall continue to forward copies of it to you, and hope that you will not want to expose yourself to unfortunate consequences in the case of cancellation.*[18]

Seduction

The flip side of the threat is the seduction:

> *"Your skin feels so beautiful," he murmured and then smiled a little sheepishly, letting his gaze meet hers. "I don't suppose I'm the first man to think your name is perfect for you. Honey. The warm color, the smooth texture . . ."[19]*

The gentleman is no doubt trying to influence Honey's behavior. But his appeal is not to reasons.

Knowing the difference between arguments and cheap substitutes is important because arguments, unlike, say, unsupported claims or descriptive passages, are held to high standards of truth and cogency and thus carry a presumption of legitimacy and rationality. Politicians, more often than not, offer cheap substitutes—lists of platitudes, flattering descriptions of the audience, scary predictions—rather than engage in argument; the poor, presumably dumb voters get the appearance, but seldom the reality, of rational thought. Advertisers are masters of the argument surrogate. Advertisers will flatter you, threaten you, amuse you, arouse you, distract your attention; they will do almost anything, short of giving you good reasons why you should buy their products.

• •

1.7 "WHAT MAKES YOU SAY SO?"

Your assignment is to experiment on your friends and family to learn how often people use arguments rather than threats, abuse, or some other way of changing your mind, and to write a research report describing your experiment, its results, and your conclusions.

Experimental method: When someone makes an unsupported claim in conversation, you (the experimenter) respond in a mild-mannered voice, "But, why should I believe that is true?" Keep a record of the responses of the people making the unsupported claims, and classify the claims as arguments (giving reasons), threats, explanations, simple repetitions of the claim, and so forth. Do this for ten responses.

Research report: Write a research report, approximately one page long, summarizing your experiments and the results you found. Do the results fit any patterns? Do they surprise you? Can you think of any explanation for your results?

• •

1.8 POLITICAL ARGUMENT

This textbook makes the claim, "Politicians, more often than not, offer cheap substitutes . . . rather than engage in argument." Yet the text offers no evidence for this claim. Is it really true?

Make or find a videotape of a debate among presidential candidates. Play the tape in class. Keep a record of how often the candidates actually formulate arguments and how often they use argument surrogates. Does your study tend to confirm or cast doubt on the textbook's claim?

Whether any writing succeeds or fails depends in part on what the author was trying to achieve. So, you cannot judge whether a piece of writing is successful unless you know its purpose. In this way, writing is like any other activity. If a runner places forty-third in a marathon, for example, has she succeeded in the race? That all depends; it depends on whether she entered the race to win, to get exercise, to join other runners, or to go the distance.

So, if you are going to evaluate the success of an "argument," be sure you *first* establish that it was intended to be an argument. By the same token, it is important to be clear about your own purpose as a writer: Are you trying to *convince* someone that a claim is true or false? If so, an argument is what you will write.

If there is any doubt that a passage is an argument, look at the relationships among the sentences. Does any one statement give a reason for thinking that any of the other statements are true? If not, the passage is not an argument.

1.9 LETTERS TO THE EDITOR

Bring in a copy of the entire letters to the editor section of a major newspaper or magazine. Working in groups, read through the letters and decide on the purpose of each.

Cut out the letters that contain arguments. Identify the claim defended in each argumentative letter. Arrange the letters in order of effectiveness. What are some of the factors that make the best letters work? What interferes with the effectiveness of the poor letters? As for those letters that are not arguments, what are they?

Choose one of the claims presented in a letter to the editor. As an individual, write a letter to the editor arguing for the opposite claim. If a letter argues, for example, that all public school classes should be taught only in English, you should argue that children in public schools should have a chance to learn in their native languages. Ask a member of your working group to read your letter and write answers to these questions:

1. Is this an argument?
2. What claim does it defend?
3. What reasons are offered in support of that claim?
4. Is the letter persuasive? Why or why not?

Argumentation and Critical Thinking

Any argument is usually an interaction between at least two people, the writer and the reader. The writer's purpose is to change you, the reader, to make you believe what you may not have believed before or to make you act in unaccustomed ways. This carries a set of risks, for a foolish or dishonest argument can persuade you to believe what is not true, to disbelieve what *is* true, or to act in ways that are inadvisable.

So, arguments call for a certain self-defensive cast of mind. In order to avoid being misled by arguments that are dishonest or defective, it is important to understand and evaluate carefully the reasons given in support of the claim. This is *critical thinking,* the art of identifying, analyzing, and evaluating arguments. People who are skilled in critical thinking have the ability to examine carefully the claims that are clamoring for admission into that select group of claims—*Coke is the real thing! There is no life after death. Your car is an embarrassment. Rhubarb is poisonous. He loves me. Apartheid is immoral. The drinking age should be lowered to 18*—that constitute their beliefs. Critical thinking skills are filters, letting in those claims that merit belief, filtering out others, and identifying questionable claims about which it is best to suspend judgment.

1.10 HABITS OF THE MIND

1. To begin an exploration of your own intellect, indicate to what extent you agree or disagree with the following statements, by putting an *X* in the appropriate place along the continuum between agreement and disagreement.

	Agree	Disagree
I am a skeptical person, hard to convince.		
I am uncomfortable with uncertainty, with not knowing what is true.		
I suspend judgment about a lot of things, adopting a wait-and-see attitude.		
I think in black/white, either/or terms.		
I think of myself as a very logical person.		
I don't like to argue with people about their beliefs; they can believe whatever they want.		
I value and seek out experiences that are mysterious, even mystical.		
I trust my intuition more than my intellect.		
When I make decisions, I "go with my gut."		
Beliefs based on faith are an important part of my life.		
I am a step-by-step thinker.		
The best way to explain something to me is with an example or analogy.		

2. Write a 250-word essay in which you describe your habits of thought to your professor, who, after all, has a professional interest in how you think. Describe what kind of thinker you are. Alternatively, think of a person whom you admire as a thinker. Write a 250-word essay in which you describe the intellectual characteristics of that person.

3. The nineteenth-century philosopher Friedrich Nietzsche said this:

> The schools have no more important task than to teach rigorous thinking, cautious judgment, and consistent inference; therefore, they should leave alone whatever is not suitable for these operations: religion, for example. After all, they can be sure that later on man's fogginess, habit, and need will slacken the bow of an all-too-taut thinking. But as far as the influence of the schools reaches, they should enforce what is essential and distinctive in man: reason and science, man's very highest power.[20]

Do you agree with Nietzsche? In an essay of approximately 250 words, take and defend a position for or against one of Nietzsche's claims.

4.   Do you agree with what Mark Twain says about human beings in the following quotation? In an essay of approximately 250 words, take and defend a position for or against one of Twain's claims.

> *Man is the Reasoning Animal. Such is the claim. I think it is open to dispute. Indeed, my experiments have proven to me that he is the Unreasoning Animal. Note his history. . . . It seems plain to me that whatever he is he is not a reasoning animal. His record is the fantastic record of a maniac. I consider that the strongest count against his intelligence is the fact that with that record back of him he blandly sets himself up as the head animal of the lot: whereas by his own standards he is the bottom one.*[21]

Making a Commitment to Reasoned Discourse

If you are going to play any game, you have to play by the rules, and the central rule of argumentation is that you will reach conclusions on the basis of reasons—evidence, data, observations—not anything else. This commitment to reasoned discourse is an implied promise you make to yourself when you try to reason through a problem. It is the central term of the implied agreement that makes it possible to reason with other people.[22]

One who makes a commitment to resolve issues on the basis of reasons must adopt certain habits of thought, a set of intellectual virtues that make reasoned discourse possible. The most important of these virtues is *intellectual honesty*, the willingness to change conclusions that conflict with the evidence rather than distort the evidence to fit conclusions already held. Another is *open-mindedness*, a willingness to take in information that may conflict with beliefs already held and a kind of intellectual inquisitiveness that keeps the door open to new ideas and information. Another virtue is *flexibility*, a tentativeness of belief that allows you to see the issue from another point of view and to change your mind when evidence suggests that you are mistaken. The last is *impartiality*, the ability to gather and weigh information without bias or blindness imposed by one's own hopes and fears.[23]

When these virtues are in place, reasoning is self-correcting. Like computers that can find errors in their own programs, reasoning can use information to redirect its own course. People who reason effectively can uncover their own errors, methodological and factual, and correct them.

A commitment to reason as the final court of appeals presupposes a world view, a way of understanding the universe, that is a legacy of the Enlightenment. This view holds that the universe is ultimately open to human understanding. To be thus, it must operate according to rules that human beings can grasp, not according to whim or whimsy. God, Einstein is said to have observed with Enlightenment faith, does not play dice with the universe. If nothing is ultimately and forever mysterious, it is realistic to have faith in human progress, to believe that, with time and with reason, human beings will come to understand more and more about the universe and their place in it. And, with a greater understanding, they will design more effective institutions to further human happiness. This world view argues for a society organized around the free flow of information and freedom of thought; if truth comes from reasons, evidence, and information, then the more information there is and the more accessible it is, the more truth will be found. All this requires a tremendous faith in the power of reason.

. . . .

1.11 MAKING DECISIONS IN OTHER CULTURES

Being children of the Enlightenment, many twentieth-century Americans take for granted that conclusions should be reached on the basis of reasoned discourse and that only certain kinds of information can function as reasons. But, in other cultures and times, far different presuppositions operate.

Go to the library or interview a person from another culture, and find information and insights that you can contribute to a class discussion on the cultural basis of "reaching conclusions," the activity of justifying claims with reasons. What kinds of reasons, denied credentials in Western intellectual culture, are admitted as good reasons in other cultures? Do other cultures share the Enlightenment commitment to rationality? Why do some feminists believe that single-minded commitment to rationality is a kind of blindness or self-limitation? How did European people during the Middle Ages justify their conclusions? How does argumentation differ in Eastern and Western cultures? Is there any reliable, noncircular way to make a judgment as to what way of justifying conclusions is the best?

You might want to consult some of the new feminist work on logic, such as *Words of Power* by Andrea Nye, or recent comparative anthropology, such as

Modes of Thought: Essays on Thinking in Western and Non-Western Societies, edited by Robin Horton and Ruth Finnegan. *How We Know* by Martin Goldstein and Inge Goldstein reviews the history of rational discourse in Europe. Remember that your classmates or parents, or you yourself, might be an excellent source of information about other cultures.

. . . .

1.12 HUNTING FOR ARGUMENTS

1. How many arguments can you find in the following selection from Sir Arthur Conan Doyle's, "The Adventure of the Blue Carbuncle"? Here, Dr. Watson and Sherlock Holmes are trying to learn the identity of a person who has run away with a fat goose, leaving only his hat. Watson speaks first:

> *"Then, what clue could you have as to his identity?"*
> *"Only as much as we can deduce."*
> *"From his hat?"*
> *"Precisely."*
> *"But you are joking. What can you gather from this old battered felt?"* . . .
>
> *I took the tattered [hat] in my hands and turned it over rather ruefully. It was a very ordinary black hat of the usual round shape, hard, and much the worse for wear. The lining had been of red silk, but was a good deal discolored. . . . For the rest, it was cracked, exceedingly dusty, and spotted in several places although there seemed to have been some attempt to hide the discolored patches by smearing them with ink. . . .*
>
> *[Holmes] picked it up and gazed at it in the peculiar introspective fashion which was characteristic of him. "It is perhaps less suggestive than it might have been," he remarked, "and yet there are a few inferences which are very distinct, and a few others which represent at least a strong balance of probability. That the man was highly intellectual is of course obvious upon the face of it . . . and the obvious fact that his wife has ceased to love him."* . . .
>
> *"You are certainly joking, Holmes. . . . I must confess I am unable to follow you. For example, how did you deduce that this man was intellectual?"*
>
> *For answer Holmes clapped the hat upon his head. It came right over the forehead and settled upon the bridge of his nose. "It is a question of cubic capacity," said he; "a man with so large a brain must have something in it." . . .*
>
> *"But his wife — you said that she had ceased to love him."*

"This hat has not been brushed for weeks. When I see you, my dear Watson, with a week's accumulation of dust upon your hat, and when your wife allows you to go out in such a state, I shall fear that you also have been unfortunate enough to lose your wife's affection."

"But he might be a bachelor."

"Nay, he was bringing home a goose. . . ."[24]

2.   In your own words, write out the arguments you found. Be sure each argument contains a claim and reasons to back it up. If all the reasons are not present in the passage, go ahead and add what you think you need to make the argument complete.

· ·

1.13 *WORLD PRESS REVIEW*

The *World Press Review* is a monthly magazine that prints "news and views from around the world." Passages one through nine are from newspapers in other countries, reprinted in the *World Press Review.*[25] For each passage,

a.   Tell what purpose(s) the author was trying to serve in writing the article. Was the author, for example, simply reporting information? trying to convince the readers of the truth of a claim? explaining a puzzling fact? or something else?

b.   Put a label on the passage. Is it, for example, an argument? an explanation? unsupported claims? Understand that a passage can sometimes be two things at once and that the identification of a passage is often controversial.

c.   If the passage is an argument, tell what claim it is defending. If the passage is an explanation, tell what statement it is explaining.

1.   *In what seems a morality play without an end, a line of once-heroic figures — each an achiever of legendary proportions — have been summoned to the off-the-field stage in front of our unbelieving eyes and turned into erring, defeated pygmies. Perhaps in no other era in sport have so many mega-stars fallen from grace or been merely embarrassed as in the late 1980s and early 1990s. . . .*

   The fastest human in the world turned out to be a cheat. The greatest soccer player in the world ended up a womanizer and a drug addict. The most powerful sportsman of them all, an awesome figure who ruled the ring, has been accused of raping a young woman and of a dozen other acts unbecoming of a former world champion. And the woman who is arguably the greatest player of her sex of all time, a nine-time Wimbledon champion, was reduced to tears in a courtroom by the actions of her former lover.

Sunday Times (independent), Colombo, Sri Lanka.

2. *[Asia is likely to see the world's next pandemic of AIDS.] WHO [the World Health Organization] notes the similarity between Asia's AIDS curve and the early days of the pandemic in sub-Saharan Africa. The worry, though, is that many more people are at risk because Asia is home to more than 50 percent of the world's population.*

Ian Steele, Depthnews, Asia (feature agency), Manila.

3. *First-rate economically, Japan is third-rate politically, at home and abroad. Inept, uninspired leaders have made this country a shrinking violet, afraid to act on its own for fear of offending Washington.*

Why are all our leaders followers? The answer, I think, is that they have never recovered from the trauma of defeat in World War II. Afraid that independent action will bring down Washington's wrath, they react meekly to their master's commands. After 46 years, obedience is second nature.

Tetsundo Iwakuni, Chanichi Shimbun (daily), Nagoya City.

4. *For the first time, the lower level of the Earth's ozone layer was perforated for several days last October, reports the Argentine National Weather Service. Argentina's observation bases at the South Pole and Marambio, on the Antarctic coast, recorded the complete destruction of the ozone layer at altitudes from 10–13 miles. Data from the U.S., Japan, New Zealand, and Britain confirm the Argentine report. In the past five years, Antarctic weather stations have reported that the region has lost up to 50 percent of the ozone in its lower atmospheric layer during the spring, meaning that living beings in Antarctica during that time could suffer serious burns from ultraviolet rays. . . . Although most of the ozone layer is still in place, it has been seriously eroded over Antarctica, and the consequences for the southern parts of Argentina and Chile are not yet known.*

Daniel E. Arias, Clarín, Buenos Aires.

5. *Japan's days as an economic superpower are numbered. The Japanese economy is being sabotaged from the top by unprincipled businesspeople, politicians, and administrators. Meanwhile, the country's declining birthrate and changing attitudes toward hard, dirty work are undermining industry from below.*

Noboru Makino, Sankei Shimbun (independent), Tokyo.

6. *An 11-year study by the German Cancer Research Center in Heidelberg suggests that vegetarians live longer and stay healthier. More than 1,000*

people participated, eating little or no meat; deaths occurred at roughly half the average rate for people of their ages. Cancer fatalities, for example, were about 50 percent lower than average.

General-Anzeiger, Bonn.

7. *The international environmental conference this June in Rio de Janeiro seems unlikely to produce any concrete agreements. Sticking points in preliminary discussions include industrialized countries' carbon-dioxide emissions ("greenhouse gas") and the level of financial aid for developing countries' environmental needs. The world's largest source of greenhouse gas—the U.S.—has opposed ceilings on carbon-dioxide emissions.*

Frankfurter Allgemeine Zeitung, Frankfurt.

8. *Peru is cracking down on illegal adoptions. Some 30 officials, including judges, attorneys, and social workers, have been indicted in a baby-trafficking ring that preyed on the country's increasing numbers of poor and dislocated mothers. A commission recommends reforming state-run adoption procedures. . . .*

Sí, Lima.

9. *Future stars of Wimbledon and other tennis tournaments may emerge from India, where the sport is booming among eight-to-16 [sic] year olds. New academies have opened to train junior players in the style of the West by providing room and board, education, coaching, and equipment.*

Indian Express, New Delhi.

10. *From a speech in the House of Representatives, by Rep. Major Owens, Democrat of New York: "[Spanking is not an acceptable method of punishment in public schools]. Those children with no advocates—the poor and minorities—will bear the brunt [of corporal punishment]. . . . If you are an adult inmate in a federal, state, or local correctional institution, you cannot be beaten or physically punished. . . . Only if you are a child sitting in a classroom can you be beaten and physically punished. Incredibly, our schools today remain the only public institution in the United States in which battery and assault are legal. This must end."[26]*

Jet, United States

Notes

1. *Webster's Third New International Dictionary* (Springfield, Mass.: Merriam, 1971), p. 1892.
2. Freewriting is the written analogue of the mental activities we call "brainstorming" and "free association." Freewriting is an effective way to generate lots of ideas. It works in part because

it allows students to get their ideas down on paper without at the same time worrying about how the ideas should be expressed. The separation of creation of ideas from expression of ideas has a surprisingly strong liberating and energizing effect on students.

Freewriting is a technique popularized by Peter Elbow in *Writing with Power: Techniques for Mastering the Writing Process* (New York: Oxford University Press, 1981).

3. Dana Tims, "Jury Selection Slated for Autzen Sniper Case," *The Oregonian* (April 22, 1986). Reprinted with permission of Dana Tims.

4. Kenneth A. Bruffee, "Teaching Writing Through Collaboration," *Learning in Groups* (San Francisco: Jossey-Bass, Inc., 1983), p. 25.

5. The answer is yes: Everybody lies to somebody, so Carol must lie to somebody. And if Carol lies to anybody, she lies to David. So Carol lies to David.

6. A leader in writing across the curriculum is Peter Elbow. See *Writing with Power* (New York: Oxford University Press, 1981).

7. See Stephen Toulmin, *The Uses of Argument* (Cambridge: Cambridge University Press, 1958), pp. 11–12, where this way of understanding claims is suggested.

8. Stephen Toulmin, *The Uses of Argument* (Cambridge: Cambridge University Press, 1958), pp. 11–12.

9. *Monty Python's Flying Circus—Just the Words,* ed. Roger Wilmut (New York: Random House, Inc., 1989), Vol. 2, p. 86. © Python Productions Ltd., 1989. Used with permission.

10. Konrad Lorenz, *On Aggression* (New York: Bantam Books, 1970), pp. 228–229.

11. This idea was inspired by an idea from Zachary Seech, "Philosophical Chairs: A Format for Class Discussion," *Demonstrating Philosophy,* ed. Arnold Wilson (New York: University Press of America, 1988), pp. 213–218.

12. Edward Abbey, *Desert Solitaire* (New York: Ballantine, 1968), p. 221.

13. Annie Dillard, *A Writer's Life* (New York: Harper and Row, 1989), p. 105.

14. *The Journals of Lewis and Clark,* ed. Bernard DeVoto (Boston: Houghton Mifflin Co., 1953), p. 279.

15. Michael H. Hart, *The 100: A Ranking of the Most Influential Persons in History* (Secaucus, N.J.: Citadel Press, 1987).

16. Michael H. Hart, *The 100: A Ranking of the Most Influential Persons in History* (Secaucus, N.J.: Citadel Press, 1987), p. 33.

17. Michael H. Hart, *The 100: A Ranking of the Most Influential Persons in History* (Secaucus, N.J.: Citadel Press, 1987), p. 39.

18. Quoted by Irving Copi, *Introduction to Logic* (New York: Macmillan Publishing Co., 1986), p. 106, who found it in *Parade* (May 9, 1971), which cited R. Grunberger, *A Social History of the Third Reich.* With a history like this, the story may be apocryphal.

19. Carole Halston, *Almost Heaven* (New York: Silhouette Books, 1985), p. 107.

20. Friedrich Nietzsche, *Epigrams,* #265.

21. Mark Twain, "The Lowest Animal," in *A Pen Warmed-up in Hell: Mark Twain in Protest*, ed. Frederick Anderson (New York: Harper and Row, 1972), p. 93.

22. Cleanth Brooks and Robert Penn Warren, *Modern Rhetoric* (New York: Harcourt Brace Jovanovich, Inc., 1972), pp. 123–124.

23. Richard Paul, *Critical Thinking Handbooks* (Sonoma, Calif.: Sonoma University Press, 1987) and John Langrehr, *Sharing Thinking Strategies* (Bloomington, Ind.: National Educational Service, 1990), p. 83.

24. Sir Arthur Conan Doyle, "The Adventure of the Blue Carbuncle," *The Adventures of Sherlock Holmes* (New York: The Popular Library, 1964), pp. 127–131.

25. Passages one through nine are reprinted from *World Press Review* (January 1992, February 1992). © 1992, *World Press Review.* Used with permission.

26. Richette Haywood, "Should Teachers Be Allowed to Spank Students?" *Jet* (May 2, 1991), p. 34. © 1991, *Jet* Magazine. Used with permission.

· ·

CHAPTER 2

Analyzing Arguments

Arguments seldom come neatly packaged and labeled like chocolates in a fancy box. More often, they are like a plate of spaghetti, with long lines of argumentation tangled together. Separating the parts, unwinding the lines of inference, and identifying the essential strands make an argument much easier to understand. And, because you must understand an argument in order to evaluate it fairly, this untangling process is an important preliminary to making a judgment about whether an argument is really good enough to change your mind and influence your actions. The untangling process is called *logical analysis.*

To *analyze* something is to break it up into its constituent parts in order to understand it. An analytic chemist takes an unknown substance and figures out what it is by breaking it up into elements. A political analyst studies the details of an election to explain who voted for what and why. A logical analyst divides an argument into its parts to learn how it fits together, or fails to fit together.

· · · · · · · · · · · · ## How to Analyze Arguments · · · · · · · · · · · ·

Argument analysis is a four-step process that leads to an understanding of an argument. These are the steps:

1. Identify the issue.
2. Identify the claim that is defended.

3. Identify the reasons used to defend the claim.

4. Represent the structure of the argument.

Identifying the Issue

To understand an argument, you first have to learn what it is about. Consider this argument:

> *The economic status [of women] has deteriorated sharply since the late 1960's. Today women — and children — are the primary beneficiaries of social welfare programs for the poor. . . . By 1980, America's poor were predominantly female; two out of three adults whose incomes fell below the official federal poverty line were women, and more than half the families who were poor were headed by women.*[1]

Who wrote this? Why did she bother? What was at stake? What difference does it make? Who listened? Who cared? The first step of argument analysis is to address questions like these by identifying what is at *issue* in the argument. The issue is the single point in question or matter in dispute. In an argument analysis, the issue should always be stated as a question: Has the economic status of women deteriorated over the past decades more than the economic status of men?

It is tempting to overlook the issue, to lose track of the fact that arguments are written to resolve a controversy. This is because examples in reasoning textbooks have been wrenched out of their settings, torn from newspapers or conversations, and alienated from the human concerns that led someone to sit down and write the argument in the first place. What you have in textbooks are often anonymous, isolated fragments with ragged edges. To compound the problem, the analytic process itself requires you to focus on the parts of the argument, the trees rather than the forest. Under these conditions, it is easy to forget that, with the possible exception of logic professors, people do not make up arguments simply for their recreational value. Arguments are made to resolve an issue, that is, to answer a question.

It is not always easy to decide what the issue is because you have to guess what an author's intentions were. The context of the argument or the circumstances that gave rise to the argument often provide the best clues to the issue. Here is an example of an argument torn from its context:

> A fetus is a human being. Killing a human being is always murder. Doctors who perform abortions are murderers. They should go to jail.[2]

Out of context, the issue is a mystery. Was this argument part of testimony before a legislative committee setting penalties for abortionists? Then the issue may be, Should abortionists be jailed? Was the argument shouted at a pregnant woman entering an abortion clinic? Then the issue may be, Is abortion murder? Only the author can say for sure what the issue is, but a good author will make the issue abundantly clear to the reader.

Notice that an issue is not the same as a *topic*. A topic is usually a noun or a noun phrase: The economic status of women. The drinking age. Abortion. Pepsi. Stating the topic may delineate the area of discussion, but it does not focus attention on the precise question to be resolved by the argument.

Consider, for example, the topic, campus racism. The topic suggests many issues: Is racism increasing on college campuses? What are the causes of racism on campuses? What are the harmful effects of racism on campuses? What can college students do to reduce racism? What can college administrators do to reduce racism on campus? Are college regulations against racist speech a violation of free-speech rights? Is there a relation between ignorance and racism? The list could go on and on. If you are analyzing someone else's argument, ask yourself: *What particular issue does this particular argument address?* This is an important step because if you do not know what question is to be resolved by the argument, you can never learn whether the argument succeeds.

The following argument illustrates the relation between a topic and an issue. Here, the topic is campus racism. The issue is, Is racial segregation increasing on college campuses?

> *"The races in the Northern universities have grown more separate since the Sixties,"* as professor Allan Bloom has pointed out in The Closing of the American Mind. *In 1987, the dean of students at Middlebury College reported that, for the first time in a long career, she had received requests from white students that they not be assigned black roommates. It has become one of the signs of the times on many campuses that black students eat at separate tables. At too many colleges and universities, "diversity" has become mere academic Newspeak for a larger, segregated minority enclave.*[3]

• •

2.1 NO MORE PARTY ANIMALS

The *Los Angeles Times* carried this article:

NEW RULES FOR USC's SORORITIES, FRATERNITIES[4]

LOS ANGELES—USC imposed strict new regulations this week on its fraternities and sororities in what officials said is an effort to change the party-animal image of Greek Row, encourage more studying and discourage date rape and alcohol abuse. . . .

The new rules, effective immediately, forbid parties on weeknights, ban most visits by members of the opposite sex to private rooms if alcohol is being used, and require that Greek organization members have higher grades on average than other students . . .

1.   At the top of a sheet of paper, write a one-paragraph argument addressing any issue you think is raised by this *Los Angeles Times* article. Pass your argument along your row, so that at least five students can read it. Ask each of the students who read your argument to write on the bottom of the page the issue they believe your argument addresses. At the same time, you will be reading arguments for other students and writing down the issues you think are addressed in those arguments.

2.   Retrieve your argument. From the list of possible issues written below your argument, choose the issue that was farthest from your mind when you wrote your argument. Now, write an argument that addresses that issue.

Identifying the Claim That Is Defended

The second step of argument analysis is to identify the claim that is defended. That claim is called the *conclusion*. Once you have identified the issue, finding the conclusion of an argument is a straightforward step; the conclusion is the answer to the question raised as the issue of the argument. The conclusion is what the writer wants the audience to come to believe, some claim about what is true or what is right or what is to be done.

For example, consider the following passage, written in 1958 in Clinton, Tennessee, by a schoolteacher whose newly integrated classroom had just been destroyed by dynamite:

> *Integration will work. It is already working in many places. It will continue to work because it is just and right and long overdue.*[5]

The issue, Will integration ever work? was an issue of great urgency and greater doubt. The teacher's answer: Yes, integration will work. This is her conclusion, what she is trying to make the reader believe. The other statements tell her reasons for believing that the conclusion is true.

Unhappily, it is not always this easy to identify the conclusion of an argument. Here is an example of an argument, out of context, in which it is not clear which statement is the conclusion:

Victor is a student. Only students can get tickets to the basketball game. Victor can get tickets to the basketball game.

A variety of strategies can be used to find the conclusion of an argument when the argument itself, like this one, does not make its conclusion clear.

First, look at the first and last statements in a passage. Most often, but emphatically not always, the conclusion is one of these. If you had to bet on which of the statements in the example is the conclusion, your best bets are "Victor is a student" and "Victor can get tickets to the basketball game." When you write, it is a kindness to your readers to put your conclusion first or last, where it can be readily found.

Second, look for words that function as *signposts*. Some words and phrases such as *therefore, thus, hence, for this reason, consequently,* and *it follows that* exist for the sole purpose of calling attention to conclusions. The more arguments you analyze, the more grateful you will become toward authors who use these special words conscientiously, skillfully, and often. See how much clearer the example becomes with the addition of one word.

Victor can get tickets to the basketball game. Only students can still get tickets. Hence, Victor is a student.

Third, in the absence of such clues (shame on the writer of a passage in which they are missing), you can probably identify the conclusion by looking for the most controversial statement. It makes sense that a statement generally accepted as true will be used most effectively as a premise and that the conclusion will be the statement most in need of support. Which statement is the most controversial depends, of course, on the context.

Fourth, when all else fails, do unto others as you would have others do unto you. That is, choose as the conclusion the statement that is most strongly supported by the others. This is, after all, what you would like your readers to do for you. Logicians call this the *principle of charity*. Try out different interpretations of the argument, and see which interpretation makes the strongest case for its conclusion. If it is true that Victor can get tickets and that only students can get tickets, it *must* be true that Victor is a student. Identifying that statement as the conclusion makes the argument the best it can be. So, that is the way it should be interpreted.

Obviously, all this trouble in finding the conclusion could have been avoided if the writer had done a better job of writing the argument in the first place. A good writer must be clear in her own mind about exactly what conclusion she wants to defend. Then, she should make that equally clear to her readers by giving the conclusion the place of honor in the paragraph, by identifying it with clear signpost words, and by making sure that the premises are less controversial than the conclusion.

•••

2.2 WRITING HEADLINES

Bring in four photocopies of the letters to the editor section of a newsmagazine. Give a copy to each member of your study group. For each letter, write down the claim you think is defended in the letter. Compare your answers with the answers of other group members. Where you have initial disagreement, try to reach a consensus. Be careful, because not all the letters will be arguments.

It may help to think of your group as doing the job of an editor writing headlines, trying to capture in a single sentence the point of the whole letter.

•••

Identifying the Reasons Used to Defend the Claim

The third step in argument analysis is to identify the statements that give reasons for believing that the claim is true. The supporting statements, the reasons, are called *premises.*

Reasons may be embedded in, or framed by, sentences that do not advance the argument. Thus, they cannot be identified by a simple process of elimination.

Consider the following example:

> At an Operation Rescue protest supervised by Randall Terry in Binghamton, New York, a protester punched a pregnant clinic worker in the stomach; she was taken to the hospital in an ambulance and miscarried several weeks later. Women trying to escort patients into clinics during protests in California report being karate-chopped in the knees and kicked in the stomach. In the "training" tapes Terry distributes to his flock, he suggests it may be necessary to "physically intervene with violence . . . , with force," because "that is the logical response to murder. [And] abortion is murder."[6]

Here, most of the sentences provide background and context for the argument, which does not appear until the final lines. The conclusion of the argument reported is ". . . it may be necessary to physically intervene with violence . . . , with force [to prevent abortions]." The premises of the argument are to be found in the final two sentences: "[Violence and force are] the logical response to murder" and ". . . abortion is murder."

In a well-written passage, the premises will be marked by signposts that make clear the supporting job done by the statements. Words such as *since, because,* and *for* tell the reader that the sentences that follow are intended to serve as premises. In the passage above, *because* tells the reader that the next two sentences are premises. When signpost words are missing, the argument analysis is more difficult because the reader faces the tasks of looking carefully for those statements that provide reasons for thinking the conclusion is true and untangling them from the sentences that are not part of the argument.

. . . .

2.3 A TREASURE HUNT

Find an editorial in the printed media. Look on the editorial pages of newspapers or in the "My Turn" column of a newsmagazine. Circle every signpost word you find. Underline every conclusion you find. Cross out all the material that frames the argument but is not part of the argument itself. Bracket all the statements that serve as premises.

. . . .

Representing the Structure of the Argument

A variety of metaphors express the relationship among the statements in an argument. Some say that the premises "lead to" the conclusion or that the conclusion "follows from" the premises—inevitably, as night follows day, or faithfully, as a dog follows its owner. Others say that a conclusion "rests on" the premises—comfortably, as if on a Beauty-Rest mattress. Many of the metaphors are architectural: The premises "support" the conclusion. The premises provide a "foundation" or a "base" for the conclusion.

What is meant is that the premises are related to the conclusion in such a way that the premises provide good reasons for believing that the conclusion is true. Invoking the architectural metaphor, this relationship between the statements of an argument may be called the logical *structure* of the argument. There are a variety of ways to represent the structure of an argument. Here are three: the argument summary, the argument diagram, and standard form.

The Argument Summary[7]

An *argument summary* is a concise statement of the main points in an argumentative passage. It leaves out all the extraneous material that does not advance the argument, organizes the information for clarity, and paraphrases the language used by the author. Where the original argumentative passage may have been wandering, thick, or abstruse, the argument summary is clear and directly to the point. It reports—without criticism—the claim advanced in the argument and the reasons that back it up. That is all.

Analyzing and summarizing an argument is not all that different from dissecting a frog in biology class. You cut away the skin that hides the essentials and lay the frog open, with all its parts clearly exposed and carefully labeled. An argument summary strips away all the extra material hiding the essential parts of the argument and clearly labels the structure that is revealed. Unlike frogs, whose parts are usually all present and in the usual arrangement, arguments sometimes present themselves in muddled disarray. So, argument summaries sometimes involve a bit of preliminary reconstruction work.

First an example, then the step-by-step directions. Here is an argument by Stacey Colino, fresh from its natural habitat:

> *[College students are living with a dangerous and false sense of security.] That's the way it's been for years at most colleges and universities across the country. . . . [T]hese institutions haven't been required by law to report campus crimes to students, parents, employees, prospective students, or the government. And because they're competing for applicants, colleges and universities have little incentive to voluntarily report just how dangerous their campus might be. After all, a school would rather stand out in a prospective student's mind for its academic standing or its idyllic setting than for its crime rate. . . . [But] students can only protect themselves if they comprehend the reality of the problem by seeing actual numbers at their schools. . . . It's a very vulnerable time for students. . . . They're on their own for the first time. So many people think that because they haven't heard about crimes, they don't exist. People need to be told; otherwise they're even more vulnerable.[8]*

The first step in writing an argument summary is to analyze the argument, identifying the conclusion and the premises. Then, put the argument back together, this time clearly and succinctly.

First, report the claim that is defended. Use phrases like "the author argues that . . ." or "the passage defends the claim that . . ." to label the statement's role in the argument. Thus, "Ms. Colino argues that campuses should be required to report campus crimes." Of course, Ms. Colino never really does come out and say that, but that is clearly the claim she means to defend and, so, that is the claim that goes in this summary.

Then, one by one, report the reasons offered in defense of the claim and any essential supporting information. "To support this claim, she notes that campuses do not voluntarily reveal crime statistics. This is because realistic reporting of crime on campus would harm college recruiting efforts."

Report the other reasons, reconstructing the case premise by premise. "She points out that hiding crime statistics is dangerous because it prevents students from seeing the need to take steps to protect themselves."

Then, put it all together, conclusion first. Frame each claim and each reason with signposting phrases that clearly identify the role each statement plays in the argument as a whole. In this argument summary, the signpost phrases are underlined. That, by the way, is not a bad idea.

> Ms. Colino argues that campuses should be required to report campus crimes. To support this claim, she notes that campuses do not voluntarily reveal crime statistics. This is because realistic reporting of crime on campus would harm college recruiting efforts. She points out that hiding crime statistics is dangerous because it prevents students from seeing the need to take steps to protect themselves.

Writing argument summaries is a useful exercise for both the reader and the writer. For the reader, summarizing an argument makes the argument clear so that its virtues can be readily evaluated. For the writer, summarizing the bare bones of an argument before it is written in all its fleshed-out glory makes it more likely that the finished product is clear, forceful, and easy to read. Moreover, writing an argument summary of your own argument is a good way to begin the revision process; if you cannot summarize your own argument, it needs help.

• •

2.4 RELIGIOUS ARGUMENTS

Here are four passages arguing that God exists, one arguing that He does not, and one disputing Jesus' moral credo. Write an argument summary for each passage:

1. Belief in God has, in times past, been supported by what is called the *argument from miracles.* It is to this effect: Miracles occur from time to

time. Since miracles are violations of natural laws, such events must therefore be explained by reference to something outside or beyond nature. Thus, a supernatural miracle-worker must exist and that is God.[9]

2. Whatever exists must have a cause of its existence. Nothing can produce itself. In tracing effects and causes, we must go on tracing an infinite regression without any first cause, or we must end at a first cause. Now the conception of an infinite regression, of utterly no beginning cause to which all others can be traced, is absurd. There must, therefore, be a first cause of all things. Such a being is God.[10]

3. *In crossing a heath, . . . suppose I had found a watch upon the ground. . . . [W]hen we come to inspect the watch, we perceive that its several parts are framed and put together for a purpose, e.g., that they are so formed and adjusted as to produce motion, and that motion so regulated as to point out the hour of the day. . . . This mechanism being observed . . . the inference, we think, is inevitable; that the watch must have a maker. [In the same way, the universe, which is also made of parts framed and put together so as to produce regulated motion, must have had a maker, whom we call God.]*[11]

4. *If the human race, taken as a whole, agrees in regarding a given conclusion as certain it is impossible to suppose that that conclusion is false. . . . This being premised, we urge that there is a veritable consensus among men that God exists. All races, civilized and uncivilized alike, are at one in holding that the facts of nature and the voice of conscience compel us to affirm that as certain truth. . . . [T]hose who admit the existence of God form so overwhelming a majority, that agnostics and atheists do not affect the moral unanimity of the race. If, then, the judgment of all mankind cannot be mistaken, we have here yet another valid proof of the existence of God.*[12]

5. *To many, the most powerful positive objection to belief in God is the fact of evil. Probably for most agnostics it is the appalling depth and extent of human suffering, more than anything else, that makes the idea of a loving Creator seem so implausible. . . . As a challenge to theism, the problem of evil has traditionally been posed in the form of a dilemma: if God is perfectly loving, he must wish to abolish evil; and if he is all-powerful, he must be able to abolish evil. But evil exists; therefore God cannot be both omnipotent and perfectly loving.*[13]

6. Sigmund Freud's opinion of the biblical injunction, "Thou shalt love thy neighbor as thyself":[14]

> *"Thou shalt love thy neighbor as thyself." Why should we do it? My love is something valuable to me which I ought not to throw away without*

reflection. It imposes duties on me for whose fulfillment I must be ready to make sacrifices. If I love someone, he must deserve it in some way. If he is a stranger to me and if he cannot attract me by any worth of his own or any significance that he may already have acquired for my emotional life, it will be wrong for me to love him. For my love is valued by all my own people as a sign of my preferring them, and it is an injustice to them if I put a stranger on a par with them. But if I am to love him merely because he, too, is an inhabitant of this earth, like an insect, an earth-worm, or a grass-snake, then I fear that only a small modicum of my love will fall to his share.

On closer inspection, I find still further difficulties. Not merely is this stranger in general unworthy of my love; I must confess that he has more claim to my hostility and even my hatred. He seems not to have the least trace of love for me and shows me not the slightest consideration.

The Argument Diagram

An *argument diagram* is another way to represent the structure of an argument. An argument diagram is a map of an argument.[15] A map is a way to represent visually the spatial arrangement of the parts of the landscape; an argument diagram is a way to represent visually the logical arrangement of the parts of an argument. On a map, lakes are represented as blue splotches and cities as yellow grids; in a diagram, premises and conclusions are represented as numbers. On a map, roadways that lead from place to place are represented as lines; in a diagram, the inferences that lead from premises to conclusion are represented as arrows. An arrow means, "This leads to that" or "This statement provides reason to believe that statement." A map shows you the lay of the land; an argument diagram "shows you," helps you "see" and "examine," the logic of an argumentative passage.

2.5 ARGUMENT DOMINOES

By playing a competitive game reminiscent of dominoes, you can sharpen the skills necessary to diagram arguments.

Form groups of four students, gathered around a clear place on the floor. Each player has seven blank three-by-five-inch index cards. Each group has a piece of chalk. The object of the game is to be the first player to get rid of all the cards in her hand.

To begin play, one player writes any statement at all (call it 1) on a card and places the card on the playing board (the floor). The player to his left then writes a statement (2) on her card. That statement can say anything at all, *as long as it follows from* statement 1. She puts her statement on the floor near statement 1 and uses the chalk to draw an arrow on the floor, pointing from the premise to the conclusion. The arrow means "therefore"; it indicates the direction of the inference. The player to her left now has two statements to work with. He writes a statement that follows from either statement 1 or statement 2 and chalks in an arrow indicating the inference. Play continues in this manner. Players may draw a conclusion from any statement on the floor.

After five plays, a playing board might look like the diagram shown here:

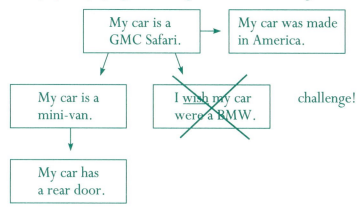

At any time after a card has been played and before the next card is played, any player may challenge the card most recently played. The challenger's job is to explain why that statement does not follow logically (even though it may follow chronologically) from the statement at the other end of the arrow. If the challenge succeeds, the challenged card is picked up off the floor, the offending statement is crossed off, and the card is replaced in the player's hand, to be played on another turn. Since the value of the game is in the nature of the discussion of "what follows from what," make sure that your group takes challenges seriously.

The winner is the first player to get rid of all the cards in her hand.

• •

The basic diagramming technique is relatively straightforward.

1.   Number the statements in the argument.
2.   Analyze the argument. To draw the diagram, you will need to know what the claim is, what the reasons are, and how the reasons are

related to the claim and to each other. You may need to supply some missing statements and to omit extraneous material.

3. Draw a diagram in which the statements are represented by their numbers and the inferences by arrows. Each arrow means "therefore." Arrange the diagram so that all the arrows point downward.

Here is a simple example: (1) Global warming will disproportionately affect third world countries, because (2) many of them are in low-lying deltas. The argument can be diagrammed as it is here:

(2)

(1)

The premise (statement 2) goes at the top of the diagram, and the conclusion (statement 1) goes at the bottom; a downward-pointing arrow leads from the premise to the conclusion. The full argument can be read from the diagram, substituting the word *therefore,* for the arrow: Many third world countries are in low-lying deltas; therefore, global warming will disproportiately affect third world countries.

Although the technique for diagramming the structure of an argument is straightforward, the structure of an argument often is not. The hard part of diagramming is figuring out the argument, the parts of which may be related in any of a variety of ways. You will need to pay attention to how the premises are related to each other. And you will need to look at how the premises are related to the conclusion.

Premises can be related to each other independently or conjointly. Premises are *independent* when any one premise, standing alone, is itself a reason for believing that the conclusion is true. Premises are *conjoint* when any one premise, taken alone, does not provide reason to believe the conclusion, but the premises, taken together, do support the conclusion.

Consider a series of arguments containing only three or four statements and displaying different logical structures. The examples are quoted from *The State of the World.*[16]

Here is an example of an argument in which each premise *independently* provides a good reason for believing that the conclusion is true. The conclusion is underlined.

(1) [It is evident that the poor are disproportionately exposed to pollution and hazardous materials.] (2) Neighborhood-by-neighborhood comparisons of income level, race, and

toxic waste site location reveal a disturbing but not so surprising pattern. The poorer the neighborhood, and the darker the skin of its residents, the more likely it is to be near a toxic waste dump. (3) Three fourths of hazardous waste landfills in the American Southeast are in low-income, black neighborhoods, (4) and more than half of all black and Hispanic Americans live in communities with at least one toxic waste site.[17]

Each of the three premises, even alone, supports the conclusion. Using numbers to represent each statement and arrows to represent each inference, the structure of the argument can be diagrammed this way:[18]

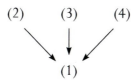

In some arguments, single premises cannot do the supporting job alone. That is, the premises independently do not provide reason to believe the conclusion, but together, *conjointly*, they do. Here is an example, again, with the conclusion underlined:

> (1) *Reports of land degradation have come from every corner of the planet.* (2) *Australian Prime Minister Robert Hawke said that "none of Australia's environmental problems is more serious than the soil degradation . . . over nearly two-thirds of our continent's arable land." (3)* Pravda *reports that the Soviet Union is suffering from a catastrophic decline in soil fertility. (4) Prime Minister Rajiv Gandhi has outlined the ecological and economic crisis India faces as the result of continuing deforestation and the associated degradation of land.*[19]

The simple fact that Australia reports problems with soil degradation does not give reason to think that reports are coming from around the world. Nor does the single fact that the Soviet Union's soil is depleted. Again for India. But all together the premises do support the conclusion. The brace indicates that the premises are conjoint rather than independent.
Look at it this way:

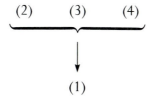

Just as there are two ways in which premises are related to each other, there are two ways in which premises are related to conclusions. One common argument structure is the *vertical* argument. Here, a premise provides reason to believe a conclusion. And that conclusion itself becomes a premise supporting the final conclusion. Here is an example:

> *(1) Bicycle transportation also uses space more efficiently than automobile transport. . . . (2) [Therefore,] replacing short car trips with bicycling . . . would save considerable space on roads. (3) <u>Cycling is thus an ever more attractive alternative to the daily grind of traffic congestion.</u>[20]*

This argument is diagrammed as a straight line of inferences, like so:

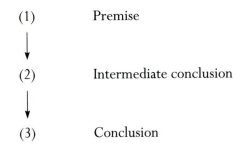

In a *horizontal* argument, at least two reasons or sets of reasons support a conclusion. Consider this example:

> *(1) [In developing countries,] <u>families spend an inordinate amount of time [gathering household necessities such as water and fuel], with women carrying the brunt of this hardship quite literally on their heads.</u> (2) A study in Kenya found that women do 89 percent of all water and firewood gathering for the family. (3) Women and children may spend three to six hours a day fetching water for the household.[21]*

The general shape of the diagram is horizontal, in that the two premises line up side by side, like so:

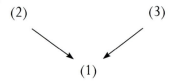

These basic forms—independent and conjoint premises, and vertical and horizontal arguments—can be combined in complex and various ways

to represent the logical structure of complex arguments. Here is an example:

> *(1) [It is a myth that increased military spending leads to prosperity.] (2) In truth, the military pork barrel turns out to be empty for most communities. (3) A recent study . . . found that 321 out of the 435 congressional districts . . . pay more in defense-obligated federal taxes than is returned to them in military salaries and contract money. (4) . . . [Moreover,] civilian spending creates significantly more jobs [than military spending.] (5) In the United States, spending $1 billion on guided missile production creates about 9,000 jobs. . . . (6) But spending the same amount on educational services would create 63,000 jobs.*[22]

There are two lines of argument supporting this conclusion. As in the following diagram, one line moves from statement 3 to statement 2 to the conclusion in a vertical line of argument. Statements 5 and 6 conjointly support statement 4, which itself supports the conclusion, statement 1.

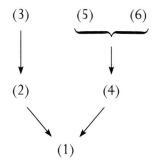

With more complex arguments, the diagram can rapidly become more complex. In some arguments, you will need to use a statement as both premise and conclusion; notice that in the preceding example statements 2 and 4 serve as the conclusion of one argument and a premise of another. In some arguments, you will need to supply missing parts. These should be added to the diagram in brackets, [ ], so that you will remember where they came from. You will sometimes need to be ruthless in cutting out information that does not do anything for the argument. This investment of time and attention is seldom wasted; the diagramming technique forces you to think carefully about how the statements in an argument are related to each other, which is exactly what an argument analysis is supposed to do.

As useful as diagramming is to a critical reader, it is even more useful to a writer of argumentative prose. Use it as a substitute for a topic outline; that is, instead of listing the topics you want to address in an essay, plan your essay by diagramming the argument you will advance. In a diagram, lay out your claim and the reasons supporting it and the reasons supporting those reasons. An essay written from such a preliminary plan will display an unusual clarity in the line of argument.

Diagramming is useful also as a first step in the revision process. After you have written an argument, sit down and diagram it. If the logical structure of your argument confuses even you, you have work to do. Better yet, ask another student to diagram your argument. Watch her struggle, hear her swear, and you will have a clear idea of where revisions are needed.

2.6 PASS IT ON

Form into groups of three or four. Each group needs one blank three-by-five-inch index card and enough "argument form" cards to give one to each member of the group. Each argument form card has one of the four following argument structures written on it:

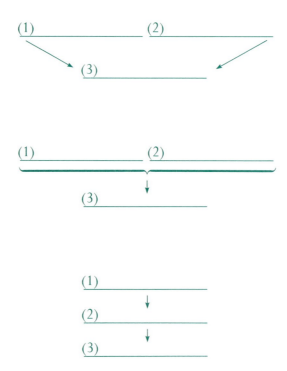

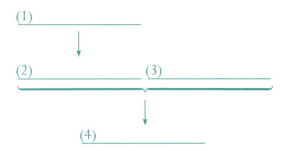

1. Fill in one of the blanks on your argument card with a statement of your choice—any statement, any line. Then, pass your card on to another student in your group. Her job is to fill in another line on your card. This will be harder because she will have to make sure that her statement relates to your statement in the way indicated by the arrows. Then she will pass your card on to another student, who fills in another line until the argument is complete.

2. As a group, study all the arguments you have put together, and make sure that they are correct; that is, make sure that each statement follows from the others as the diagram indicates. An easy way to do this is to try reading the argument out loud, saying "therefore" each time an arrow leads from one statement to another. Make any corrections you need.

3. Choose your group's best argument, and write it *in paragraph form* on the blank card. Exchange cards with a neighboring group, whose job is to diagram your argument while you diagram theirs. Compare their diagram of your argument with the diagram you used to write your argument. Was your argument's structure clear to readers? How might you improve its clarity?

2.7 CIVILIZATION ALONG THE AMAZON

Diagram the argument in each of the following paragraphs. The statements in the argument are numbered for your convenience, but you may decide not to use all the statements in each paragraph.

Archeologists have long dismissed the idea that a great prehistoric civilization might have grown up along the steamy, snake-infested banks of the Amazon River. But new research by Anna C. Roosevelt, curator of archaeology at Chicago's Field Museum of Natural History, indicates that the Amazon may have been one of the world's great cradles of civilization.[23]

1. Before Roosevelt's work, scientists believed that (1) the complex culture of the Americas grew up on the northwestern coasts of South America and spread to the great civilizations of the Incas, Maya, and Aztec. (2) This interpretation of history made sense. After all, (3) the coastal areas had temperate climates and rich soils, and (4) when European explorers arrived in the New World, this is where they found the great civilizations. Besides, (5) scientists did not think that the deep forests along the Amazon could support complex population centers.

2. (1) Roosevelt claims to have found pieces of pottery in ancient refuse dumps along the Amazon that were made 7,000 to 8,000 years ago. (2) Pottery is considered to be a sign of a culture that has advanced beyond hunting and gathering. This is because (3) making pottery requires sophisticated knowledge of clay deposits and furnaces at just the right temperature and because (4) pottery indicates that a culture has developed a sustainable food source. Thus, Roosevelt believes that (5) the Amazon basin, far from being a cultural backwater, was home to a sophisticated culture as many as 7,000 to 8,000 years ago.

3. (1) Until now, scientists believed that the plant communities in the Amazon valley were pristine, unchanged by human beings. (2) But researchers now believe that the great forests were planted, or at least nurtured, by humans. (3) More of the plants in the forest produce edible fruits and nuts, or contain medically useful compounds than would be expected by chance alone. So, (4) it is likely that people who lived in the valley long ago either planted the trees deliberately or planted them accidentally by discarding their seeds after using them.

4. (1) The quality of life along the Amazon may have been unusually good. (2) The skeletons of Amazonians average nearly five inches taller than Indians in the same area today. This indicates that (3) the people living along the Amazon were very well nourished, because (4) people who are properly nourished grow taller than those who are less well nourished. Moreover, (5) large river valleys tend to produce great amounts of food. (6) The Amazon basin is a large river valley, like the valleys of the Nile, the Ganges and other former breadbaskets of ancient civilizations. So it stands to reason that (7) the Amazon valley provided good nourishment for its inhabitants.

5. (1) Roosevelt found a huge midden, a refuse dump, along the Amazon River. (2) The midden is twenty feet high and covers fifteen acres. (3) This means that towns were thriving in this area for thousands of years. (4) It takes a long time for a group of people to accumulate that much garbage. (5) The midden contained fish bones and the shells of freshwater mussels. Thus, Roosevelt claims, (6) the people enjoyed abundant fish and shellfish from the river. (7) In the midden, Roosevelt also found hammerstones, scrapers, and grinding and cooking stones.

Standard Form

The final method for displaying the logical structure of an argument is *standard form.* An argument is in standard form when its premises are numbered and stacked on top of a horizontal line; the order of the premises does not matter. The conclusion is written beneath the line and is preceded by three dots in the shape of a pyramid, the symbol for *therefore.*

(1) First premise.
(2) Second premise.
∴ Conclusion

Consider, for example, this argument: "Age is the most terrible misfortune that can happen to any man; other evils will mend, but this is every day getting worse." In standard form, the argument looks like this:

(1) Other evils will mend, but [age] is every day getting worse.
∴ Age is the most terrible misfortune that can happen to any man.

This form is similar to the standard form for an addition problem:

$$
\begin{array}{r}
356 \\
+\ 345 \\
\hline
701
\end{array}
$$

In the argument, as in the addition problem, the information in the premises "adds up" to the conclusion.

This representational method is most useful when the arguments are most simple. Thus, standard form is most often used to present the logical structure of simple three-line arguments.

• •

2.8 GETTING INTO AN ARGUMENT[24]

1. When you come into the classroom, your professor will hand you a three-by-five-inch index card containing one of the following statements:

> The production of pornographic material should not be supported by funds from the National Endowment for the Arts.
>
> The results of AIDS tests must be kept confidential.
>
> Political speech is protected by the Constitution of the United States.
>
> The rivets on my car door popped out on July 1.
>
> Robert Mapplethorpe's photographs of nude men are pornographic.
>
> Student athletes who do not maintain 2.0 grade-point averages are disqualified from participating in intercollegiate sports.
>
> If people at risk of AIDS avoid being tested for the disease, AIDS will spread more quickly through the population.
>
> It is immoral to hurt or kill innocent animals.
>
> Ready access to cigarettes through vending machines is partly responsible for the rapidly increasing numbers of teenagers who smoke.
>
> The costs of repairing the rivets on my car door will not be covered by the warranty.
>
> It is immoral to wear fur coats.
>
> The center on the basketball team did not maintain a 2.0 grade-point average during the last academic year.
>
> Teenagers can readily buy cigarettes in vending machines.
>
> Flag burning is protected by the Constitution of the United States.
>
> The center on the basketball team is disqualified from participating in intercollegiate sports.

The warranty on this car expired on June 30.

Cigarette vending machines should not be put in places where teenagers can go.

Robert Mapplethorpe's photographic work should not be supported by the National Endowment for the Arts.

Wearing fur coats is responsible for the suffering and death of innocent animals.

If the results of AIDS tests are not confidential, many people will avoid testing.

Burning a flag is a kind of symbolic political speech.

2. Move around the room and find two other students whose statements, with yours, make up an argument. Using the principle of charity, decide among yourselves which statement is the conclusion.

3. Write the full argument on the chalkboard *in standard form*.

• •

2.9 HARSH WORDS ABOUT PROFESSORS

1. Higher education has recently been the target of savage attacks by legislators, students, and—often—professors themselves.[25] Ten of the most common criticisms are listed below. Choose one of those claims, and write a one-page (250-word) essay in which you use your own academic experiences as evidence for or against the statement. *Be sure that you write an argument, not an explanation.*

    a. The institution of tenure, which guarantees professors that they will not be fired no matter how poorly they perform, creates professors who are free to ignore their obligations to their students and concentrate on improving their golf games instead.

    b. By teaching students almost exclusively about the past, about the history of ideas and cultures, universities are graduating people who will be unable to function in the future.

    c. The modern university is actively hostile to good teaching. The more time a teacher spends advising students and preparing up-to-date class materials and effective lectures, the lower her salary will be and the less likely she is to be promoted and tenured.

    d. In order to save money, universities are offering fewer courses and fewer sections, forcing many students to spend an extra year in college to fulfill their course requirements.

    e. Students should study their own culture and not be forced to spend time learning about cultures and ideas from other parts of the world and from other times.

    f. Listening to a lecture is a lousy way to learn.

    g. Professors often neglect their students in order to spend time writing books, doing outside consulting, and chasing federal research dollars—activities more likely than teaching to bring them significant dollars.

    h. More and more, classes are likely to be taught by undergraduate and graduate teaching assistants, many of whom can barely speak English.

    i. Colleges and universities are not doing a good job of preparing students for the job market.

    j. Students choose the easiest courses, the "guts," in order to avoid writing term papers and final exams. Professors are happy to offer easy courses in order to improve their teaching reviews and keep their classrooms filled with a minimum of effort. As a result, students can graduate from college knowing little more than they knew when they arrived, which is not much.

2. Exchange papers with a partner. Represent the structure of your partner's argumentative essay in two different ways: argument summary, diagram, or standard form. Return the paper to your partner along with your representations, and see what your partner has done with your argument.

Finding the Missing Parts of Arguments

Sherlock Holmes once solved a mystery by focusing his attention on something that did not happen: A dog did not bark in the night. Often the key to understanding an argument is something that does not appear in the argument, a premise that is not stated, a conclusion never drawn, a value judgment or assumption never revealed.

Replacing Missing Premises and Conclusions

In some arguments, the job of representing the argument becomes a job of reconstruction since an essential part of the argument is missing. The missing part could be a premise or the conclusion. An argument in which a statement is understood but not stated is called an *enthymeme,* from the Greek words meaning "in the mind"—*en,* "in," + *thymeme,* "mind"— rather than on paper. "Richard Nixon cannot be elected president of the United States, no matter how rehabilitated he may become, because he has already served two terms" is an enthymeme because the premise that makes the argument work, "Presidents may serve only two terms," is understood and unstated.

Pieces of arguments go unexpressed for many reasons. Most often the omitted premise is a general principle that is so obvious, so familiar, that including it would make an argument tedious.

> Registrar: I'm sorry, I can't enroll you in that class because the class is full.

Understood is the premise, "I can't enroll students in classes that are full." But adding the premise would only add insult to injury because the student is not only closed out of the class but patronized as well.

Sometimes the omitted premise is left out because it is the weakest part of the argument and the writer is reluctant to call attention to it. An advertisement for cologne, for example, shows a close-up photograph of an extremely handsome man. Under the photo is this phrase:

> The extra-special cologne for an extra-ordinary man.

The reader who is willing to supply the missing premise—"Why yes, thank you, I guess I am an extra-ordinary man"—will surely reach the hoped-for conclusion—"This cologne is especially for me."

Occasionally, the missing part of an argument is false or indefensible, and the advertiser omits it to avoid trouble with the law: "The bigger the burger, the better the burger. The burgers are bigger at Burger Barn." If *you* want to draw the conclusion that the burgers are better at Burger Barn, you are welcome to do so, but then don't blame Burger Barn if the conclusion you draw turns out to be false.

Missing statements pose a special problem for argument analysis. To make an analysis complete, the missing statements should be supplied and included in brackets in the representation of the argument. This is particularly true of dubious or questionable claims. Statements that are generally accepted by the argument's audience can safely be ignored in an analysis.

How can you determine the content of a missing premise? How can you learn about something that is not there? When you have one piece missing from a puzzle, there is no mystery about the shape of that piece. The missing piece is precisely the shape of the empty space. The same holds true of missing premises: The missing premise is what is needed to make the connection between the stated premise and the conclusion. It is usually a general statement.

Here is an argument with a missing piece: "Jeremy will surely have a parking ticket on his car because he forgot to put money in the meter." What makes the connection between forgetting to feed the meter and getting a ticket is the general statement that people who do not put money in the meter get parking tickets.

Finding a missing premise is a three-step process: (a) Identify the conclusion, (b) identify the stated premise, and (c) ask what else must be true to make that conclusion follow from that premise. The answer to that question is the missing premise. One last example:

(1) She will probably speak English. (2) After all, she was educated in Swedish schools.

The conclusion? She probably will speak English.

The premise? She was educated in Swedish schools.

What else must be true if the ability to speak English is likely to follow from a Swedish education? English is generally taught in Swedish schools.

The diagram will look like this:

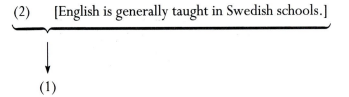

(2)   [English is generally taught in Swedish schools.]

(1)

* *

2.10 ADVERTISING ENTHYMEMES

Advertisements are arguments that are often missing important parts, perhaps because truth in advertising is required by federal regulations and so advertisers must hide false premises.

1. For the following six advertising enthymemes, state the unstated premise, the unstated conclusion, or both.

a. Thousands of callers have been amazed by the <u>accurate results</u> of their past psychic readings. . . . Call now! Your psychic is waiting! . . . $3.50/min.

b. WHEN COLLEGE STUDENTS HAVE THE FREEDOM AND RESPONSIBILITY TO THINK FOR THEMSELVES, THEY LEARN TO MAKE GOOD DECISIONS.

—Peter H. Coors

c. Tropical Delite Fruit Drink tastes just like its name. You'll be "delited."

d. Hyde-bound Furniture Company has been in the Hyde family for four generations. So you are guaranteed reliable, home-style service.

e. *Frederick Forsyth's Rolex watch is like his novels. [His novels are] tough, accurate, and very stylish.*

f. Joe Morino does a big volume of business. So you know he'll give you a good trade-in on your car.

2. Search through your own magazines for advertisements that can be understood as arguments that are missing a premise, a conclusion, or both. Cut out three or four and bring them to class. In working groups, reconstruct the arguments by supplying the missing parts.

• •

2.11 NAME THAT TUNE

Each of the following arguments is missing a premise or conclusion. Find the conclusion of the argument if you can. Identify the stated premises. Then, use these statements to determine the missing statement. In each case, the missing statement will be a line from a song.

1. Mary went to the opera. So, her lamb went to the opera also.

2. Every beautiful flower has its thorn. Every rose is a beautiful flower.

3. Towns like New York are rife with crime. A town rife with crime is a helluva town.

4. I drove my Chevy to the bank of the canal. The bank of a canal is a levee.

5. If you gotta get up in the morning, then get to bed early. Therefore, you will have to go to bed early.

6. I'm too sexy for my wardrobe. My shirt is part of my wardrobe.

7. Old MacDonald had a farm or he had a ranch. Old MacDonald did not have a ranch.

8. If you keep dancing with your eyes closed, you will step on my blue suede shoes. So, quit dancing with your eyes closed.

9. All teapots are short and stout. So, I am short and stout.

10. If I wanted to be safe, I would walk on the tame side. So, I obviously don't care about being safe.

Identifying Underlying Value Judgments

The most interesting and most critical part of an argument is the nebulous net of hopes and fears, of commitments and aversions, of values and disparagement that leads a person to say, "This reason counts," "This is an important consideration," or, alternatively, "That reason has no weight," "That may be true, but so what?" At some level, it is possible to understand an argument without concerning yourself with its underlying value assumptions. But for a deep understanding, you need to inquire into the value judgments that have shaped the selection of reasons in a given argument.

A *value* is a belief about something's relative importance, about its status on a scale of preferences. A person's values determine what reasons have weight in an argument, for that person. Suppose, for example, that there is dispute about whether a grove of redwoods should be cut. One person argues that the trees should be cut because doing so would create jobs for unemployed people. Another argues that the trees should be cut because they are infested with a disease that will destroy the remainder of the forest. Another argues that the trees should be cut because it is profitable to sell them. Which of these arguments is a *good* argument depends on what you value. Is it more important to you that a forest be saved or that jobs be saved? Which has a higher value, the aesthetic value of a forest or the monetary value of the cut lumber?[26]

Value judgments do an undercover job in argumentation. They validate reasons. They give reasons the power, the credentials, needed to support a conclusion. If you can uncover the value judgments operating in an argument, you gain insight into the strengths and weaknesses of that argument.

For example, Detroit schools are in federal court arguing for the right to set up all-male schools with Afrocentric curricula, higher standards, and longer hours. They support their plan by pointing out that the education of black males is in profound crisis in Detroit, where the leading cause of death among black males older than ten is homicide, and that all-male schools show some promise of improving academic performance. Behind the argument, empowering the reasons given, are a set of value judgments. The argument works only if one accepts a judgment that is never said out loud: that a primary goal now is the education of black males and that this is more important than integration and more important than equal treatment of female students. A federal judge who shares these assumptions will probably support the new school plan. A judge who does not will probably decide that although the reasons offered for all-male schools are true, they do not have sufficient importance to support the conclusion.

When you write an argument, think about the value judgments that drive your selection of reasons. Think about the value judgments that your audience is likely to make. If they are similar to yours, assumptions about values are unlikely to see the light of day; they function smoothly and below the surface. But if you and your audience do not share the same values, it may be wise to articulate your values in the interest of clarity. When you are analyzing an argument, even an argument that seems to be entirely factual, look for the value judgments that explain the selection of reasons offered in support of a conclusion.

· ·

2.12 KOREMATSU v. UNITED STATES

The Japanese attack on Pearl Harbor on December 7, 1941, which destroyed or immobilized much of our Pacific fleet, provoked fear of attack on the West Coast of the United States, [an attack] which might be aided by Japanese agents among the large numbers of American citizens of Japanese ancestry. It was assumed that there was inadequate time for screening [Japanese-Americans] for such disloyal persons and that in the emergency it was necessary immediately to isolate all persons of Japanese ancestry from military installations and remove them from critical areas. A combination of an act of Congress and an Executive Order of the President and orders of the military commander on the Pacific Coast brought . . . [for many Japanese-Americans] incarceration in what were called relocation centers—all without any findings of fact as to misbehavior of any kind and in spite of the fact that most of the persons involved were American citizens.[27]

In the 1944 case of *Korematsu* v. *United States*,[28] Mr. Korematsu argued that his incarceration in a relocation camp, in the absence of any evidence that he was an enemy but solely on the basis of his race, was a violation of his constitutional rights.

1. If you are on the left side of the classroom, write a one-paragraph argument to support the conclusion that Mr. Korematsu's imprisonment was improper. If you are on the right side of the classroom, write an argument to support the conclusion that Mr. Korematsu's imprisonment was proper. (If you think this will be a difficult argument to make, note that when this case came to trial in 1944, Korematsu lost. Try to imagine why.)

2. Both sides: Meeting with the others on your side of the classroom, read over the arguments your side wrote, and choose the most convincing three or four different arguments. Read these aloud to the entire class.

3. Both sides: As you listen to the arguments of the other side, jot down a list of the unstated value assumptions underlying their arguments. Do the others on your side agree with your list? Come up with a common list. Read it to those on the other side. Do they agree with your assessment of their assumptions? Are *they* correct about *your* assumptions? Does anything on their list surprise you or conflict with what you really believe?

4. Arguing for the majority of the U.S. Supreme Court in *Korematsu*, Justice Black said in part:

    > . . . *[E]xclusion of those of Japanese origin was deemed necessary because of the presence of an unascertained number of disloyal members of the group, most of whom we have no doubt were loyal to this country. It was because we could not reject the finding of the military authorities that it was impossible to bring about an immediate segregation of the disloyal from the loyal that we sustained the validity of the . . . order as applying to the whole group.*
    >
    > *We uphold the exclusion order. . . . In doing so, we are not unmindful of the hardships imposed by it upon a large group of American citizens. . . . But hardships are part of war, and war is an aggregation of hardships. . . . When under conditions of modern warfare our shores are threatened by hostile forces, the power to protect must be commensurate with the threatened danger.*

What value judgments are implicit in Justice Black's argument?

● ●

How to Evaluate the
•••••••••••••• Worth of an Argument ••••••••••••••

The analysis of an argument will help you understand what the argument is asking you to believe or to do and on what grounds. To decide whether you ought to believe what the argument urges or do as the argument advises requires an additional step: the evaluation of the argument. What are the criteria for deciding whether an argument merits agreement? What makes an argument a good argument?

To make good bread, a baker must have good ingredients, must combine them according to a good recipe, and must produce a final product that appeals to the taster. In much the same way, the worth of an argument depends on the content of its statements, the relationships between those statements, and the way the argument is received by the listener. In a good argument, the premises are *true,* the premises provide good reason to believe that the conclusion is true, and the combination of premises and conclusion is convincing.

So, to evaluate an argument, it is important to ask three questions:

1. A question of content: Are the premises true?
2. A question of form: Are the premises and conclusion logically related in such a way that the premises support the conclusion?
3. A question of effectiveness: Is the argument convincing?

A Question of Content

A good argument begins with true premises. If you start with false or dubious premises, even if you put them together correctly, there is no reason to think you will arrive at a true conclusion. For example, the following argument is correctly constructed but completely worthless because its premises are false:

> Crack cocaine is nonaddictive. Nonaddictive drugs do no harm. Therefore, crack cocaine does no harm.

A good argument conveys the truth of the premises to the conclusion. If the premises are false in the first place, all bets are off.

A Question of Form

It is not enough for an argument to start with true premises. For the truth of the premises to be conveyed to the conclusion, the argument must be correctly constructed. For example, in the following argument, every statement is true. But the argument is worthless because the premises do not *give reason* to think that the conclusion is true.

> Paula Abdul sang "Opposites Attract." You should brush your teeth after every meal. Therefore, crack cocaine is addictive.

In a good argument, the premises and conclusion are related in such a way that true premises increase the likelihood of a true conclusion.

A Question of Effectiveness

Rhetoricians, people who study the persuasiveness of argument, would add another criterion to the list of factors that make one argument better than another. This is the effectiveness of the argument, its power to change people's minds or alter their behavior.

Aristotle, a Greek philosopher of the third century before Christ, analyzed the factors that combine to make an argument convincing. There are three such factors, he claimed: *Logos* refers to reason, the logical grounds or evidence for a claim. Persuasive arguments rest on good reasons, Aristotle believed, since the truth is more powerful than falsehood. *Ethos* refers to the credibility of the speaker or writer. Much of the effectiveness of an argument depends on a relationship of trust and respect that the speaker is able to develop with the audience. *Pathos*, the third element of effective argumentation, refers to the emotions of the audience. An argument will be more effective if it builds not only on the minds but also on the hearts of the audience.

An argument with true premises and correct form may or may not be persuasive. An argument that is persuasive may or may not have true premises and correct form. But an argument that is persuasive *and* has true premises *and* has correct form is as good as an argument can get.

● ●

2.13 SLASHER FLICKS

Slasher films like *Night of the Living Dead* and *The Texas Chainsaw Massacre* are the center of heated controversy about blood and violence in the movies. Here you have an argument in defense of violent films, followed by four possible replies.[29] *Analyze* each of the arguments. That is, for each argument:

1. Identify the issue.
2. Identify the claim that is defended.
3. Identify the reasons used to defend the claim.
4. Represent the structure of the argument.

IN DEFENSE OF VICIOUSNESS AND VIOLENCE

By Ima Fan

It is easy to criticize "splatter flicks," the bloody and vicious horror movies so popular among teenagers. After all, they portray our worst nightmares in living color and focus attention on vicious, twisted criminals. All the same, I think it is important to pay attention to the good effects of slasher flicks.

Our society is a scary place. There is terrible violence in public schools, vicious drug-related crime, adult abuse of children, random death on city streets. So, teenagers have to deal with real fears. It helps to watch real fears acted out in the safety of a movie theater, where the audience can—if they choose—simply walk away. Because splatter flicks scare us in a setting where we have ultimate control, they help us learn to cope with our deepest fears, dreads, and anxieties.

Violent behaviors are not popular because of violent movies; violent movies are popular because they reflect the violence that already exists. No one claims that people are loving because they watch *Bambi*. So why do critics claim that people turn into murderers because they watch *Nightmare on Elm Street?*

1. Ima Fan's claim that graphic violence helps us to deal with our deepest fears, dreads, and anxieties might be true for adults. But many children and adolescents watch horror films, and their reaction is different. Research shows that children act out what they see; when they see someone acting in violent, cruel ways, their own aggressive behaviors increase measurably. So I think that Ms. Fan is wrong: The

violence in the slasher films is a cause of, not merely a reflection of, violence in society, especially violence among young people.

2. The "Texas Chain Saw Massacre" is a good way to reduce stress and fear?! If slasher flicks really were effective means of learning how to deal with our deepest fears, dreads, and anxieties, then you would think that psychologists would have learned to treat anxious patients by prescribing large doses of horror movies. Until that happens, I remain skeptical.

3. When Alexander Pope wrote "An Essay on Man," he said something important to people like Ima Fan:

> Vice is a monster of so frightful mien,
> As to be hated needs but to be seen.
> Yet seen too oft, familiar with her face.
> We first endure, then pity, then embrace.

4. Ima Fan is absolutely wrong about the positive effects of slasher flicks. The horror in the films desensitizes people to violence and makes them think it is an unremarkable part of life.

     Psychologists have known this for a long time. When they want to help a person overcome a phobia, they expose the person to continual, small doses of the object of his fear. The slasher flicks are helping cure viewers of the fear of violent death, maiming, and vicious assault.

5. In Massachusetts, Sharon Gregory was killed by a youth who believed he was Jason in "Friday the Thirteenth," a popular horror movie. By producing slasher flicks, film makers are providing role models for potential murderers and sadists.

• •

2.14 IS AFFIRMATIVE ACTION CONSTITUTIONAL?

In each of the following paragraphs, students work with the topic of affirmative action.

For each paragraph:

a. Tell whether it is an argument or something else.

b. Write out the issue and the conclusion.

c.   Represent the structure of the argument with a diagram, an argument summary, or standard form. Be sure to include any missing, but essential, premises or conclusions.

1.   Taking minority status into account for hiring, scholarships, and school admissions is another way to promote discrimination. By doing this, the affirmative action group is excluding the people who may not fall under the minority category. This is clearly discrimination against those who aren't minorities because they're giving a privilege or an edge to certain groups over others. After all, when it comes to hiring someone for a particular job, the important thing to take into account is if that person has the qualifications, such as experience, dependability, and punctuality.[30]

2.   What this country needs is an affirmative action program for white males!

3.   I would have to be for the affirmative action idea that race and gender should sometimes be taken into consideration for hiring, scholarships, and admissions because, in many instances, minorities are not taken into consideration, basically because it seems easier to choose from the majority. Being a minority, it is difficult to find a job but, with the help of affirmative action policies, minorities would have doors open to new opportunities. Most scholarships are also very limited. Males seem to receive them more easily than females on account of the demand for male college sports.[31]

4.   Biologists can find no differences in ability between ethnic groups, men and women. Why then do certain ethnic groups do poorly in school? Why do women and minorities have trouble getting good jobs? The answer has to be environment. Society must try to make things fair. Minority scholarships may seem unfair. But, when these minorities grow up educated, they are more likely to have educated children who live in a more equal environment. Also, the minority or woman probably has a greater actual potential, because they have persevered through an adverse environment. Women and minorities will not be accepted in high positions of society until there are already some in these high positions. This apparent paradox can only be solved by affirmative action programs, giving opportunities to people who would otherwise be denied them.[32]

5.   Race and gender should never be used as acceptable criteria in hiring, scholarships, or school admissions. The only criterion that should be

used is the material pertinent to the issue. Can you do the job and do it completely? Do you deserve to receive a scholarship? Do you qualify with the set academic standards? What sex you are and what the color of your skin is tell nothing of your qualifications and say nothing about your future prospects. Race and gender should not be used when deciding who works, who receives money, or who goes to school.[33]

6. The United States has a long history of racism and sexism. Affirmative action is designed to counteract this. Affirmative action forces people to facilitate the hiring of minorities and women. Quite often, in instituting social change, they tend to be resisted. Affirmative action requires that people hire equally. This will be a necessary law until fair practices are used automatically. Therefore, affirmative action is necessary.[34]

· ·

· **Notes** ·

1. Barbara Ehrenreich and Frances Fox Piven, *Dissent* (Spring 1984); quoted in *Social Justice: Opposing Viewpoints,* ed. David Bender (St. Paul, Minn.: Greenhaven Press, 1984).

2. This example is from Kathleen Dean Moore, *A Field Guide to Inductive Arguments* (Dubuque, Iowa: Kendall/Hunt, 1989), p. 3.

3. Thomas Sowell, "The New Racism on Campus," *Fortune* (Feb. 13, 1989), p. 115. Thomas Sowell, FORTUNE, © 1989, The Time, Inc. Magazine Company. All rights reserved. Used with permission.

4. Larry Gordon, "New Rules for USC's Sororities, Fraternities," *Los Angeles Times* (August 29, 1991), pp. B1, B4. Copyright © 1991, Los Angeles Times. Used with permission.

5. Margaret Anderson, "The Southern Crucible," *Background and Foreground* (New York: Channel Press, 1960), p. 211.

6. *Mother Jones* (Nov. 1989), reprinted in *Utne Reader* (May/June 1990), p. 38.

7. Arnold Wilson, logic professor and editor of *Teaching Philosophy,* emphasized the usefulness of argument summaries in his "Sourcebook for Student Logic Portfolios" © Arnold Wilson, 1990. The approach here follows the system he encourages his students to use.

8. Stacey Colino, "Crime on Campus," *Seventeen* (September 1991), pp. 138–139. Copyright © 1991, Los Angeles Times Syndicate International. Used with permission.

9. Alburey Castell, *An Introduction to Modern Philosophy* (New York: Macmillan, 1943), p. 42 (paraphrased).

10. David Hume, *Dialogues Concerning Natural Religion* (New York: Hafner, 1948), p. 80 (paraphrased).

11. William Paley, *Evidences of the Existence and Attributes of the Deity* (New York: Sheldon and Co., 1875).

12. G.H. Joyce, *The Principles of Natural Theology* (London: Longmans, Green, and Co., 1923).

13. John Hick, *Philosophy of Religion* (Englewood Cliffs, N.J.: Prentice-Hall, 1983).

14. Sigmund Freud, "Aggression, Guilt, and Conscience," see *The Life and Work of Sigmund Freud,* ed. E. Jones (New York: Basic Books, 1953).

15. Stephen Naylor Thomas, *Practical Reasoning in Natural Language* (Englewood Cliffs, N.J.: Prentice-Hall, 1986).

16. Lester R. Brown, et al., *State of the World 1990* (New York: W.W. Norton and Co., 1990). Copyright © 1990, W.W. Norton and Company. All selections used with permission.

17. *State of the World 1990*, p. 148. Underline added.

18. Analyzing arguments by diagramming them is an idea developed and popularized by Stephen Naylor Thomas, *Practical Reasoning in Natural Language* (Englewood Cliffs, N.J.: Prentice-Hall, 1986).

19. *State of the World 1990,* p. 60. Underline added.

20. *State of the World 1990,* p. 124. Underline added.

21. *State of the World 1990,* p. 126. Underline added.

22. *State of the World 1990*, pp. 156–157. Underline added.

23. Information for this exercise is drawn from Boyce Rensberger, "Ancient Remnants of a Complex Civilization," *The Washington Post National Weekly Edition* (December 23–29, 1992) p. 38.

24. This idea is suggested by Arnold Wilson, "Getting Into an Argument," *Demonstrating Philosophy* (New York: University Press of America, 1988), pp. 93–94.

25. One of the more provocative books, and one that has caused the most stir among professors and administrators, is Charles J. Sykes, *Profscam* (New York: St. Martin's Press, 1990).

26. Lisa Ede, *Work in Progress: A Guide to Writing and Revising* (New York: St. Martin's Press, 1989), p. 232, suggests that disputes about forest-management plans are especially value-laden.

27. Carl Brent Swisher, *Historic Decisions of the Supreme Court* (Princeton, N.J.: D. Van Nostrand Co., 1958) pp. 160–161.

28. 323 U.S. 214 (1944).

29. The fictional essay and the responses that follow are broadly based on an article by the director of *The Night of the Living Dead*, John Russo, and the responses his article stimulated. See John Russo, " 'Reel' vs. Real Violence," *Newsweek* (February 19, 1990), p. 10.

30. Kristi Huynh, Philosophy 121 (Winter 1992), Oregon State University. Used with permission.

31. Lorie Krois, Philosophy 121 (Winter 1992), Oregon State University. Used with permission.

32. Matthew Harrison, Philosophy 121 (Winter 1992), Oregon State University. Used with permission.

33. George Goesch, Philosophy 121 (Winter 1992), Oregon State University. Used with permission.

34. Ellener G. Peavyhouse, Philosophy 121 (Winter 1992), Oregon State University. Used with permission.

Putting Arguments Together

According to Chapter 2, you must analyze an argument in order to understand it; you must strip it down to its skeleton and examine how its claims and their supporting reasons are joined. Chapter 3 addresses the exact opposite task. How do you take a skeleton and make it into a flesh-and-blood argument, living and working in the real world? Chapter 2 introduced the techniques for taking an argument apart. In this chapter, you will use the same techniques in reverse, to put an argument together.[1]

The chapter is divided into three sections: planning an argument, drafting an argument, and revising the draft. This format is instructive in one respect, and potentially misleading. The format correctly suggests that the actual writing of an argument is a relatively small segment of a larger endeavor. But the format should not be taken to suggest that the three parts of the writing job—planning, writing, and revising—follow each other rigidly like soldiers marching up to the top of the hill. These steps often occur simultaneously. People write to plan, they plan to write, they revise before they even get to the end of the first sentence, and there is nothing wrong with any of that. But if you are trying to understand the process, to improve it, it may be well to divide the process into discrete steps.

·········· Creative and Critical Thinking ··········

All three stages of the writing process require skills of creative and critical thinking in constant interaction, sometimes working together, sometimes working against each other. Writing an argument means thinking of ideas (a creative endeavor) and cutting and shaping these ideas to fit with each other and with the occasion (a critical endeavor).

The creative process itself has never been satisfactorily explained. Where do ideas come from? Why do they arrive unbidden and abundant at some times and at other times vanish like spit on a griddle? Medieval scholars thought creative people were literally inspired, infused with the Holy Spirit, taking down divine dictation. A present-day insight is that the most creative people seem to have broad knowledge reaching into disparate and distant fields, knowledge that allows them to see something from a new angle or to discover a new connection.

In the past two decades, composition teachers[2] have developed a set of techniques for generating a flow of ideas. Each technique involves writing, and each takes advantage of the way the mind works. On the chance that they will help you think of ideas for your arguments, three of the techniques are briefly summarized here: brainstorming, freewriting, and looping.

- *Brainstorming* is the unrestrained offering of ideas and suggestions. Like storms—uncontrolled, unpredictable, chaotic, often windy events, where a lot of stuff falls out of the sky—brainstorms generate ideas quickly and uncritically. *Group brainstorming* is an idea-generating or problem-solving process whereby all the members of a group offer all their ideas spontaneously, randomly, freely. Ideas are not criticized or praised, just recorded. The process is disorderly and often noisy. The interplay among all the minds, the interaction of all the ideas, generates a pile of options from which the group can later, in a quite separate process, select the best.

- *Freewriting* is simply thinking on the page, recording whatever ideas come into your head. The process itself is simple: Get out a blank piece of paper or call up a blank screen. Now, for ten minutes, write without stopping. It does not matter what you write or what you write about as long as you are writing. Freewriting is just that—writing that is free. You are free of self-consciousness because the writing is for your eyes only; free of the constraints of self-criticism because the goal is to come up with lots of ideas, good and bad; free of rules because spelling, grammar, and such are absolutely irrelevant at this point in the process; free of all expectations because surprise, unexpected directions, and arbitrariness are to be valued over a direction or destination.

    Some of what you write will be trash. Some of what you write will be incoherent, disjointed. Some of what you write will be simple repetition of an empty mantra: "I don't have anything to say." It doesn't matter. The goal of freewriting is to get thoughts down on paper.

- *Looping* is a variation of freewriting.[3] The process combines freewriting with analysis in a way that allows a direction to emerge from the writing. First, freewrite for five minutes. Then, examine what you have written. Find the heart or central concept or most interesting theme of what you have written. Write a sentence that summarizes this theme. Then, freewrite about that topic for five minutes. Examine what you have written. Summarize the central theme of that writing. Continue in this pattern, spiraling through your ideas like a tornado.

In each of these procedures, keep one thing in mind: The time of creativity is absolutely not the time to be critical. Any idea is, at least, an idea, and that is all you are looking for at this point. Forbid yourself absolutely to censor, to second-guess, to judge, even to plan. There will be plenty of time for that. In Peter Elbow's words:

> If you are trying to be inventive and come up with lots of interesting new ideas, it's usually the worst thing in the world if someone comes along and starts being critical. Thus, the power of brainstorming [and of other idea-generating techniques] is that no one is allowed to criticize any idea or suggestion that is offered—no matter how stupid, impractical, or useless it seems. You can't get the good ones and the fruitful interaction among the odd ones unless you welcome the terrible ones.[4]

Courage to Risk and Revise

Two related misconceptions bedevil student writers. One mistake is to think that writing must be (or even *can* be) done right the first time. The other mistake is to think that a first draft might ever be a finished product. A truly finished product is almost always the result of writing and revising, rewriting and revising again, as many times as it takes. Thus, good writing is partly a matter of putting words on paper; but it is also a matter of throwing out what is not good enough and replacing it with what is better. Write, cut, fix, replace, chop out, write, rearrange, try again: This is the slash-and-burn approach to the writing process.

This way of thinking about the writing process both gives and takes courage. You know that, in the end, you will need to produce a piece of writing that is grammatically perfect, logically compelling, true in every detail, and persuasive. But it should *give* you courage to know that your writing doesn't have to be all these things the first time through. So, you don't have to worry about everything at once. You are free to work first on one aspect of the writing (say, the logical structure) and then another (the grammar, for example) until you have put together all the elements of good writing. It's as if an Olympic ice skater were allowed to skate her program until she did it perfectly.

On the other hand, this way of thinking about the writing process *takes* courage. You have to be brutal with your own creation, cutting out and discarding what doesn't work, starting over again when you have to. And, of course, it takes time.

· ·

3.1 SLASH AND BURN

1. Freewrite for five minutes by the clock. It doesn't matter what you write about; it doesn't matter if what you write makes sense; it doesn't matter if you have complete sentences or correctly spelled words. Just put pen to paper and start writing. Don't stop to think. Don't stop to revise. Don't stop to pick the right word. If you can't get started, write down one of these phrases and keep on writing.

    > In the middle of the night, last night . . .
    >
    > My brother . . .
    >
    > It hurts my feelings when . . .
    >
    > Tomorrow, when I get a chance, . . .
    >
    > It's hard to start writing, because . . .

2. When your five minutes are up, shake out your writing hand, read what you have written, and pick out *one* sentence that interests you. *Throw the rest away.* Write that sentence at the top of a new piece of paper and continue writing for three minutes by the clock.

3. When your three minutes are up, shake out your writing hand, read what you have written, and pick out the one, two, or three parts that are interesting. *Throw the rest away.* Using the parts that you've saved and adding whatever else you need, write a short paragraph.

4. Look over the paragraph and mark it up, making any changes you think will help make it more interesting, more coherent, or more lively. Copy that paragraph to keep. *Throw everything else away.*

· ·

• •

3.2 THE AGONY AND THE ECSTASY

The great sculptor Michelangelo was chipping away at a block of marble while a young boy watched closely. Slowly, chip by chip, a lion emerged from the block. Amazed, the little boy asked the great sculptor, "How did you know there was a lion in there?"

This story is told by composition teacher Peter Elbow,[5] who believes that writing is like sculpting; a good writer generates lots of material, then chips away at it. An essay is first the creation, then the selection, of ideas.

Is this how you write? Think carefully about the mental processes that accompany your writing process. Then, write a paragraph in which you describe how you think when you write.

• •

• • • • • • • • • • • • • Planning an Argument • • • • • • • • • • • • •

A good argument has two characteristics. First, it is correct in form and content; that is, all the claims made in the argument are true, and together the claims provide strong support for the conclusion. Second, it is effective; it is likely to succeed in affecting the readers' opinions or actions. The correctness and the effectiveness of an argument are inextricably connected.

Effective Argument

To write an effective argument, an argument that succeeds in changing the way readers think or act, you need a clear idea of why you are going to the trouble of writing the argument: What is your purpose? And you need a clear picture of the people to whom your argument is addressed: Who is your audience?

What Is the Purpose?

People usually write arguments for a good and compelling reason: They want to change another person's mind or behavior. When you write an argument, be clear about what change you are trying to bring about.

You may want to change a person's behavior, as these two letters are designed to do:

Dear Mom and Dad,

My textbooks cost lots more than we figured. And I need to pay a damage deposit on my apartment. So please send at least $450.

Your loving daughter,
Karen

Sirs:

The VCR I purchased from your company on June 3 is defective. It eats tapes. The guarantee that came with the VCR says that the purchase price is "cheerfully refunded if not fully satisfied." Yet, when I returned my VCR to the store, the manager was not the least bit cheerful; in fact, she refused to take back the machine and refused to return my money.

Since I am not fully satisfied, and since you have promised to return the purchase price if I am not fully satisfied, please send me a check for $345.99.

K.V.R.

Or you may want to effect a more or less dramatic change in a person's mind, nudging it a little in an unaccustomed direction, or opening it to a blaze of light. Here is an unusually ambitious argument, an attempt to change the minds of university professors, a particularly intransigent lot:

It is common in faculty discussions to degrade the value of athletics on campus. To many, athletics represents the worst side of academia. . . . However, North Carolina State University received a 40 percent increase in applications in the wake of its championship victory in 1983. . . . Boston College received 16,200 freshman applications in 1985 compared with 12,500 applications the previous year. Boston College admissions director, Charles Nolan, gave much of the credit for this increase to Heisman Trophy winner Doug Flutie, his 1984 teammates, and the attention they brought the school. . . . The preceding stories suggest a symbiosis between athletics and academics very different from the adversary relation common in faculty club discussions. If, as these stories suggest, athletic success breeds increases in applications, then there is a link between athletic success one year and the quality of the incoming freshmen in the future.[6]

Before you even begin to write, decide how ambitious you want to be. Would you be satisfied if the reader simply understood why you hold the view you hold? Are you trying to raise doubt in a reader's mind? Are you trying to reinforce a belief that is already present but only weakly? Are you trying to achieve a 180-degree shift in a reader's opinion?

• •

3.3 THE BOTTOM LINE

1. As a class, choose a situation on your campus or in your community that needs to be changed. Identify the individual who could make that change.

2. As individuals, write to that person, advocating a particular change that will solve the problem.

3. Invite that person to come to class to discuss the letters, answer questions about their effectiveness, and help the class determine what makes an effective letter effective.[7]

Think along these lines. Are people unhappy with the bookstore's textbook-selling policies? Invite the manager of the bookstore. Does your community need new legislation to protect student renters? Draft some legislation, and invite the head of the town council. Do the police treat minority students fairly? Invite the police chief. Is registration a disaster, term after term? Invite the registrar. Are lots of animals used in experiments on campus? Invite the head of the cancer research lab. Is industrial waste contaminating the creek on campus? Invite the president of the polluting company.

• •

Who Is the Audience?

Before you begin to write, have a clear mental image of the people to whom your argument is directed. Who will the readers be? What do they already believe? How firmly do they believe it? How much do they already know? Where are they likely to be confused or of two minds? What interests and values color their decisions?

Answers to these questions will help you select reasons to include in your argument. Knowing what your audience knows will help you avoid boring them or offending them by telling them what they already know, or, worse yet, omitting a crucial piece of information from the case you are making. Knowing what your audience believes will tell you where to start: If you are up against a rock-solid set of beliefs, you may have some major ground-leveling to do. And knowing your audience's hopes and fears will allow you to choose the line of argument most likely to be heard.

Even if your argument is not addressed to an individual, the argument will be better if you *pretend* you are writing to a particular reader, either a real person or one you make up for this purpose.[8] Think of someone in your life who represents the audience you have imagined: your mother-in-law, perhaps, or Tom Brokaw. Keep in mind the things that would turn this person away: an over-stated position, probably, or overblown rhetoric or sarcasm. Keep in mind that person's intelligence, concerns, and reasoning ability. If you would not feel comfortable presenting your argument to that person, you probably need to think it through again.

. . . .

3.4 ARGUMENTS FROM A SLAVE NARRATIVE

In 1789, the African slave and writer Equiano wrote two arguments against the slave owners' common practice of separating slaves who love one another. The first argument simply and powerfully tells the story of his separation, then reunion, then final separation from his sister.

> . . . One evening, to my great surprise, whom should I see brought to the house where I was but my dear sister! As soon as she saw me she gave a loud shriek and ran into my arms—I was quite overpowered: neither of us could speak, but for a considerable time clung to each other in mutual embraces, unable to do anything but weep. Our meeting affected all who saw us. . . . When these people knew we were brother and sister they indulged us to be together, and the man to whom I supposed we belonged lay with us, he in the middle while she and I held one another by the hands across his breast all night; and thus for a while we forgot our misfortunes in the joy of being together: but even this small comfort was soon to have an end, for scarcely had the fatal morning appeared when she was again torn from me forever! I was now more miserable, if possible, than before.[9]

The second argument is more elaborate. Equiano describes the clamor and confusion of the slave market in the West Indies, where slaves are purchased and sent in all directions, regardless of their relationships. Then he says,

> O, ye nominal Christians! might not an African ask you, Learned you this from your God who says unto you, Do unto all men as you would men should do unto you? Is it not enough that we are torn from our country and friends to toil for your luxury

and lust of gain? Must every tender feeling be likewise sacrificed to your avarice? Are the dearest friends and relations, now rendered more dear by their separation from their kindred, still to be parted from each other and thus prevented from cheering the gloom of slavery with the small comfort of being together and mingling their sufferings and sorrows? Why are parents to lose their children, brothers their sisters, or husbands their wives? Surely this is a new refinement in cruelty which, while it has no advantage to atone for it, thus aggravates distress and adds fresh horrors even to the wretchedness of slavery.[10]

1. In a paragraph, describe what you would infer to be the characteristics of the audience for the first argument. What do they know about the slave trade? What do they probably believe about it? What do they value? Do the same for the second argument.

2. Describe an entirely different audience (perhaps slave owners). Then write an argument to that audience, trying to convince them that slaves should not be parted from those they love.

• •

3.5 LETTERS TO THE FAMILY

Families are often called upon to make important decisions as a group. Should the family move to another city? Should the family buy a house? Should a single parent marry? Should the family have another child? Should an elderly parent be moved to a nursing home? Decisions like these are often very difficult because the outcome will affect different family members in different ways.

Think back to a time when your family faced a difficult decision. (Or, look forward to a decision your family is about to make.) What is the issue your family faced? What did you think they should do?

For three minutes, write to your mother, trying to convince her that your advice is correct. For three minutes, write to your youngest sibling, trying to convince him or her. For three minutes, write to your father, trying to convince him.

Join classmates whose families faced similar problems. Share your letters with one another. Then, prepare answers to the following questions:

1. Did each of you use different reasons when writing to different people? What characterized the reasons you presented to your mother? to your sibling? to your father?

2. What do the letters presuppose about the values and interests of the mother? the sibling? the father?

3. Did all three letters have the same purpose? If not, how do the letters vary?

4. Did any member of your group have an approach to a family member that was dramatically different from the approaches used by the other group members? How can that variation be explained?

5. Generally, what are the characteristics of the most convincing reasons?

• •

Effective arguments focus on a particular goal and fit a particular audience. Correct arguments begin with information that is true and then put that information together in a way that clearly supports the conclusion.

Correct Argument

Chapter 2 suggested that you could understand an argument written by another person by analyzing it, that is, by asking a set of questions designed to isolate the parts of the argument. These were the analytic questions:

1. What is the issue addressed in the argument?
2. What is the claim defended in the argument?
3. What reasons are offered to back up the claim?
4. How can the relations among the statements be represented?

Now the task is not to analyze but to synthesize an argument. Any argument you write will need to have all the same parts, so you can collect the pieces that you will craft into an argument by asking yourself the same analytic questions. Then, just as the diagram laid out the structure of the argument you were analyzing, you can use a diagram to plan the structure of the argument you will write. Thus, for example, you can plan a simple argument by filling in the blanks of a generic diagram like the one shown on the next page. Then you can use this diagram as a writing outline to draft your argument. Of course, this is only one of infinitely many possible argument forms.

The topic: _____ _____

The issue: _____ ?

Support for reason 1, if necessary.	Support for reason 2, if necessary.	Support for reason 3, if necessary.
_____	_____	_____
_____	_____	_____
↓	↓	↓
Reason #1	Reason #2	Reason #3
_____	_____	_____
↘	↓	↙

Claim _____

Here are the steps:

What Is the Issue?

It is hard to overemphasize the importance of having an issue clearly in mind. When an argument fails, when it wallows in detail, when it shifts direction and wanders, it is almost always because the writer did not know what issue she was addressing. Alternatively, when an argument succeeds, it almost always has a single issue to provide a focus, a point, a direction.

Distinguishing Topics from Issues

It is not enough to have a topic. A *topic* is a noun or noun phrase that defines a content area to be addressed. Skiing. The Weather during the Constitutional Convention. Chow Mein. Grandmother's Dog. Highways. An *issue* is a particular arguable point arising in the context of some doubt or controversy. Should a new ski area be built next to the wilderness area? Did the extreme heat during the Constitutional Convention shape the compromises that were reached? Is chow mein authentic Cantonese food? Is grandmother's dog actually a rat? Should this neighborhood be cut by a new highway?

Since you will have to choose a topic before you can choose an issue, here is some general advice about topics:

Generating ideas for topics   In real life, choosing a topic to write about is seldom a problem. You write about love or refrigerators or trash pick-up or Yugoslavia because you want to convince your lover to love you, because you want to sell your refrigerator, because you want to improve your trash pick-up service, or because you want to convince your readers that Yugoslavia should be divided among its ethnic minorities.

In class, it is sometimes a different story. In class, where the point is to practice writing, the choice of topic is sometimes left entirely up to you. The first step in choosing a topic is to come up with a lot of topic ideas from which you can choose the best. Begin by examining your own experience. It is likely that a promising idea is on your mind already.

- Examine your emotions. What have you been angry about lately? In the last few days, why have you said, "That's not fair," or "That's stupid," or "That's not true"? When you mutter under your breath, what do you mutter about? Chances are these emotions have been triggered by a situation or policy that is worth arguing about.

- Examine your living situation. The dimensions of your life—your partner, your apartment, your job, your social life—have been shaped almost entirely by decisions you have made. Which of those decisions do you really believe in? What mistakes have you made? What changes would make your life easier, more rewarding? What hard decisions are you facing?

- Examine your classes. Do your professors always tell you the truth? Do you always agree with their interpretation of facts? What objections would you have made in class if you had had the courage or the facts to back up your claim? Have you noticed any contradictions among the claims that are made in various classes?

Criteria for selecting topics   In choosing a topic from all the ideas you have generated, keep the following criteria in mind:

1. Choose a topic that you know something about or can learn something about.

2. Choose a topic whose scope matches the scope of the assignment. It is better to do a good job on a narrowly defined topic than barely to scratch the surface of a complex, global subject.

3.   And, of course, choose a topic that you care about. It does not have to be a topic that will save the world, but it does have to matter to you.

Once you have a topic, you still have lots of work to do. Choosing a topic is like choosing a state for your vacation; it provides you some limits but does not give you much direction. Within that topic, you need next to define an issue.

Defining an Issue

Generating ideas for issues   The issue is the single point in question or matter in dispute. Issues generally fall into one of three categories: issues of fact, issues of value, and issues of policy. So, you can brainstorm by asking three different sorts of questions[11] about the topic you have chosen. For purposes of illustration, assume that you have chosen to write about the topic national Greek organizations, that is, fraternities and sororities.

1.   *What are the factual issues?* Within the topic, what sorts of questions of fact are unsettled? Where are the controversies about what is true? Of the factual claims that are made within this topic, which may be debatable or simply false?

> Do fraternities still engage in dangerous hazing activities? Do sororities encourage race discrimination? Does the membership of Greek organizations show racial balance? Do "Greeks" have a greater chance of later success in business? Have any fraternities or sororities been able to control alcohol use among their members? How does membership generally affect members' grades? What effect would banning fraternities and sororities have on university enrollment? Does date rape occur more frequently in Greek houses than in off-campus apartments and dorms?

2.   *What are the issues related to values?* Are there controversies within this field about what is important, what is to be valued? What are the goals of the practice? Is there disagreement about what is right? what is good? what is better? what is beautiful? What value judgments need to be made, and on the basis of what criteria? Are there conflicts between competing values?

> Are the purposes of Greek organizations consistent with the purposes of a university? Is the cohesiveness, the network, fostered in sororities and fraternities a positive or negative factor? Are the public service projects of Greek organizations important? Does it matter that fraternities, by defi-

nition, exclude women and that sororities exclude men? Are the organizations good things? Do their positive aspects outweigh the negative?

3.   *What are the policy issues?* What should be done? What policy is the best? What problems need to be resolved? What changes do you advocate?

Should the university ban hazing? Should the university ban national Greek organizations? Should fraternities and sororities develop affirmative action programs to increase their minority membership? Should fraternities and sororities with exclusively minority membership be encouraged? How should police deal with alcohol-related offenses in Greek houses? How can Greek houses combat date rape? How can fraternities and sororities improve their public image?

. . . .

3.6 TOPICS AND ISSUES

1.   Here is a list of topics. Choose any one of them, and write down a list of ten issues that fall under that general topic. Remember to phrase the issues as questions.

disposable diapers	rain
minimum-wage work	sexually transmitted diseases
2 Live Crew	global warming
date rape	Japanese-American relations
organ transplants	the American automobile
marriage	alcohol
the Olympics	intercollegiate athletics

2.   Now, choose one of those issues. Write three further questions raised by that issue.

3.   Look over your issues. Write *F* next to each item that presents a factual issue. Write *V* next to each one that presents a question of values. Write *P* next to each one that presents a policy issue.

4.   In class, your professor may take a class vote to see which topic most students wrote about and which issue was most often raised under that topic and may ask you to write a short (250-word) essay on that issue.

. . . .

Criteria for choosing an issue   When you choose an issue, here are some things to think about:

1.   Is this an issue about which people have *reason-based* differences of opinion? Some issues are not subjects of reasoned discourse. It is not profitable, for example, to argue about matters purely of taste.

"Window-shopping is my favorite way to spend a Saturday afternoon."

"I'd rather have my teeth pulled."

A statement of taste preference is a description of yourself; it is true if you are truly describing yourself and false if you are lying. But since you are the only one with access to corroborative evidence, an argument about taste is futile. Moreover, your tastes are not usually based on reasons. So, arguments about matters of taste are likely to be boring. Even claims like "I enjoy tearing wings off houseflies" are not claims you can argue about, although you should of course engage the issues "Is it a moral failing to enjoy dismembering insects?" and "How are you going to prevent yourself from enjoying this 'pleasure'?"

Another set of issues about which there can be no rational argument is beliefs based on faith, not reason. Some beliefs are held for no reason whatsoever. Moreover, some beliefs are valued only because they are unreasonable, or perhaps nonreasonable. Many religious beliefs have this character, and so are not suitable subjects for argument. The claim that Jesus was the son of a virgin could perhaps be refuted by displaying its logical contradiction. Believing it anyway, without any reason whatsoever or in the face of reasons to the contrary, may be an important sign of faith.

. . . .

3.7 *FIDES ANTE INTELLECTUM*

A medieval Latin proverb advocates "faith over intellect." Twentieth-century Americans with an Enlightenment heritage are more likely to pride themselves on being creatures of reason, choosing to believe only claims that are supported by the weight of evidence. Yet within most people is a core of beliefs that cannot be touched by reasons. And some people take pride in having beliefs that are immune to any rational examination whatsoever.

Do you have any beliefs that you hold on faith alone? Or, to phrase the question another way: Is there anything you believe so firmly that no amount of counterevidence could shake your belief?

Freewrite on this issue for five minutes.

. . . .

2. Is this an issue that cannot be resolved by direct observation? It is pointless to debate issues that can be resolved by direct observation. "There are twenty people in this room." "No, there are only nineteen." Obviously the sensible thing to do is go together and count them. "My $5 bill is green." "No, it is red." Save time; pull it out and look at it.

In contrast, "There are too many people enrolled in this class" and "My $5 bill is counterfeit" are claims worth arguing about.

3. Is this an issue about which you can get reliable information? Choosing an issue is just the first step. You will soon have to make a claim and back it up with evidence. If the evidence is not available, or not available to you, save yourself the trouble.

4. Does this issue give you an opportunity to study, learn more about, or grapple with something you find intriguing? This question is not asking whether the issue is of earth-moving significance. It does not have to be. But if you do not care about it at all, you will be hard-pressed to make a reader care about it. Life is too short to spend on matters of no account.

What Claim Will You Defend?

The next question to answer is What claim will you defend in the argument? Decisions about what position to take should be made on the *weight of the evidence*. Given that there are good reasons on both sides of the issue, a careful thinker ponders the issue (*ponder*, "to deliberate," from the Latin *ponderare*, "to weigh"). She decides which side of the issue has the preponderance of evidence (*preponderance*, "superior importance," from the Latin *praeponderare*, "to weigh more"). Then, all other things being equal, she reaches the conclusion that is most strongly supported by the evidence. If there is no clear preponderance of evidence, she reaches no conclusion at all. "I don't know yet" is not a weak-kneed response to a difficult dispute; it is an honorable and honest response and one least likely to lead to error.

For this reason, it is not until after the evidence is in that you are in a position to draw a conclusion. Topic → issue → evidence → conclusion is the correct *logical* order. That is not to say that most people are usually this deliberate in choosing a claim to defend. What you already believe no doubt influences the evidence you seek and determines the evidence you value. If you had not already reached some sort of conclusion, the issue would probably not interest you enough to write about it.

What is important is that if you reach a judgment before you go out to look for evidence, you must treat the judgment you begin with as *tentative*. Note that the word *tentative* is from the same Latin roots as the word *tempt*, "to entice to do wrong, to allure into evil." Treat your claim as an enticing but dangerous idea. Let it lead you to a search for evidence for and against it. And if the evidence contradicts your tentative conclusion, you can always change your mind.

Whatever you do first, part of planning an argument is writing out a clear statement of the claim your argument will defend. Having an idea of it is not enough; write it down. You will notice that the claim turns out to be an answer to the question raised in the issue. For example,

> Issue: How does membership in a fraternity affect a student's grades?
>
> Claim: Membership in a fraternity generally results in higher grades.

How strongly you state your claim will depend on how strong your evidence is. If you have *overwhelming* evidence of an effect, say so: Membership in a sorority causes a dramatic drop in a new member's grades. If you have *some* indication of an effect, say so: Membership in a fraternity may be a factor in higher grade point averages for new members.

This *claim* will become the most important part of your finished argument, with a prominent place in your paragraph. It is your *position*, your *conclusion*, your *thesis statement*, depending on what vocabulary you use. It will be the main point of your paragraph, the claim that you defend.

• •

3.8 THE ADMISSIONS COMMITTEE

This is a role-playing and reflection exercise. Six of you will play the roles and speak with the voices of the members of the admissions committee for the medical school at a major state university. The rest of you will listen to their discussion and provide written responses to the questions provided.

The situation. The admissions committee is meeting to reconsider its admissions policy. In the past, admissions were based on GPA, MCAT score, and an interview. The committee is considering a new proposal:

> The goal of the admissions process shall be to admit a student body that is of the highest academic quality and that reflects the racial balance of the community. Without resorting to formal quotas, the admissions committee shall divide the applications by race of applicant and shall admit the most outstanding students in each racial category, in numbers proportional to their numbers in this community. The basis for judgment of ability (GPA, MCAT, interview) shall remain unchanged.

The roles. Martin, the white, middle-aged dean of the medical school and chair of the committee; Julia, a representative of the Latino community and the director of public health projects for the state; Candice, a white neuroanatomy professor; Jeffrey, an African-American medical student and head of the black student caucus at the school; Jonathan, a white physician and wealthy benefactor to the medical school; Stefan, a physiology professor and recent immigrant from Poland.

The plan. For fifteen minutes, the student role-players will discuss the proposed change. They should be careful not to break character; on the other hand, they should be thoughtful people, not caricatures. As they debate, listen to the discussion and write responses to the questions on the Student Response Form. Your professor will give you time before the discussion begins to answer question one and will provide time for you to ask questions of the "committee" after their discussion.[12]

Student Response Form

1. Before any current reflection or discussion, I hold that:

2. Based on the discussion of the "admissions committee," I now hold that:

3. The major factors that lead me to this tentative conclusion are as follows:

    a.

    b.

    c.

4. My main questions for the "admissions committee" are:

    a.

    b.

    c.

5. All things considered, I now/still conclude that:

• •

What Evidence Will You Use?

The next step in planning an argument is to explore the reasons for and against your claim and to select the reasons you will use in your argument. Reasons take the form of *statements of fact* (statements about what is true) or *statements of value* (statements about what ought to be). To find out what is true, you may need to do some research. This could be library research, of course, but consider also other rich sources of information. For example, your own experience may be a source of information, insight, and examples. Other people—experts—might be able to help you. Where you go for information and how much information you need will depend on the nature of the issue.

Students are often surprised to see that statements of value serve as good reasons. "How can he put that in his argument? That's just his opinion!" This objection rests on a confusion between a "mere" opinion and a value judgment. A "mere" opinion is a belief carelessly acquired and largely unexamined and unsubstantiated. Given this definition, an opinion probably does not have enough substance to support a conclusion and so should not be part of an argument. But a value judgment does not have to be a mere opinion; if it is carefully examined and buttressed by reasons, it can be a reasoned judgment and thus provide strong support for a conclusion.

Moreover, many arguments must use value judgments to support their conclusions. In order to resolve issues of value and issues of policy, it is necessary to take a stand on what is important, what is intolerable, what is essential—all value judgments. Thus, value judgments are vital premises in some kinds of arguments. When they reflect the values of the audience, they are very effective reasons indeed. When they do not, the writer must be prepared to defend them, with reasons.

As an illustration, consider this excerpt from Thurgood Marshall's opinion in the landmark legal case *Brown* v. *Board of Education*.[13] The Supreme Court's value judgment that education is important, along with its factual evidence of the harm segregation does to education, allowed it to reach the judgment that segregation is unconstitutional.

> *Today, education is perhaps the most important function of state and local governments. . . . In these days, it is doubtful that any child may reasonably be expected to succeed in life if he is denied the opportunity of an education. Such an opportunity, where the state has undertaken to provide it, is a right which must be made available to all on equal terms. . . . Segregation of white and colored children in public schools has a detrimental effect upon the colored children. . . . We conclude that in the field of public education the doctrine of "separate but equal" has no place.*

How Writing Can Help You Select Reasons

When you are trying to think of reasons for and against a claim, the idea-generating techniques of brainstorming, freewriting, looping, and group brainstorming are always available to you. But several other techniques are better designed to help you explore the evidence and reasons on either side of an issue. The first two are variations on the freewriting theme.

- *Dialogue writing.* Begin with a question that can be answered with "yes" or "no," such as: Should universities abolish sororities? Imagine two people who hold contrary views, one an avid defender of sororities and the other their most rabid attacker. What might they say to each other? Write it down. Get them started, and then just keep on writing down whatever you imagine they might say. You will find that your characters take on lives of their own and come up with reasons to defend their own points of view that are far more complete and compelling than any you would think of yourself, even though this is all a product of your imagination.

  As with all freewriting, there is no reason to think that all the reasons generated in this imaginary discussion will be splendid reasons or even that most of them will be usable. But the discussion gives you a rich assortment of ideas from which you can choose the best.

- *Role-playing.* Pretend you are the president of the Sigma Chi chapter on campus. Pretend that, much to your surprise, you are called on to defend fraternities to the guests at an alumni picnic. Quick, what do you say? Write it down. Pretend that you are an anti-fraternity parent, talking to the dean of students, trying to persuade her to ban fraternities. Quick, what do you say? Write it down. Don't censor yourself here or stop to think or polish. Speak with the voice of your imaginary spokesperson. Get the ideas down on paper, just as you would be forced to get your ideas out in an extemporaneous speaking situation.

- *Listing.* Work on a big sheet of paper or a chalkboard. Write the issue at the top. Draw a line down the center of the paper to form two columns: *Yes* and *No*. As ideas come to you, list all the reasons you can think of on each side of the issue. This is a method that works very well as an organizational framework for group brainstorming. Get your study group to help you brainstorm. Or engage the entire class. There is no limit to what develops when twenty or fifty minds start their motors in an enclosed space.

How to Select the Best Set of Reasons

Coming up with lots of reasons requires a fund of background knowledge about the issue, insight into the nature of the problem, flexibility, empathy, and imagination. What you produce is a pile of reasons on both sides of an issue. The next step is to choose the best set of reasons to support the claim you decide to defend. These will be the reasons that are likely to be most effective, given the purpose of the argument and the nature of the audience.

Part II of this textbook, "Developing a Repertoire of Argument Strategies," will help you develop and select supporting arguments for your claims.

• •

3.9 THIS IS YOUR DEATH[14]

KQED, the public television station in San Francisco, brought suit in a California district court, claiming the right to televise the execution of criminals. KQED hoped that it would be allowed to broadcast electrocutions on special news shows, with the permission of the person being executed. If you were the judge, would you allow executions to be televised?

Your professor will write the issue across the top of the chalkboard and then divide the board into two halves, labeled *Yes* and *No*.

Think of one good reason either for or against televising executions. Go up and write it on the chalkboard in the appropriate space. If you think of another, go up and write it, too. When every student has written a reason and the board is full of reasons "on each side" of the issue, come to a class consensus on the following:

1. Which reasons are weakest? That is, which reasons are based on false or questionable presuppositions? Which are not to the point? Erase these.
2. Which reasons are strongest? That is, which reasons are true, relevant, and likely to be effective? Star these.
3. Which side has the strongest support overall?
4. Selecting what you think is best from the reasons starred on the chalkboard, write a quick (ten-minute) essay defending a position on the issue.

• •

3.10 EXTRA CREDIT

Divide into groups of three to six students. One-third of the people in each group will get a significant number of extra credit points for the day's work; the others will get none. You have eight minutes to decide as a group how to assign those points. Tape-record the discussion that leads to a decision.

Replay the tape and keep score. How many statements made in the course of the discussion are statements of fact, descriptive of a state of affairs ("I have the lowest GPA already." "If she gets the points, she'll have an unearned advantage.")? How many statements reflect a value judgment ("This isn't a fair assignment." "We should draw straws.")?

Your professor will decide exactly how many points go to the lucky students.

• •

If you were analyzing an argument, you would now, having identified all the parts of the argument, diagram its structure. Since you are writing an argument, you will plan your argument by putting the pieces together in an argument diagram.

What Is the Structure of the Argument?

What is your topic? Put it at the top of the page. What issue will you address? Write it below the topic. What claim will you defend? Write it next. What reasons will you offer to support your claim? Connect these with arrows to the claim. Do any of those reasons need support? Connect the supporting reasons to the main reasons with arrows. When you are done, you may have something hat looks like this argument, drawn from an article in *Time* magazine:[15]

The topic: Dieting

The issue: Are Americans as diet-conscious as they have recently been?

Data came from a report by the Calorie Control Council

The number of dieters in the U.S. has leveled off from 65 million in 1986 to about 48 million currently.

Many weight-loss clinics across the nation have closed or are failing.

Makers of liquid and powder diets are avoiding bone-thin models and choosing heftier people to hawk their products.

People are losing their appetite for diet books.

The claim: The American preoccupation with dieting is moderating.

This argument is organized in a horizontal fashion, with four different, independent reasons all emphasized equally, all, so to speak, on the same horizon.

If you want to organize an argument so that each claim is supported by another, you can set up a vertical argument, with a structure something like this:[16]

The topic: Dieting

The issue: Is dieting healthy?

In a study of 3,130 men and women, ages 30 to 62, participating in the Framingham Heart Study, researchers found that yo-yo dieters ran a 70% higher risk of dying from heart disease than did people whose weight stayed fairly steady, even if they were overweight.

$$\downarrow$$

Dieters who swing through cycles of weight loss and gain may actually be cutting their lives short.

$$\downarrow$$

Claim: Dieting is unhealthy.

Once you have a diagram, your planning is complete. The diagram outlines exactly what you plan to write. Now you have to write it.

. . . .

3.11 A PROGRESSIVE ASSIGNMENT

For progressive dinners, each stage of the dinner, from hors d'oeuvres to dessert, is at a different person's home. Having a progressive dinner is one way to force lots of people to clean house. This is a progressive writing assignment, where each stage of the writing process is done by a different person.

1. At the top of a clean sheet of paper, write down a topic. Pass the paper to the person on your right.

2. On the paper you now hold, write down an issue that falls under that topic. Check to make sure it is a question. Check to make sure it satisfies the criteria for a workable issue (that is, the issue is something

the writer knows or can learn about, the issue's scope matches the scope of the assignment, and the issue makes a difference). Pass the paper to the person on your right.

3. On the paper you now hold, write down a short description of an audience to whom the argument will be addressed and the purpose of the argument. Pass it to the person on your right.

4. On the paper you now hold, write two or three good reasons on each side of the issue. Check to make sure they satisfy the conditions for a good reason (that is, that they are both true and persuasive). Pass the paper to the person on your right.

5. Weigh the reasons, decide what claim will be defended. Write down a clear statement of the claim. Pass the paper to the person on your right.

6. Diagram an argument, using all the materials provided you. Return it to the person who chose the topic.

Drafting the Argument

Now, after a long, laborious section on planning an argument, squeezed in front of an equally detailed section on revising an argument, comes what was promised in the first place: a little advice on writing an argument. The diagram will serve you as a writing outline.

Making the Issue Clear

Because readers may not want to invest the time it takes to read an argument unless they know from the beginning what is at stake, the first part of a paragraph containing an argument should raise the issue. For example, in the following argument, the issue is raised in the first sentence.

> [How much longer will Americans be preoccupied with the unending struggle to be slender? Several factors indicate that the preoccupation with dieting is moderating.] According to the Calorie Control Council, . . . the number of dieters in the U.S. has leveled off from 65 million in 1986 to about 48 million currently. Many weight-loss clinics across the nation have closed or are failing. People are also losing their appetite for diet books. . . . [And] makers of liquid and powder diets are avoiding bone-thin models and choosing heftier people to hawk their products.[17]

Stating a Clear Claim

The most important element of an argument is a clear statement of the claim you will defend. Many writers put the claim within the first one or two sentences of the paragraph. The advantage to this is that it helps the reader anticipate the direction of the argument. Other writers put the claim at the end of the paragraph as a sort of goal reached. Either way is fine; just don't bury the claim somewhere in the middle of the argument. And worse yet, don't forget to include it or assume that your audience will figure it out themselves. They won't.

In the following argument, the conclusion is put in the second sentence, right after the issue:

> [Researchers are looking again at the widespread belief that "thin is healthy, fat is doomed." New research suggests that the effort to achieve ideal thinness is unhealthy.] Dieters who swing through cycles of weight loss and gain may actually be cutting their lives short. [Evidence comes from] a study of 3,130 men and women, ages 30 to 62, participating in the landmark Framingham Heart Study. Researchers found that so-called yo-yo dieters ran a 70% higher risk of dying from heart disease than did people whose weight stayed fairly steady, even if they were overweight.[18]

Signposting

When you make an argument, you, the writer, have a certain destination in mind. You want to "get to the point," "arrive at a conclusion." What makes the job difficult is that you have to take your readers along with you. For the argument to be effective, to "lead" readers to the conclusion, you need somehow to guide your readers from statement to statement until they can "see" the conclusion. This guiding is done by "signposts."

A *signpost* is a word that indicates the job a given statement does in an argument. Words like "thus," "therefore," and "so" tell the reader that the statement that follows is the claim defended in the argument. Words like "since," "because," and "given that" tell the reader that the statement that follows is offered as a reason for believing the claim is true. Carefully signposted, the dieting argument might read like this:

> According to the National Center for Health Statistics, "only 10% of dieters who lose 25 pounds or more will remain at their desired weight beyond two years." So most people will gain back all the weight they lose on strict diets. Since nothing is more frustrating than doing a job and then having to do it all over again, it follows that dieting is frustrating.

Adroit and abundant signposting dramatically improves the clarity of an argument. This is true for two reasons: First, it leads your readers in the direction you want them to go. Second, it forces writers to know where they want to go. Whenever signposting an argument is a hard job, the argument needs revision.

• •

3.12 REDUCE SPEED

Suppose that a friend brought you the following diagram for an argumentative essay and asked you to change it into a well-written essay.

Topic: The Speed Limit

Issue: Should the 65-mph speed limit be reduced on interstate highways?

Studies conducted in Connecticut showed that highway deaths increased by one percent with each 1 mile per hour increase in the speed limit.

From birth, when government requires your footprints to be registered, to death, when government tells you where you can be buried, laws govern our lives.

Reason 1: The higher the speed limit, the higher the death rate.

Reason 3: The government already has too many rules that govern our lives.

It is estimated that 12,000 people in the U.S. die every year from lung disease brought on by air pollution.

Reason 2: Cars emit more pollution when they are driven at higher rates of speed.

Conclusion: Speed limits on interstate highways should be reduced from 65 mph to 55 mph.

Help her out; that is,

1. Correct any mistakes in the logic displayed in the diagram. (Be careful; there are several terrible mistakes.) Supply unstated premises. Omit or change irrelevant or false reasons. Make sure the claim is supported by the reasons. Add reasons if you think that is necessary.
2. Use the diagram to write a first draft of an essay.
3. Evaluate and revise the essay.
4. Rewrite.
5. Proofread.

. . . .

3.13 THE PROGRESSIVE ASSIGNMENT: DESSERT

Pull out the argument diagram you and your classmates created in Exercise 3.11. Using the diagram, write out a clearly signposted argument in defense of the claim provided you.

. . . .

3.14 CATALOG COPY

For each of the following lists of statements, figure out the logical relationships among the statements: Which supports which? Which is the main claim? Which are reasons? Which are reasons supporting reasons?

Diagram the logical relation among the statements.

Write a *clearly signposted* argument, using only the statements provided and all the signposts you want.

1. From Lands' End:[19]

Commuter Oxfords [are] better than most.

They're lined with Thinsulate.

Thinsulate lining has microfibers that trap air to insulate your foot against the cold.

Rubber bottoms keep water out.

Water-resistant leather uppers have comfortable padded leather collars.

2. Order a portable canvas umbrella.
    The umbrella is perfect for beach sand or lawns.
    The umbrella has a wooden shaft and a stake at the bottom to shove into the soil.
    A swivel joint allows you to easily adjust the umbrella toward the angle of the sun.
    The umbrella can be folded into a package only 3 feet long.
    Comes with a canvas carrying case.
    Convenient for family trips to the beach.

3. Ours are the best polarized sunglasses available for the price.
    The optic lenses are precision-ground.
    The glass is impact-resistant.
    You will not find finer lenses at any price.
    The glasses are especially designed for performance in all fishing situations.
    They provide full protection from UV light.
    The glasses cut through glare on the water.
    The glasses allow you to see fish that are swimming under-water.

4. In one of your own catalogs, find an advertisement that expresses an argument. Diagram it. Rewrite the argument, making good use of signposts.

Evaluating and Revising
•••••••••••••••••••• the Argument ••••••••••••••••••••

The critical evaluation and revision of writing is an essential part of the writing process. Especially with an approach to writing like the one offered here, in which critical judgment is deliberately suspended during the initial stages of writing, this is a step that cannot be omitted. Save as much time for this part of the process as you devoted to the creative part of the process. Do this, even if the only way to do it is to set a stopwatch when you begin work on your assignment: Figure out how much time you have by the clock. Start to evaluate and revise when half that time period has passed.

Evaluating Your Own Work

When you have finished writing your argument, set it aside. What you need for an objective evaluation is distance. Letting time pass between writing and rewriting is one way to acquire distance.

When you are ready to evaluate your work, read it out loud. This also provides distance. What "sounds good" echoing in the head does not always sound good when it comes in through the ears. Simply reading your work aloud will probably show you some points that need to be reworked.

Write down the issue your argument addresses. Write down the main claim defended in your argument. Briefly describe the audience. Diagram your argument. If you can do this much, so far so good; at least, your argument has all its parts in place.

Now check your work on these points:

1. Does the argument defend one clearly identifiable claim?
2. Is everything the argument says true?
3. Is everything the argument says relevant to the main claim?
4. Does the argument move clearly from one point to the next?
5. Toward what sort of audience is the argument directed? Is it consistently written for that audience?
6. What is the purpose of this argument? Is that purpose achieved?
7. What do you like best about your argument? What should you work on next?

On the basis of the information you have discovered about your argument, revise and rewrite.

3.15 A SECOND CHANCE

Look in your notebook for the argument you wrote for Exercise 1.2, the argument about the stadium murders. Evaluate it according to the criteria offered here. Then revise it and rewrite it. Turn in both the original and the revised versions.

Peer and Group Evaluation

No matter how hard you try, it is not in your nature as a human being to be your own best critic. So it is well at this point to seek out the help of another person. That other person can give you feedback about the two important aspects of your argument, its cogency and its effect on the reader. The reviewer could be one of your peers—a friend, a classmate, or a group of your class-mates. Alternatively, you could seek feedback from a professor or a tutor. Many universities have writing centers for just this purpose.

It is important to go after feedback with the right attitude, the attitude of an owl seeking a mouse.[20] The analogy is instructive: Go after criticism systematically and industriously, knowing that your life as a writer depends on it. When you get it, gulp it down, rejecting nothing, not even the most dismaying tails and paws. Then, let it digest slowly. Keep the parts that are useful to you. As for the parts that are not useful, spit them out.

Since a good argument is both effective and cogent, it makes sense to seek information about how the argument has affected readers and to seek information about the logical correctness of the argument. The first kind of information comes from reader-based evaluations, where readers pass along their reactions to the argument. The second kind of information comes from criteria-based evaluations, where a trained reader checks the argument against a set of standards.

Reader-based Evaluation

These questions are designed to elicit detailed information about the effect of an argument on a reader:[21]

Reader-based Evaluation

1. Read the first two or three sentences. Do you already know where the argument is headed? Where?

2. Read on. Write a question mark at each and every point where you start to get confused, or where you have to back up to catch the train of thought, or where you wonder where you are headed.

3. Read on. Write *zzz* at each point where you start to lose interest.

4. When you began reading, what was your position on this issue? How did the argument affect that view?

5. How do you feel about the writer of this piece when you have finished reading?

6. Write a summary of the argument. As a guideline, you may fill in these blanks: "The writer argues that _____ . The writer's primary reason is that _____ . The writer backs this up by noting that _____ . As added support for the claim, the writer says that _____ ."

7. Tell one thing you wish the writer had done but did not do.

• •

3.16 THE CASE OF THE TWISTED T.A.[22]

A week before she was to graduate, a female student confided to the dean that she had been offered a passing grade in a statistics class in exchange for sex with the instructor, a graduate teaching assistant. Fearful of failing, she had accepted the offer.

The dean in whom she confided encouraged her to file a formal complaint of sexual harassment. She was reluctant to do so because she was worried about retribution from the teaching assistant. But after some persuasion, she filed the complaint. When confronted with the accusation, the teaching assistant admitted trading grades for sex, not just in this case but in others as well. He resigned from graduate school.

There the matter might have ended. But the chair of the statistics department was outraged. He demanded that academic dishonesty charges be brought against the undergraduate who filed the complaint. "She was given a grade she did not deserve, for reasons having nothing to do with her performance in class," the chair complained to the dean. "She knew what she was doing. Her grade and class credit must be withdrawn."

The dean was horrified. He had promised the student she would not suffer any retribution if she filed charges. And he had hoped that her example would help uncover other sexual harassment cases.

What should the dean do?

1. Write a one-paragraph argument in which you take a position on this problem and defend it with reasons. Make three copies of your argument.

2. In class the next day, divide into groups of four. Taking turns, ask the group to provide information that will help you improve your argument, as follows:

> Give each member of the group a copy of your argument.
>
> Read the argument aloud as each group member reads along.
>
> Ask each group member to answer the "Reader-based Evaluation Questions" above. While they do that, you do it, too.

3. On the basis of the suggestions and insights you gained from the group, revise and rewrite your argument. Your professor may choose to give you a group grade on this assignment, the average of the grades of all the members of your group. The quality of a piece of writing is, after all, very much a function of the quality of feedback it receives.

Criteria-based Evaluation

Another approach is to ask others to review your argument and respond, not about its effects on them, but about its success or failure to meet a set of standards of quality in argumentation. This takes a more sophisticated reader. The following questions are designed to elicit information about the cogency of an argument:[23]

Criteria-based Evaluation

Quality of content

1. Is the argument in support of a single claim?

2. Is it supported by reasons that are
    a. true?
    b. to the point?

3. Are the reasons suited to its audience and the purpose?

4. Are the ideas clearly expressed?

5. Are important points missing?

Quality of form

6. Does the evidence really support the claim?

7. Are the parts arranged in a coherent and logical sequence?

8. Are the inferences clearly labeled?

Revising the Argument

With the information gained from feedback, revise your paper. Evaluation and revision can be done as many times as you like or have time for. With this option, a piece of writing suddenly becomes not a product but an ongoing, mutable process, subject to improvement at any time.

Proofreading

Students take great pains with their appearance—their hair, their clothes, their makeup—because they know that people will judge them by how they look. Turning in a piece of writing without proofreading it is like walking out the door without checking yourself in a mirror. Your zipper might be open. And there might be spinach between your front teeth.

Thus, before your writing job is complete, it is important to proofread what you have written, checking for errors in spelling, grammar, punctuation, and usage. This will prevent you from misleading the reader about your meaning. And it will prevent hostile readers from dismissing your work out of hand.

Proofreading will also prevent you from misleading the reader about your intelligence. Writers are judged by their writing; writing is judged in part by its appearance. If a piece of writing is sloppy, full of misspelled words and misplaced commas and mismatched verbs, readers will make a quick first judgment of the writer: This person is a dummy. And it will take quite a bit of work to dispel that first impression, even if what you say is brilliant.

If you don't trust yourself to catch errors, don't give up. Look around for help. Your computer can check your spelling for you, but only if you ask it to. It will not catch you, though, when you have used the wrong word—"their" instead of "there," for example. Friends and fellow students can sometimes help. And most schools have writing centers, where student tutors can help other students learn to proofread their own work. For your birthday, ask someone to give you a good writing handbook that will explain the basic rules. Keep it on your desk, next to your dictionary.

• •

3.17 SHOULD THE LEGAL DRINKING AGE BE REDUCED?[24]

Below are five arguments defending a position on the issue Should the legal drinking age be reduced to eighteen? All five are *first drafts* of arguments written by students. Thus, the arguments are rough, as first drafts should be. No one can write perfectly the first time through.

First, working alone, rank the arguments, ordering them from weakest to strongest. Then, working in groups, try to reach a consensus on your ranking. Evaluate, revise, and rewrite one argument. Write the revised argument on an overhead transparency, so that you can share it with the class.

1. The drinking age should either be reduced to 18 years old or the legal age to be an adult should be increased to 21 years old. I say this because it is unfair to say an 18 year old has the right to be an adult and vote or to fight and or die for his/her country but then they are not able to take on an adult responsibility—like drinking at that same age. My concern is not that 18 year olds should be able to drink. In fact I think it's too young an age and too big a responsibility. If the age of becoming an adult was increased to the age of 21 or 20 then maybe there would be a better solution. If this were to happen there would be less contradiction. Also there would be more responsible kids. Therefore either the drinking age should be combined or lowered to the age of adulthood.[25]

2. The drinking age should not be lowered to 18. Enough people who are under the age of 21 already drink. If they drink with friends away from bars, that's their option. But if they are under 21 they are still not allowed to go into bars. Enough of what minors do, such as parties, are directly related to alcohol and whatever else they choose to do. Not many people really give a hoot when they finally do turn 21 because they have previously had ID that says they are legal or they drink as minors. Therefore I feel 21 is a good age to become legal.[26]

3. I do not think the drinking age should be reduced to 18. The problems that would result would be enormous. With people age 18 drinking, many of whom are in high school, it would result in more abuse than use. Any form of lowering the drinking age would result in an increased amount of abuse by people who may not be mature enough to handle the responsibility. If someone between 18 and 21 wanted to drink now they pretty much could, as it is fairly easy to obtain. With the drinking age at 21 it at least keeps it a little more difficult to obtain, resulting in fewer problems. Therefore, the drinking age should not be 18.[27]

4. The drinking age should be lowered to age 18. I think that the drinking age may as well be lowered to the age of 18 because so many

18-year olds drink now as it is. Alcohol is readily accessible to these minors through friends who are 21 and older and also brothers and sisters. Some liquor stores and other places that sell beer and wine will knowingly sell to people under the age of 21. If people are considered legal adults by the age of 18, that is they have all rights including being old enough to defend their country, then they should have the one right that they don't get until they are 21. Therefore the right to buy and drink alcohol should be legal for 18-year-olds.[28]

Notes

1. For pedagogical philosophy as well as for specific ideas, I am deeply indebted to Peter Elbow, whose book *Writing with Power* (New York: Oxford University Press, 1981), I highly recommend. Many of the ideas for exercises came from a seminar in teaching writing-intensive courses, taught by Lex Runciman, Director of the Writing-Intensive Curriculum at Oregon State University. Another rich source of ideas is Lisa Ede, author of *Work in Progress: A Guide to Writing and Revising* (New York: St. Martin's Press, 1989).

2. Under the leadership of Peter Elbow. See his *Writing with Power* (New York: Oxford University Press, 1981).

3. See also Lisa Ede, *Work in Progress: A Guide to Writing and Revising* (New York: St. Martin's Press, 1989), p. 77.

4. Peter Elbow, *Writing with Power* (New York: Oxford University Press, 1981), p. 8. Copyright © 1981, Oxford University Press. Reprinted by permission.

5. Peter Elbow, *Writing with Power* (New York: Oxford University Press, 1981).

6. "Athletics versus Academics? Evidence from SAT Scores," *Journal of Political Economy* (October 1985), p. 1103.

7. The idea comes from Peter Elbow, "A Method for Teaching Writing," *Ideas for English 101*, eds. Richard Ohmann and W.B. Cooley (Urbana, Ill.: National Council of Teachers of English, 1975), p. 20.

8. Rise Axelrod and Charles R. Cooper, *The St. Martin's Guide to Writing* (New York: St. Martin's Press, 1988), p. 209.

9. Equiano, *Equiano's Travels: His Autobiography*, ed. Paul Edwards (London: Heinemann, 1989), pp. 20–21. Reprinted with permission.

10. Equiano, *Equiano's Travels: His Autobiography*, ed. Paul Edwards (London: Heinemann, 1989), p. 32. Reprinted with permission.

11. This categorization of questions is standard in rhetoric textbooks, both for speech classes (see Karyn Rybacki and Donald Rybacki, *Advocacy and Opposition* [Englewood Cliffs, N.J.: Prentice Hall, 1991], pp. 27–31) and for composition classes (see, for example, Lisa Ede, *Work in Progress: A Guide to Writing and Revising* [New York: St. Martin's Press, 1989], pp. 234–235).

12. This questionnaire is based on one prepared by Professor James M. Kilbride, Department of Psychology and Education, Miami–Dade Community College South; reprinted in *Using TAKING SIDES in the Classroom* (Guilford, Conn.: Dushkin Publishing Group, Inc., 1991), p. 54.

13. *Brown v. Board of Education of Topeka*, 347 U.S. 483 (1954).

14. The title of this exercise and the summarized information come from Jacob Weisberg, "This is Your Death," *New Republic* (July 1, 1991), p. 23.

15. Anastasia Toufexis, "Forget About Losing Those Last 10 Pounds," *Time* (July 8, 1991), p. 51. Copyright © 1991, Time, Inc. Reprinted by permission of the publisher.

16. From Anastasia Toufexis, "Forget About Losing Those Last 10 Pounds," *Time* (July 8, 1991), p. 51. Copyright © 1991, Time, Inc. Reprinted by permission of the publisher.

17. Anastasia Toufexis, "Forget About Losing Those Last 10 Pounds," *Time* (July 8, 1991), p. 51. Copyright © 1991, Time, Inc. Reprinted by permission of the publisher.

18. Anastasia Toufexis, "Forget About Losing Those Last 10 Pounds," *Time* (July 8, 1991), p. 51. Copyright © 1991, Time, Inc. Reprinted by permission of the publisher.

19. *Lands' End, Direct Merchants*, 26:13 (December 1990), p. 93. Copyright © Lands' End, Inc. Reprinted courtesy of Lands' End catalog.

20. The analogy is a common one among composition texts, originating, I believe, with Peter Elbow.

21. For ideas, I am indebted to Lex Runciman, Director of the Writing-Intensive Curriculum at Oregon State University and a rich source of information, inspiration, and ideas. He has adapted his list of reader-based responses from ideas in Peter Elbow's, *Writing with Power*.

22. Thanks to Dean John Minahan, Western Oregon State College, for this fictional case study.

23. Thanks, again, to Lex Runciman, Director of the Writing-Intensive Curriculum at Oregon State University, who distributed this list in a seminar for faculty. The list has its origin in the ideas of Peter Elbow. See Elbow, *Writing with Power*.

24. The idea for this exercise was adapted from Beverley Lyon Clark, *Talking About Writing* (Ann Arbor, Michigan: University of Michigan Press, 1985).

25. Becky Justus. Used with permission.

26. Amy Mortensen. Used with permission.

27. Patrick Thomas. Used with permission.

28. Kristin Sheets. Used with permission.

DEVELOPING A REPERTOIRE OF ARGUMENT STRATEGIES

SUMMARY OF PART TWO

Part II introduces a series of argument strategies, abstract reasoning formulas that have proved their usefulness over a long period of time and in a variety of contexts. These are the basic, simple patterns by which people put information together, learn from experience, and seek to persuade others. The student who acquires a set of argument strategies is equipped to put information together to reach reliable conclusions in simple and complex ways, in a variety of contexts, about a multitude of subjects.

The deductive arguments are formal patterns of reasoning that provide conclusive grounds for conclusions. Inductive arguments are patterns of reasoning that provide persuasive, but not conclusive, support. These include arguments by analogy, arguments that draw conclusions about one thing on the basis of its similarity to another. Inductive generalizations, hypothetical reasoning, and causal arguments are other patterns of inductive reasoning, all ways to learn from experience and experiment.

CHAPTER 4

Deductive Argument Strategies

During Teddy Roosevelt's presidency, his daughter Alice caused a national scandal by driving her new automobile at speeds approaching twenty-five miles per hour. Her flustered father admitted that he could rule the nation or he could rule Alice, but he could not do both. Since he was the president, bound by law to rule the nation, Alice would have to be allowed to do as she chose.

President Roosevelt's argument is an example of a type of argument that is so strong, so airtight, that it falls into a special category of arguments called *deductive arguments.* Like all deductive arguments, Roosevelt's argument is put together in such a way that it is impossible for the conclusion to be false if the premises are true.

•   •

4.1 STRETCHING EXERCISES

Deductive reasoning is something you do naturally and often. Here are some puzzles that make use of your native deductive reasoning abilities.

In groups of four, solve the following puzzles and write the answers. After you hand in your work, your professor may ask you to put an answer on an overhead transparency to share with the class. Or, she may ask your group members to circulate among the groups that are still working and help them reach solutions.

1.   On the following page is a stack of five blocks.[1] Each block is either green or red. Block B is green and block D is red.

A	
B	green
C	
D	red
E	

Is there, in this stack, a green block directly on top of a red block? Yes or no? Explain how you know.

2.   There has been a terrible murder at the manor house, where the characters in the Clue™ game have gathered. Detectives know only this much:

If Ms. Scarlet was the murderer, then the weapon was a rope.

The murder was committed with either a knife or a rope.

The murder did not occur in the library.

Either Col. Mustard did it, or Ms. Scarlet did it.

If Col. Mustard did it, then the murder took place in the library.

Who dunnit? With what weapon? Explain how you reached those conclusions.

3.   God is perfectly benevolent.

God is infinitely powerful.

Terrible things happen to good people.

Suppose all three claims are true. What problem does that pose for believers? Explain the problem.

After you have solved all three puzzles, go back through them and rephrase your explanations, using only the following four kinds of sentences:

If _____, then _____.

_____ or _____.

It is not the case that _____.

It is the case that _____.

• •

Characteristics of
• • • • • • • • • • • • Deductive Arguments • • • • • • • • • • • • • •

A deductive argument is defined as an argument "whose premises are claimed to provide *conclusive* grounds for the truth of its conclusion."[2]

Deductive arguments are significantly different from the kinds of arguments in Part I. The first difference is this: In Part I, an argument is defined as any claim supported by reasons. This is a broad understanding of "argument," with the focus on content. With deductive arguments, the focus is on form, independent of content. When you have acquired a repertoire of deductive argument strategies, what you will have is a set of argument forms, or patterns.

Thus, deductive arguments are said to be *formal* in two senses of the word. They are formal in that the essence of the argument is its form rather than its content; the structure, the skeleton, of the argument is what counts. Deductive arguments are formal also in that there can be nothing relaxed or casual about them; the form must be followed exactly. In deductive arguments, the claim to be justified is called the *conclusion*. The reasons are called *premises*. The skeletal pattern of reasoning is called *standard form*.

A second difference between the broad definition of argument and deductive arguments is this: Unlike all other arguments, the deductive argument forms come with a guarantee. They guarantee that if you fill in the blanks in the argument forms with true premises, the argument will carry you to a true conclusion.

> *A deductive argument is an argument that is intended to be constructed in such a way that it is impossible for its premises to be true without its conclusion being true also.*[3]

How can this be? How can any argument guarantee a true conclusion? Deductive arguments can offer this kind of guarantee because of another peculiarity of deductive reasoning. In a deductive argument, the information in the conclusion is drawn—pulled out, *deduced*—from information already contained in the premises. When the conclusion does not contain any information other than the information in the premises, the conclusion must be true when the premises are true.

This characteristic can be most clearly seen in a simple deductive argument like this one:

> All Chicago residents are Illinois residents.
> Solomon is a Chicago resident.
> ———————————————————
> Therefore, Solomon is an Illinois resident.

In all possible worlds, on any planet including Mars, whenever it is true that all Chicago residents are Illinois residents and that Solomon is a Chicago resident, it must also be true that Solomon is an Illinois resident. This is because the information in the conclusion is provided by the premises, as this diagram shows:

Be careful, however, about the nature of the guarantee. A deductive argument does not have to have true premises and a true conclusion. What is required is that *if* the premises are true, the conclusion must be true. It is certainly possible that Chicago is not in Illinois. And maybe Solomon has recently moved to Los Angeles. It doesn't matter. What matters is that the form of the argument is such that it is logically impossible for the argument to have true premises and a false conclusion. The statement "All Chicago residents are Illinois residents, and Solomon is a Chicago resident; however Solomon is not an Illinois resident" is self-contradictory.

Good deductive arguments are said to be *valid*. This word is the highest praise. Like Prince Valiant, who is known for his valor, a valid argument is the strongest in the world of argumentation. A valid argument is a perfect conveyor of truth from premises to conclusion.

An argument that is not valid is said to be *invalid* (in-val′id). This word is to be distinguished in pronunciation, but not in spelling or meaning, from an *invalid* (in′val-id), a chronically ill person. The conclusion of an invalid argument might be true, but it might also be false. There is no guarantee.

An argument that is valid in form and has true premises is said to be *sound*.[4] The word comes from the same ancient roots as *Gesundheit,* meaning "robust good health." A sound argument, by definition, necessarily has a true conclusion: When an argument has true premises and has a form that requires that the conclusion be true when the premises are true, the conclusion must be true.

$$\text{Sound argument} = \text{True premises} + \text{Valid form}$$

• •

4.2 GEOGRAPHICAL REASONING

This is a fill-in exercise. First, fill in each box on the next page with a three-statement deductive argument that fits the description for that box. For example, in box 1, put an argument that is *valid* and has *true premises and a true conclusion.* Use only the sentences provided here:

True Statements	False Statements
Rome is in Italy.	Tokyo is in Yugoslavia.
Peru is in South America.	Yugoslavia is in Asia.
Italy is in Europe.	Tokyo is in Africa.
Lima is in Peru.	Peru is in Africa.
Tokyo is in Asia.	Lima is in Africa.
Rome is in Europe.	Tokyo is in Peru.
	Italy is in Rome.
	Lima is in Yugoslavia.

Notice that one box must remain empty. Put an *X* in that box.

	Valid	Invalid
TRUE PREMISES, TRUE CONCLUSION	1.	2. Example: Rome is in Italy. Peru is in South America. ∴ Rome is in Europe.
AT LEAST ONE FALSE PREMISE, TRUE CONCLUSION	3.	4.
TRUE PREMISES, FALSE CONCLUSION	5.	6.
FALSE PREMISES, FALSE CONCLUSION	7.	8.

Now, use the completed boxes to fill in these blanks:

a. Box _____ demonstrates that an invalid argument can have a true conclusion.

b. Box _____ demonstrates that a valid argument can have a false conclusion, but only if _____.

c. The only sound argument in this entire chart is in box _____.

d. If an argument is valid and its premises are true, then its conclusion must be _____.

e. The following argument from Mars goes in box _____ since all its statements are true:

> Wetaohn is in Abaeoi.
> Abaeoi is in Nsfena.
> Therefore, Wetaohn is in Nsfena.

f. Box _____ must remain empty because a valid argument cannot have true premises and a false conclusion.

········· **The Uses of Deductive Arguments** ·········

It is handy to have several deductive argument strategies in your set of argumentative skills. Using any one of these forms, you can plug in appropriate information and create deductive arguments for different uses. The forms are extraordinarily adaptive. Once you master them, you will find them very useful argumentative strategies for at least three purposes.

First, deductive argument forms can be used to test the validity of an argument. The validity of a deductive argument is a function of its form, not its content; any argument with a valid form is valid. So, you can show that an argument is valid by showing that its form matches the form of one of the arguments in your repertoire of valid deductive arguments.

Second, deductive arguments can make for powerfully persuasive prose since there is no denying the power of an argument that is logically perfect. Valid deductive arguments are steel traps. Once a person walks into the trap by accepting the premises, there is no escape; the conclusion follows necessarily.

Third, deductive argument forms can be used to clarify a complex and diffuse line of reasoning. Given a confusing set of inferences, it often helps to represent the arguments in the form of standard-form deductive arguments. Then, those arguments can be used as a guide to writing a clear, easy-to-follow argument.

Eight Valid Deductive
•••••••••••••• Argument Strategies ••••••••••••••

This chapter introduces eight of the most useful and common valid deductive arguments:

> Disjunctive syllogism
> Hypothetical syllogism
> Two kinds of conditional syllogisms
> Two kinds of dilemmas
> Two categorical syllogisms

Despite their names, these deductive argument forms are exceedingly simple. Sherlock Holmes acknowledged their simplicity in his famous line:

> "Excellent," [Watson] cried.
> "Elementary, my dear Watson," said he.[5]

Sherlock Holmes prided himself on his deductive methods. He understood, even if Watson did not, how simple deductive arguments are and, consequently, how powerful.

Do not be put off by the esoteric names assigned to these argument forms. In fact, the names are a kind of code that tells you exactly what the arguments are like. All the deductive arguments presented here are syllogisms. *Syllogism* is the Greek word for a valid argument with two premises and a conclusion. So, the "syllogism" label tells you that each of the argument forms you will learn has only three statements. The first word in the name of each argument form, a word such as *disjunctive* or *conditional,* refers to the kind of statement that serves as the first premise for that syllogism. So a *disjunctive syllogism,* for example, is a valid three-statement argument with a disjunctive statement as the first premise.

The statements in deductive arguments are either simple or complex. A *simple statement* is either a statement that does not contain another statement or the negation of a simple statement. A *complex statement* is a statement that contains another statement as a component part. Here are the kinds of statements that occur in the deductive arguments:

Name of Statement	Statement	Example
Simple statement	A.	The party is tomorrow.
Complex statements:		
Disjunctive statement	B or C.	Parents should volunteer to help, or they should send in a check.
Hypothetical or conditional statement	If A, then D.	If the party is tomorrow, then today is Thursday.
Categorical statements	All E is F.	All parents are members of the cleanup committee.
	No G is H.	No students are members of the music volume committee.

. . . .

4.3 WHAT CAN YOU LEARN FROM A STATEMENT?

Here is a list of all the statements that, along with simple statements, make up deductive arguments. Your job is to learn all you can about one of these statements and to share your expertise with the class.

A or B.
If A, then B.
All A is B.
No A is B.

Together with members of your study group, choose one statement from the list, or consider the statement your group has been assigned. Then do the following:

1. Write two examples of the kind of statement you have chosen. Then, write another example, using entirely different words. For example,

write a sentence of the form "All A is B" without using the words *all* and *is*.

2. Write the technical name for your assigned statement.

3. Reverse the positions of A and B in your statement; what kind of difference does that make? Add "It is not the case that" to the beginning of that sentence; what can you immediately infer from the new statement?

4. In each item below, an underlined statement is followed by a set of four related statements. Circle the number of each statement that *must be true if the underlined statement is true.*

    a. <u>All the people on W. 47th Street are invited to the block party.</u>

        (1) Only people on W. 47th Street are invited to the block party.
        (2) Everyone invited to the block party lives on W. 47th Street.
        (3) Some of the people on W. 47th Street are invited to the block party.
        (4) Some of the people invited to the block party do not live on W. 47th Street.

    b. <u>If James has a stepdaughter, then James is a stepparent.</u>

        (1) James has a stepdaughter.
        (2) James is a stepparent.
        (3) If James does not have a stepdaughter, then James is not a stepparent.
        (4) If James is a stepparent, then James has a stepchild.

    c. <u>Only odd-numbered houses are permitted to water their lawns on Wednesday.</u>

        (1) Even-numbered houses are permitted to water their lawns on all days except Wednesday.
        (2) Even-numbered houses are not permitted to water their lawns on Wednesday.
        (3) All odd-numbered houses are permitted to water their lawns on Wednesday.
        (4) If your house is not odd-numbered, you may not water your lawn on Wednesday.

    d. <u>If you do not have a car, it is difficult to get around in Los Angeles.</u>

        (1) If you do have a car, it is difficult to get around in Los Angeles.

      (2)   If you can get around easily in Los Angeles, you have a car.

      (3)   All those who have cars can get around easily in Los Angeles.

      (4)   If you do have a car, it is not difficult to get around in Los Angeles.

  e. No one may graduate without a demonstrated proficiency in a foreign language.

      (1)   Everyone who graduates must have a demonstrated proficiency in a foreign language.

      (2)   If you have graduated, you have a demonstrated proficiency in a foreign language.

      (3)   If you have a demonstrated proficiency in a foreign language, you can graduate.

      (4)   Only those with demonstrated proficiency in a foreign language may graduate.

  f. All people born in the United States are U.S. citizens.

      (1)   If you are a U.S. citizen, you were born in the United States.

      (2)   If you are not born in the United States, you cannot be a U.S. citizen.

      (3)   All U.S. citizens are people born in the United States.

      (4)   No people born in the United States are not U.S. citizens.

The Disjunctive Syllogism

When you know that at least one of two statements is true and you know which one is false, you can be sure that the other one is true. This small piece of common sense translates into the disjunctive syllogism, a powerful little piece of reasoning.

The Form of the Disjunctive Syllogism

The disjunctive syllogism, as its name reveals, begins with a *disjunctive statement.* A disjunctive statement is an either-or statement, like these:

A university can allow racist speech on its campus, or it can enact strict penalties for racist speech.

The squeak in your car is a problem with the power steering, or it is a worn bearing.

> Single mothers can stay home with their little children, or they can put the kids in day care and get a job.

The second premise of a disjunctive syllogism adds a crucial piece of information. The second premise is a simple statement that claims one of the alternatives is false or impossible. The following statements would qualify as second premises:

> Strict penalties for racist speech have been struck down by the Supreme Court as unconstitutional violations of free speech.

> The problem cannot be caused by the power steering.

> Staying home with the children is not an option for women who are the breadwinners in the family.

The combination of a disjunctive statement and a simple statement denying one of the options yields the conclusion, again a simple statement. The three statements together make up the syllogism. Here are the entire disjunctive syllogisms:

> A university can allow racist speech on its campus, or it can enact strict penalties for racist speech. Strict penalties for racist speech have been struck down by the Supreme Court as unconstitutional violations of free speech. Therefore, a university must allow racist speech on its campus.

> The squeak in your car is either a problem with the power steering, or it is a worn bearing. The problem cannot have been caused by the power steering. So, it must be a worn bearing.

> Single mothers can either stay home with their little children, or they can put the kids in day care and get a job. But staying home with the children is not an option for women who are the breadwinners in the family. So, single mothers must put the kids in day care and get a job.

Notice that the support for the conclusions is very strong. If the premises are true, then it is not simply that universities *may* allow racist speech; they *must*. The squeak *must* be caused by a loose bearing. Single mothers *must* go to work. The imperative nature of the conclusions comes from the deductive nature of the argument. If the premises are true, then the conclusion must be true. In any world it is possible to imagine, if single mothers must choose between two options and one of them is impossible, the other must be chosen.

In standard form, the disjunctive syllogism looks like this:

(1) A or B.   First premise (disjunctive statement, outlines two options)
(2) Not A.   Second premise (simple statement, denies one option)
Therefore, B.   Conclusion (simple statement, the only remaining option)

or like this:

(1) A or B.
(2) Not B.
Therefore, A.

Common Mistakes to Watch Out For

As you start to use disjunctive syllogisms in your writing or when you encounter them in other people's reasoning, you should be aware of two different
ways in which disjunctive syllogisms often go wrong. The first mistake has to
do with content, the second with form.

Faulty Content

The most common downfall of the disjunctive syllogism occurs when the
first premise is false. The first premise claims that there are only two alternatives. However, life being what it is, there are usually more. A university, for
example, does not have to choose between allowing racist speech and forbidding it on pain of expulsion. It can educate its students about the harmful
effects of racist speech. It can encourage efforts to make racist speech socially
unacceptable. It can reprimand or fine students who make racist remarks. So,
even if forbidding racist speech is unconstitutional, the university is not forced
to tolerate it. This argument has a false premise and, so, it is unsound. Since
it is unsound, its conclusion is untrustworthy.

This sort of mistake is so common that it has earned its own name—*the
either-or fallacy.* Sometimes people call it the *fallacy of bifurcation* or *false dichotomy.*
Whatever you call it, it is a mistake to think that there are only two options
if, in fact, there are others.

Faulty Form

The second prize in the mistake category goes to a common error in the
form of the disjunctive syllogism. A valid disjunctive argument claims that since
one option is false, the other is true; this much you can be sure of. But it is
risky to argue that since one option is true, the other is false.

This is because the word *or* is ambiguous. There are exclusive and inclusive meanings of *or*. The *exclusive or* means that only one option can be true:

He is registered to vote, or he is not.

Either the block is green or it is not green.

You can have the pound cake or the cheesecake, but not both.

But sometimes *or* is an *inclusive or,* indicating that at least one of the options—and maybe both—is true. These are inclusive uses of *or* since both options can be true at the same time:

For my birthday, I would like a check or cash.

This semester, I could take history or I could take sociology.

Is she your neighbor or your friend?

Since a deductive argument offers a guarantee that true premises will lead to a true conclusion, there can be no ambiguity in a deductive argument. So, it is necessary to play it safe and not assume that only one option can be true. That assumption adds extra information that may or may not be in the premises; thus, it introduces the possibility of error. Assume, then, that the *or* in a disjunctive syllogism is inclusive.

Consider again the squeal in the car that is caused, the mechanic says, by faulty power steering or a loose bearing. For all anyone knows, the squeal in the car could, by some terrible misfortune, be caused by *both* faulty power steering and a loose bearing. Then it would be a mistake to assume that once one found a fault in the steering system, one could assume that the bearings were sound. The following argument, therefore, is invalid; so, even if the premises are true, the conclusion may or may not be true:

The squeal in the car is caused either by faulty power steering or by a loose bearing. Tests show that the power steering is indeed faulty. Therefore, none of the bearings are loose.

. . . .

4.4 THE KEY TO YOUR CLASSMATES

A dichotomous key is a means of classifying something, using a series of choices between alternative characteristics. Dichotomous keys require the reader to make a series of judgments, using the reasoning form of the disjunctive syllogism. This, for example, is how you would identify the subalpine larch, using a key to trees on the Pacific coast.[6] The statements in boldface are from the key. The other statements are decisions made by the reader.

1. **The tree has needles (go on to #2), OR it has ordinary leaves (go on to #6).**
    It does not have ordinary leaves.
    So, the tree has needles (go on to #2).

2. **The needles are narrow (go on to #3), OR the needles are scalelike and pointed (go on to #7).**
    The leaves are not scalelike and pointed.
    So, the needles are narrow (go on to #3).

3. **The needles are bundled together (go on to #4), OR the needles are unbundled (go on to #8).**
    The needles are not unbundled.
    So, the needles are bundled together (go on to #4).

4. **The bundles have fewer than six needles (go on to #5), OR the bundles have more than six needles (go on to #9).**
    The bundles do not have fewer than six needles.
    So, the bundles have fewer than six needles (go on to #5).

5. **The needles are three-sided (SUBALPINE LARCH), OR the needles are four-sided (WESTERN LARCH).**
    The needles are not four-sided.
    So, the needles are three-sided (SUBALPINE LARCH).

If your class is small, work together to make up a dichotomous key for the identification of the members of your class. If your class is larger, divide into groups of ten to twelve and make a key to the members of your group. See if your professor can use the key to determine the name of a given student in your group.

• •

Arguments Made from Conditional Statements

Conditional statements are the building blocks of the hypothetical syllogism and of two valid forms of the conditional syllogism.

Conditional Statements

A *conditional statement* is an *if-then* statement. Another name for a conditional statement is a *hypothetical statement.* Here are some examples:

> If today is Cinco de Mayo, then this must be May.
>
> If he did not have something to hide, then he would not have run from the police.
>
> If Rita were Princess Diana, then she would be married to Prince Charles.
>
> If an animal is a raccoon, then it has a striped tail.

The statement in the *if* part of a conditional statement is called the *antecedent* because it comes before the rest of the statement. The statement in the *then* part is called the *consequent.*

Conditional statements do an unusual sort of job in the language. They describe a logical relationship between the antecedent and the consequent. We are accustomed to statements that describe *events, people, or things:* "The Burfords were a family of woodcutters: a stringy little father, a plump mother, and four sons the size and intelligence of pickup trucks."[7] And we have no trouble understanding statements that describe *relationships* of various sorts, whether they be *temporal* relationships ("First he pried open the trunk, then he flicked the beam of his flashlight into the corner"), *spatial* relationships ("Behind the spare tire was a case of bootleg Scotch"), *family* relationships ("The big one was Maudie's son"), and even *relationship*-relationships ("He was desperately in love with the Morton girl, but she thought they were 'just friends' ").

The conditional statement, however, describes a *logical* relationship between two statements. A conditional statement claims that two statements are related in such a way that whenever the antecedent is true, the consequent must be true as well. "If today is Cinco de Mayo, then this must be May" claims that whenever it is true that today is Cinco de Mayo, it must also be true that this is May.

Since a conditional statement describes a logical relationship, it follows that the statement is true when the logical relationship is correctly described. Consider "If Rita were Princess Diana, then she would be married to Prince Charles." Rita is not Princess Diana. And certainly Rita is not married to Prince Charles. Yet the conditional statement is true. What makes it true? It is true that *if* Rita were Princess Diana, *then* she would be married to Prince Charles since Princess Diana and Prince Charles are still married (at least they were when this book went to press).

Note that conditional statements work only in one direction. That is, a conditional statement's meaning shifts dramatically when the antecedent and the consequent switch places. Compare the meanings of these two conditional statements:

1. If this animal is a raccoon, then it has a striped tail.
2. If this animal has a striped tail, then it is a raccoon.

The first statement is quite a different claim from the second. Barring highway accidents, the first statement is true: If this animal is a raccoon, then it has a striped tail. But the second version—If this animal has a striped tail, then it is a raccoon—is not necessarily true since an animal with a striped tail could be a zebra lizard or a skunk or a pheasant instead of a raccoon.

For any true conditional statement, the antecedent is a *sufficient condition* for the consequent: The truth of the antecedent is all it takes to establish the truth of the consequent. But the consequent is merely a *necessary condition* for the antecedent: That is, the antecedent cannot be true unless the consequent is true. Knowing that an animal is a raccoon is sufficient to inform us that the animal has a striped tail, and having a striped tail is necessary to being a raccoon.

There is another way to talk about the truth of conditional statements.[8] "If-then" is an example of what is called a *truth-functional connective.* That means that the truth of the conditional statement depends completely on the truth of the simple statements that make it up, that is, the antecedent and the consequent.

The only time a conditional statement is false is when it has a true antecedent and a false consequent. It follows that when a conditional statement's antecedent is false, the conditional statement itself is true ("If Acapulco is in California, then I'm a monkey's uncle!"). But when the antecedent of the conditional statement is true, you cannot know if the conditional statement itself is true until you check the truth value of the consequent: If the consequent is true, the entire conditional statement is true ("If Acapulco is in Mexico, Acapulco is in North America"); and alternatively, if the consequent is false, the entire conditional statement is false ("If Acapulco is in Mexico, then Acapulco is in Africa").

This table lists the possibilities:

If the antecedent is . . . ,	and the consequent is . . . ,	then the entire conditional statement is . . .
True	True	True
True	False	False
False	True	True
False	False	True

• •

4.5 WRITE YOUR OWN STATEMENTS

By combining the following simple statements, write four true conditional statements:

> The person sitting next to me is a student.
>
> The person sitting next to me is not King Louis XIV.
>
> The person sitting next to me is a sophomore.
>
> The person sitting next to me is a professor.
>
> The person sitting next to me is not a student.
>
> The person sitting next to me has paid tuition.
>
> The person sitting next to me is a mother.
>
> The person sitting next to me is a female.
>
> The person sitting next to me is a father.
>
> The person sitting next to me is not a male.
>
> The person sitting next to me is not a father.

Ask a classmate to look over your work to make sure that each conditional statement is true.

• •

The Hypothetical Syllogism

In a heated dispute over whether police officers need to be monitored by an independent civilian authority, a citizen said, "If you give a person a gun, you give him power. If you give him power, you corrupt him. So, if you give a person a gun, you corrupt him." The citizen's argument is an example of a hypothetical syllogism.

A hypothetical syllogism is an argument made up of three conditional statements. The name is easier to understand if you remember that *conditional statement* is just another name for a hypothetical statement.

The Form of the Hypothetical Syllogism

In form, the hypothetical syllogism is a simple sequence of three conditional statements, with the consequent of each conditional statement serving as the antecedent of the next. If statement A is true, then statement B is true. And if statement B is true, then statement C is true. Eliminate the middle statement, and you get a conclusion: If statement A is true, then statement C is true.

Think of the conditional statements in a hypothetical syllogism as making up the links in a chain. The first link is connected to the second, which is connected to the third. No matter how many links there are in the chain, no matter how many intermediate conditional statements, the first link is connected to the last.

In standard form, the hypothetical syllogism looks like this:

(1) If A, then B.	(Conditional statement)
(2) If B, then C.	(Conditional statement)
Therefore, if A, then C.	(Conditional statement)

Hypothetical syllogisms can be extended indefinitely, with the addition of more intermediate premises. Here is an example based on information in *Jane Brody's Good Food Book:*

If you go on a drastic diet and eat significantly fewer calories than your body needs, then a calorie-conservation system begins. If a calorie-conservation system is operating, then your body lowers its metabolic rate so that fewer calories are used. If fewer calories are used, weight loss stops even though less food is eaten. If weight loss stops even though less food is eaten, you will not lose weight. It follows that if you go on a drastic diet, you will not lose weight.[9]

The hypothetical syllogism can sometimes play a clarifying role in your writing. Use it when you want to spell something out, when you need to lead your reader by baby steps to a conclusion. Car mechanics sometimes have to talk to car owners this way:[10]

Car owner:	Should I worry about that whimpering noise in my front end?
Mechanic:	Absolutely. If you ignore that noise, then you're ignoring a problem in the tie rods or the ball joints. If you ignore a problem in the tie rods or ball joints, then either one can break while you're driving. If one of them breaks when you're driving at 50 or 60 miles per hour, the wheel falls off. If the wheel falls off, you're dead. So if you ignore that noise, you're dead.

Common Mistakes to Watch Out For

As long as you move step by step, with the consequent of each statement becoming the antecedent of the next, it is hard to make a mistake in the form of a hypothetical syllogism. The danger with hypothetical syllogisms is that the premises might not be true. Among all those conditional statements may be one—or many—for which the antecedent could be true while the consequent is false. A false premise like this breaks the logical sequence and destroys the support for the conclusion.

Consider, as an example, Frank Julian Warne's 1913 argument against unrestricted immigration into the United States:

> If the United States allows unrestricted immigration, it will soon have a surplus of cheap labor. If there is a surplus of cheap labor, then wages will fall. And if wages fall, it will detrimentally affect the standards of living of other workers. So if the United States allows unrestricted immigration, it will hurt hundreds of thousands of workers.[11]

As events unfolded in the 1920s, it became clear that a surplus of immigrant labor did not cause a drop in wages. On the contrary, immigrant workers were among the fiercest defenders of a living wage.[12] A false conditional statement breaks the logical chain, making the argument unsound and the conclusion untrustworthy.

• •

4.6 GOOD ADVICE

Suppose a friend wrote to you and asked for advice on a matter of some importance. Suppose your friend said, "Should I get married before I graduate?" Or suppose your friend said, "Should I quit school and work for a while?" or "Should I tell my parents about my abortion?" or "Should I move in with my boyfriend?" or, "Should I get my hair straightened?" or something else.

Suppose also that you have very strong feelings on the issue and want to make your case as strongly and as clearly as possible.

Write a one-paragraph note to your friend in which you state your opinion and spell out the reasons behind it. Use the form of the hypothetical syllogism. Before you hand in your note, run it by a classmate to make sure that all the statements in your argument are likely to be true.

• •

The Conditional Syllogism

The conditional syllogism is the second kind of argument that makes use of conditional statements.

Imagine this: Tonight is the Big Game. If the Portland Trailblazers win this one, they will advance to the semifinals. You flip on the TV, and (it has been a long day) you fall fast asleep. The next morning, you want to know what happened. Your roommates could give you either of two valuable pieces of information. Suppose they tell you that the Trailblazers won. You will quickly conclude that the Trailblazers will advance to the semifinals. Suppose, instead, they tell you that the Trailblazers will not advance to the semifinals. You can be sure, on the basis of this information, that the Trailblazers lost the game.

The Forms of the Conditional Syllogism

This familiar scenario illustrates the two valid forms of the conditional syllogism. The first is the argument form called *affirming the antecedent*. This is a valid three-statement argument, the first premise of which is a conditional statement. The second premise is a simple statement that affirms that the antecedent is true. Since a true antecedent is sufficient to establish the truth of the consequent, the premises tell you beyond a doubt that the consequent must be true. Here is the argument in standard form:

(1) If A, then B.   (Conditional statement)
(2) A.   (Simple statement affirming antecedent)
Therefore, B.   (Simple statement affirming consequent)

If the Trailblazers won, then they will go to the semifinals.
The Trailblazers won.
Therefore, they will go to the semifinals.

The second argument form is the conditional syllogism called *denying the consequent*. This also is a valid three-statement argument that starts with a conditional statement. Its second premise adds a different piece of information: The consequent of that conditional statement is false. Remember that in any conditional statement the consequent is a necessary condition for the antecedent. That is, the antecedent cannot be true unless the consequent is true. (For example, consider this statement: "If she is a mother, then she is a female." "She is a mother" cannot be true unless "she is a female" is true.) So, since a true consequent is a necessary condition for a true antecedent, whenever the consequent is not true, the antecedent cannot be true either. Here is the standard form:

(1) If A, then B.   (Conditional statement)
(2) Not B.   (Simple statement denying consequent)
Therefore, not A.   (Simple statement denying antecedent)

If the Trailblazers win, then they will go to the semifinals.

The Trailblazers will not go to the semifinals.

Therefore, the Trailblazers did not win.

Denying the consequent is probably the most commonly used of all the simple valid argument forms. It is particularly useful in testing explanations. It is central to scientific reasoning. In the following passage, a bicyclist uses it to diagnose the nasty noise her bike makes when she pedals. The argument itself is in boldface.

The manual says, "To find the source of the noise, get going at a good clip on a quiet, level place and then just coast. **If the noise is caused by the power train, then the noise will stop when you stop pedaling.**" Okay, let's see what happens . . . (She coasts along for a few minutes.) No, **the noise does not stop when I stop pedaling. So the problem is not caused by the power train . . .**

Here is the argument in standard form:

If the noise is caused by the power train, then the noise will stop when you stop pedaling.

The noise does not stop when you stop pedaling.

Therefore, the noise is not caused by the power train.

• •

4.7 TESTING HUCKLEBERRY FINN

One evening, Huckleberry Finn disguised himself as a girl and went to town to "find out what was going on." But he didn't fool Mrs. Judith Loftus, who soon had proof that Huckleberry was not a girl. Read the following passage from *The Adventures of Huckleberry Finn.*[13] Here, barefoot in bonnet and dress, Huck knocks on the door of an isolated cabin.

> . . . I knocked at the door, and made up my mind I wouldn't forget I was a girl. "Come in," says the woman, and I did. She says: "Take a cheer." . . .
>
> Well, the woman fell to talking about how hard times was, and how poor they had to live, and how the rats was as free as if they owned the place. . . . She was right about the rats. You'd see one stick his nose out of a hole in the corner every little while. She said she had to have things handy to throw at them when she was alone, or they wouldn't give her no peace. She showed me a bar of lead twisted up into a knot, and said she was a good shot with it generly, but she'd wrenched her arm

a day or two ago, and didn't know whether she could throw true now. . . . Then she told me to try for the next one. . . . I got the thing, and the first rat that showed his nose I let drive, and if he'd 'a' stayed where he was he'd 'a' been a tolerable sick rat. She said that was first-rate, and she reckoned I would hive the next one. . . .

"Keep your eye on the rats. You better have the lead in your lap, handy." So she dropped the lump into my lap just at that moment, and I clapped my legs together on it and she went on talking. But only about a minute. Then she . . . looked me straight in the face, very pleasant, and says . . .

"You do a girl tolerable poor. . . . [W]hen you throw at a rat or anything, hitch yourself up a-tiptoe and fetch your hand up over your head as awkward as you can, and miss your rat about six or seven foot. Throw stiff-armed from the shoulder, like there was a pivot there for it to turn on, like a girl; not from the wrist and elbow, with your arm out to one side, like a boy. And, mind you, when a girl tries to catch anything in her lap she throws her knees apart; she don't clap them together, the way you did when you catched the lump of lead. Why I spotted you for a boy . . . and I contrived the other things just to make certain. . . ."

How did Mrs. Loftus reach the conclusion that Huck was not a girl? Answer the question by writing down two deductive arguments representing Mrs. Loftus's reasoning. Formulate both arguments as conditional syllogisms.

● ●

Common Mistakes to Watch Out For

Two types of mistakes commonly occur in conditional syllogisms. Both mistakes rest on a misunderstanding of what a conditional statement means.

The first mistake occurs when one assumes that because the antecedent of a conditional statement is false, the consequent must be false. It makes sense to call this the *fallacy of denying the antecedent.* Those who make this mistake forget that although a conditional statement says that if the antecedent is true, the consequent is true, it makes no claim about what happens when the antecedent is false.

A quick example shows the nature of the mistake. Consider again the statement, "If today is Cinco de Mayo, then this must be May." Suppose the antecedent is false: Today, alas, is not Cinco de Mayo. Then the consequent may or may not be false: It might be any one of thirty other days in May. The antecedent is *sufficient* to establish the truth of the consequent. But many other antecedents are also sufficient for the same job.

The second mistake occurs when one assumes that because the consequent of a conditional statement is true, the antecedent must be true. It makes sense to call this the *fallacy of affirming the consequent*. Consider the same example: "If today is Cinco de Mayo, then this must be May." Suppose one knows only that the consequent is true: Today is indeed a May day. It does not necessarily follow that today is Cinco de Mayo; that is, the antecedent may or may not be true. The consequent is a necessary condition for the truth of the antecedent (today could not be Cinco de Mayo if it were not also a May day); but it is not sufficient (to be Cinco de Mayo, it must be not only a May day but a particular May day, of which there are thirty others).

Affirming the consequent is, unhappily, a very common mistake. It occurs, for example, when people accept as proof of a theory the existence of a fact that could be explained by lots of other theories. Consider this:

> I am convinced that vitamin C prevents colds. I put it to the test. I figured that if vitamin C prevents colds, then I won't get colds while I am taking vitamin C. Right? Well, I have been taking vitamin C since Christmas, and I haven't had a single cold.

Here is the same argument in standard form:

> If vitamin C prevents colds, then a person taking vitamin C will stay healthy.
> A person taking vitamin C in fact did stay healthy.
> _____
> Thus, vitamin C prevents colds.

The argument fails to reach a reliable conclusion because many other factors are sufficient to explain the speaker's continuing good health. Maybe, on the advice of his mother at Christmas, he adopted the practice of washing his hands before he ate. Maybe it's the extra glass of water he drinks when he downs the vitamin pill that does the trick. The point is that the information needed to reach a reliable conclusion is not present in the premises of this argument.

· ·

14.8 ARGUMENT SCRABBLE

If you know how to play Scrabble, you know how to do this group activity. Instead of making words, you make valid arguments.

The object of the game is to get more points than any other player. To play, you need four people and a set of "tiles," small pieces of paper with words or statements and point values on them, as follows. For simplicity, your professor may photocopy pages of these tiles and let each group cut out its own set.[14]

6 — or	2 pts.	4 — Polly has only two legs.	1 pt.
6 — if	1 pt.	1 — Polly can swear like a pirate.	3 pts.
6 — then	1 pt.	2 — Polly is a mammal.	1 pt.
8 — it is false that	2 pts.	2 — Polly has fur.	1 pt.
12 — therefore	2 pts.	2 — Polly has feathers.	1 pt.
2 — Polly is a parrot.	1 pt.	2 — Polly is a puppy.	1 pt.
4 — Polly is a bird.	1 pt.	1 — Polly chews up slippers.	3 pts.

Designate one player to be scorekeeper. Place the tiles face down on the table. Each player draws six tiles. To begin play, a player uses one to six of her tiles to make a statement. From the extra tiles, she draws as many tiles as she used.

The next player has a number of options. He can start an entirely different statement; he can add to a statement that is already on the table, making it into a complex statement; he can put another statement under one already on the board to make the two premises of an argument; or he can complete an argument that other players have started. The only restriction is that the complex statements must be true and the inferences valid. The conclusion of an argument can be used as the first premise in another argument. During one turn, a player can do only one of these things *unless* if he has the tiles to complete an argument. If he has them, he can complete an argument during that turn.

If a player constructs an argument that is invalid, the argument is broken up, the tiles in that argument are divided among the other players, and the offending player is thrown out of the game.

The game ends when no one can play. The student with the highest point value when the game ends is the winner.

Scoring: A player who makes a statement or adds to a pre-existing statement earns only the point value of the tiles she plays. But a player who completes an argument earns the point value of all the tiles in the argument.

• •

The Dilemmas

Anyone who has experienced a forced choice between two unwelcome alternatives will already have an intuitive understanding of the deductive argument form called the *dilemma*. Say you have only two alternatives. If you choose one alternative, it will result in one unwelcome consequence. If you choose the other, it will result in another unwelcome alternative. You must choose one or the other. So you will face one or the other unwelcome alternative. Here is an example of what school officials saw as a dilemmatic situation, given what they believed about AIDS. The conclusion is underlined.

> School officials face a dilemma when trying to decide how to handle school children with AIDS. If they let them go to school as usual, they are exposing the other children to an increased chance of contracting AIDS. If they deny the children admission to school, they are adding the pain of rejection to the very real pain of a lingering death. Officials must choose between letting them come to school and forcing them to stay at home. So, they have to choose between risking the health of the healthy children and hurting the sick children.

The dilemma posed by the AIDS-stricken children is called a *complex dilemma* because the end result is a choice between two different consequences. In this case, the school officials thought they had to choose between risking the health of the well children and hurting the sick children.

Some dilemmas, however, are *simple dilemmas.* Simple dilemmas put you in an even tighter spot: You are faced with only two alternatives. Each alternative leads to the same result. So, no matter what you do, you cannot escape that result.

Here is an example. In 1991, six police officers pursued a driver through the dark streets of Los Angeles at speeds faster than 100 miles per hour. When they finally stopped the car, two of the officers dragged the driver out, threw him to the ground, kicked him repeatedly in the head, and clubbed him with their nightsticks. The other four officers watched. When a secret videotape of the beating was released, indignant Los Angelenos demanded the resignation of Daryl Gates, the chief of police. Gates defended his job, saying that he did not know the beatings were occurring. His critics responded by pointing out Gates's simple dilemma. Again, the conclusion is underlined.

> It does not matter whether Gates knew of that particular beating or not. If Gates was aware that his officers sometimes beat up suspects, he should resign on the grounds that he tolerated police brutality, and if he wasn't aware that his officers sometimes beat suspects, he should resign because he was derelict in his duty. Either he knew about beatings or he did not. So, either way, he should resign.

Although the events had very complicated and tragic consequences, this is a *simple dilemma* because the conclusion does not offer a choice of alternatives.

The Forms of the Dilemma

Like a true-life dilemma, the argument form called the complex dilemma begins with a choice between alternatives, formulated as a disjunctive (either-or) statement:

The AIDS-stricken children are admitted to school, or they are not.

The second premise is the combination of two conditional (if-then) statements. Each conditional statement draws out the consequences of one of the alternatives:

If the AIDS-stricken children are admitted to school, then there is an increased risk to the health of healthy schoolmates; *and* if the AIDS-stricken children are *not* admitted to school, then those children feel rejected.

The conclusion is the disjunction of the two consequences:

So, there is an increased risk to the health of healthy schoolmates, or the AIDS-stricken children feel rejected.

In standard form, the complex dilemma looks like this:

(1) A or B.	(Disjunctive statement)
(2) If A, then C; AND if B, then D.	(Conjunction of two conditionals)
Therefore, C or D.	(Disjunctive statement)

The form of the simple dilemma differs from the form of the complex dilemma only in that both alternatives in a simple dilemma have the same consequence. So, the simple dilemma begins, as usual, with a choice between alternatives, expressed as a disjunctive statement.

Chief Gates knew about police beatings, or he did not.

The second premise tells about the consequences of each alternative:

If he did not know about the beatings, he should resign *and,* if he did know about the beatings, he should resign.

There is only one consequence, no matter what. So the conclusion is simple:

Therefore, Chief Gates should resign.

In standard form, the simple dilemma looks like this:

(1) A or B.	(Disjunctive statement)
(2) If A, then C; AND if B, then C.	(Conjunction of two conditionals)
Therefore, C.	(Simple statement)

When dilemmas are sound, they skewer the opponent on the two alternatives of a dilemma just as surely as a bull can skewer a matador on its two horns. In fact, logicians speak of the two conditional statements in the second premise (if this, then this; if that, then that) as the *horns* of a dilemma.

• •

4.9 "CROSS TALK: WOMEN AND MEN TALKING"

Author Deborah Tannen believes that women "use language to create connection and rapport; men use it to negotiate their status in a hierarchical order. . . . The implication of these different conversational habits and concerns in terms of office interactions are staggering."[15] Here are some details:

> [W]omen in positions of authority are inclined to phrase their requests as suggestions and to assume they will be respected because of their authority. . . . Many men complain that a woman who is indirect in making requests is manipulative: she's trying to get them to do what she wants without telling them to do it. . . . But if a woman gives direct orders, the same men might complain that she is aggressive, unfeminine or worse.
>
> Women are in a double bind: If we talk like women, we are not respected. If we talk like men, we are not liked. . . .
>
> What if you're the subordinate and your boss is a man who's offending you daily by giving you orders? If you know him well enough, one potential solution is "metacommunication"—that is, talk about communication. Point out the differences between women and men, and discuss how you could accommodate to each other's styles. . . . But if you don't have the kind of relationship that makes metacommunication possible, you could casually, even jokingly, suggest he give orders another way. . . .
>
> Many women find it difficult to speak up at meetings; if they do, they may find their comments ignored, perhaps later to be resuscitated by a man who gets credit for the idea. . . . Women, on the other hand, are often worried about appearing to talk

too much — a fear that is justified by research showing that when they talk equally, women are perceived as talking more than men.

How many different dilemmas do you find in this passage?
Circle each one.
Write each in standard form.
Which are simple dilemmas? Which complex dilemmas?

Choose one of the dilemmas, and write a paragraph illustrating it with an instance from your own experience. Put your own experience in the form of a dilemma.

• •

Common Mistakes to Watch Out For

Dilemmas sometimes have a false premise that weakens the entire argument. The first premise, the disjunctive statement, may be false; that is, it may not be true that there are only two mutually exclusive alternatives. The AIDS case above, for example, claims that either the school administrators must let the sick children go to school as usual or they must force them to stay at home. But surely there are other alternatives. Maybe the children can go to school with a restricted schedule. Or maybe they can be admitted to school once everyone has been taught how the disease is communicated.

When there are really more than two alternatives, it is possible to refute the dilemma by *going between the horns of the dilemma.* This amounts simply to pointing out that the disjunctive premise is false, by showing that there is a third alternative.

Sometimes the fault of a dilemma lies with the second premise. The second premise is the premise that outlines the consequences of each alternative. If one of the consequences does not really follow from an alternative, the second premise is false. The AIDS example has a fault in the second premise. The argument claims that if AIDS-infected children are allowed to go to school, they expose the other children to a higher risk of catching the disease. Given the way AIDS is transmitted, this is probably false.

When a consequence does not really follow from an alternative, it is possible to refute the dilemma by *seizing the bull by the horns.* This amounts to pointing out the error in the second premise.

4.10 AS THE WORLD TURNS

1. At the top of a full sheet of paper, write a paragraph describing a situation in which you were faced with a choice between unwelcome alternatives. Describe your alternatives. Describe what you thought would happen as a result of choosing the different alternatives. What did you finally decide to do? Why? Pass your paper to the person on your right.

2. Read over the dilemmatic situation that your classmate has described at the top of the paper you now hold. On that paper, put your classmate's dilemma in standard form. Is it a simple dilemma or a complex dilemma? Pass that paper to the person on your right.

3. Read over the standard-form dilemma on the paper you now hold. How might that dilemma have been avoided if the student had "seized the bull by the horns"? Write down your ideas. Pass that paper to the person on your right.

4. Read over the standard-form dilemma on the paper you now hold. How might that dilemma have been avoided if the student had "gone between the horns of the dilemma"? Write down your ideas. Pass the paper back to the original author.

Read what your classmates have written about your personal dilemma.

The Categorical Syllogism

Categorical Statements

A categorical statement makes a claim about the relationship between two categories, or sets. Here are two such relationships: It is possible that all the members of one set are members of the other. That is: All A is B. It is also possible that none of the members of one set is a member of the other. That is: No A is B. When a categorical statement refers to all the members of a set, as both of these statements do, it is called a *universal* categorical statement. The following statements are all universal categorical statements:

All A is B.

Knowledge is power. (Francis Bacon, John Kennedy)

Power is an aphrodisiac. (Henry Kissinger)

Injustice anywhere is a threat to justice everywhere. (Martin Luther King)

No A is B.

No one has been barred on account of his race from fighting
    and dying for America. (John Kennedy)

No Presidential act is illegal. (Richard Nixon)

No man is an island . . . (John Donne)

The Forms of the Categorical Syllogism

Categorical statements can be combined in many ways to form valid arguments
called categorical syllogisms. Here are two:

All A is B.	All knowledge is power.
All B is C.	All power is an aphrodisiac.
Thus, all A is C.	Thus, all knowledge is an aphrodisiac.
All A is B.	All knowledge is power.
No B is C.	No power is uncorrupting.
Thus, no A is C.	Thus, no knowledge is uncorrupting.

The information content in the premises can be represented with overlapping
circles, like so:

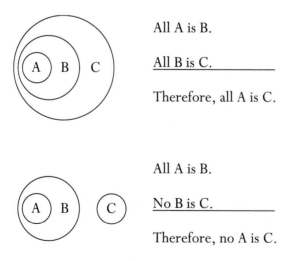

All A is B.

All B is C. ⎯⎯⎯⎯⎯⎯

Therefore, all A is C.

All A is B.

No B is C. ⎯⎯⎯⎯⎯⎯

Therefore, no A is C.

From this information about the relation between A and B, and between B and
C, it is possible to draw conclusions about the relation between A and C.

The arguments look simple-minded, and they are. But there is power in simplicity. So, you will find that categorical syllogisms are often used when someone wants to hammer home a point:

> Teenagers do not make the decisions in this home. You are still a teenager. So, you do not make the decisions in this home.

or make a classification:

> This thing is an eastern wood tick. Eastern wood ticks are members of the order *Acarina.* So, this thing is a member of *Acarina.*

or decide on a course of action:

> Hester Prynne committed adultery. All those who commit adultery shall be severely punished by whipping on the naked body not exceeding thirty-nine stripes, and stigmatized, or burned on the forehead with the letter A, on a hot iron. Therefore, Hester Prynne shall be severely punished.

or justify a legal decision:

> Flag burning is a kind of political speech. All political speech is protected by the First Amendment to the Constitution. So, flag burning is protected by the Constitution.

Common Mistakes to Watch out for

Categorical syllogisms, like all other arguments, can fall prey to mistakes of form and mistakes of content.

Mistakes of form

To avoid mistakes, it is important to be clear about what a categorical statement does, and does not, say. The claim "All horses are mammals," is quite a different claim from "All mammals are horses." The first claim, as diagrammed here, is that horses are a subset of mammals—a true statement.

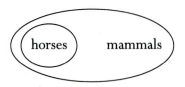

The second claim, which is diagrammed next, is that mammals are a subset of horses—a clearly false statement.

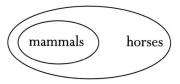

Failure to be clear about this can lead to faulty inferences like this:

This young man is out after curfew. Gang members typically come out after curfew. So, this must be a gang member.

The premises claim that "this young man" and "gang members" are both subsets of "people who are out after curfew." But the premises do not tell us whether those subsets intersect. So, the conclusion contains more information than the premises convey and is therefore suspect. The overlapping circles demonstrate that the premises don't provide enough information to be sure about how the categories intersect.

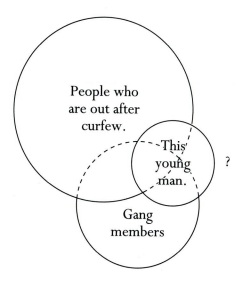

Mistakes of content

Since categorical syllogisms are made up of categorical statements, they suffer from the same problems that generalizations do. Whenever you take it upon yourself to deal in generalizations ("All salt is bad for your heart." "All welfare recipients are lazy." "All athletes are indifferent students." "All graduates of Harvard Law School are elitists."), you open yourself up to a wealth of opportunities for error. The argument forms of the categorical syllogisms will carry the mistake through to the conclusion.

· ·

4.11 LISTENING FOR UNIVERSAL STATEMENTS

For two days, keep a list of all the universal categorical statements you encounter. They can be spoken (your professors are probably a rich source) or written (watch advertisements and announcements). They can be explicit (said in so many words) or implied (suggested or presupposed but not explicitly stated). They can be positive (All A is B) or negative (No A is B).

In class, sort all the statements into four piles:

Universal positive categorical statements, likely to be true.

Universal negative categorical statements, likely to be true.

Universal positive categorical statements, probably false.

Universal negative categorical statements, probably false.

What can you learn from the piles? Here are some questions to ask yourself: Which pile is biggest? Why do you suppose that is so? What is the most common source of false generalizations? Why do you suppose that is so? Did any particular categorical statements show up on the lists of several students? What are some of the richest hunting grounds for categorical statements?

Choose a statement from each pile. Treat each statement as a conclusion, and write a categorical syllogism to prove that it is true.

· ·

······ Putting Deductive Arguments to Work ······

The table on the next page summarizes all eight simple valid deductive argument forms and the most commonly made errors.

Deductive Argument Forms

Name	Valid Forms	Invalid Forms
Disjunctive syllogism	A or B. Not A. Thus, B is true.	A or B. A. Thus, B is false.
Hypothetical syllogism	If A, then B. If B, then C. Thus, if A, then C.	
Conditional syllogism, affirming the antecedent	If A, then B. A. Thus, B is true.	If A, then B. B. Thus, A is false.
Conditional syllogism, denying the consequent	If A, then B. Not B. Thus, A is false.	If A, then B. Not A. Thus, B is false.
Simple dilemma	A or B. If A, then C; and if B, then C. Thus, C.	
Complex dilemma	A or B. If A, then C; and if B, then D. Thus, C or D.	
Categorical syllogisms	All A is B. All B is C. Thus, all A is C. All A is B. No B is C. Thus, no A is C.	

Testing the Validity of Deductive Arguments

Since validity is a function of the form of an argument, it follows that any argument whose form matches a valid form is itself valid. So, one way to test the validity of an argument is to try to paraphrase it in a way that matches one of these eight forms.[16] If the argument can be paraphrased as a disjunctive syllogism, hypothetical syllogism, conditional syllogism, dilemma, or categorical syllogism—without changing the meaning of the argument—then the argument is valid.

For example, is the following argument valid?

I know you say you love me. But if you loved me, you would treat me well, and you treat me like garbage. So don't talk to me about love.

The argument is indeed valid since its meaning can be accurately reproduced in the form of a conditional syllogism:

If you loved me, then you would treat me well.
You do not treat me well._____
Therefore, you do not love me.

Translated into standard form, the argument is revealed to be an instance of denying the consequent:

If A, then B.
Not B._____
Therefore, not A.

Notice that this does not show that the argument is sound. Even though it is formally valid, the argument may have a false premise: Maybe it is possible to mistreat a loved one. If so, the conclusion does not come with a guarantee.

Notice also that if you cannot represent an argument as an instance of a valid form, you cannot be sure that the argument is invalid. Your inability may prove only that you need to work on your translating skills.

• •

4.12 TESTING THE VALIDITY OF ARGUMENTS

The following are all simple arguments that someone has put forward. Your job is to judge whether the arguments are valid. You can check their validity by trying to paraphrase them or cast them into the form of a valid deductive argument. If you can cast the argument into the same form as a valid argument, it is valid. If you cannot, you can't be sure it is invalid. After all, the failure may be your own.

1. John Kennedy's speech to the citizens of Allied-held West Berlin: "All free men, wherever they may live, are citizens of Berlin. And

therefore, as a free man, I take pride in the words 'Ich bin ein Berliner.' "

2. To reduce acid rain, electric power companies that burn coal have two options: They can switch to low-sulfur coal and pay more for it, or they can install pollution control devices known as scrubbers that remove sulfur dioxide gases. But scrubbers cost about $125 million to install on each power plant, and millions more to operate. So, the power plants will have to switch to low-sulfur coal.

3. Doctors and coaches are excited about the possibility of using human growth hormone (HGH) to produce superathletes. If normal children are given HGH, they will show significant increases in height and muscular strength. This increase would give them tremendous advantages in sports. So, many current sports records will probably fall before the decade is over.

4. Some people complain that the war on drugs leads to the violation of civil liberties. Well, so what? When you are at war, you have to make sacrifices. Either the people of this nation show the courage to solve the drug problem, or we will have to surrender to the drug lords. I believe that the American people do have the courage to solve the drug problem and, thus, will never turn this country over to the drug lords.

5. The judge told Margaret that if she would complete an alcohol-treatment program, he wouldn't suspend her license for driving under the influence of alcohol. She must have taken the course because I saw her out driving yesterday.

6. It must have rained during the night because there are worms on the sidewalk. And worms always come out after a rain.

7. How can I be sure I truly exist, philosopher René Descartes fretted. It's possible that some Evil Genius has planted in my mind the false belief that I exist. But wait! If I am deceived, then I must be something that is deceived. And if I must be something that is deceived, then I must exist. So even if I am wrong about existing, I exist!

8. I have no use for God, said the skeptic, since he is either irrelevant or he is a bungler. It works this way: God created the universe, right? Well, did He create it so it runs perfectly without His interference? Or did He create it so He has to tinker with it continually to keep it working properly?

9. You are a traitor. Anyone who thinks Boris Yeltsin would be a better president than George Bush is a traitor.

10. From a *Time* report on the extinction of dinosaurs:

> *If a comet or asteroid massive enough to kill off the dinosaurs had struck the earth, it would have left a crater hundreds of kilometers wide. . . . Now, after a decade-long search, [scientists have found] a circular basin some 180 km in diameter, . . . centered beneath the town of Chicxulub, on the northern tip of Mexico's Yucatan Peninsula. . . . Says Boynton, "This is as near a certainty as one can get in science."*[17]

The Persuasive Power of Deductive Arguments

Consider the persuasive possibilities of deductive arguments. Deductive arguments, alone among all arguments, provide conclusive proof of a conclusion if the premises are true. So, if your audience agrees with your premises, they will have to agree with your conclusion, provided you argue deductively. Thus, deductive arguments have a kind of power to persuade that is unique among arguments. The question is how to put that power to use in persuasive essays.

No one would suggest that a persuasive essay be made up entirely of deductive arguments. That would look silly, as if a robot or android had written it. Far better to use deductive arguments selectively to bring a diffuse topic into sharp focus, to summarize an argument, or to drive home a point.

Here is an example of how a deductive pattern is used to bring a diffuse topic into sharp focus: There is a general understanding of the difficulties faced by women sports reporters who have to decide whether to interview male athletes in the locker room. The locker rooms are sweaty and steamy. The athletes are often naked or barely covered with a wet towel. The reporters are often harassed with obscenities and nasty gestures. But the locker room after a game is where useful information about a game is conveyed, and women who stay out of the locker rooms will not get the news stories that their competitors will get.

See how much clearer the issue becomes when it is framed in the pattern of a complex dilemma:

Women sports reporters face a dilemma. They can pursue their stories into the men's locker room after a game, or they can wait to interview the athletes when they emerge. If they go into the locker room, they are often forced to interview sweaty, naked or half-naked men who sometimes harass them with obscenities and obscene suggestions. But if they stay out of the locker rooms, they cannot compete with other journalists. So they have to choose—endure the unpleasantness or give up the story.

Deductive argument patterns can be used to summarize an argument, to present it in compact, easy-to-follow form. An argument that natters on and on can lose its audience either through boredom or confusion. So, it is often useful to recapture the reader with an argument that goes directly to the point. Here the deductive argument is in boldface type.

What is clear is that frogs and other amphibians are disappearing from much of their former ranges. Ponds that used to echo with the spring mating calls of tiny frogs have fallen silent. What is not so clear is the cause of their disappearance. Some scientists have suggested that acid rain is responsible. Acid rain, the residue of coal-fired power plants, has increased the acidity of many lakes and streams on the East Coast. But other scientists dispute this suggestion, noting that the pattern of disappearances does not match the pattern of acid rain. **If acid rain were causing frogs to disappear, then they would be disappearing only where acid rain is a problem. But frogs are disappearing all around the world. So, acid rain cannot be the only culprit.**

Here is an example of the use of a deductive argument pattern, the simple dilemma, to drive home a point. Notice that the argument is embedded in a letter that gives it context. The dilemma appears in boldface.

To the Editor:

We have all been reading about the new hotel complex proposed for the downtown area. **I** am opposed to the project because I think nothing good can come of it. **If the hotel complex is a big success, then it will generate traffic that will clog up the entire downtown area. If it is a failure, then the city will be stuck with an empty shell in the middle of town. So success or failure, the complex is a failure.**
I would urge all voters to reject the project.

Sincerely,
K.D.M.

What is usually thought of as a tool for mathematicians and logicians can, in these ways and in others, be useful in everyday persuasive prose. The characteristics that make deductive arguments useful in specialized contexts—that they are clear-cut, that they demonstrate conclusions conclusively—also make them useful as rhetorical tools for writers in many workaday contexts.

• •

4.13 *FLORIDA v. RODRIGUEZ*

Read the following news summary of the state of Florida's manslaughter prosecution of a father for failing to put his child in a seat belt.[18]

FATHER OF DEAD GIRL GOES ON TRIAL OVER FAILURE TO USE SAFETY SEAT

MIAMI (AP)—Jury selection began Monday in the trial of a man charged with vehicular homicide in his 3-year-old daughter's death because she wasn't in a seat restraint.

A defense lawyer said 30-year-old Ramiro de Jesus Rodriguez was singled out for prosecution to teach other parents a lesson. A prosecutor said Rodriguez' driving was to blame for the fatal accident.

It's rare for a parent to be held legally responsible for failing to restrain a child killed in an auto accident. In 1983, a Cincinnati man was acquitted of vehicular homicide in the death of his 2-year-old son in a crash five days after an Ohio law took effect requiring child restraints.

Attorneys screened more than half of 40 prospective jurors in the courtroom of Circuit Judge Sidney B. Shapiro. Almost all said they were familiar with the case. Selection of the six-member jury was set to resume Wednesday and the trial was expected to last a week.

Rodriguez said he is still grieving for his daughter Veronica, who flew out of her mother's arms when Rodriguez made a left turn and his car collided with a van Aug. 3 as they returned to their Hialeah home from a store.

"What will they accomplish if they send me to prison? It won't bring my daughter back and it will destroy the rest of my family," Rodriguez said.

The vehicular homicide charge carries a maximum penalty of five years in prison, but prosecutors said they will seek probation.

Florida law requires motorists to use seat belts or a secure safety seat for children under age 6.

With impetus from the case, state legislators approved a bill that would raise the penalty for failing to use a child-restraint seat for children 5 and under from $37 to $150 starting in October. The measure has not yet gone before the governor.

Defense attorney Reemberto Diaz questioned why prosecutors are pursuing the case [against] Rodriguez, an immigrant from Nicaragua.

"You have a poor Hispanic immigrant who has been selected for this prosecution and I think that's unfair," Diaz said.

Do you think the state should continue its prosecution of Mr. Rodriguez? Or do you think it should drop the charges?

List the four or five best reasons to support your decision.

Now choose two of those reasons and express each one in the form of a deductive argument.

After you have written your arguments, your professor may divide the class into a prosecution and defense team (depending on whether students would argue for or against continuing the case), and ask each team to prepare and present its best case, using only deductive argument forms.

• •

Increasing Clarity with Simple Deductive Arguments

Think of the deductive arguments as strategies or patterns for thinking through problems. Usually, our thoughts do not follow a rigid series of steps; humans come to conclusions—who knows how?—all at once by considering the information as a whole. But, sometimes, when a problem is too complicated, it helps to slow down and move step by step in a line. This is when simple deductive arguments can be very useful. Here are some ideas about how you can put deductive argument forms to work to increase clarity.

The categorical syllogism. Use the categorical syllogism to organize information. Seemingly unconnected pieces of information can come together in meaningful ways if you think of them as telling you how different sets interconnect.

The dilemma. Use the dilemma to figure out the consequences of the different possibilities. There are two alternatives. What happens if one occurs? What happens if the other occurs?

The hypothetical syllogism. Use the hypothetical syllogism to figure out the long-term consequences of a decision. If they turn out to be disastrous (or beneficial), that will be useful information for your argument. If this happens, then what? If that happens, then what?

The conditional syllogism, affirming the consequent. Brainstorm with the conditional syllogism. Use it to figure out the options. If this is true, then what? On the other hand, if that is true, then what?

The conditional syllogism, denying the consequent. This is a versatile way to test a claim. If this is true, then this consequence will follow (first premise). But that consequence is false (second premise). So, this cannot be true.

The disjunctive syllogism. This is often a useful way to put together the information from other arguments. Either this happens or that. Which alternative is impossible? Let that be your second premise. Then, draw the conclusion.

For mathematicians, philosophers, puzzle addicts, and scientists, deductive argument forms are tools of the trade. But it is not just academics who can be helped by the clarifying qualities of deductive reasoning. Anyone who has a difficult decision to make can sort out the options with deductive patterns of thought.

For example, Governor Richard Celeste of Ohio had some heavy thinking to do just before he left office. Thirteen women were in Ohio jails because they had killed their husbands. Each one was a battered wife who had endured repeated life-threatening assaults. Were they really murderers? Or were they victims who cracked under pressure? Should he keep them in jail? Or should he pardon them?

No one knows how he worked through his decision. But he could have reasoned this way:

The situation certainly posed a dilemma. If he pardoned them, then he might encourage battered women to kill their husbands. If he did not pardon them, then the state of Ohio would be punishing women who were not really morally blameworthy. He had to decide to pardon them or not. So, either he encouraged battered women to kill their husbands, or he allowed Ohio to punish people who could not be blamed. (Complex dilemma)

The consequences were quite serious. If he pardoned the women, then other battered wives might reasonably expect they would not be punished for killing their own husbands. If other battered wives thought they could escape punishment, then they might be encouraged to kill their husbands. So, if he pardoned the women, then he might be encouraging other women to kill their husbands. (Hypothetical syllogism)

Under the law, the matter was fairly straightforward. All people who unlawfully kill another human being without malice are guilty of man-slaughter. And the thirteen women undoubtedly killed another human being without malice. So, they are guilty of manslaughter. (Categorical syllogism)

Still, he had to weigh the consequences of failing to pardon. If he did not pardon the women, then he would be allowing the state of Ohio to punish people who could not be blamed for moral wrongdoing. Punishing people who cannot be blamed is unjust. So, he could not fail to pardon the women. (Conditional syllogism)

It came down to a simple decision. Either he pardoned them or they would stay in jail the rest of their lives. He could not allow them to stay in jail. So, he pardoned them. (Disjunctive syllogism)

4.14 PREPROFESSIONAL TESTS

It is a measure of the importance of deductive reasoning skills to a person's reasoning ability that many preprofessional exams test applicants' abilities to use deductive argument forms. The following questions, for example, are from the Law School Admission Test.[19] The assumption is that deductive reasoning skill is a predictor of success in law school. Now that you have studied deductive reasoning, can you ace this test?

Since the LSAT is a timed test, your professor may decide to make this exercise into a race.

1. All people seek happiness. Some people are accident-prone. Accident-prone people seek self-punishment.

    Which one of the following conclusions can be properly drawn from the statements above?
    a. Accident-prone people are the exceptions that prove the rule of the universal search for happiness.
    b. Accident-prone people are not human in the fullest sense.
    c. Those people who seek self-punishment also seek happiness.

    d.   Accidents are the only form of self-punishment that accident-prone people seek.

    e.   Those people who seek happiness also seek self-punishment.

2.   The jewelry store doesn't care about its customers. I was looking for a birthday present there last week, and it took me ten minutes to get the attention of a salesperson.

       Which one of the following statements best expresses the assumption underlying the author's conclusion?

    a.   Customers who shop for birthday presents do not like to wait.

    b.   Stores that care about the customer do not allow their salespersons to keep customers waiting.

    c.   Ten minutes is too long for anyone to wait for a salesperson.

    d.   A salesperson should be able to get the customer's attention.

    e.   The jewelry store is a bad place to shop.

3.   If a person doesn't study hard in college, she won't get a good job after college; and if a person doesn't get a good job after college, she won't be happy after college.

       Which one of the following is a conclusion that can be properly inferred from the above premises?

    a.   One should study hard in college.

    b.   One should get a good job after college.

    c.   One should be happy after college.

    d.   One who studies hard in college will be happy after college.

    e.   One who doesn't study hard in college won't be happy after college.

4.   Fred will come to the party, and, since he will, so will Mary. Furthermore, if Mary and Sue both come, then John will come, drink too much, make a fool of himself, and leave. Therefore, John will make a fool of himself and leave.

       Which of the following, if true, would allow the author to properly draw the conclusion in the argument above?

          I.   John will come to the party.

         II.   Sue will come to the party.

       III.   Mary will come to the party.

    a.   I only

    b.   II only

    c.   III only

    d.   II and III only

    e.   I, II, and III

5. All professional hockey players are good skaters. Therefore, some good skaters wear red uniforms.

    Which one of the following assumptions is necessary to support the conclusion expressed above?
    a. Some good skaters are not professional hockey players.
    b. Some professional hockey players wear red uniforms.
    c. All professional hockey players wear red uniforms.
    d. Some people who don't wear red uniforms are professional hockey players.
    e. Some people who don't wear red uniforms are not professional hockey players.

6. When there is a rainstorm, the streets get wet; but it hasn't rained recently, so the streets must not be wet.

    Which one of the following is logically most similar to the argument above?
    a. When people are patriots, they criticize their country's follies; but our country has no follies, so it must have no critics.
    b. When a country has follies, it also has critics; our country has many follies, so it must also have many critics.
    c. When people criticize their country's follies, they're patriots; but no one is criticizing our country's follies, so we must have no patriots.
    d. When a country has critics, it must also have follies; our country has many critics, so it must have many follies.

7. If banks pay interest on checking account balances, customers will leave more money in their checking accounts. If so, bank customers will put less money into long-term bank notes. If that happens, there is an increased likelihood of bank failures. Thus, if banks are permitted to pay interest on checking account balances, bank failures will be more likely.

    Which one of the following arguments uses reasoning that is most similar to that used in the argument above?
    a. The federal government, obviously, can either condone or forbid interest-bearing checking accounts. Allowing U.S. banks the option of paying interest on checking accounts may stimulate the economy, but disallowing the practice will only perpetuate the recession. Between these two alternatives, the choice is only too clear.
    b. Because of an increased likelihood of bank failures following a slump in long-term investments, banks in New York are hereby

forbidden to offer interest-bearing checking accounts to their customers.

c.   The more money left in the interest-bearing checking account, the greater the gain to the checking account customer. The greater the gain to the customer, the better customer relations with the bank will become. This may result in the opening of more new accounts. Thus, if banks are permitted to pay interest on checking account balances, bank business may improve.

d.   Unless banks are permitted to offer interest-bearing checking accounts, the likelihood of bank failures will increase. The government is unlikely to change its opposition to such checking accounts, so bank failures will probably increase.

e.   Ninety percent of all the banks and credit unions in New York offer interest-paying checking services to their customers, 78 percent of whom take advantage of the service. At the same time, the rate of failure of such businesses is lower in New York than in any other state. Interest-bearing checking accounts, then, do not pose a threat to the success of any bank.

Your professor may ask you to compose other, similar exam questions on overhead transparencies to further test your classmates' understanding of deductive reasoning.

4.15 JUDGE ACQUITS FATHER

A series of arguments follows each passage below. For each argument:

a.   Put the argument in standard form, paraphrasing the argument without changing its meaning and adding missing premises or conclusions if necessary.

b.   Tell the name of the deductive argument form that the argument exhibits.

c.   Tell whether the argument is valid or invalid, and sound or unsound.

1.   A judge dismissed the case of *Florida* v. *Rodriguez,* in which a father had been charged with vehicular homicide in the death of his three-year-old daughter, who was killed in an automobile accident that occurred while she was not wearing a seat belt.

a.   After the verdict ended the four-day trial, a juror said, "I felt he was at fault. He disobeyed the rules of the road. People who disobey the rules of the road are at fault. And that was that."

b. The state presented evidence showing that if Veronica had been properly restrained, she would have survived. That she was killed in the accident is evidence that she was not safely secured in the car.

c. The judge said that reckless driving and failing to put the child in a restraint seat were really only traffic infractions. No one guilty only of traffic infractions should be charged with homicide. So, Rodriguez could not be charged with homicide.

2. Two cartoons:

a. TOOTH AND JUSTICE by Shannon Wheeler—A college student is standing in the bookstore next to a row of books. "Should I go ahead and buy the books for the classes I'm planning to take?" he asks. "Or should I wait until I know which classes I'm actually in? If I buy now I'll probably end up with lots of useless books. But if I wait, then I fall behind in my classes." New frame: "Wow. My first intellectual challenge of the semester."

b. WIZARD OF ID by Johnny Hart and Brant Parker—The jester is sitting on a bar stool, talking to the bartender. "Gimme 'nother one, Sam." The bartender thinks hard: "If I don't cut him off, I could lose my license. . . . But if I do, he might not come in anymore. (Sigh) Either way I'm out of business." He pours another drink.

3. Editorial comments about the nomination of Judge Clarence Thomas to the Supreme Court of the United States (be careful—each comment is missing a premise or conclusion):

a. Here we have Clarence Thomas and Anita Hill, two intelligent, articulate people, both lawyers, both under oath, telling diametrically opposite stories. Somebody is lying.

b. If Judge Thomas thinks particular groups—the Democrats or women's rights organizations—tried to ruin his chances for nomination, then it will be impossible for him to disassociate himself from those feelings in a case in which one of those groups is involved. So, I do not think that Judge Thomas can be impartial in future cases involving Democrats or women's groups.

c. Anita Hill and Judge Thomas cannot both be telling the truth: either Hill is lying or Thomas is lying. And Hill seems to be telling the truth.

d. Talking to women about sex is not a crime. So what Judge Thomas did was not a crime.

4. On January 1, the grandson of C. Nicholas Conchas accidentally killed himself with Conchas's .22-caliber revolver. Under a California law, the Children's Firearm Accident Protection Act of 1991, Conchas was charged with a felony.

   a. If a child is injured or killed by a loaded weapon negligently stored within reach of a child, the adult who owns the gun can be jailed for up to three years. So Conchas faces a possible prison sentence because his grandson shot himself with Conchas's loaded gun.

   b. Friends and family worry that Conchas will be deported since he is not a citizen and, under federal law, people who are not citizens and who are convicted felons can be deported.

   c. Prosecutors recognize Conchas's grief but still plan to press charges: "If the state wants to protect children, then they have to enforce the Accident Protection Act. And if they are going to enforce the act, then they will have to press charges against people who break the law, even when those people have already suffered the loss of a loved one. So, if the state wants to protect children, then they have to press charges, even in hard (even cruel) cases.

   d. The penalty for the offense is either three years in jail or a $10,000 fine. Conchas was fined. So, he will not have to go to jail.

5. Two auto mechanics from Cambridge, Massachusetts (one with a Ph.D. from M.I.T.), talk about car repair problems:[20]

   a. [Here is why you should change the fuel filter on your car regularly]. "Eventually that fuel filter will get plugged up. If you're lucky, the car will stop. If you're not, it'll keep running long enough to plug up your injectors and do some real damage. [Either way, you should] change the fuel filter once a year. I don't care what the book says."

   b. "There's a lot of confusion about pinging and knocking. . . . If the gasoline gets too hot, or if it has too low an ignition temperature, it can be ignited by hot spots in the combustion chamber. [If it is ignited, then] it begins to burn in various places all at once. [If it's burning in different places, then the] walls of flame collide. [When the walls of flames collide,] the sound you hear is the knock or ping inside the engine." [So, if gasoline gets too hot, you hear a knock or ping.]

   c. [The burning that causes pinging is to be avoided.] ". . . [T]he places where these walls of burning gasoline collide are very hot.

And if they're always occurring at the same spot, they can burn valves or even burn holes in the pistons. Not a nice thought, especially if you're a piston."

Notes

1. This puzzle was suggested at the Seventh Annual Conference on Critical Thinking and Educational Reform, August 4, 1987.
2. The definition is from Irving Copi's classic introductory logic textbook: Copi, *Introduction to Logic,* 7th ed. (New York: Macmillan, 1986), p. 169.
3. Copi, *Introduction to Logic* (New York: Macmillan, 1986), p. 169. Copyright © 1986, Macmillan. Reprinted by permission of the publisher.
4. Logic textbooks are not consistent in how they label the best sort of reasoning. This text uses "valid" to refer only to deductive arguments; however, some (Hurley, *A Concise Introduction to Logic*) use "valid" to refer to both deductive and inductive arguments. This text uses "cogent" to label only inductive arguments that begin with true information and put that information together correctly; but others use "cogent" to refer to good arguments of all sorts. Students should be aware of the potential for confusion here.
5. Sir Arthur Conan Doyle, "The Crooked Man," *The Complete Sherlock Holmes* (New York: Doubleday and Co., 1927), p. 411.
6. Tom Watts, *Pacific Coast Tree Finder* (Berkeley: Nature Study Guild, 1973), pp. 6–9.
7. Patrick E. McManus, *Rubber Legs and White Tail-Hairs* (New York: Henry Holt and Company, 1987), p. 12.
8. In this explanation, I follow Merrilee Salmon's lucid explanation in *Introduction to Logic and Critical Thinking* (New York: Harcourt, Brace, Jovanovich, 1989).
9. Jane Brody, *Jane Brody's Good Food Book* (New York: Bantam Books, 1985), p. 166.
10. For the information in this example, I am indebted to Click and Clack, the Tappett Brothers. See Tom and Ray Magliozzi, *Car Talk* (New York: Dell Publishing, 1991), pp. 40–41, 47.
11. Frank Julian Warne, *The Immigration Invasion* (New York: Dodd, Mead and Company, 1913), reprinted in an Opposing Views Pamphlet, "Historical Debate: Should Immigration Be Restricted?" (San Diego: Greenhaven Press, Inc., 1990), pp. 33–34. The argument is paraphrased.
12. Peter Roberts, *The New Immigration* (New York: Arno Press, 1970), reprinted in Opposing Views Pamphlet, "Historical Debate: Should Immigration Be Restricted?" (San Diego: Greenhaven Press, Inc., 1990), p. 42.
13. Mark Twain, *The Adventures of Huckleberry Finn* (New York: Bantam Books, 1981), pp. 54–61.
14. The playing "tiles" can be photocopied from the pages in the instructor's manual.
15. All quotations are from Deborah Tannen, "Cross Talk: Women and Men Talking," *The Professional Communicator* (Fall 1990), pp. 6–7. Published by Women in Communications, Inc. Used with permission.

16. The English language has myriad ways to express the logical relationships that are here referred to as "A or B" and "If A, then B." To help with paraphrasing ordinary language into logical language, here are some translations.

The following are some English language logical words that express a disjunction:

Or	Otherwise
Either . . . or . . .	With the alternative that
Or else	Alternatively

The following are some English language logical words that express conditional relationships. It is important to know which logical order these words indicate. In these, the *antecedent* occurs first in the sentence:

If . . . , then . . .	So long as . . . , . . .
If . . . , . . .	. . . means that . . .
Given that . . . , . . .	Insofar as . . . , . . .
. . . implies . . .	. . . lead to . . .
Whenever . . .	. . . only if . . .
. . . is a sufficient condition for . . .	

In these, the *consequent* occurs first in the sentence:

. . . if . . .	Only if . . .
. . . in case . . .	. . . provided that . . .
. . . whenever . . .	. . . so long as . . .
. . . insofar as . . .	. . . is implied by . . .
. . . is a necessary condition for . . .	

Reprinted with permission of the author, Jon Dorbolo.

17. Leon Jaroff, "At Last, the Smoking Gun?" *Time* (July 1, 1991), pp. 60–61.
18. *Corvallis Gazette-Times* (April 30, 1991), p. 1. Copyright © 1991, The Associated Press. Used with permission.
19. Law School Admission Services, "Logical Reasoning Workbook," *The Official LSAT PrepKit* (Newtown, Pa.: Law School Admission Services, Inc., 1990). Copyright © 1990, Law School Admission Services. Reprinted by permission.
20. Tom and Ray Magliozzi, *Car Talk* (New York: Dell Publishing, 1991), pp. 150–151. Copyright © 1991, Dell Publishing Group. Reprinted with permission.

CHAPTER 5

Arguments by Analogy

The mind makes extensive use of similarities to create images and emotional responses, to make sense of new experiences, to justify claims. The mind uses similar sights or smells to call up images and evoke emotional responses. In *Remembrance of Things Past*, Marcel Proust described how a familiar taste conjured up a scene from his past:

> *Once I had recognized the taste of the crumb of madeleine soaked in her decoction of lime flowers which my aunt used to give me, . . . immediately the old gray house upon the street, where her room was, rose up like the scenery of a theater.*[1]

The mind uses similarities to make sense of new experiences. Much learning is a matter of making connections between what one has already observed and something similar but less familiar. Similarities are thus the primary means by which people learn from experience. A child learns to avoid campfires and candles, for example, when he is burned by the flame on a cigarette lighter. For the same reason, an effective way to teach people about something new is to compare it to something they already know about. People who have never seen the Grand Canyon would get a fairly clear picture of it if it were compared to something they are familiar with:

> The Grand Canyon is like the little gully that washed down into the driveway, but it is long enough to cover the distance between New York City and Cincinnati.

Most important for one who is developing a repertoire of argumentative strategies, the mind uses similarities to justify claims. Similarities can justify judgments about even the most difficult, inaccessible topics. Judgments about matters of fact and predictions about the future, complex moral and legal judgments, decisions about policies—all can rest on similarities between what people already know and what they are not sure about. An argument that is based on the similarity between two things is an *argument by analogy.*

The word *analogy* comes from the Greek word *analogia,* meaning "proportion" or "correspondence." Thus, an analogy is a correspondence, or similarity, between two things. An *analogue* is something that is similar to something else. Two similar things are said to be *analogous* to one another. An *argument by analogy* is an argument based on a similarity between two things. It proceeds on the principle that if two things are alike in many relevant observable respects, there is a good chance they are alike in another, unobserved respect as well.

Analogies are powerful strategies of inference that can be used to mislead or, equally, to inform. As Samuel Butler said, "Though analogy is often misleading, it is the least misleading thing we have."[2] It is well worth the time to learn to write good analogies and to identify, analyze, and evaluate analogies in the writing of others.

The Uses of Analogies

Using Analogies to Create an Image or Emotional Response

To call up images and feelings in the readers' minds, many poets and other writers make extensive use of analogies.

"Ah, Celeste, my pretty jewel, I love you as a pig loves the mud," croons a Louisiana folk song. The hopeless romantic who sings these words of love expects that, because Celeste is well acquainted with a pig's attraction to mud, she will instantly understand the depth and intensity of his love for her. This explicit use of a similarity between two things, where the similarity is expressed in words such as "is like" or "as" is a *simile.*

A *metaphor* is an implied comparison, where the similarity between two things is not explicitly stated but only understood. When our romantic calls Celeste a "pretty jewel," he is speaking metaphorically, implying that Celeste—like a jewel—is beautiful, and glowing, and priceless. Like the singer, poets and professors, songwriters and politicians, evoke ideas and emotions about a new experience by identifying it with something the reader is already familiar with.

An *implied analogy* is an even more subtle use of analogy. An implied analogy uses a word or phrase that applies to one thing in reference to another to suggest a likeness between them. For example, "the ship plowed the seas" tells very clearly how a ship moved through the water. The use of the word "plowed" takes advantage of readers' knowledge of how a plow moves through the earth. The implicit analogy thus links what is unfamiliar with what is familiar, thereby creating a new image or idea in the readers' minds.

A critical thinker needs to be aware of how subtly and effectively implicit analogies can be used to plant misleading impressions in a reader's mind. Implicit analogies are misleading when language associated with one thing is used in sentences describing another thing when, in fact, there is no real similarity between the two things.

For example, a four-star general briefing reporters about the progress of the 1991 Gulf War used language usually heard on Monday Night Football: "Well, we've got all the players on the field, and it's just a matter now of following the game plan." The implicit analogy is between the conduct of a war and a football game. The language suggests that war, like football, is just a game—a comforting, and dangerous, idea.

It is equally misleading, although perhaps more benign, when sports announcers use the language of war. "The blitz is on. Joe Montana throws a long bomb all the way to the 20-yard line. Jerry Rice is buried under defenders." The language here suggests that football, like war, is not to be taken lightly.

When the language associated with children or babies or small animals is used in reference to adults, the effect is equally misleading. "Hey, *boy,* come over here." "The *Bunnies* take drink orders." "I'd like to invite all the *girls* in the office to lunch." All these sentences contain implicit analogies that demean their subjects by subtly suggesting that they do not have the qualities or status of adult human beings. These are some of the more common uses of implied analogies.

• •

5.1 THE IMAGES OF WAR

An implied analogy occurs whenever a word or phrase that applies to one thing is used in reference to another to suggest a likeness between them.

1. In the following descriptions of war, underline each word used to imply an analogy; state the analogues (that is, explain what two things

are being implicitly compared); and explain what attitude change the implicit analogy is intended to bring about. Some passages may contain multiple, mixed analogies.

a.   President Franklin Roosevelt, 1937:

> *It seems to be unfortunately true that the epidemic of world lawlessness is spreading. When an epidemic of physical disease starts to spread, the community approves and joins in a quarantine of the patients in order to protect the health of the community against the spread of the disease. . . . War is a contagion, whether it be declared or undeclared. It can engulf states and peoples remote from the original scene of hostilities. We are determined to keep out of war, yet we cannot insure ourselves against the disastrous effects of war and the dangers of involvement. . . .* [3]

b.   Abraham Lincoln, 1863:

> *Fourscore and seven years ago our fathers brought forth, on this continent, a new nation, conceived in Liberty, and dedicated to the proposition that all men are created equal.*
>
> *Now we are engaged in a great civil war, testing whether that nation, or any nation so conceived, and so dedicated, can long endure. . . .*
>
> *[W]e here highly resolve that these dead shall not have died in vain—that this nation, under God, shall have a new birth of freedom—and that government of the people, by the people, for the people, shall not perish from the earth.* [4]

c.   General Norman Schwarzkopf, 1991:

> *We have an integrated campaign plan we are going to continue to execute until we have accomplished the objectives of the United Nations resolution. . . . Saddam Hussein is literally destroying his own nation right now. Clearly we are doing everything we can to avoid killing innocent people, and that has given him a shield behind which he can hide. We're willing to demonstrate to the world that this is not a war against the Iraqi people. I don't know how long we will continue to do that. I don't know what the limits of American tolerance would be before the rules of the game change. If he starts using chemical weapons and kills large numbers of innocent people, I'm not certain I'd be willing to sit back and say we're the guys with the white hats.* [5]

d.   James Fallows, quoting American soldiers in the Gulf War, 1991:

> Last week, after Iraqi and Coalition ground forces were engaged for
> the first time, an American soldier said that the encounter had been
> "like a turkey shoot." Over the next three days, one U.S. briefer said
> that fighting Iraqis is like "swatting gnats," another that the Iraqi army
> was "swarming like ants." And another, in the most memorable line,
> said that when U.S. war planes surprised an Iraqi ground unit, Iraqi
> soldiers "scrambled like cockroaches when the kitchen light goes on."[6]

e.   Winston Churchill, broadcasting on June 22, 1941, the day after
Germany invaded the Soviet Union:

> Hitler is a monster of wickedness, insatiable in his lust for blood and
> plunder. Not content with having all Europe under his heel, or else
> terrorized into various forms of abject submission, he must now carry
> his work of butchery and desolation among the vast multitudes of
> Russia and Asia. The terrible military machine which we and the rest
> of the civilized world so foolishly, so supinely, so insensately allowed the
> Nazi gangsters to build up year by year from almost nothing, cannot
> stand idle lest it rust or fall to pieces. It must be in continual motion,
> grinding up human lives and trampling down the homes and the rights
> of hundreds of millions of men. Moreover it must be fed, not only with
> flesh but with oil. . . .
>
>   I see advancing upon all this in hideous onslaught the Nazi war
> machine, with its clanking, heel-clicking, dandified Prussian officers,
> its crafty expert agents fresh from the cowing and tying down of a
> dozen countries. I see also the dull, drilled, docile, brutish masses of
> the Hun soldiery plodding on like a swarm of crawling locusts. I see
> the German bombers and fighters in the sky, still smarting from many
> a British whipping, delighted to find what they believe is an easier and
> a safer prey.[7]

2.   Choose one of the passages above, and transform it by substituting a
different implicit analogue. That is, delete every word you have underlined, and substitute a word that is associated with some other
analogue. For sports imagery, for example, you might choose to substitute the language of the surgical operating room. Your professor
may ask you to read the new passages aloud in class.

Using Analogies to Explain

People create meaning by interpreting information in light of what they already know.[8] An idea that is totally new, unlike anything ever encountered before, is literally inconceivable—you cannot even think about it. Imagine the difficulty, for example, of explaining a river to a Martian whose planet is without flowing water. "It's like the wind," one might decide to say, trying to think of something remotely similar, "only it's thicker and cooler." How much easier it is to explain a river to an earthling: "A river is like a stream, only bigger."

Because it is easier to understand new ideas by connecting them with old familiar ideas, analogies are often very useful as a means of explanation. In general, the more abstruse and abstract an idea, the more useful analogies become as explanatory tools. For example, to help nonscientists understand the secrets of the universe, scientists often use elaborate analogies. This analogy explains energy levels in atoms.

> *The various electron orbits or atomic energy levels in Bohr's model can be compared to the rungs of a ladder. When you are standing anywhere on a ladder, your feet are on one rung or another. You cannot stand between rungs. The potential energy corresponds to standing on the first rung, the second rung, and so forth. Your potential energy cannot correspond to standing in midair between two rungs. The potential energy of your body with respect to the ground is thus subdivided into small, definite amounts—the energy is quantized. In the same way, an electron can be in one orbit or another, but not in between.*[9]

Textbooks in the most abstruse of subjects, such as quantum mechanics, organic chemistry, and cosmology, are full of analogical explanations.

• •

5.2 "I HAVE NEVER UNDERSTOOD HOW . . ."

1. To do this exercise, you will need to divide into sets of approximately four students, grouped by expertise. So, your class will first have to agree on a list of subject areas in which students consider themselves to be experts. It might include such areas as car repair, flying, infant care, stereo equipment, Mexican culture, dating, etiquette, computer equipment, popular music, weight lifting, Islam, and weather.

    This is everyone's chance to ask for explanations of things they have never understood. On small pieces of paper, write out questions—as many as you want—and hand them to the appropriate group. For example, to the weight-lifting group: "I have never understood how lifting weights would make your muscles bigger." Or "I have never understood why weight lifters wear those thick belts." Or "I have never understood why bodybuilders put oil all over themselves." To the Islam group: "I have never understood how a war could be a holy war." To the weather group: "I have never understood why it is warmer in summer than winter." And so forth.

As a group, sort through your questions and find one that can be clearly answered using an analogy. Prepare an answer to present to the class. The answer should take the form of an explanatory analogy: "It's like this: Think of your muscle as a bundle of strings . . ." If there is enough time, prepare an answer to another question.

Present your explanatory analogies to the class. The measure of your success will be the number of "Oh, *now* I understand" comments that come from the other students.

2. Find and photocopy an explanatory analogy from one of the textbooks for your other courses. Post it in the classroom for everyone to read. Try to reach agreement as a class about which explanation works best and which fails most dramatically. Then, come up with a list of the three or four most important things to keep in mind when writing an effective analogical explanation.

• •

To help their listeners understand abstract religious ideas, prophets used analogies. This one, from the *Koran,* dramatizes the insignificance of the words of unbelievers.

> As for the unbelievers, their works are as a mirage in a spacious plain which the man athirst supposes to be water, till, when he comes to it, he finds it is nothing; . . .
> Or they are as shadows upon a sea obscure, covered by a billow above which is a billow, above which are clouds, shadows piled upon one another; when he puts forth his hand, wellnigh he cannot see it. And to whomsoever God assigns no light, no light has he.[10]

A very elaborate form of explanatory analogy is the *parable,* a vivid story that helps listeners understand an abstract idea. By setting up an analogy between the idea and the action in the story, the idea is clarified and explained. According to the Bible, when Jesus wanted to make a point with the common people, he used parables.

"Listen!" Jesus said. "A farmer went out to sow his seed. As he was scattering the seed, some fell along the path, and the birds came and ate it up. Some fell on rocky places, where it did not have much soil. It sprang up quickly, because the soil was shallow. But when the sun came up, the plants were scorched, and they withered because they had no root. Other seed fell among thorns, which grew up and choked the plants so that they did not bear grain. Still other seed fell on good soil. It came up, grew and produced a crop, multiplying thirty, sixty, or even a hundred times." Then Jesus said, "He who has ears to hear, let him hear." [11]

A parable sets up an *analogia*, or proportion. The seed is to the soil as the word of God is to the listener. Just as the successful growth of a seed depends on its landing on good soil, successful understanding of God's word depends on its being heard by a receptive mind.

5.3 WRITING PARABLES

1. Write a parable of about 250 words to explain one of the following quoted abstract ideas, or one you have chosen.

    Life shrinks or expands according to one's courage. (Anaïs Nin)

    Don't get mad; get even. (Joseph Kennedy)

    Man, if you gotta ask, you'll never know. (Louis Armstrong, when asked what jazz is)

    Only when he has ceased to need things, can a man truly be his own master. (Anwar Sadat)

    Power in defense of freedom is greater than power in behalf of tyranny and oppression. (Malcolm X)

    Imagination is more important than knowledge. (Albert Einstein)

    We have nothing to fear but fear itself. (Franklin Roosevelt)

    In spite of everything, I still believe that people are really good at heart. (Anne Frank)

2. Read another person's parable, and write out the proportion expressed by the parable, by filling in these blanks:

    In this parable, _____ is to _____ as _____ is to _____ .

Using Analogy as Argument

An *argument by analogy* is an argument in which the similarity between two sets of facts is offered as grounds for believing that a conclusion about one of those sets of facts is likely to be true of the other.

When the Reverend Martin Luther King, in jail in Birmingham, wanted to *explain* to white moderates why he was organizing civil disobedience in the South, he compared injustice to an infected boil.

> *Like a boil that can never be cured as long as it is covered up but must be opened with all its pus-flowing ugliness to the natural medicines of air and light, injustice must likewise be exposed, with all of the tension its exposing creates, to the light of human conscience and the air of national opinion before it can be cured.*[12]

His analogy between a boil and the injustice of segregation explained his purposes far more effectively than a lengthy explanation ever could.

But Dr. King was called upon not only to clarify the goals of civil disobedience but also to *justify* civil disobedience to those who believed that actions precipitating violence are violent themselves. That required a different use of analogy—analogy as argument. An analogy can be used as a reason, to justify a claim. This is because what is true of one thing is often true of its analogue. Consider, for example, Dr. King's argument by analogy.

> *In your statement you asserted that our actions, even though peaceful, must be condemned because they precipitate violence. But can this assertion be logically made? . . . Isn't this like condemning Jesus because His unique God-consciousness and never-ceasing devotion to His will precipitated the evil act of crucifixion? We must come to see, as federal courts have consistently affirmed, that it is immoral to urge an individual to withdraw his efforts to gain his basic constitutional rights because the quest precipitates violence.*[13]

Dr. King's argument began with a claim about which there is general agreement: The fact that Jesus' preaching prompted his own violent death is no reason to condemn his preaching. Dr. King then suggested that civil disobedience is like Jesus' acts. If the two sets of actions are the same, then it stands to reason that you should make the same moral judgment of them. Jesus' acts were morally justified even though they resulted in violence. Thus, civil disobedience—a similar set of acts—is morally justified as well.

Arguments by analogy are often used to justify moral judgments, as in Dr. King's argument. But they are also often used to justify claims of fact or predictions about the future, moral judgments, legal decisions, and decisions about policy.

Analogy as a Basis for Claims of Fact and Predictions About the Future

In many fields, in many ways, people draw conclusions about something they have not observed, on the basis of its similarity to what they have observed. Many facts about the world cannot be directly verified. People must rely instead on analogical inference, that is, drawing conclusions about what they *cannot* directly experience on the basis of its similarity to what they *can* directly experience.

For example, it is impossible to verify directly that animals feel pain. But an argument by analogy can give good reason for thinking that they do.

> Do laboratory animals feel pain? No one can directly experience what a white rat experiences. Yet we have all had firsthand experiences of our own pain, and we know what kinds of treatment make us squeal. If a rat's nervous system is similar to our own, it is a reasonable inference that laboratory rats feel much the same kind of pain a human would feel under similar circumstances.

In this case, the analogy is between a rat and a human being. Humans know from experience that, under certain conditions, they will feel pain. They also know that there are some parallels between rat and human nervous systems. To the extent that the two nervous systems are similar, it is reasonable to infer that rats feel pain under circumstances similar to those that cause humans to feel pain.

It is possible to use arguments by analogy to make predictions about the future based on experiences of the past. Suppose, for example, that you are in the market for a new car. You have been very happy with the performance of your Toyota over the past ten years. So, you decide to replace it with another Toyota, expecting that since the old car was reliable and since the old and new Toyotas are very similar, it is likely that the new car will be reliable as well. The expectation is a reasonable one if the cars really are similar in relevant ways.

In a sense, many people are professional fortune-tellers. Loan officers, tax assessors, judges, parents, used-car sellers, farmers, politicians—all depend on their abilities to make reliable predictions about what will happen in the future.

A loan officer has to decide if an applicant is likely to repay a loan. A judge has to decide if offenders are likely to repeat their crimes. A farmer has to predict the effect of a fertilizer on a crop. They make their decisions on the basis of past experience and on the basis of the similarity of the present situation to situations that occurred in the past.

• •

5.4 STUDENTS CHOOSING COURSES

As a student, you make many predictions about the future. Quickly, jot down a description of how you chose this class. What did you think it would be like? What made you think it would be like that?

Now, go back to your description and circle all the inferences based on analogical reasoning; that is, find places where your expectations about this class were based on similarities between it and your own past experiences or the experiences of your friends.

• •

Analogy as the Basis for Moral Judgments

Judgments about whether an act is right or wrong are some of the most difficult judgments to make. Moreover, moral judgments are some of the most difficult judgments to defend. Once one person has said, "Abortion is right," and another has said, "Abortion is wrong," one might wonder what more they can say to each other. The answer is that they can offer reasons to support their judgments. A moral judgment that is supported by good reasons is more likely to be correct than one that is based on mere preference or unthinking appeal to authority or nothing at all. But what kinds of reasons can be offered in support of moral judgments?

Sometimes arguments by analogy can serve as the basis for moral judgments. When two fact situations are similar in important respects, it is likely that the moral judgment that is correct in one situation is correct in the other. Thus, the argument by analogy makes it possible for people to move from moral judgments that they are quite sure of, in situations that do not seem to be morally ambiguous, to problematic moral judgments in difficult, ambiguous situations.

Consider an example of moral reasoning using analogical arguments.

Scientists at a hypothermia research laboratory at the University of Minnesota, plan to use the results of Nazi experiments in their research program. The Nazis studied the effects of cold on humans by deliberately freezing concentration camp prisoners—Jews, Poles, and Gypsies. The scientists' plans have come under heavy criticism. Some people believe the information from the Nazi studies should be used. Should we never gaze at the pyramids, they ask incredulously, because the Egyptians built them with slave labor? It would be foolish to waste information that could help people, they argue, just as it would be foolish to ignore the pyramids.

These scientists compare the data from Nazi experiments to the pyramids; both were obtained at terrible cost to innocent human beings, and both are potentially beneficial to humankind. Since it is right to study the pyramids despite their origin, the scientists reasoned, it is probably right to use the Nazi data.

With similar arguments, people have sought to justify problematic moral judgments by comparing them to situations in which the right thing to do is clear. Many of these arguments are very familiar: Abortion is wrong because killing a fetus is like killing a baby. Capital punishment is wrong because it is like murder. Adultery is wrong because it is like breaking a promise.

In all moral arguments by analogy, the strength of the argument depends utterly on a real similarity between the situations. And not only that: The situations must be similar in ways that are morally significant. Is killing a fetus like killing a baby, or is the difference between a potential person and an actual person enough to destroy the analogy? It is not enough that fetuses and babies are similar—that they are all made of human cells, that they have fingers, that their hearts beat. Their similarities must be morally significant. Ask, what is it about a baby that makes it wrong to kill it? Do fetuses also have that characteristic?

Again, there are numerous similarities between capital punishment and murder. In both cases, someone ends up dead. In both cases, someone wanted that person dead and took a hand in making it happen. But, what is it about murder that makes it wrong? Is that also true of capital punishment? Moral arguments by analogy must be made carefully and with a clear eye for significant similarities and significant differences.

There is one more way in which analogical argument is central to moral reasoning: Notice that the biblical injunction, "Do unto others as you would have others do unto you," is an invitation to analogical reasoning. It is often unclear to people how they should act in relation to other people. But everyone knows how they would like people to act in relation to them. Through argument by analogy, they can take advantage of this knowledge to clarify the right course of action in problematic situations.

• •

5.5 IS BUSINESS LIKE POKER?

1. Read the following excerpts from a *Harvard Business Review* article that defends lying in business deals:

Most executives from time to time are almost compelled to practice some form of deception when negotiating with customers, dealers, labor unions, or government officials. By conscious misstatements, concealment of pertinent facts, or exaggeration—in short, by bluffing—they seek to persuade others to agree with them. If he is to reconcile personal integrity and high standards of honesty with the practical requirements of business, he must feel that his bluffs are ethically justified. The justification rests on the fact that business, as practiced by individuals as well as by corporations, has the impersonal character of a game—a game that demands both special strategy and an understanding of its special ethics.

We can learn a good deal about the nature of business by comparing it with poker. . . . No one expects poker to be played on the ethical principles preached in churches. In poker it is right and proper to bluff a friend out of the rewards of being dealt a good hand. . . . Cunning deception and concealment of one's strength and intentions, not kindness and openheartedness, are vital in poker. No one thinks any the worse of poker on that account.

And no one should think any the worse of the game of business because its standards of right and wrong differ from the prevailing traditions of morality in our society. . . . As long as [business leaders] comply with the letter of the law, they are within their rights to operate their businesses as they see fit. . . . [F]rom time to time every businessman, like every poker player, will bluff—and bluff hard.[14]

Reprinted by permission of *Harvard Business Review.* "Is Business Like Poker?" An excerpt from "Is Business Bluffing Ethical?" by Albert Carr, (January/February 1968). Copyright © 1968 by the President and Fellows of Harvard College; all rights reserved.

2. Team up with four or five other students who share your belief that this is a sound (or unsound) argument by analogy. Appoint a spokesperson. Prepare to present to the class the strongest case for (or against) the argument. In preparing your case, you may want to consider these questions:

   - In precisely what ways are business and poker alike? Are these important, relevant similarities?

   - In precisely what ways are business and poker disanalogous? Are these important, relevant differences?

   - Is *all* behavior "fair" in poker, or are some things cheating? Can any conclusions be drawn about business ethics from what you know about how to cheat at poker?

- • Think about the last time you bought a car. During negotiations, did you believe you were playing a game? If so, how did that affect your behavior? If not, how did that affect your behavior?

3. Present your defense (or criticism) of the business–poker analogy to the class, and listen to the ideas of other groups. If an opposing group convinces you, feel free to go over and join that group.

4. Interview a car salesperson. Through adroit questioning, determine whether the salesperson believes he or she is playing a game with different ethical rules. What are some of those special rules? Report your findings to the class.

· ·

Analogy as the Basis for Legal Decisions

In Anglo-American law, legal judgments are made according to the *doctrine of precedent*. The doctrine of precedent requires that every legal case be decided in the same way as similar cases in that jurisdiction have been decided in the past. In many cases, this is a straightforward judgment. It is straightforward when the preceding cases are consistent among themselves and when the facts of the present case clearly match the facts of the precedent cases.

Here is an example of analogical reasoning in law, drawn from the facts and reasoning in *People* v. *Dlugash.*[15] Dlugash was charged with attempted murder for firing five shots in the head and face of his victim with a .22-caliber pistol. The case was complicated by the fact that Dlugash apparently did not know that the victim was already dead, shot through the heart several minutes before. Can a person be charged with attempting to commit a crime that is factually impossible to commit?

To resolve this issue, the court in *Dlugash* turned to the case of *United States* v. *Thomas,*[16] where,

> It was held that men who had sexual intercourse with a woman, with the belief that she was alive and did not consent to the intercourse, could be charged with attempted rape when the woman had, in fact, died from an unrelated ailment prior to the acts of intercourse.[17]

On the basis of this case, the Court ruled that Dlugash could indeed be charged with attempted murder.

The facts of the *Dlugash* and *Thomas* cases are similar in important ways: both victims were dead, both of the accused were unaware that the victim was dead, and the definitions of both crimes require the intent to hurt the victim. Thomas was found guilty of attempted rape. So, Dlugash can be found guilty of attempted murder, given the doctrine of precedent. This is analogical argument of a fairly straightforward (and appalling) sort.

However, it often happens in law that there are *competing precedents;* that is, it is often possible to argue that a given case is similar to precedents that were decided one way *and* similar to precedent cases that were decided another way. Then, the judge has to decide which of the competing precedents is most analogous to the present case. Each attorney's job is to convince the judge that precedent cases decided in a way that favors her client are more like the present case than precedent cases decided in a way that would hurt her client. An example comes from *United States* v. *Walker.*

Laurie Walker was a Christian Scientist who believed in treating illness with prayer rather than medical care. When her four-year-old daughter became ill, Mrs. Walker prayed but did not seek any medical treatment. After seventeen days, the child died. Laurie Walker was charged with involuntary manslaughter.

In support of the position that Mrs. Walker was guilty, the state cited the case of *People* v. *Atkins,* in which the court affirmed the involuntary manslaughter conviction of a parent whose child died for want of medical care when the parents did not seek medical care, even though they knew that their child was seriously injured.

In support of their position that Mrs. Walker was innocent, her attorneys cited the case of *People* v. *Rodriguez,* in which a mother who had left her children alone at home, where one died in a fire, was found innocent of manslaughter.

The Court decided that the *Rodriguez* case was "clearly distinguishable," that is, not analogous to Mrs. Walker's case. "The failure of defendant to seek medical attention for a child who sickened and died over a seventeen-day period is plainly more egregious than the decision of Mrs. Rodriguez to leave her children alone at home for an afternoon." Thus, the jury could find Mrs. Walker guilty as charged.

Since analogous reasoning is central to legal decisions, good attorneys fill their briefcases with briefs (short descriptions of cases) and come to court prepared to argue by analogy.

· ·

5.6 YOU BE THE JUDGE

According to statute, burglary is defined this way: "Every person who breaks and enters any building or any part of any building, room, booth, tent, railroad car, automobile, truck, trailer, vessel or other structure in which any property is kept, with intent to steal therein or to commit any felony, is guilty of burglary in the second degree."

To determine whether a person is guilty of burglary, it is therefore important to know whether there was "breaking and entering." This is not always clear and must be determined by analogy to precedent cases.

A useful precedent case is *Houchin* v. *State:*

> *Houchin . . . removed a box containing a television set from the trunk of a car belonging to Dorothy Davis. He was observed placing this television set in the trunk of his car and arrested by Officer Kerlick. The evidence further discloses that the trunk of Davis' car was not closed because of the height of the box containing the television set, and that it had been secured by a nylon cord which was broken when the defendant opened the trunk.*[18]

The court decided that this was indeed a case of breaking and entering. The cord, which had been put on the car to secure the trunk lid, was broken. And the defendant, to remove the television, put his hands inside the trunk, a case of entering.

You be the judge. In each of the following cases, is there breaking and entering? Justify your answer by explaining how the facts of the case are (or are not) like the facts of the precedent case, *Houchin* v. *State.*

1. The defendant pried apart the bars covering a window in a street-level apartment building. The window itself had already been raised to let in cool air. He reached in and seized a silver teapot, a silver tray, and a silver creamer and carried them away.

2. The defendant used a garden rake to break a basement window. Then he pushed the rake through the shattered glass, hooked the tines over the cord on a radio, and pulled the radio through the window. He was arrested when he tried to sell the radio on a street corner for $50.

3. The defendant lived as a renter in a second-story apartment overlooking the patio of Dr. Wayne Williams. One night after a late party, Dr. Williams left seven jugs of wine on his patio table. All the jugs had handles formed of the glass of the bottle. The defendant, a skillful fisherman, fastened large hooks to a stout line. Casting carefully, he hooked all seven bottles of wine and hauled them into his own apartment.

Analogy as the Basis for Policy Decisions

A policy decision is a decision about what general plan or course of action to take. Like moral judgments, policy decisions are judgments about what ought to be rather than descriptions of what is. When policy decisions are difficult, it is often helpful to compare the problematic situation to a relatively clear-cut one. If two situations are alike in relevant ways, a policy that is correct in one of those situations is likely to be correct in the other.

Using analogical arguments to make policy decisions allows people to take advantage of what they already know by applying it to a new, ambiguous situation. But the strategy is dangerous unless two things are true: The first decision must have been correct, and the two situations must be truly similar in ways that really count.

In the first days of 1991, President George Bush was faced with the terrible policy decision of whether to go to war with Iraq. The two armies facing off in the desert represented a complex and ambiguous situation. But George Bush was a student of World War II and was convinced that if Hitler had been forcibly stopped when he moved his armies into Poland, World War II could have been prevented. Saddam Hussein's ambitions, Bush believed, were much like Hitler's. He reasoned by analogy that destroying Iraqi ability to wage war would similarly prevent further aggression and bloodshed. Whether or not Saddam is a Hitler, Bush is no Chamberlain; he went to war. History will judge the strength of President Bush's argument by analogy.

When you start looking for arguments by analogy, it becomes clear that they are very common in debates about public policy. Here are some examples:

- Debates about the legalization of marijuana. The effects of marijuana and alcohol are very similar, yet alcohol use by adults is legal. Should marijuana use be legal, too?

- Debates about beer advertisements on TV. Because cigarette smoking is harmful to health, cigarette advertisements have been pulled off the air. But beer is harmful to health, too. Shouldn't beer ads be pulled off the air, too?

- Debates about laws requiring seat belts. Wearing a seat belt and wearing a motorcycle helmet both save lives at minimal inconvenience. Many states require people to wear helmets. Shouldn't states also require motorists to wear seat belts?

For these and other public policy issues, the argument by analogy is a way to extend consensus into new, more difficult areas.

5.7 WOMEN ON THE FRONT LINES

Do you believe that women should serve in combat positions during wars? Write a short (250-word) essay in which you use an analogical argument to defend your view. As you plan your argument, it may be helpful to think through answers to these questions: What are the important similarities between men and women? the important dissimilarities? What characteristics are essential to being a good soldier? What characteristics are essential to being a person who deserves equal protection of the law? Refer to "Writing Analogical Arguments," the next section in this chapter.

In class, trade essays with another student. Analyze and evaluate that argument. (See the sections later in this chapter headed "How to Analyze Arguments by Analogy" and "How to Evaluate the Strength of Arguments by Analogy.")

5.8 A COOPERATIVE CONTROVERSY ABOUT DRUGS[19]

Gather in groups of four students, divided into two teams of two people each. Working with your partner, write the best analogical argument you can think of to support the claim that marijuana should be legalized. While you do that, the other pair in your group will write the best analogical argument they can think of to support the claim that marijuana should not be legalized.

Then, do the reverse: without looking at what the other members of your group have written, write the strongest analogical argument you can think of for the contrary claim. That is, those who wrote in favor of the legalization of marijuana now write an argument opposing legalization, and vice versa.

Read all the arguments your group members have written. As a group, discuss the merits of the arguments, and reach a consensus about the legalization of marijuana. Together, prepare and present to the class a group report stating your consensus position on the issue and supporting it with your group's best analogical argument.

·········· Writing Analogical Arguments ··········

The key to writing a good argument by analogy is thinking up an appropriate analogue, one that is truly similar in relevant respects to the subject of your argument and one that will· yield the conclusion you want to justify. Here are the steps in the process, illustrated by the step-by-step construction of an argument about skin cancer and the destruction of the ozone layer.

1. Be clear in your own mind about the claim you want to defend. Write the claim down to be sure you have it clearly in mind.

    The hole in the ozone layer over Europe and New England will result in increased incidence of cataracts and skin cancer.

2. Then, look for good reasons to back up the claim. What is it about the hole in the ozone layer that makes an increase in these diseases likely?

    The hole will allow more ultraviolet light to reach people on the ground.

3. Then, brainstorm: Under what other circumstances has ultraviolet light reached living beings *and* caused increased rates of disease?

    Mice exposed to ultraviolet rays at an intensity like that expected to reach Europe and New England showed a tenfold increase in the incidence of cataracts and the mutations in cell structure that cause skin cancers.

4. Then you are in a position to compile the pieces of an argument by analogy, by these steps:
    a. Make clear what two things are being compared.

        The people who live under the hole in the ozone are compared to mice exposed to high levels of ultraviolet radiation in laboratory experiments.

    b. Explain how they are similar.

        Mice and human beings have similar cellular structures. And they are exposed to similar rates of ultraviolet radiation.

        c. State what is already known about the familiar case.

        Mice exposed to the higher levels of ultraviolet light showed a tenfold increase in the incidence of cataracts and the mutations in cell structure linked to skin cancers.

    d.   Draw the conclusion.

> It is likely that people who are also exposed to higher levels of ultraviolet radiation will also experience higher rates of cataracts and skin cancer.

5.   Then, put the pieces of the argument together:

> Residents of Europe and New England, living under a new hole opening in the ozone layer, find themselves in a position similar to that of mice exposed to high levels of ultraviolet radiation in the laboratory. Both are being exposed to far higher levels of radiation than are normal. The mice showed a tenfold increase in the incidence of cataracts and mutations in cell structure that cause skin cancers. Thus, given the cellular similarities between humans and mice, it is likely that the damage to the ozone layer will result in increased incidence of eye and skin diseases among the residents of those areas.

To be sure that all the parts of the argument are present and clearly identifiable, check a draft of your argument against the list of analytical questions in the next section, headed "How to Analyze Arguments by Analogy." Then, you may want to alter the argument to make the argument clearer.

• •

5.9 TO THE EDITOR

1.   Write a letter to the editor of your local newspaper in which you use an argument by analogy to defend your position in regard to one of the policy statements listed below. The letter should be short (one paragraph) and should be based on a single argument by analogy.

2.   Post your letter on the wall so that all the other students can read it.

> It (is, is not) right to kill and eat animals for food.
>
> Mandatory drug testing in the workplace (is, is not) a violation of a citizen's rights.
>
> Requiring companies to hire a certain percentage of minorities (threatens, enhances) the rights of other citizens.
>
> America should (encourage, discourage) immigration.

People with AIDS (should, should not) be allowed to hold jobs in the medical, restaurant, or teaching professions.

It is best for society if women (stay, do not stay) in the home.

Capital punishment (should, should not) be abolished.

The heads of corporations that cause environmental disasters (should, should not) go to jail.

People (should, should not) wear fur coats.

Religious student groups (should, should not) be allowed to meet in public schools during school hours.

Homosexuals (should, should not) be allowed to serve in the armed forces.

Looting (is, is not) a legitimate response to long-term economic injustice.

Analyzing and Evaluating Analogical Arguments

The Fallacy of False Analogy

An analogy is said to be *false* when the two things compared have fundamental differences, although the differences are often masked by a superficial resemblance. An analogical argument is said to be *fallacious* when it rests on a false analogy. While some false analogies are obviously flawed, others are subtle and seductive. As the logician R.H. Thouless said in 1932, "To an extraordinary extent, intelligent people become convinced of highly improbable things because they have heard them supported by analogies whose unsoundness would be apparent to an imbecile."[20]

Some analogies are obviously flawed. Defending state executions of those convicted of adultery, Iran's former ruler, the Ayatollah Khomeini, exploited a false analogy between moral corruption and physical corruption: "If your finger suffers from gangrene, what do you do? Letting the whole hand and then the body become filled with gangrene, or cutting the finger off? . . . Corruption, corruption. We have to eliminate corruption." It is not clear that adultery spreads through a population like gangrene spreads through the blood. Nor is it clear that adultery is as dangerous as gangrene. The weakness of the argument is not hard to detect.

On the other hand, it often requires all the skills of intelligent people to decide whether an analogy is misleading. Analogical arguments are not true or false, all or nothing. Their virtues are a matter of degree. So, judgments about analogies often require subtle judgments of relative strength.

An example of an analogy that has been the subject of heated debate is found in a famous argument by the estimable Oliver Wendell Holmes in *Schenck v. United States.* During World War I, Schenck distributed an antidraft document to men who had been drafted into the military. Quoting the Constitution, the document claimed that draftees had a right to oppose the draft. Did Schenck have a right to circulate that document? Justice Holmes argued that "the most stringent protection of free speech would not protect a man in falsely shouting fire in a theatre, and causing a panic." Likewise, the First Amendment would not protect Schenck in encouraging draft resistance during a war. The similarity, Holmes argued, lay in the fact that, in both cases, "words are used *in such circumstances* . . . as to create a clear and present danger" of an evil Congress has the right to prevent.[21]

Does circulating a document really create a clear and present danger of harm as serious as a stampede to the exits? Is circulating the document more like shouting "Fire!" in a burning theater? The issues are still debated.

The ability to distinguish weak from strong analogical arguments rests on two things: first, the ability to analyze, and thus to understand, an argument by analogy; second, an understanding of the criteria for evaluating arguments by analogy.

How to Analyze Arguments by Analogy

To get a clear understanding of an argument by analogy, break it up into its parts. This series of analytic questions can be helpful:

1. *What two things are being compared?* Do this first step conscientiously and you will be well rewarded; confusion at the start muddles the entire analysis. Understand that it is the rare analogical argument in which the analogues are clear on the face of it.

2. *Of these two analogues, which is the one you know about already, and which is the one you are trying to draw a conclusion about?* For convenient reference, call the analogue you already know about, the *familiar case;* call the analogue you want to draw a conclusion about, the *unfamiliar case.*

3. *In what specific ways do these two cases resemble each other?* The entire analogical argument rests on the similarity between cases. Does the author provide any grounds for saying that the cases are indeed similar? What are the similarities?

4. *What important fact do you know about the familiar case?* What characteristic have you observed in the familiar case? This is the characteristic that you will infer belongs also to the unfamiliar case.

5. *What conclusion is drawn about the unfamiliar case?* The conclusion will be a claim about the unfamiliar case.

The skeletal structure of an argument by analogy is not complex. The argument rests on the similarity between two things. This similarity should be clearly expressed as a first premise:

(Familiar case) and (unfamiliar case) are alike in that (similarities).

The second premise sets forth what is known about the familiar case:

(Familiar case) is (attribute).

The conclusion puts these two pieces of information together. Given that two things are alike and that one of these has an additional attribute, it is probable that the second will have that additional attribute also:

Thus, (unfamiliar case) probably also is (attribute).

The argument by analogy, in standard form, looks like this:

(1) _____ and _____ are alike in that _____ .

(2) _____ is _____ .

Therefore, _____ probably also is _____ .

If you can answer the analytical questions clearly and put the argument in standard form, you have a clear grasp of the essentials of the argument. Then (and only then) can you proceed to evaluate its strength.

Some arguments by analogy are clearly stated. Far more often, the analogical argument is hidden and confusingly stated. Consider this:

A new kind of job is available for women: surrogate motherhood. It is possible for a woman to earn up to $10,000 while she stays at home or works another job if she is willing to undertake a pregnancy for another couple. Here's how it works. A woman consents to have the couple's fertilized ovum implanted in her own uterus. She carries the baby to term.

Then, when the baby is born, she gives it up to be adopted by the biological parents.

The problem is that many legislatures are passing laws making surrogate motherhood illegal. This hardly seems fair. If men can sell blood for money, why should it be illegal for a woman to sell the use of her body for nine months?

The analysis of this argument would proceed this way:

1. *What two things are being compared?* Selling blood for money and undergoing a pregnancy for another couple in exchange for money are compared.

2. *Of these two analogues, which is the one you know about already, and which is the one you are trying to draw a conclusion about?* Selling blood for money is the familiar case. Undergoing a pregnancy for another couple in exchange for money is the unfamiliar case.

3. *In what specific ways do these two cases resemble each other?* The author does not make any argument for their similarity. So, it is up to the reader to note that, while both procedures involve some risk, neither is particularly dangerous. Both involve a part of the body. Both involve giving up part of the body, at least temporarily, for profit.

4. *What important fact do you know about the familiar case?* We know that the practice of selling blood for money is legal.

5. *What conclusion is drawn?* Surrogate motherhood should be legalized.

5.10 ANALOGIES: THE GOOD, THE BAD, AND THE UGLY

All the following passages contain analogical arguments—more or less. You will find that some of them are incompletely formed, some are muddled, and some are generically awful. Your job is to rewrite the passage so that the analogical argument is clearly expressed. This is a three-step process:

1. First analyze the argument; that is, answer these questions:

   - What two things are being compared?
   - Of these two analogues, which is the familiar case and which is the unfamiliar?
   - In what specific ways do these two cases resemble each other?

- What important fact do you know about the familiar case?
- What conclusion is drawn?

2. Write the argument, following standard form.

3. Then, revise your sentences to make a graceful paragraph. You may choose to make use of indicator words such as *therefore* and *since*. You may choose to put the conclusion first. You may choose to eliminate the obvious or add details to make the meaning clearer.

   a. Indiana state law makes public nudity a Class A misdemeanor. So the Indiana state troopers arrested Darlene, Gayle, and Carla, nude go-go dancers at the Kitty Kat Lounge. On appeal, the U.S. Circuit Court upheld the right of the dancers. They cited the dance of Salome in the Richard Strauss opera, an erotic, sensual expression, the legality of which has never been challenged.[22]

   b. *It has been said that a comparison can be made between the Independence Movements in the Baltic region and the American Civil War. Such a scenario would equate Estonia, Latvia, and Lithuania with the secessionist southern states of 19th century America and Mikhail Sergeyevich Gorbachev with Abraham Lincoln. [This comparison would lead one to believe that Gorbachev had a right to use his armies to force the Baltic countries to remain in the Soviet Union.]*[23]

   c. *Suppose that someone tells me that he has had a tooth extracted without an anaesthetic, and I express my sympathy, and suppose that I am then asked, "How do you know that it hurt him?" I might reasonably reply, "Well, I know that it would hurt me. I have been to the dentist and know how painful it is to have a tooth [filled] without an anaesthetic, let alone taken out. And he has the same sort of nervous system as I have. I infer, therefore, that in these conditions he felt considerable pain, just as I should myself."*[24]

   d. In an *Outland* cartoon, a TV is pictured, blaring this advertisement:

      FURS!! FURS!! Ya want furs? We got furs! Come on down! Come on down to "Fashion Frank's Unfinished Furs!!" Outland's family discount, do-it-yourself fur emporium!! Pick from among our vast inventory of fur coats on-the-hoof including truck driver! Plumber! Dock worker! Plus exotic imports like Middle Eastern 7-Eleven clerk! Bring the kids! Pick your personal fashion statement . . . And as we say here at "Fashion Frank's Unfinished Furs" . . . WOMP 'EM! STOMP 'EM! SKIN 'EM AND WEAR 'EM![25]

e. A poster tacked to a telephone pole showed two photographs side by side. The first was labeled "Jews in Germany: inmate bodies piled into a cart, Gusen concentration camp (Austria, 1945)"; this was indeed what the photo showed. The second was labeled "Babies in North America: trash can full of aborted bodies (Canadian teaching hospital, early 1970s)"; the photograph showed a black plastic garbage bag opened to reveal parts of fetuses.

f. From a review of *The Dreaded Comparison: Human and Animal Slavery* by Marjorie Speigel:

> *Historians have long reported that African slaves were treated like animals. But the book turns that analogy around: Should even animals be treated that way?*
>
> *Speigel is a young animal rights activist from Seattle. Her basic premise is that living creatures are living creatures and oppression is oppression.*
>
> *"Both humans and animals share the ability to suffer from restricted freedom of movement; from the loss of social freedom, and to experience pain at the loss of a loved one. Both groups suffer from the fear of being hunted, tormented or injured."*
>
> *She likens the belief that humans are on a higher evolutionary plane to all other animals as "speciesism" akin to racism.*[26]

How to Evaluate the Strength of Arguments by Analogy

In an argument by analogy, the fact that two things are similar in important, observed ways is used as grounds for arguing that they are likely to be similar in another, unobserved respect. So, the strength of an argument by analogy depends utterly on the degree of similarity between the two things compared.

So, the first important question to ask of an argument by analogy is this:

Is the similarity strong enough to support the inference?

This is going to be a judgment call. It is possible to find similarities between any two things. And it is possible to find differences between any two nonidentical things. The important point is to ask: Are the two things similar in important and essential ways? Conversely, are they different in important, essential ways?

In part, the judgment will be based on the *number of similarities.* Usually, the more, the better. But this does not get you very far in your evaluation. Apples and oranges are alike in many, many ways: cell structure, vitamin content, genesis, shape, edibility, usefulness as missiles; yet people are repeatedly warned not to compare them. On the other hand, handing a soldier an antidraft document and shouting "Fire!" in a crowded theater seem to be alike in only one way: both are likely to incite people to dangerous actions. But that similarity, Oliver Wendell Holmes believed, is essential.

In part, the judgment will be based on the *number of differences.* But, again, not all differences are equal. Differences are irrelevant if they are not causally or logically connected to the quality at issue. For example, differences in the colors of two cars are irrelevant to a judgment of whether both cars will start equally well since color is not causally related to mechanical quality. But difference in the age of two cars may well make a difference in how well the two cars start.

The important point is to be clear about just what similarities and differences exist between the observed and unobserved cases and to make a critical judgment about whether those similarities and differences make it likely or unlikely that what is true of one case will be true of the other.

• •

5.11 ANSWERING LETTERS TO THE EDITOR

Read over the letters to the editor that your classmates wrote and posted on the wall, in Exercise 5.9. Select a letter that you think is dead wrong. Write a letter to the editor responding to that letter. Your response should include three paragraphs: (1) a summary of the argument your classmate has made, (2) a discussion of the relevant differences between the analogues in that letter, and (3) a counteranalogy, that is, an analogy supporting the opposite conclusion. Post your letter on the wall next to the letter it answers. You will want to take time to read any responses students have written to your original letter.

The following example can help you see how you might frame such a response. Follow this format as closely as you can.

To the Editor:

In his letter to the editor of May 16, Mr. Bial argues that capital punishment is like cutting off the hands of thieves or putting out the eyes of voyeurs. Since these punishments are cruel and unusual, it follows, he claims, that capital punishment is cruel and unusual.

But there is an important difference between maiming a thief or blinding a voyeur and killing a killer. In the first cases, the punishment imposes a harm far exceeding the harm done by the thief or the voyeur. But killing a murderer imposes exactly the same harm as the murderer did to the victim. Thus, while I agree that it is wrong to maim thieves and blind voyeurs, that does not mean that it is wrong to kill killers.

Capital punishment is more like paying off a debt. A person who has borrowed money and a person who has taken a life both owe payment in return. Just as the borrower must pay his debt, so murderers must give their lives to pay for the lives they have taken.

. . . .

Even if an argument by analogy is based on a strong similarity, and even if no essential differences undermine the analogy, there is another question that needs to be addressed:

Are the facts about the familiar case correctly reported?

Suppose you are considering purchasing a new Yugo. You ask the Yugo dealer about the past service record of Yugos, reasoning correctly that if past Yugos had good service records, the new one is also likely to need few repairs. The dealer assures you that the service record has been exemplary. You buy the car, only to spend the next few years of your life having the car hauled in for repairs. What went wrong? The similarities between past and present Yugos were certainly strong enough to support the inference. But the facts about the old Yugos were incorrectly—in this case, deceptively—reported.

It is possible that the Ayatollah Khomeini's argument in favor of execution for adultery fails on this criterion. One may assume that moral corruption and gangrene are similar in essential ways: they both spread; they both destroy. But the ayatollah may be wrong that the best way to treat gangrene is by amputation. Antibiotics are now available to eliminate the infection in its earliest stages and save the victim's life. Perhaps there are less drastic ways to deal with adultery as well.

Both these examples illustrate the second way in which arguments by analogy can fail: Any mistaken observation about the familiar case can be carried along through the argument to become a mistaken inference about the unfamiliar case.

Analogies are adaptable, colorful, and persuasive ways to support claims and justify decisions. Used carefully, they are indispensable tools for learning from experience. Used carelessly, though, they quickly lead us astray. Using an analogy, Mark Twain noted the risks of analogical reasoning in *Pudd'nhead Wilson's Calendar:*[27]

> *We should be careful to get out of an experience only the wisdom that is in it—and stop there; lest we be like the cat that sits down on a hot stove lid. She will never sit down on a hot stove lid again—and that is well; but also she will never sit down on a cold one anymore.*

• •

5.12   COLLABORATIVE QUIZ TAKING[28]

Take the following quiz. When you are done, hold on to your answer sheet, but do not make any changes in it.

Analogy Quiz

Directions. Circle the letter of the best answer *or answers.* You will notice that, unlike most multiple-choice quizzes, this one is designed to exercise your ability to make reasoned judgments about ambiguous situations.

1. The Beavers lost the last two away basketball games. They are about to play another. A fan predicts that since they lost the last two games and since the next game is away also, they will probably lose this one, too.
    Which of the following additional pieces of information would weaken the fan's argument?
    a. The past two games were coached by the head coach. The next game will be coached by the assistant coach.
    b. The center has found his lucky wristband, a talisman that had been lost for the first two games.
    c. The last two games were against Pac-10 opponents. So is the next game.
    d. The last two games were played during driving rainstorms. However, weather forecasts for the next game predict clear skies.

2. The argument is advanced that guns cause accidental deaths in private homes. This, of course, is true. So also do power tools. It seems to me that people who wish to assume the risk of having guns in their homes ought to be permitted to do so. After all, no one suggests that we should ban power tools.
    Which of the following additional pieces of information would strengthen the argument above?
    a. Power tools have lots of constructive uses, such as building birdhouses. Guns can be used only to shoot holes in things.

b. Both hammers and the butt ends of guns can be used to drive nails into wood.

c. Like power tools, guns become less dangerous when used only by well-trained adults.

d. Once a man killed his wife with a power drill.

e. In some parts of the country, chain saw accidents cause as many injuries as gun accidents.

3. After I ate chicken-fried steak at the Horned Toad Bar and Grill last weekend, I became very sick to my stomach. Once again, I have ordered chicken-fried steak at the Horned Toad Bar and Grill.

Which conclusion, if added to the premises, would make the strongest argument?

a. I will probably get very sick to my stomach.

b. I will get very sick to my stomach.

c. I'll surely throw up.

d. I may get sick.

4. Consider this argument: There is nothing morally wrong with having an abortion. The fetus is just a mass of unwanted and potentially harmful tissue in the woman's body. If she does not want it there, she should have it removed, just as she would have a tumor removed if it were likely to cause her trouble.

This is a relatively weak argument, because:

a. A fetus is not made of cells as a tumor is.

b. Women do not create their own tumors, but women play a large part in the creation of the fetus.

c. A tumor, if left alone, will not develop into a human being. A fetus will.

d. Sometimes women die from the effects of pregnancy just as they sometimes die from the effects of tumors.

5. Consider this TV commercial from the government's war on drugs:

This is your brain.

[Shows a raw egg]

This is drugs.

[Shows a frying pan]

This is your brain on drugs.

[Shows an egg being broken into a hot frying pan]

Any questions?

The conclusion of this "argument" is most likely to be:

a. If you don't use drugs, your brain will be runny.

b. Taking drugs hurts your brain.

c. If you do use drugs, your brain will solidify.

d. Eggs should not do drugs.

6. Mars may be a likely place for life. The Earth and Mars are very much alike. (a) There is water on Mars. (b) There are high levels of carbon dioxide on Mars. (c) The temperatures on Mars are more extreme than those on Earth, but there are places, under the soil, for example, where temperatures are very Earthlike. (d) Mars revolves around the same sun the Earth revolves around. (e) Mars has polar ice caps just like Earth's. (f) Mars has a rock formation that looks just like the smiley faces found all over Earth. These conditions were conducive to the development of life on Earth. So, it seems that there are good reasons for thinking there is some kind of life on Mars as well.

   Which of the similarities above, if any, is/are not relevant to the conclusion?

7. With very few exceptions, research on cosmetic products—lipstick, for example—is performed on laboratory animals. It is not that researchers care what effect lipstick has on monkey lips; rather, researchers believe that studying lab animals will reveal what effects the substances will have on humans.

   Which of the following differences between monkeys and humans will the lipstick researchers not worry about (that is, which are not relevant differences)?

a. Monkeys do not wear lipstick in nature.

b. Much of a monkey's skin is protected by fur.

c. Monkeys are generally smaller than humans.

d. The monkeys in the experiment are held in small cages, and their lipstick is applied by scientists, in contrast to human wearers of lipstick (except scientists).

e. In past studies, monkeys have shown a higher sensitivity to environmental toxins than humans.

8. If you wanted to argue by analogy that governments should have the right to control citizens' access to information that is false or injurious, you would want to compare a government to which of the following?

a. A parent

b. A teacher

c. A jailer

        d.   A Hitler

        e.   A lawyer

9. Here's the situation: Your friend is drunk. She pulls her car keys out of her purse and walks out to the parking lot, announcing that she is going to drive to another bar. You urge her not to go. She replies that unless you plan to use force, you cannot prevent her. Is it right to use force to prevent a drunk friend from driving? You ask four friends and get the following answers. Which answer is supported by the strongest argument by analogy?

    a.   Yes. A drunk driver is like a child with an Uzi. She does not have the ability to keep from harming others or herself. You would surely wrest the Uzi from a child. So, you should use force to keep your friend from driving.

    b.   Yes. A drunk driver is like a suicidal person. Just as you should use force to keep a person from throwing himself off a cliff, you should use force to keep your friend from driving.

    c.   No. Using force in this situation is like swatting a fly with a SCUD missile. Talk to your friend, persuade her, trick her—but the use of force is not called for.

    d.   Yes. A drunk driver is like a murderer. No one doubts the authority of the police to use force to keep a murderer from killing again. So, use all necessary force to keep your friend from driving.

As soon as most students have finished taking the quiz, your professor will assign you to study groups. Take the quiz again, working as a group. Share your knowledge, discuss and debate answers, reach a consensus, and record your answers. Signal your professor when you have finished; make no changes after that.

As your professor reads the answers, correct both your individual and group exams, and compute your grade. Your grade is the average of your own score and your group's score.

Your professor may give your team time to prepare and submit written appeals on items on which you disagree with the given answer. These need to be well-reasoned arguments exhibiting a clear grasp of the concepts.

• •

5.13 DRUG USE IN RELIGIOUS CEREMONIES[29]

You and your classmates will serve as attorneys and judges in the case of *Department of Human Resources of Oregon* v. *Smith*. Here are the facts of the case:

The Native American Church has for many years used the hallucinatory drug peyote in its religious rituals. Church members believe that the peyote plant embodies their deity. Thus, eating it is an act of worship and communion. Church doctrine forbids the nonreligious use of peyote.

Smith, an Oregon member of the Native American Church, ingested a small amount of peyote in a religious ceremony. As a result, he was fired from his job. Subsequently, the State of Oregon denied unemployment benefits on the grounds that Smith's use of peyote violated the conditions of his employment.

Smith sued Oregon, arguing that the First Amendment to the Constitution protects the religious use of peyote.

The Oregon Supreme Court ruled that it was unconstitutional to forbid the religious use of peyote and, thus, the state could not deny unemployment benefits. The United States Supreme Court agreed to hear the case on appeal to decide this issue: Is a law forbidding the religious use of peyote a violation of the First Amendment to the Constitution?

For classroom purposes, the Court's procedures are simplified to the following steps:

1. From the members of the class, form a team of attorneys to represent the State of Oregon, a team of attorneys to represent Smith, and a panel of Supreme Court Justices.

2. Either in or out of class, attorneys and judges prepare for oral argument before the Supreme Court Justices.

    To prepare for the arguments, the *Justices* should familiarize themselves with the case documents and formulate questions they may decide to ask the attorneys.

    Each *team of attorneys* should prepare an argument to present to the Court. Attorneys for the State of Oregon will argue that forbidding religious use of peyote is not a violation of the Constitution. Attorneys for Smith will argue that forbidding religious use of peyote is a violation of the Constitution.

    Carefully outline the presentation so that it includes all of the following elements:

    -   A clear statement of the position your team will defend.
    -   A short summary of a previous court decision that supports your position.
    -   An argument showing that the precedent case and the *Smith* case are so similar that they should be decided the same way.
    -   A short summary of a previous court decision that offers the strongest challenge to your position.

- • An argument showing that the competing precedent case and the *Smith* case are so different that they should not be decided the same way.

3. During the Court proceedings, the Chief Justice of the Supreme Court directs the moot court, calling for the arguments of both teams of attorneys. Justices may ask questions at any time during an argument. After the arguments, the Chief Justice leads the panel of justices in a discussion of the issues and arguments. The case is decided by a vote of the Justices.

Case Documents

The following information may be useful to your team as you prepare your case. But feel free to use any other information you may have.

The First Amendment to the Constitution reads, in part, "Congress shall make no law respecting an establishment of religion, or prohibiting the free exercise thereof."

* * *

In *Reynolds* v. *United States,*[30] the defendant, a Mormon, was indicted for bigamy under a federal statute. Reynolds was a member of the Church of Jesus Christ of Latter-Day Saints and a believer in its doctrines. One of the doctrines of that church was that it was the duty of male members of the church to practice polygamy.

The Supreme Court found that Reynolds was properly convicted of the crime of polygamy even though the Mormon religion held polygamy to be proper and desirable.

* * *

KENTUCKY MAN KILLED BY RATTLER IN RITE OF SNAKE-HANDLING CULT

A rattlesnake bit a man at a snake-handling religious ceremony in a church in the mountains of southeast Kentucky yesterday and the man died nearly eight hours later at his home here. The state police said they had been told that the man was bitten at a snake-handling service. The funeral home confirmed the report.

Snakes have been handled for years at religious services in the mountains of Kentucky, Tennessee, Virginia, North Carolina, and

Georgia. The venomous snakes have claimed many victims but the practice has continued as a "demonstration of faith."

The continuing practice is in violation of an injunction issued by Circuit Judge George Shepherd. The same judge sentenced Rev. Liston Pack to 30 days in jail and a fine of $100 for violating his injunction against snake-handling.[31]

* * *

[The case of Wisconsin v. Yoder *addressed the issue] of whether the state of Wisconsin could force an Old Order Amish family to send its children to school beyond the eighth grade. The Amish lead a simple, rural farm life in cohesive, self-supporting religious communities, stressing "a life of goodness rather than a life of intellect. . . ." In their view, by sending their children to high school, "they would not only expose themselves to the danger of the censure of the church community, but . . . endanger their own salvation and that of their children. . . . [T]he Court held that in view of the kind of life for which the Amish children were being trained . . . , the state did not have a sufficiently compelling interest in the additional years of schooling to warrant interfering with the free exercise of religion.*[32]

* * *

PEOPLE v. *WOODY*[33]

On April 28, 1962, a group of Navajos met in a hogan in the desert near Needles, California, to perform a religious ceremony that included the use of peyote. Police officers, who had observed part of the ceremony, arrested defendants, who were among the Navajos present. Defendants were convicted of violating laws prohibiting unauthorized possession of peyote. The California Supreme Court refused to allow the state to ban the drug peyote when used by the Native American Church, basing its decision on the history of the church and the sincerity of its members.

* * *

In 1960, the State of Pennsylvania terminated the welfare rights of a Native American, Stephen Roy. Roy had refused to get a Social Security number for his daughter, Little Bird of the Snow. His refusal was based on his religious beliefs.

The Supreme Court ruled that the state had not violated Roy's constitutional rights to the free exercise of religion, saying that "some religious practices must yield to the common good."[34]

5.14 BRAVES AND TOMAHAWKS

For each of the following examples:

a.   Tell the purpose to which the analogy is put (to evoke an image or emotion, to explain a concept, or to justify a conclusion).

b.   Tell what two things are being compared.

c.   If the analogy is intended to serve as an argument, analyze and evaluate the argument.

d.   Circle any similes, metaphors, or implied analogies.

1.   The following adaptation is reprinted courtesy of SPORTS ILLUS-TRATED from the October 28, 1991 issue. Copyright © 1991, The Time Inc. Magazine Company. ("Let's Bust Those Chops," by Rick Reilly.) All rights reserved.

a.   *Would you be offended if your dog fetched a morning paper that had this item inside?*

> CHICAGO — *The Chicago Jews defeated the Houston Astros 2 – 1 Friday in front of a stadium full of wild fans waving yarmulkes and singing Hava Nagila.*

You would be? Then why shouldn't the two million Native Americans in this country be offended when they read something like this?

> ATLANTA — *The Atlanta Braves defeated the Houston Astros 2 – 1 on Friday in front of a stadium full of wild fans waving foam-rubber tomahawks and chanting war cries.*

b.   *Roger Head, a Chippewa who heads the Minnesota Indian Affairs Council, commenting on the use of Native American traditions in sports settings:*

> *"It hurts. It's not a true depiction of the Indian people. They wear headdresses, which are very spiritual in nature, very ceremonial. It would be like if we went to a game with a lot of Catholics and started giving communion in the stands or hearing confession."*

c.   *Oh, my, even people who should know better don't get it. Twenty-one years ago, Jane Fonda was on Alcatraz Island in San Francisco Bay with Native Americans who had occupied the island, demanding that it be turned into an Indian cultural-education center. . . . But during the National League Championship Series, there she was—sandwiched between Ted Turner and Jimmy and Rosalyn Carter—chop-chop-chopping away, bellowing pseudo-Indian war cries, having a wonderful time cheering on Ted's Braves.*[35]

2.   Heard on TV:

Looking at the AIDS problems today is like looking at the stars. What we are seeing now happened years ago. Who knows what is happening today?[36]

3.   From eco-warrior Edward Abbey:*

If a stranger batters your door down with an axe, threatens your family and yourself with deadly weapons, and proceeds to loot your home of whatever he wants, he is committing what is universally recognized—by law and in common morality—as a crime. In such a situation the householder has both the right and the obligation to defend himself, his family, and his property by whatever means are necessary. . . .

The American wilderness, what little remains, is now undergoing exactly such an assault. With bulldozer, earth mover, chainsaw, and dynamite the international timber, mining and beef industries are invading our public lands—property of all Americans—bashing their way into our forests, mountains, and rangelands and looting them for everything they can get away with. This for the sake of short-term profits in the corporate sector and multimillion-dollar annual salaries for the three-piece suited gangsters (MBA—Harvard, Yale, University of Tokyo, et alia) who control and manage these bandit enterprises.[37]

4.   When tennis star Martina Navratilova heard that Magic Johnson had slept with hundreds of women before he learned he was infected with the HIV virus, she pointed out a double standard. If a woman announced she had slept with 200 or 300 men, she would be called a slut. But no one seems to think that Magic Johnson's behavior was shameful.

5.   From a biology textbook:

Plasma cells are weapons factories: they secrete about 2,000 antibody molecules per second into the extracellular fluid! . . . The antibodies they

* From ONE LIFE AT A TIME PLEASE by Edward Abbey. Copyright © 1978, 1983, 1984, 1985, 1986, 1988 by Edward Abbey. Reprinted by permission of Henry Holt and Company, Inc.

secrete cannot destroy a target directly; rather, they bind to it and mark it for disposal by other agents.[38]

6.   From Isak Dinesen (Karen Blixen), *Out of Africa:*

> *Out on the safaris, I had seen a herd of buffalo, one hundred and twenty-nine of them, come out of the morning mist under a copper sky, one by one, as if the dark and massive, iron-like animals with the mighty horizontally swung horns were not approaching, but were being created before my eyes and set out as they were finished. . . .*
>
> *I had seen a herd of elephant traveling through dense native forest . . . pacing along as if they had an appointment at the end of the world. . . .*
>
> *The giraffe, in their queer, inimitable, vegetative gracefulness, as if it were not a herd of animals but a family of rare, long-stemmed, speckled gigantic flowers slowly advancing.*[39]

Notes

1.   Marcel Proust, *Remembrance of Things Past* (New York: Random-House, 1934).

2.   Samuel Butler, "Music, Pictures and Books," quoted in *Bartlett's Familiar Quotations,* ed. Emily M. Beck (New York: Little, Brown and Co., 1980), p. 620.

3.   Franklin Delano Roosevelt, speech at Chicago, October 5, 1937 (the "Quarantine the Aggressors Speech").

4.   Abraham Lincoln, Address at Gettysburg, November 19, 1863.

5.   Dean Fischer, "We're Not Going to Lose," *Time* (Feb. 4, 1991), p. 29.

6.   James Fallows, "Morning Edition," National Public Radio (Feb. 4, 1991).

7.   Winston Churchill, "The German Invasion of Russia," reprinted in *Winston S. Churchill: His Complete Speeches 1897–1963,* ed. R.R. James (New York: Chelsea House Publishers, 1974), pp. 6428–6429.

8.   Bette LaSere Erickson, "Presenting and Explaining," Instructional Development Program, University of Rhode Island (unpublished paper).

9.   Excerpt from *Modern Chemistry* by Nicholas Tzimopoulos, copyright © 1990 by Saunders College Publishing, reprinted by permission of the publisher.

10.   *Koran* 24:399–40.

11.   Mark 4:1–8.

12.   Martin Luther King, "Letter from Birmingham Jail," in Robert L. Holmes, *Nonviolence in Theory and Practice* (Belmont, Calif.: Wadsworth, 1990), p. 72. Copyright © 1990, HarperCollins Publishers. Used by permission.

13.   Martin Luther King, "Letter from Birmingham Jail," in Robert L. Holmes, *Nonviolence in Theory and Practice* (Belmont, Calif.: Wadsworth, 1990), p. 72. Copyright © 1990, HarperCollins Publishers. Used by permission.

14. Reprinted by permission of *Harvard Business Review.* "Is Business Like Poker?" An excerpt from "Is Business Bluffing Ethical?" by Albert Carr, (January/February 1968). Copyright © 1968 by the President and Fellows of Harvard College; all rights reserved. Used with permission. Thanks to Jon Dorbolo for calling the article to my attention.

15. *People* v. *Dlugash,* 41 N.Y.2d 725 (1977).

16. *United States* v. *Thomas,* 13 U.S.C.M.A. 278 (1962).

17. 41 N.Y.2d 725.

18. *Houchin* v. *State,* 473 P.2d 925.

19. The pedagogical pattern of this exercise is drawn from "Models for Developing Critical Thinking," by Joanne Kurfiss, Teaching and Learning Center, Santa Clara University.

20. R.H. Thouless, 1932; quoted in Alburey Castell, *A College Logic* (New York: Macmillan, 1935), p. 58.

21. *Schenck* v. *United States,* 249 U.S. 47, 39 S. Ct. 247, 63 L. Ed. 470 (1919) (emphasis added).

22. Paraphrased from information in James Kilpatrick, "Naked issue of nation's Constitution," *Corvallis Gazette-Times* (February 6, 1991), p. A7.

23. Adapted from Chuck Kelley, "Gorbachev courageous, savvy, but he's no Lincoln," *Corvallis Gazette-Times* (February 8, 1991), p. A7.

24. A.J. Ayer, *The Problem of Knowledge* (Baltimore: Penguin, 1966).

25. Dialogue from OUTLAND by Berke Breathed. Copyright © 1990, Washington Post Writers Group. Reprinted with permission.

26. Wiley Hall III, "New book makes persuasive case that experimentation is the same as slavery," *Corvallis Gazette-Times* (March 3, 1989).

27. Mark Twain, *Pudd'nhead Wilson's Calendar,* Chapter 11.

28. This method of instruction is explained and recommended by Joanne Kurfiss, Teaching and Learning Center, Santa Clara University.

29. The format for this moot court simulation is adapted from a similar exercise, "*California* v. *Greenwood* Moot Court Simulation," *Update on Law-related Education* (Fall 1989), pp. 21–24.

30. *Reynolds* v. *United States,* 98 U.S. 145 (1878).

31. "Kentucky Man Killed by Rattler in Rite of Snake-Handling Cult," *The New York Times* (October 30, 1973). Copyright © 1973, by The New York Times Co. Reprinted by permission.

32. From Robert F. Cushman, *Cases in Constitutional Law* (Englewood Cliffs, N.J.: Prentice-Hall, 1975), p. 603.

33. *People* v. *Woody,* 61 Cal. 2d 716; 394 P. 2d 813 (1964).

34. Adapted from James Kilpatrick, "Live and let live on peyote," *Corvallis Gazette-Times* (Nov. 17, 1989), p. A9.

35. Rick Reilly, "Let's Bust Those Chops," *Sports Illustrated* (October 28, 1991), p. 110.

36. KEPB, Eugene, Oregon, November 2, 1991.

37. From ONE LIFE AT A TIME PLEASE by Edward Abbey. Copyright © 1978, 1983, 1984, 1985, 1986, 1988 by Edward Abbey. Reprinted by permission of Henry Holt and Company, Inc.

38. Cecie Starr and Ralph Taggart, *Biology: The Unity and Diversity of Life* (Belmont, Calif.: Wadsworth, 1989), p. 423.

39. Isak Dinesen, *Out of Africa* (1937), Pt. I, Ch. 1.

CHAPTER 6

Reasoning from Experience

"Experience," conventional wisdom says, "is the best teacher." But how much can people learn from direct experience alone? How much would they know if all they knew was what they learned directly from the senses?

People see only those things that are of a certain size, not too big and not too small. They experience only the present, not the future and not the past. They see only surfaces, not inside and under or too far away. They directly experience individual things and events, not things in general and in the abstract. They see only colors and shapes, not causes and consequences. These are the things people learn from experience.

And yet people have knowledge of things larger than the galaxy and smaller than an atom. They know what happened in the past and what will happen in the future. They know what is under their skin and beyond the moon. They know rules and principles and kinds. They know what events will follow other events, and why. How can these be learned from experience?

Direct experience provides the raw material for learning. But a very powerful set of inferences allows the human mind to "make something of it." Because people are able to use what they have seen to draw conclusions about what they can never see, they have knowledge that ranges far beyond the limits of their direct experience. How to draw those conclusions reliably is the subject of this chapter.

6.1 WHAT DID YOU KNOW, AND HOW DID YOU KNOW IT?

Start writing a list of everything you know, a list of statements that you are fairly sure are true. Just start writing, and don't stop for five minutes. Look over the list. Cross out every claim that you did not learn from your own *direct* experience.

What percentage of claims did you have to cross out?

Group the claims you crossed out into categories. For example, you might have a category of statements about the past or a category that includes generalizations. What kinds of claims do you believe are true without their having been corroborated by your experience?

Inductive Reasoning

The patterns of reasoning that allow one to draw conclusions from experience and experiment are called *inductive arguments* or *induction*. These are arguments that "push information together" into conclusions (as opposed to deductive arguments, that "pull information out" of claims). Because the conclusions of inductive arguments contain more information than the premises, inductive arguments provide only *persuasive* support for their conclusions (as opposed to deductive arguments, that provide conclusive support).

Induction is often equated with *scientific reasoning* since inductive patterns of reasoning are the workaday intellectual tools of scientists. When scientists predict the orbit of a satellite or explain the behavior of honeybees or disprove the big bang theory of the origin of the universe, they are using the patterns of inductive reasoning explained in this chapter. Scientists are, after all, only people who learn from experience in an elaborate and ritualized manner.

But if induction is to be called "scientific reasoning" because scientists use it, it may as well be called "infantile reasoning" because babies use it or "athletic" reasoning because athletes use it. When a baby cries when his mother puts on her coat, when a quarterback decides to fall on the ball, when a mechanic turns on the headlights to test the battery, they use inductive patterns of reasoning. Induction is the most common way to draw conclusions.

The terminology used in praise of good inductive arguments is somewhat different from that used in praise of deductive arguments. An inductive argument that is formally correct, that is, constructed in such a way that the evidence provides good grounds for thinking the conclusion is true, is called *strong.* An inductive argument that has true premises and a strong form is called *cogent. Cogent* comes from the Latin word meaning "to drive together." The metaphor is apt; like skilled riders on a cattle drive, a cogent argument gathers up all the information and sends it toward a particular point.

In this chapter, you will learn about three different patterns of inductive reasoning. The first is the *inductive generalization,* in which a conclusion about all the members of a given set is based on information about some of the members of that set. The second is *hypothetical reasoning,* in which the results of experimental tests provide evidence against and for explanations and general rules. The third is the *causal argument,* a specialized form of hypothetical reasoning in which evidence is used in support of causal claims. You are already well acquainted with yet a fourth kind of inductive argument, the argument by analogy of Chapter 5.

The Difficulties of Reasoning
••••••••••••••••••• from Experience •••••••••••••••••••

The deductive arguments described in Chapter 4 are relatively straightforward and risk-free. All the information needed is present in premises assumed to be true; drawing a conclusion is a matter of drawing out or recombining that information. In contrast, inductive arguments offer abundant opportunities to go wrong.

All inductive arguments are based on a deep uncertainty. Consider: When your alarm rang this morning, did you just dump yourself out of bed? Or did you reach out tentatively with one foot, hanging onto the sheets, unsure if you would drop to the floor or lodge against the ceiling? If you did not hesitate, why not?

> "I've never had any problems with floating before," you might respond, "and besides, bodies—mine included—respond to certain rules, like the law of gravity. Unless the law of gravity has changed, I'm not going to float away."

But how do you know that the law of gravity did not change while you slept?

> "Look, it hasn't changed yet," you might respond with growing exasperation, "so I don't expect it to change."

Does the fact that the law of gravity has operated without fail in the past give reason to believe that it will operate without fail in the future? Not necessarily; it is possible—not probable but logically possible—that gravity will change overnight.

This reasoning, like all reasoning from experience, is reasoning from *past* experience. But conclusions tell not only about the past but about the present and future as well. So, any conclusion supported by past experience depends utterly on the assumption that the future will resemble the past. This assumption cannot be proved. It follows that all conclusions based on past experience are only *probably* true. This is the uncertainty that plagues all inductive reasoning, as philosopher of science Bertrand Russell pointed out.[1]

Russell illustrated the perilous nature of inductive reasoning by telling a sad story about a very reasonable chicken. Every morning, a farmer came to the barnyard to throw feed to the chicken. The chicken reasoned from past experience that the farmer's appearance would always signal feeding time. This turned out to be true—until the day the farmer grabbed the chicken, wrung its neck, and made it into soup. The moral of the story is that all inductive reasoning must be done carefully and with a clear sense of the logical risks assumed.

. . . .

6.2 PATTERNS, THE INDUCTION GAME

Patterns is a simple game that mirrors inductive reasoning processes and thereby illustrates the problematic nature of inductive reasoning. The game was invented by Sidney Sackson[2] and reported by Martin Gardner, whose *Scientific American* column is a rich source of scientific reasoning adventures.

1. Three to six people can play. Each player needs a pencil and a sheet of paper. On the paper, each player draws a six-by-six-square grid. One player is the Designer.

2. The Designer secretly fills in each of the squares in his grid with one of four symbols (a star, a plus sign, a circle, or a triangle). The arrangement may exhibit a strong pattern or no pattern at all; any or all of the symbols may be used. However, the scoring of the game is such that the Designer benefits from a pattern that is easily recognized by one player but not recognized by another.

3. The goal of the other players is to determine the pattern of symbols on the Designer's grid. A player may gain information by putting a

check in the corner of any squares on his own grid and passing the grid to the Designer. Without revealing the answers to the other players, the Designer fills in the checked squares with the correct symbol and returns the grid to its owner. Players can ask for as much information as they want, whenever they want. However, the key to winning this game is to make the most of the least information.

4. When a player believes she knows the pattern, she fills in all the squares. When all players have collected all the information they wanted and have made their guesses, the Designer reveals his grid and the pattern he designed. Players check their guesses against the Designer's pattern.

5. A player's score is the number of squares that the player (but not the Designer) correctly filled in, minus the number of squares incorrectly filled in. The Designer's score is twice the difference between the highest player's score and the lowest player's score.

As you play this game, you will find yourself using inductive reasoning. Play several times, and then discuss and prepare answers to these questions: Did you have any strategy in mind when you selected squares to ask about? How did you know when you had enough information to quit asking questions and start making guesses? What made a pattern easy to discern? What made a pattern difficult to discern? If you made any mistakes, why? Explain in detail how this game is analogous to the "game" scientists "play" when they try to figure out the patterns of the universe.

• •

• • • • • • • • • • • • • Inductive Generalization • • • • • • • • • • • • •

Inductive generalization is a pattern of reasoning that uses observations about some of the members of a given set (class or category) to support a conclusion about all the members of that set. Here are two examples of inductive generalization:

A gardener noticed that her sunflowers turn their faces to the sun. She noticed that the branches of her ivy reach toward the sunlight coming through the window of her office. Although she directly observed only one patch of sunflowers and one houseplant, she believed that she had discovered something about plants in general: Plants grow toward the sun.

A shopkeeper was annoyed when a boy with a torn T-shirt and shaved head swiped a six-pack of Pepsi. The next day, a different boy, also with torn T-shirt and shaved head, stole a magazine. The shopkeeper drew a conclusion about boys with torn T-shirts and shaved heads: You have to watch them like a hawk because they are likely to rip you off.

Generalizations

The conclusion of an inductive generalization is a *universal generalization*, a statement that describes all the members of a given class or set: "All the clocks in the house stopped at midnight." Universal generalizations can be *affirmative*, telling what characteristics the members of the set have: "All the clock faces had been smashed with a blunt instrument." Or universal generalizations can be *negative*, telling what characteristics the members of the set do not have: "None of the residents remembered hearing any unusual noises."

Probably the most familiar generalizations are generalizations about people. In *I Know Why the Caged Bird Sings*, Maya Angelou described the generalizations she made as a child in Stamps, Arkansas:

> *I remember never believing that whites were really real. . . . Whitefolks couldn't be people because their feet were too small, their skin too white and see-throughy, and they didn't walk on the balls of their feet the way people did—they walked on their heels like horses. People were those who lived on my side of town. . . . These others, the strange pale creatures that lived in their alien unlife, weren't considered folks. They were whitefolks.[3]*

Science is awash in generalizations. In fact, a scientist's goal in life is to generate true generalizations. Almost every sentence in a science textbook is a generalization:

> *In the human brain, as in the brains of other vertebrates, the cerebral hemispheres are the most complex constellations of neurons. Inside each hemisphere is a core of white matter . . . The surface layer, the cerebral cortex, is gray matter about three millimeters thick.[4]*

These statements do not refer to the brains measured and then stored in jars on a shelf somewhere. The statements describe the nature of all brains—your brain, your grandmother's, and your unborn child's—even though no scientist has seen those brains and, one hopes, never will.

Causal explanations are a particular kind of generalization, *causal generalizations*.

> *The "magic mushroom" of Mexico,* Psilocybe mexicana, . . . *produce[s] hallucinations or psychoses.*[5]

Causal generalizations make a general statement about the causal connection between two events.

The Logical Pattern of the Inductive Generalization

The form of the inductive generalization is simplicity itself:

> One (or some or many) A's are B's.
> ———————————————————————
> Therefore, all A's are probably B's.

The *probably* in the conclusion acknowledges that although the observed cases provide some evidence for the conclusion, the evidence is by no means perfect.

In any example of inductive generalization, the class or set to which the generalization refers is called the *population*. In the formula above, "All A's" make up the population; the shopkeeper generalized about the population of "all boys with torn T-shirts and shaved heads," the gardener about "all plants." The observed cases, the examples actually experienced, compose the *sample*. In the formula above, "One (or some or many) A's" make up the sample; the shopkeeper's sample was two boys, and the gardener's sample was a dozen sunflowers and an ivy plant.

The Reliability of Inductive Generalization

Making inductive generalizations involves a kind of risk-benefit analysis. The benefits are great. Information about *particular events* is simply not very useful. What good does it do to know that one person stole a magazine or that one ivy plant grew toward the sun in January? General information — information about what sorts of people are likely to be shoplifters or about how plants grow — this is information you can do something with.

Unfortunately, the risks are also great. General information is not directly observable; even if one were willing to devote the time to it, one could not observe every case, past, present, and future. So, general information must be put together from whatever particular information one has or can obtain. Some generalizations are very strong: If pure water at sea level boils at 100 degrees centigrade today, it is likely that it always will. Other generalizations are terrible; even if water drawn from this stream is pure, water drawn from the next stream may be pestilential.

So, while inductive generalization has a high payoff, it is risky. Since one cannot avoid generalizing, at least one must avoid generalizing carelessly. Here are three principles about the reliability of generalizations:

1. *The more observations, the more reliable the generalization.* It is generally true that the more observations supporting a generalization, the more reliable the generalization. Suppose the chief inspector for a candy bar company needs to determine whether all the candy bars boxed for shipment contain sufficiently few insect body parts to meet federal standards. She pulls one candy bar from one box, tests it, and finds that it meets the standards. An inductive generalization from this single observation to a conclusion about all the candy bars would be exceedingly untrustworthy. A generalization based on observations of two candy bars would be minimally stronger and so forth.

2. *The more variety among the observations, the stronger the generalization.* The wider the variety of situations in which the generalization is confirmed, the more confident you can be of that generalization. If the chief inspector pulled ten candy bars out of the same box and found them insect-free, she would have some evidence for a generalization about all the candy in the shipment. But that box of candy might have been made under unusual conditions, maybe immediately after the exterminator sprayed the factory or while the CEO was leading the board of directors on a tour of the factory. The chief inspector's conclusion would rest on a firmer foundation if the foundation were wider—if, of the ten candy bars sampled, one was made in September and another in October; one was made by the night shift and one during the day; one was a Baby Ruth and one a Heath Bar. The reliability of the generalization increases with an increase in the variety of situations in which it has held true.

3. *The less variation within the population, the stronger the generalization.* It is generally true that the less variation there is among the population generalized about, the stronger the generalization is likely to be. The reason that one can confidently generalize about the boiling point of water is that pure water is pure water; there is little variation from one cupful to another. Streams, on the other hand, may flow through alpine meadows or feedlots. So, what is true about one is not really very likely to be true of another. The candy inspector could draw more reliable generalizations on the basis of fewer observations if all candy bars were pretty much the same when it comes to insect body parts.

Each of these principles is based on a single, commonsense characteristic of inductive generalizations:

> The most reliable generalizations are those in which the portion of the population sampled—the observed cases—is most truly representative of the population as a whole.

Increasing the number and variety of observations increases the reliability of the sample by reducing the chances of accidentally sampling an atypical subset of the population; if there are exceptions, you are more likely to find them. Having less variation in the population is also likely to increase the reliability of the sample since any member is more likely to share the characteristics of the others.

Generally, there are two ways to achieve a representative sample. In relatively homogeneous populations or in populations that vary in unpredictable ways, the sample should be *random*. A sample is random when every member of the population has an equal chance of being selected. In populations that vary in predictable ways, the most representative sample may be a *stratified sample*. A stratified sample is one in which the population is subdivided into categories, and then samples are randomly chosen from each category in numbers proportional to their numbers in the population as a whole.

. . . .

6.3 ANALYZING INDUCTIVE GENERALIZATIONS

For each of the following inductive generalizations, underline the conclusion. Tell whether the conclusion is a negative or an affirmative universal generalization. Identify the population, and identify the sample. Then, tell whether each additional piece of information would strengthen, weaken, or have no effect on the inference. Explain why.

1. . . . *[T]here are signs that [Christian] theologians are beginning to think more seriously about the idea of hell than they have in decades. A Roman Catholic bishop in New York startled church members who had not heard much of hell recently when he warned pro-abortion-rights Catholic politicians a few months ago that they were in serious danger of going there.*
    a. Martin Marty, a professor at the University of Chicago Divinity School, observed that "hell has disappeared and no one noticed."
    b. "A recent Gallup Poll showed more Americans believe in hell today than did in the . . . 1950s."
    c. "In Islam, . . . [believers fear] a 'lake of fire,' a burning 'bed of misery' where the wicked and the infidel suffer endlessly, . . . with only 'boiling, fetid water' to drink."[6]

2. Salaries for professional baseball players are climbing to ridiculous levels. Robin Yount of Milwaukee makes more than $3 million.[7]
   a. Two hundred and twenty-three players are making more than $1 million, according to an Associated Press survey.
   b. The salaries for Houston athletes have actually decreased during the last season.
   c. Robin Yount is an exceptionally talented and sought-after athlete.

3. *That beavers react aggressively to the presence of a trespasser's scent mound was demonstrated in another experiment. D. Muller-Schwarze and fellow researchers introduced alien mounds into the territories of two beaver colonies. . . . As soon as the resident animals got a whiff of the foreign odors, they began hissing. . . . One of them summoned up courage to mount the bank and cancel out the unwanted scents with a blast of his or her own excretions.*[8]
   a. The beavers in the experiment were captives at a zoo.
   b. Muskrats also react aggressively to the presence of a trespasser's scent.
   c. The early trappers in Canada reported similar beaver behaviors.

4. *The poor know that government officials and rich white men "loot" the public treasuries in a thousand different ways. They have heard about the savings-and-loan scandals, the Housing and Urban Development deals that make white men rich. They know about Jim Baker and John Sununu's fancy trips at government expense. They are not unaware of the check-bouncing scandals by members of the U.S. House.*[9]
   a. When a Polish jetliner crashed near Warsaw in 1987, many Poles stole rings and cash from the crash victims.
   b. In the 1992 Los Angeles riots, looters were blacks, whites, Hispanics, and Asians.
   c. Each of the last five U.S. Presidents has left the White House a millionaire.
   d. By flying on military jets, Secretary of State James Baker cost U.S. taxpayers $371,599 for eleven flights.
   e. The Chief Justice of the Supreme Court gets a Cadillac limousine and a driver; other Justices ride free in Lincoln Town Cars—all at taxpayer expense.

5. Public universities across the nation are facing unprecedented budget problems as states cut funds and the costs of educational programs rise. The Oregon State System of Higher Education cut ten percent last year and faces losses of state revenue of up to 20 percent next year. California state colleges and universities are trimming their

budgets, as are New York and North Carolina. Reduced budgets and rising costs are a nationwide problem for higher education.

a. Oregon's economy was particularly hard hit by the recession because reductions in building starts reduced the demand for timber, one of Oregon's primary industries.

b. Apparently, the State of Colorado has not cut its higher education budgets.

c. Huge private endowments shelter many private schools from budget problems caused by the economic ups and downs of the states in which they are located.

• •

6.4 STUDYING CAMPUS

Divide into groups of approximately five students. Designate one of the five to be recorder. Your group's assignment is to answer, *as accurately as possible,* one of the following questions. You must collect all the data yourselves (no fair calling the registrar to find out the answer). Since you have only this class period to complete this assignment, you will have to plan carefully to maximize the results of your efforts. Feel free to leave the classroom to collect data, but be sure to return in time to compile the data and help the recorder complete the record. The questions:

In order of popularity, state the make and model of the three cars most often driven by American college professors.

What is the ratio of evergreen to broad-leaved trees on campus?

What percentage of the college students in America wear beards?

What is the most popular brand of bicycle on campus?

What percentage of students on campus know the name of the vice president or provost of the university?

What percentage of students on campus will answer in a friendly manner when a passing stranger greets them with a smile and says, hello?

The recorder's job is to keep an ongoing account of the group's reasoning process by consulting with the group and answering the following questions.

Before the group leaves to collect data:

1. What question will your group answer?
2. For your study, what is the population?

3. For your study, what is the sample?

4. How will the sample be selected? How large is your sample in relation to the size of the population? How will you assure that the sample is representative of the population?

After the group returns with its data:

5. What did you learn about the sample?

6. What conclusion do you draw about the population?

7. If you had to bet on your conclusion, how much would you bet? What makes you confident of your conclusion? What makes you worried about your conclusion?

8. Find another group that answered the same question as your group. Did they reach the same conclusion? If so, does this fact strengthen your own conclusion? Why? If not, which conclusion is more trustworthy? Why?

● ●

The Fallacies of Inductive Generalization

Mark Twain, ever an astute observer of humanity, had the greatest faith that humans would abuse the inductive generalization:

> . . . [T]he world will not stop and think — it never does, it is not its way; its way is to generalize from a single sample. . . . It has no reflection, no logic, no sense of proportion. With it, figures go for nothing; to it, figures reveal nothing, it cannot reason upon them rationally; it would say, for instance, that China is being swiftly and surely Christianized, since nine Chinese Christians are being made every day; and it would fail . . . to notice that the fact that 33,000 pagans are born there every day, damages the argument. It would say, "There are a hundred lynchers [in Missouri], therefore the Missourians are lynchers"; the considerable fact that there are two and a half million Missourians who are not lynchers would not affect their verdict.[10]

So predictable are the logical errors that arise in inductive generalization that the reasoning pattern has its own set of fallacies. Here are three of the most common.

Hasty Generalization

A *hasty generalization* is a generalization based on a sample that is too small. When a sample is very small—when a generalization is based on very few examples—the chances are astronomical of having accidentally made observations about members that are not typical of the population as a whole. For example, a little girl was asked what philosophy was. Her quick reply: "Oh, it's just something women do." How many philosophers did she know? Exactly one, her mother. As a matter of fact, only 14 percent of all American philosophers are women, a generalization that is reliable only because a large number of philosophers were sampled.

Biased Sample

It is not enough to have a large sample size. The sample must truly reflect the characteristics of the population. The fallacy of *biased sample* occurs when the sampling technique is not random, when it systematically excludes a subset of the population. All these generalizations are based on biased samples:

> "Americans must be very wealthy," said the Parisian as she watched American tourists shopping along the Champs Elysées.

> "No handicapped people are unhappy about a lack of accessibility on this campus," said the university president in his office at the top of five flights of stairs.

> "Minorities do not need special admissions programs to get into law school," concluded the law student after talking with minority members of the entering class.

Stereotyping

Originally, a stereotype was a printing plate made by casting a mold in metal. To produce many identical copies of one printed page, a stereotype was a most useful invention. *Stereotype* has come to mean a conventional, standardized image of something or someone, a universal generalization: the Blonde, the Capitalist, the Urban Black Youth, the Migrant Worker, the Preppie, the Jew. It is easier to adapt one's perceptions of people to fit a stereotype than to adapt a stereotype to fit people one meets. A stereotype, after all, is cast in metal. Since people are definitely not cast from the same mold, stereotyped descriptions of people are almost always misleading.

· ·

6.5 STEREOTYPING[11]

Think of a stereotype through which other people may have viewed you. Write it at the top of a piece of paper. On one side of that paper, list the characteristics about you that others might perceive through the lens of that stereotype (these perceptions could be either accurate or inaccurate). On the other side of that page, list characteristics about you that others might fail to perceive through the lens of that stereotype.

· ·

6.6 EXPERIENCING A NEW CULTURE[12]

Divide into two groups of different sizes. One group is approximately 20 percent of the class; these are the "Outsiders," who will try to learn as much as they can about a new culture. The other group, the remaining 80 percent, are the "Insiders," the designers and members of the new culture.

Directions for Outsiders. You will be asked to leave the room for approximately five minutes. During this time, the Insiders will design a new culture. When you return, your job will be to find out as much as you can about the new culture. You may do this by asking yes and no questions of the Insiders.

Directions for Insiders. The directions for the Insiders are in the endnotes[13] for this chapter. Insiders should read them and follow them very, very carefully.

The Outsiders leave the room for five minutes. When they return, they have approximately ten minutes to learn as much as they can about the new culture by circulating among the students and asking questions of individual Insiders. After ten minutes of questioning, discuss the experience as a class.

Questions for discussion:

1. Outsiders, describe what you have learned about the new culture. (Don't worry if your reports conflict with each other.)

2. Outsiders, how did it feel to interact with the new culture?

3. Insiders, explain to the Outsiders the rules you followed.

4. Insiders, describe your feelings as you answered the Outsiders' questions.

5. Is there any connection between this exercise and what goes on in universities?

6. Can you generalize about the kinds of difficulties people of different cultures face when they try to understand one another?

· ·

•••••••••••• Hypothetical Reasoning ••••••••••••

Human beings seek not just an awareness of events that occur but also an understanding of those events. Understanding comes with the achievement of satisfactory explanations for why events occur as they do. In other words, humans seek to put observations in the context of general principles or patterns that govern the order and operation of the world. For this, they use *hypothetical reasoning*. Hypothetical reasoning is a strategy for testing explanations by determining whether their logical consequences are consistent with experimental observations.

••

6.7 THE BLACK BOX EXPERIMENT[14]

A scientist trying to understand a system, such as hormonal control of growth, the dynamics of a double star, or canine perception of color, sometimes thinks of the system as a "black box." The reason is that, in the case of both black boxes and systems under investigation, you can see what goes in and you can see what comes out, but you can only make educated guesses about what goes on inside.

In this exercise, you make a black box and see if a classmate can figure out its system.

At home. To make a black box, you will need a shoebox and four 2-foot lengths of string. Punch four holes in the box, and label them A, B, C, and D. Push the ends of the strings through the holes in the box, leaving an equal length of each string showing. Knot the outside ends of the strings so that they cannot be pulled through the box. Tie the ends of string *inside* the box in any arrangement you choose. The diagrams show two possible arrangements. Close up the box, tape it shut, and bring it to class.

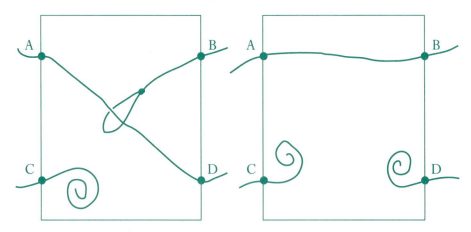

In class. Exchange boxes with another student. Your job now is to determine the arrangement of strings inside your partner's box. You may not open the box. You may not shake it. All you may do is pull on the strings that stick out of the box. Pulling the exposed end of a string will give you indirect information about how the strings are arranged inside the box. You are allowed only four pulls, or experiments, so, think through your moves very carefully.

These questions will guide your research:

1. How much can you learn from direct observation? That is, does looking at the box give you any clues as to the arrangement inside?

2. Perform an experiment like this: What is one possible arrangement of the strings? Just take a guess. If the strings are arranged that way, what will happen when you pull on a string? Go ahead and do that. Did the other strings move the way you thought they would? What does that tell you about your guess? Using the same procedure, experimentally test three other guesses.

3. When your experiments are completed, draw your best guess as to the arrangement of the strings:

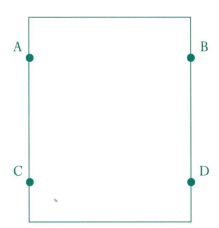

4. Open the box. Were you right? If so, were you lucky or were you smart? If you were wrong, generalize about the source of your error; that is, what was it about the evidence that misled you?

5. Try to reconstruct the logic behind each experiment by filling in the blanks of this form. Since you performed four experiments, you will end up with four arguments.

> If (hypothesis) , then (prediction) .
> The prediction was (true/false) .
> Therefore, the hypothesis is probably (true/false) .

6. In what ways is this exercise analogous to the job scientists do? In what ways is it different? Why do you think the exercise limited you to four experiments?

Exercise adapted from Kathleen Dean Moore, *A Field Guide to Inductive Arguments.* Copyright © 1986, Kendall/Hunt Publishing Company. Adapted with permission.

The Steps of Hypothetical Reasoning

Hypothetical reasoning can be understood as a sequence of the following steps:

1. Collecting observations
2. Formulating a question
3. Generating alternative hypotheses
4. Testing alternative hypotheses
5. Drawing tentative conclusions

The story of the search by nineteenth-century doctors for the cause of the disease pellagra illustrates the reasoning sequence. The story is told by Martin and Inge Goldstein, philosophers of science.[15]

The Goldsteins explain that nineteeth-century doctors noticed a set of symptoms that afflicted some of their patients: first, a red, rough rash on the skin and tongue, then diarrhea, swelling of the stomach, depression, mental dullness, and a peculiar sucking reaction. Finally, death. Recognizing a similarity among all the cases, they generalized that all the patients were suffering from the same syndrome. They labeled it "pellagra."

The cause of pellagra was unknown, although certain observations were suggestive. The disease had long been common in America. It came to Europe at about the same time as corn became a staple in European diets. The disease afflicted the poor almost exclusively. Doctors and nurses who treated the sick never became ill with pellagra. But once one member of a family contracted pellagra, the other members of the family often sickened too. Not everyone who ate corn became ill; but the disease rarely afflicted those who did not eat corn.

A variety of explanations was offered: Maybe it was a disease caused by a toxin in corn. Maybe it was an infectious disease, spread by close and continuous contact. Maybe it was a disease carried by the rodents that hide in corncribs or by corn-boring insects.

Some of the explanations offered were quickly rejected, the Goldsteins point out, because they were inconsistent with observations at hand. If pellagra were caused by a toxin in corn, then the more corn people ate, the sicker they would become, rich or poor. But this was clearly not what was happening. If pellagra were caused by infection, then the doctors and nurses attending patients would fall victim to the disease more often than the patients' field hands or children. But this was not the disease's pattern. The only explanation that was consistent with all that had been observed was an explanation that focused on nutrition; maybe pellagra was caused by a nutritional deficiency brought about by eating corn, which lacks certain vitamins, rather than by eating a varied diet of more nutritious food.

In 1915, the Goldsteins say, Joseph Goldberger suggested that the disease was brought on by deficiencies in B-complex vitamins, which are lacking in corn. He predicted that the disease could be cured by supplementing a patient's diet with ample quantities of the vitamin missing from corn. In clinical trials, the prediction proved true. Now pellagra is rarely seen except in the poorest parts of the world.

The Logical Pattern of Hypothetical Reasoning

Step by step over a century, the medical researchers seeking the cause of pellagra moved through the logical sequence of hypothetical reasoning.

Collecting Observations

Every piece of hypothetical reasoning begins with observations. The observations have a dual role. They raise a question to be investigated, and they provide the parameters that determine the directions the search for an explanation will take. When doctors observed patient after patient with the appalling symptoms of pellagra, they knew they had a problem to solve: What causes this disease, and how can it be controlled? At the same time, they knew that any explanation would have to be consistent with what they had already learned by observing their patients.

While observations direct the search for an explanation, the search for an explanation itself determines what observations are made. Even in the initial stages of hypothetical reasoning, one's educated guesses guide the initial search for information. The doctors did not ask what powerful practitioners of occult arts the patients had recently offended. They did not ask what mortal sins the patients had recently committed. They did not record the color of the bedspreads in the sickrooms. They made note instead of who got the disease, and where, and when—a search for initial information already delimited by their general understanding of the causes of disease.

Formulating a Question

Hypothetical reasoning seeks to "make sense" of observations, by explaining them in terms of general rules or principles that govern the universe. The entire endeavor presupposes some such underlying order and sets out to understand just what it is. The next step in hypothetical reasoning is to formulate this search as a particular question.

The search for the causes of pellagra presupposed that all events have causes and that diseases have natural causes. The question is, what is that cause?

Generating Alternative Hypotheses

The next step is to put forward a variety of explanations that are consistent with observations already made. These tentative explanations are called *hypotheses*. A hypothesis is a general principle or explanation tentatively assumed in order to test its truth against facts that may be observed. The doctors' educated guesses about the causes of pellagra were alternative hypotheses: Maybe corn is poisonous. Maybe the animals associated with corn carry a disease-causing agent. Maybe corn is nutritionally deficient.

Generating alternative hypotheses is *the* central creative tool of scientists and probably the key to the extraordinary effectiveness of hypothetical reasoning. If scientists were to put forward a single explanation—a favorite—and then sought evidence to show that it was true, they would, with enough searching, come up with that evidence. Soon they would become conspirators in their own deception. But if a scientist puts forward several possibilities, she can seek evidence for and against all of them, and the results are less likely to be distorted by the protectiveness of an intellectual parent.

Hypotheses must meet certain conditions before they qualify as scientific hypotheses. Primary among these is the condition of *defeasibility*. This means that it must be logically possible to provide evidence against the hypothesis. There must be some conceivable observation that, if it were true, would count against the hypothesis. The hypothesis "Ice is frozen water" is defeasible, even though it is true, because it is possible to imagine evidence that would count against it. For example, if a block of ice in your kitchen melted into a puddle of beer (at least a logical possibility), that would raise doubts about the composition of ice.

A hypothesis like this one is not defeasible, and thus not scientific: "God created the earth in 4004 B.C., complete with a fossil record of a past that never existed." What observation could possibly count against this? Paleontologists date fossil plants at a million years old, but that doesn't damage the hypothesis because God could have made those fossils when He made everything else. Geological strata in the Grand Canyon show that the canyon was formed long before 4004 B.C., but that is not inconsistent with the hypothesis because God might have made the Grand Canyon to look just that way. A hypothesis that protects itself against any possibility of refutation may or may not be true, but it is not scientific.

• •

6.8 UNEXPLAINED PHENOMENA

Each of the following "factual" descriptions can be explained in many different ways. One explanation—often an extraordinary one—is provided in each case. For each case, write down the explanation given, and then make up and list three alternative explanations.

1. *Henry Gris [of the* National Enquirer*] has scored another exclusive scoop: "Russians Float in Midair—Lifted Only by Hypnosis." Gris claims to have witnessed floating cosmonauts in a secret research lab somewhere near Moscow. "I'm absolutely convinced it was real," says Gris. A Soviet scientist reportedly explained that "as they are put under hypnosis, their nervous system is ordered to become insensitive to the actual physical weight of their bodies."[16]*

2. *Another tabloid, the* Weekly World News, *reports: MYSTERY OF THE TALKING WALL: Experts record voices from 700 years ago. It seems that the bricks of an ancient tavern in Wales have allegedly stored the sound of thirteenth-century merrymaking. After the owner of the pub reported hearing voices and organ music, two engineers investigated the phenomenon and reportedly succeeded in making tapes of the eerie sounds. A journalist who heard the*

tapes said that he could make out voices and music, adding, "It certainly isn't a hoax. I heard the voices of men laughing and talking. It was clear enough, but not a language I could understand. It must have been in some ancient Welsh dialect." One of the researchers theorized that "the walls contain a mixture of silica and ferric salts just like those on recording tape. There is no reason why it shouldn't be able to record sound."[17]

3. *Outside Fostoria, Ohio, hundreds of people have been assembling by the roadside to see an image of Christ on the side of a soybean-oil storage tank. They claim to see the life-sized image of a long-haired, bearded man, with the profile of a child alongside. The company that owns the tank says they are seeing just shadows, lights, and steam vapors from the soybean processing plant.*[18]

4. *[Backward masking is a process by which secret messages are recorded backward over other sounds.] Apparently Satanists are not the only ones with sneaky messages that can be heard by playing their recordings backward. According to an aide for Rhode Island Senator Claiborne Pell, backward masking of a secret code word was detected in speeches . . . given by President Bush [and others]. . . . When the three officials' statements about Iraq were played backwards, they appeared to contain the code word "Simone."*[19]

5. *Farther south, in Orange County, . . . another famous prognosticator, Oscar the Fish, is said to have registered the effects of the big quake by swimming on his side. Oscar, a tropical fish with only one good eye, who used to live in the biology lab in the Corona del Mar High School is said to have predicted 15 to 20 quakes in three years by swimming sideways, the Associated Press reported. Indeed, Oscar may even have given advance warning of the big quake up north, but no one was present to heed. Oscar had been sequestered in protective custody because of death threats.*[20]

Testing Alternative Hypotheses

Given a set of alternative hypotheses, the next step is to learn which hypotheses are false. Some hypotheses can be *directly* tested against experience; you can learn if they are true by going out and looking. But most (and the most interesting) hypotheses cannot be confirmed or disconfirmed by direct experience. Scientists could stare at corn and sucking, diarrhea-stricken people for the duration of their lives and never learn whether pellagra is caused by a toxin in corn.

However, most hypotheses can be tested *indirectly* by determining whether their logical consequences are consistent with experimental observations. This is a two-step experimental process. First, from the hypothesis, deduce an observable consequence. The observable consequence is the prediction that a fact deduced from the hypothesis will, upon investigation, turn out to be true. Nineteenth-century doctors reasoned that if pellagra were caused by a toxin in corn, it would follow as a logical consequence that "the more corn people ate, the sicker they would become." That is a prediction that can be tested. Again, the hypothesis that pellagra was an infectious disease implied a different testable prediction: Those who tend the sick will get sick themselves.

Second, determine whether that prediction is in fact true. A hypothesis that makes a false prediction must be false. The truth or falsehood of a given prediction can often be determined by library research into the reported results of other scientists' experiments. When this is not possible, scientists do experiments themselves to test their predictions. *Experiments* are systematic attempts to test whether predictions derived from a hypothesis are correct. Although medical researchers cannot directly observe whether corn causes pellagra, they can directly observe whether a person who eats more corn gets sicker than one who eats less.

A legendary example of this reasoning process is Galileo's experimental test of Aristotle's theory of motion. Aristotle believed that bodies of different weights fall at different speeds. As the legend has it, Galileo climbed to the top of the leaning tower of Pisa and simultaneously dropped two balls of different weights. If Aristotle were correct, Galileo reasoned, then the balls would hit the streets of Pisa at different times. The prediction turned out to be false: The balls hit the ground simultaneously.

Unfortunately for this example, the story is probably apocryphal: Galileo probably never actually dropped anything off the tower of Pisa. It serves nevertheless as an example of a hypothesis that had to be abandoned because what one would expect to be true, given that hypothesis, was shown experimentally to be false.

In this decade, global warming, the hypothesis that increased carbon dioxide in the atmosphere will cause irreversible heating of the earth, is turning out to be a very difficult hypothesis to test. This is because it is so difficult to predict what will actually be the result of the carbon dioxide buildup: Will the warmth be evenly distributed around the globe? Will there be wide variation in temperatures from year to year? Will nighttime temperatures rise? Should sea levels be expected to rise, or will more water be trapped in glaciers when the earth warms? The only thing known for certain is that scientists are generating quantities of hot air, as they debate how to come up with a prediction that will test whether global warming is actually occurring.

Drawing Tentative Conclusions

Disconfirming Hypotheses

With experimental results in hand, researchers are in a position to draw a tentative conclusion. If the results of the experiment are inconsistent with the prediction—that is, if what you expected, given the hypothesis, was not what you found—the hypothesis that gave rise to that expectation is probably false. The hypothesis falls because it is inconsistent with what was learned from experimental observation. Darwin put it this way:

> I have steadily endeavoured to keep my mind free so as to give up any hypothesis, however much beloved (and I cannot resist forming one on every subject), as soon as facts are shown to be opposed to it. Indeed, I have had no choice but to act in this manner . . .[21]

In its form, the reasoning process by which hypotheses are disconfirmed is the same as the conditional syllogism called denying the consequent:

If A, then B.
Not B.
Therefore, not A.

If the hypothesis is true, then this prediction is likely to be true.
The prediction is not true.
Therefore, the hypothesis is probably not true.

This is a valid deductive argument and is therefore highly trustworthy, but not entirely so. There are always worries about whether the premises are true, whether the prediction would always be true when the hypothesis is true.

Confirming Hypotheses

If the results of the experiment are as predicted, researchers need to proceed with great caution. There is always more than one explanation that is consistent with any given set of experimental observations; so, the observations alone do not provide conclusive evidence that one of those explanations is true and the others false. A true prediction calls for further experimentation to determine whether the hypothesis is consistent with a wide variety of predictions.

In this regard, scientists must be as careful as Prince Charming, searching, glass slipper in hand, for his beloved Cinderella. If the glass slipper does not fit a villager, she is definitely not Cinderella. But if the slipper does fit, the villager may be Cinderella or she may not be, because the slipper will presumably fit more than one person.

In form, the argument one is tempted to make when a prediction turns out to be true is an invalid deductive argument, affirming the consequent.

If A, then B.
B is true.
_____
Therefore, . . . what?

If the hypothesis is true, then the prediction is true.
The prediction is true.
_____
Therefore, . . . what?

The only conclusion you can draw with any assurance is that you have not yet disconfirmed the hypothesis. It is still a live possibility.

Medical researchers found that increased ingestion of corn did not result in a correlative increase in symptoms. Thus, they were reasonably sure that corn did not contain a toxin that was causing pellagra. Had they found that symptoms increased as ingestion of corn increased, this would have provided some evidence that corn is toxic. But the results would have been equally consistent with other explanations; maybe rat feces in the corn caused the problem, or maybe corn silk caused it. So, they would have had to conduct further experiments. Each confirmed prediction, in the absence of disconfirming instances, would have increased the plausibility of the hypothesis.

• •

6.9 COLONEL MUSTARD IN THE LIBRARY WITH THE ROPE

Scientists are not the only people to use hypothetical reasoning. It is useful also to detectives who have to decide who commited the murder, in what room, and with what weapon. The board game Clue™ — is invariably won by the person who is best at hypothetical reasoning — and who is lucky.

The object of this exercise is to make close observations about the thought processes used by people trying to solve a mystery (and win at Clue). Your class will need one Clue game for every four students.

Divide into groups of four. Play the game once. When you have determined a winner, interview the winner to learn how the winning player thinks while playing the game. Just to get you started, you might ask such questions as these: How do you know what to guess at the beginning of the game? How do you know what to guess toward the end of the game? How do you learn what is false? How do you learn what is true? What are the sources of your information?

As a group, write a step-by-step "Guide to Effective Thinking for Clue Games." Read over the preceding section, "The Steps of Hypothetical Reasoning." How does your list differ from, and resemble, the list in that section?

• •

The reasoning steps of the hypothetical method look something like the diagram shown here[22] (diagram adapted from Kathleen Dean Moore, *A Field Guide to Inductive Arguments.* Copyright © 1989, Kendall/Hunt Publishing Company. Used with permission.).

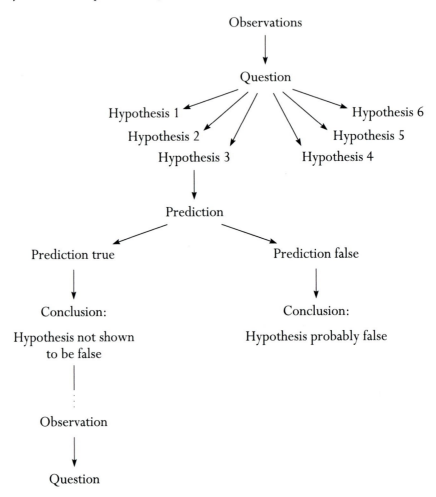

Note that the reasoning process is a continuing one since each tentative conclusion drawn becomes an observation that raises further questions in a process that becomes more sophisticated and focused as the researcher's understanding increases.

Note also that hypothetical reasoning involves a process of elimination as the researcher seeks to eliminate each alternative hypothesis in an ever-narrowing search for the truth.

. . . .

6.10 MYSTERIOUS EXPLOSION AT TUNGUSKA

Natural History magazine reported research about the origin of a brilliant fireball that destroyed a Siberian forest in 1908.

Read the following account of that research and study its logic:

a. State each of the hypotheses suggested to explain the explosion.

b. For each hypothesis, state the prediction that follows from it.

c. State whether the prediction was true or false.

d. Then, using statements a through c, write a standard-form argument for or against each hypothesis.

WHAT STRUCK TUNGUSKA?

Three-quarters of a century after a massive object from interplanetary space exploded over the Tunguska region in central Siberia, astronomers are still debating what it was. . . .

The forest was leveled for hundreds of square miles along the trace of the incoming projectile. Reindeer were killed, but no human fatalities were recorded. Many persons felt the tremors from the explosion. Possessions were hurled to the floor in some homes, and at least one farmer was said to have been knocked unconscious from his porch, about thirty-seven miles from ground zero. All around this point, trees were leveled, their trunks falling in a radial pattern. At ground zero itself, some trees remained standing but were shorn of their limbs. . . .

Soon after the event, a Siberian newspaper reported that the explosion was due to the fall of a meteorite near a railway junction, where a train crew and passengers allegedly saw a red-hot fallen meteorite from a safe distance. . . . In fact, the Siberian newspaper account was blatantly false, since freshly fallen meteorites are not red-hot but rather cold to the touch and sometimes covered with frost. . . .

Early Soviet accounts of the Tunguska event assumed that the incoming object actually struck the earth. This is unlikely in view of the failure of several expeditions to find evidence of a crater and the lack of reliable eyewitness reports that the fireball continued beyond the point of explosion. . . .

If the Tunguska object was a comet, as previously suggested by several astronomers, it would have entered the earth's atmosphere at a speed of about nineteen miles per second. At this tremendous velocity, the air would seem to pile up in front of the falling object and exert a tremendous aerodynamic pressure . . . [that] would have exceeded the compressive strength of iron, let alone of cometary ice. Thus, if it was a comet, the Tunguska object should have exploded or broken up much sooner than it did. . . .

If the Tunguska object was a very large stone meteoroid (or small stone asteroid) . . . its compressive strength would have been large enough to withstand the pressure of atmospheric entry until it reached just about the altitude where it exploded. . . .

A core from the icecap shows that precipitation in the Antarctic during 1908 contains four times more iridium than earlier years (found in lower layers of the ice core). During 1909 and the next few years, the ice was similarly enriched in iridium. Then the iridium content dropped back to its original level. This is strong evidence that particles from the shattered Tunguska object . . . were born around the world by atmospheric currents.[23]

Causal Reasoning

When the hypothesis to be tested is a causal generalization, special care must be taken since causes are notoriously easy to get wrong. Consider this:

The citizens of a small town in the pickle-producing region of Ohio were upset. Every summer, when the town filled up with migrant workers who came to pick the cucumbers, the rape statistics increased. Residents were blaming the migrant workers. "Be careful," an unusually clear-thinking (and courageous) resident[24] said. "The only evidence you have that these two events are causally related is that they occur at the same time. But there may be other explanations for the coincidence. All across the country, every year, rape statistics rise in the summer. An increase in rape and an increase in migrant laborers are both causally related to the season, but otherwise there is no evidence that they are anything but independent events."

If the eighteenth-century philosopher David Hume had been privy to that conversation, he would have nodded in approval. For he is the philosopher who pointed out the problematic nature of all reasoning about causation. What kind of evidence does one have, he asked, that any event A causes event B? Only this, he claimed: that events A and B occur in the same place at the same time. A dog owner believes that calling his dog causes the dog to come, since every time he calls his dog, the dog comes. The governor believes that tougher drug laws cause a reduction in drug use, since drug use declined after the new laws were put into place. If each time you pointed at something, it exploded, wouldn't you be sorely tempted to believe that pointing caused the explosion?

But, Hume pointed out, these are all unreliable inferences. They are unreliable inferences because A and B could happen together for a variety of different reasons, only one of which is that A causes B. A and B could be independent events, occurring together by chance alone; or A and B could occur together because B causes A; or they might occur together because they are both caused by another factor—call it C. The point is that the mere fact that two events occur together does not require that they be causally related, or causally related in the way you think. *Correlation* (two events occurring together or changing in relation to one another) does not prove *causation* (one event making another happen).

The Particular Perils of Causal Reasoning

Consider this correlation: Between 1965 and 1968, the number of new handgun permits issued in Detroit and the number of murders committed in Detroit increased at almost exactly the same rate, as the two graphs show.[25, 26]

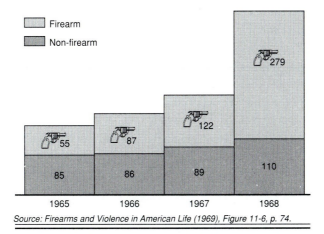

Source: Firearms and Violence in American Life (1969), Figure 11-6, p. 74.

Murders Committed in Detroit

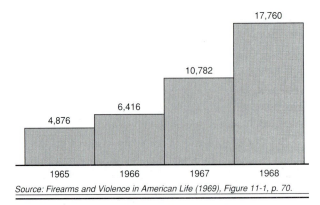

Source: *Firearms and Violence in American Life (1969), Figure 11-1, p. 70.*

Handgun Permits Issued in Detroit

Is it safe to conclude, on the basis of this correlation, that the increase in guns caused an increase in murder? Not with any assurance, since the same data could be explained in any of these alternative ways:

1. On the basis of this evidence alone, it is equally possible that the increase in the number of murders caused an increase in handgun purchases. Maybe B caused A rather than A causing B.

2. Alternatively, it is possible that another factor caused both an increase in gun purchases and an increase in murders. One can speculate about what that third factor might be: a simple increase in population? an increase in drug use? rising unemployment? urban gang warfare? Any of these could result in both increased gun sales and increased homicide rates.

3. Alternatively, it is possible that the correlation is merely coincidental; that is, *co-* ("together") + *incidental* ("happening"). After all, at the same time that murders increased in Detroit, the price of Buicks rose. But no one would postulate a causal connection between the price of Buicks and murders or guns. These years were also years of dramatic rise in the popularity of the Beatles. Did the Beatles cause a rise in the price of Buicks? Things happen at the same time. They cannot all be causally related.

The point of this list of alternative explanations is to try to induce a degree of caution about making causal generalizations. To be even moderately confident that two events are causally related, it is not enough to observe that they occur together, even again and again. Yet this is the only evidence that stands behind causal generalizations. The logic of the causal generalization looks like this:

(1) <u>In one case (or several), event A is accompanied by event B.</u>   (Premise)

(2) <u>Therefore, events A are always accompanied by events B.</u>   (Intermediate Conclusion)

(3) Therefore, event A causes event B.   (Conclusion)

Statements 1 and 2 make up a standard inductive generalization. The reasoner observes two events occurring together and infers they always occur together. He sees gun sales rise and murder rates rise; he infers that murder rates always go up when gun sales go up. Statements 2 and 3 are the causal inference. The reasoner believes that two events always occur together; he infers that they are causally related. The more guns there are, the more murders there are; so, guns must cause murders. Two dubious inferences, added together, yield a very dubious conclusion.

Causal Fallacies

Three common kinds of mistakes are associated with reasoning about causal relations.

The Backward Fallacy

When events A and B occur together, it may be because they are causally related. But it is easy to make a mistake about which of the two events is the cause and which is the effect. The *backward fallacy* occurs when an effect is mistaken for a cause.

For example, educators take great satisfaction from statistics proving that people with a college education have higher incomes than those whose education ends with high school. They draw the conclusion that a college education increases earning power (and thus justifies the breathtaking cost of higher education). But, given that college can cost as much as $20,000 a year, is there not reason to suspect that the causal relation goes in the other direction, that a high income gives access to a college education?

The Third-Factor Fallacy

When events A and B occur together, it may be because they are causally related. Alternatively, they may be independent events that occur together because they are both causally linked to a third factor. The *third-factor fallacy* occurs when two independent events that occur together because they have a common cause are mistakenly assumed to be causally related themselves.

Learn a foreign language, guidance counselors recommend, because foreign language study will improve your English language skills. The evidence? "Students who study a foreign language score higher on the SAT Verbal Test than students who do not." It is possible that foreign language study increases English language ability. But it is equally possible that the factors that cause a student to study a foreign language—academic ambition, facility with words—are exactly the factors that would cause a student to do well on the SATs. Academic ambition and facility with words are a "third factor" that may explain the link between foreign language study and high SAT scores.

Coincidence Fallacy

When events A and B occur together, it may be because they are causally related. Alternatively, they may be independent events occurring together by chance alone. The *coincidence fallacy* occurs when two independent events are mistakenly assumed to be causally related.

In 1348, the Black Death swept into Europe. A quarter of the population of Europe was wiped out. Seeking a causal explanation, people immediately focused on the sinfulness of society and its deviation from the doctrines of the Christian church. Iniquity, they decided, brought the Black Death as God's vicious revenge. True, the bubonic plague came at a time of heresies and public and private immorality. But coincidence in time seems to be the only connection between the events.

The coincidence fallacy is sometimes given a Latin name, *post hoc ergo propter hoc,* or the *post hoc* fallacy. The phrase translates, "after this, therefore because of this." Because event B occurred after event A, event B occurred because of event A. A baseball player pitched a perfect game wearing a new cap, and so he inferred that the perfection was brought on by the cap. A student got a terrific headache after she ate oysters, and so she inferred that the headache was caused by the oysters. Maybe so. But maybe not.

• •

6.11 A SEARCH FOR CAUSAL FALLACIES

Complete one of the following projects, each of which is designed to illustrate the ubiquity of causal fallacies:

1. Write a 250-word narrative essay in which you describe a causal fallacy that misled you. Include information about how you were led

into the error, what the error was, and how you discovered that you had been misled. If you cannot immediately think of such a situation, consider these questions: Do your parents tell cute stories about causal errors you made as a small child? Have you been misled by advertising? Do you have a lucky charm/ritual/clothes? Have you misinterpreted the cause of another person's behavior?

2. Put together a poster, collage, notebook, or videotape of advertisements in which the consumer is encouraged to infer a causal relationship from correlation alone. Look especially carefully at advertisements based on testimonials ("I used Magic Hair Restorer and now I have more hair than a road-kill raccoon") and advertisements based on statistics ("Nine out of ten people who tried our new Heart-Attack Prevention Bracelet are still alive today!!").

3. Design and present to the class an original advertising campaign based on faulty causal reasoning.

4. Interview a person whom you know to be superstitious, perhaps a classmate who wears a lucky charm or an athlete who follows a lucky pregame routine. Ask them to tell you about how they acquired their belief. Ask them what evidence they have for it. Ask them what evidence it would take to disconfirm it. Share what you learned with the class.

How to Test Causal Hypotheses

Fortunately, it is possible to test the truth of causal generalizations. A causal generalization (A causes B) can be treated like any hypothesis and tested by hypothetical reasoning. As in all cases of hypothetical reasoning, a causal hypothesis cannot be confirmed or disconfirmed by *direct* observation. But causal hypotheses do have logical consequences, and these can be tested in the real world. In his textbook *Understanding Scientific Reasoning*,[27] philosopher of science Ronald Giere described the logical process, suggesting that students begin by asking, What are the logical consequences of a causal hypothesis?— What follows if A causes B? This is not an easy question. "A causes B" does not mean that every time A occurs, B occurs. "Exposure to sun causes skin cancer," for example, does not mean that everyone who is exposed to sun will develop skin cancer. Nor does it mean that B can only occur when A occurs; not everyone with skin cancer has been excessively exposed to the sun. "A causes B" does mean, Giere says, that B will occur more frequently in the presence of A, than in its absence. If excessive exposure to the sun causes skin cancer, it follows that skin cancer will be greater among those who have been excessively exposed to the sun than among those who have not:

> If A causes B, then B will be more frequent when A is present than when A is absent.

Now, *this* is the kind of claim one can test. Professor Giere outlines three different sorts of experiments one could design to see whether this prediction is true. By far the best, logically speaking, is the randomized experimental design.

1.   *Randomized experimental design.* An experiment using a randomized experimental design yields a causal generalization that is protected from the possibility of all three causal fallacies. Here is the procedure, illustrated by the problem of skin cancer but applicable to any causal hypothesis: Randomly select experimental subjects, in this case human beings. Randomly divide the subjects into two groups. If the groups are large enough and the divisions truly random, it is safe to assume that the two groups are roughly similar. In this case, the groups must be similar when it comes to other factors that may be causally related to skin cancer; that is, people in both groups have roughly the same distribution of ages, races, diets, and so forth. Expose one group to excessive sunlight over a long period of time. This group—the group that has the suspected causal factor—is called the *experimental group.* The other group is the *control group.* It differs from the experimental group in only one respect: in the control group, the suspected causal factor is absent. That is, the control group is entirely protected from the sun's rays.

Observe the two groups over a period of time. If skin cancer occurs with roughly the same frequency among those exposed to the sun and those protected from the sun, then the prediction is false. Consequently, there probably is no causal effect. If there is a significant difference between the skin cancer rates of the two groups, then the causal hypothesis has not been disproved. This finding would help guide further research into the causes of skin cancer.

2.   *Prospective design.* There is, of course, a terrible flaw in the procedure outlined above. It is not a logical flaw, but a serious moral failing. It is wrong to expose people to a causal factor that is suspected of causing cancer. In this and in many other situations, randomized experimental design is impossible. The prospective design is a second-best substitute.

The prospective design takes advantage of the fact that the experimental group and control group needed for the experiment already exist naturally. Among humans, there are those who routinely fry themselves in the sun, and there are those who assiduously protect themselves from the sun. The researcher can draw the experimental and control groups from these two preexisting groups. From sun worshipers, randomly select a group to serve as the experimental group. From those who avoid the sun, randomly select a control group. Observe both groups carefully over time. If skin cancer occurs with the same frequency in both groups, then the prediction is false: it is not the case that cancer occurs more frequently among those who bask in the sun than among those who avoid the sun. Thus, there probably is no causal effect.

However, if a difference in cancer rates is found, researchers performing prospective experiments have to be very cautious about drawing conclusions. The reliability of the experiment rests on the assumption that the experimental and control groups are alike in all respects except one: the presence or absence of the suspected cause. But this is an unsupported, and often false, assumption; there may be a hidden factor found primarily among those who seek the sun or among those who do not. Then, if the experiment shows a difference between the two groups, it is difficult to know whether to attribute the difference to the presence or absence of sun exposure or to pre-existing differences between the two groups. Maybe sun seekers are exposed to more chlorine in swimming pools, and it is this that causes skin cancer. Or maybe emissions from TV screens somehow protect people who stay inside.

3. *Retrospective experimental design.* There is a third way to design this experiment. A researcher could study two groups of people, those in whom the *effect* is present and those in whom it is absent, those who have skin cancer and those who do not. Then she could conduct interviews or in some other way delve into the past to determine whether the subjects sought or avoided exposure to the sun. If she finds that those with skin cancer had no more sun exposure than those without, she can cautiously conclude that the causal hypothesis connecting sun and skin cancer has been damaged.

If, however, the researcher finds that people who have developed skin cancer have had more sun exposure than those who did not, she must draw conclusions with extreme care. For it may be that the difference in cancer rates can be explained by some unnoticed difference between those with skin cancer and those without.

• •

6.12 "I'M SICK AND I'M SCARED"

Read the following excerpts from football great Lyle Alzado's account of his use of performance-enhancing drugs and his fight against brain cancer.

I've got cancer—a brain lymphoma—and I'm in the fight of my life. . . . I was a giant. Now I'm sick. And I'm scared . . . I wobble when I walk. . . .

I know there's no written, documented proof that steroids and human growth hormone caused this cancer. But it's one of the reasons you have to look at. You have to.

When I was playing high school football . . . , I hadn't heard about steroid use by anybody. . . . Then I went to Yankton College . . . [and] I started taking steroids. I don't remember now where I got them or how I even heard about them, but I know I started on Dianabol, about 50 milligrams a day.

As I progressed, I changed steroids whenever I felt my body building a tolerance to what I was taking. . . . I mixed combinations like a chemist.

My first year with the Broncos was 1971. I was like a maniac. I outran, outhit, outanythinged everybody. . . . All along I was taking steroids, and I saw that they made me play better and better. I kept on because I knew I had to keep getting more size. I became very violent. . . . I got moodier and moodier. I had a couple of divorces. I yelled all the time.

I decided to take human growth hormone. . . . I started taking it in mid-June and used it right up until this March along with testosterone cypionate, an anabolic steroid. . . .

If you're on steroids or human growth hormone, stop. I should have.

The above article is reprinted courtesy of SPORTS ILLUSTRATED from the July 8, 1991 issue. Copyright © 1991, The Time Inc. Magazine Company. ("I'm Sick and I'm Scared," by Lyle Alzado.) All Rights Reserved.

1. Mr. Alzado makes or implies a variety of causal generalizations. List as many as you can find.

2. Mr. Alzado is reluctant to insist on a causal connection between the cancer and his drug use. Which causal fallacy is he taking care to avoid? But he has no doubt that the steroids really did increase his performance. Why is that, do you suppose? Why, in other words, is the inductive generalization that links steroids and cancer a weaker argument than the inductive generalization that links steroids and performance?

3. Suppose that you wanted to test the hypothesis that the combined use of steroids and human growth hormone causes brain cancer.
    a. What would you predict?
    b. How would you test the prediction?
    c. Which experimental method is that?
    d. If your prediction turned out to be correct, what would prevent you from claiming you had proved a causal connection?

6.13 A GRANT PROPOSAL

The grant proposal, the peculiar literary form of the scientist, is a request for funding to support research. It requires applicants to put all their skills of scientific reasoning and writing to work. Your assignment is to write a modest grant proposal and to serve on a "review panel." The proposal can be on any aspect of any subject. It certainly does not have to be narrowly scientific. Nor does it have to be technical in any way. Here are some ideas to help you brainstorm a project: Are threats or persuasion more effective at quieting midnight party animals? Does sitting in the front of the classroom improve performance on quizzes? Is it a weak battery that is causing problems in your motorcycle? What are some of the causal factors related to drug use among college students? Does washing a car make it rain? Does stress increase susceptibility to colds and other infections?

Directions for writing. (For the sake of authenticity, these directions are adapted from the "Application for Public Health Service Grant" from the U.S. Department of Health and Human Services.)

Specific Instructions

An application may be returned if it fails to observe the page limitations.

Research Plan. Organize sections A–C of the Research Plan to answer these questions: (A) What do you intend to do? (B) What has already been done? (C) How are you going to do the work?

A. Specific Aims. State the broad, long-term objectives and describe concisely and realistically what the specific research described in this application is intended to accomplish and any hypotheses to be tested.

B. Background. Briefly sketch the observations that led to this research and the question to be answered.

C. Experimental Design and Methods. Outline the predictions that will be tested and explain the experimental design of the procedures to be used to test them. Discuss the potential difficulties and limitations of the proposed procedures and how they may be overcome.

Submit five copies of the proposal.

Usually, a review panel made up of the applicant's distinguished peers determines which proposals will be funded. Before the panel members meet, they receive a cardboard box full of proposals and a set of instructions. They review the proposals, following those instructions. Then they meet to discuss their comments and rank the proposals. Starting with the highest-ranking proposals, grant proposals are funded until the money runs out.

Directions for review. Form review panels of five people, each panel to review five grants (none of which was written by members of that panel and each of which is numbered to assure anonymity). Take the proposals home and review them, using the following form. Then, in class, discuss and rank the proposals. Your professor will figure out what will be analogous to research dollars, for the purposes of this exercise. (These instructions are also adapted from the procedures of the U.S. Department of Health and Human Services.)

Instructions for Reviewer's Comments

Please provide:

1. Brief description of project
2. Critique
   a. State whether the hypothesis is clear.
   b. Comment on the appropriateness and adequacy of the proposed experimental design. Do the predictions follow from the hypotheses? Are they testable? Are there flaws in the experimental design? Will the experiment yield the information needed to draw a conclusion about the hypothesis?
3. Summary and recommendations
   Assign a priority score:
   - 1-2   Highest quality, most meritorious
   - 2-3   Better than average quality
   - 3-4   Less than average quality
   - 4-5   Poorest quality, marginal acceptability

• •

• • • • • • • • • • • • • • • **Scientific Writing** • • • • • • • • • • • • • • • • • •

There is a great irony about scientific writing. Many—not all, but many—scientists choose science as a career because they do not like to write. Science appears to be a career that allows you to tramp around in mud flats or manipulate numbers or pour chemicals into beakers and thereby avoid all painful contact with commas and clauses. This appearance is deceiving. A scientific lackey—a lab tech or a dishwasher—may not have to write. But a successful scientist is a professional writer. Successful scientists spend most of their time writing grant proposals and scientific papers and critically reading and reviewing the written work of other scientists.

To compound the irony, scientific writing is a particularly exacting and exasperating art form. This is for two reasons. First, scientific writing is severely compressed. Grant proposals and research reports must be squeezed into strict word and page limits. There is no time for a leisurely exploration of the scientist's thought processes and laboratory procedures. Second, scientific writing must communicate exactly. If the reader of a poem is slightly misled about the exact shade of purple in the gentleman's passion, no harm is done. But if the reader of a research report misinterprets a procedure, he will not be able to build on the research reported; and if an engineer cannot understand the specifications for a bridge, she cannot build anything at all.

As a result, the primary values of scientific writing are efficiency and clarity. The best scientific writing communicates information quickly and unmistakably.

Using Argument Analysis Skills in Scientific Writing

Scientific writing takes many different forms, each of which is highly formal and rule-bound. So, it is not helpful to talk in general terms about the content of scientific writing. But all the formats share a single problem, and that is the problem of organizing information. When a scientist sits down to write, she sits in the middle of a more or less sloppy pile of information—graphs, hypotheses, other people's research results, descriptions of procedures, predictions, bad guesses, good guesses, tentative conclusions, leads, research data, statistics. The task at hand is to pick through that pile to find the pieces of information that are relevant and to organize them in such a way that they add up to something. Here are some general suggestions.

Think carefully about the audience. Who will read this work, and why? What will they already know? What will they already believe?

Think carefully about the purpose of the writing. Are you giving directions for another person to follow? Are you simply presenting information? Or (what is most likely to be the case) are you actually presenting an argument? Much scientific writing, almost everything in scientific journals, is argument, presenting evidence for or against a claim.

If your writing is, in fact, an argument, treat it like an argument. First, take advantage of what you know about argument analysis to organize the information. For this, use the question schema of argument analysis, adapted to fit hypothetical reasoning. Sort through the pile of information to find answers to these questions:

1. What is the issue to be addressed in this piece of writing? What background information defines that issue?
2. What is the conclusion to be defended?
3. What is the evidence?
   a. What is the hypothesis to be indirectly tested?
   b. What is the prediction to be directly tested?
   c. What are the procedures for testing the prediction?
   d. Was the prediction true or false?

Now, "make something" of this information. Put your argument together into standard form. The standard form of hypothetical reasoning is as follows:

If (hypothesis) , then (prediction) .
Experiments showed that the prediction is (false/true) .
Therefore, the hypothesis (is/is not) shown to be false.

This gives you a clear outline of your argument. It tells you the place of each piece of information in the argument. It provides a map of your argument around which you can organize the details you want to include. Once *you* understand the logical direction of your thought, you can present the information in a way that makes it easy for your readers to follow your reasoning in directions you want to take them.

• •

6.14 BUILDING FROM SCIENTIFIC RUBBLE

Each item below contains a chaotic set of facts. Your job is to transform it into a clear and effective paragraph. Do so by first casting the arguments into the standard form of hypothetical reasoning. Then use the standard-form argument as a writing outline. In each paragraph, in this order:

1. Present the issue.
2. Present the conclusion.
3. Provide the evidence for the conclusion.
   a. Plants generally curve toward the light. When researchers cut the tips off of growing oat plants, the plants did not curve as rapidly toward the light as did plants that still had their tips. But when

researchers covered all but the tips of the plants, the plants still grew toward the light. There must be something in the tips of the plants that stimulates growth on the side of the plant away from the light. If the cells on the shadowed side of a plant grow bigger and faster than the cells on the lighted side of a plant, then the plant will curve toward the light.[28]

b. Planaria are little flatworms with big, crossed eyes. Some years ago, there was quite a stir when experiments with planaria appeared to show that learning can be stored chemically in the brain. Scientists trained some planaria to avoid the light, and then they ground up the "educated" animals and fed them to "ignorant" animals. To the surprise of scientists, the ignorant animals learned to avoid light much more quickly than animals that had not been fed the ground-up bodies of their educated siblings. There must be some chemically stored knowledge that was transferred to the planaria in their diets, scientists thought. People got quite excited, thinking they might have found a substitute for a college education. But then other scientists, who were very suspicious, decided to grind up "ignorant" flatworms and feed them to other "ignorant" flatworms. It turned out that those flatworms also were quicker to learn to avoid the light. So much for that idea!

c. *"Before the mid-1800s, a speckled light-grey form of the [speckled] moth was prevalent [in England]. A dark-grey form also existed at that time but was extremely rare. . . . Between 1848 and 1898, however, the dark form increased in frequency. . . .*

In the 1930s, the geneticist E. Ford suggested that natural selection was causing the increased frequency of the dark form in industrial areas, [where pollution had darkened the trees. Since this made the dark moths harder for birds and other predators to see,] the dark form began surviving and reproducing at a greater rate than its light-colored kin. . . .

In the 1950s, H. Kettlewell . . . test[ed] Ford's hypothesis. He bred both kinds of moths in captivity, then marked hundreds of them. He then released them . . . in two areas, one near the heavily industrialized area around Birmingham, and the other in the unpolluted area of Dorset. As many moths as possible were recaptured during the days that followed. More dark moths were recaptured in the polluted area—and more light moths were recaptured in the pollution-free area.[29]

•••••••••••••••••••••••• Notes ••••••••••••••••••••••••

1. Bertrand Russell, "On Induction," *The Basic Writings of Bertrand Russell*, eds. Robert Egner and Lester Denonn (New York: Simon and Schuster, 1961), pp. 148–155.

2. See Sidney Sackson, *A Gamut of Games*. The description of the game that appears here comes from Martin Gardner, *Mathematical Circus: More Games, Puzzles, Paradoxes, and other Mathematical Entertainments from Scientific American* (New York: Vintage Books, 1979), pp. 45–53.

3. Maya Angelou, *I Know Why the Caged Bird Sings* (New York: Random House, 1969), p. 25. Copyright © 1969. Reprinted by permission.

4. Cecie Starr and Ralph Taggart, *Biology: The Unity and Diversity of Life,* 3rd ed., (Belmont, Calif.: Wadsworth Publishing Company, 1981), p. 335.

5. Jean Starobinski, *A History of Medicine* (New York: Hawthorne Books, 1964), p. 93.

6. All the material for this example comes from "Hell's Sober Comeback," *U.S. News and World Report* (March 25, 1991), p. 56.

7. This information comes from Martha Hernandez, "Salaries Skyrocket," *Corvallis Gazette-Times* (December 4, 1990).

8. Hope Rydeh, *Lily Pond: Four Years with a Family of Beavers* (New York: HarperCollins, 1989), p. 109.

9. Claude Lewis, "L.A. poor 'mugged' by verdict," *Corvallis Gazette-Times* (May 5, 1992), p. A9.

10. *A Pen Warmed-up in Hell: Mark Twain in Protest*, ed. Frederick Anderson (New York: Harper-Collins Publishers, 1972), p. 152.

11. The exercise was written by John Lenssen, Oregon Department of Education. He presented it during a workshop at the annual meeting of the American Association of Philosophy Teachers, San Jose State University, July 17, 1991. Reprinted by permission of the author.

12. Thanks to John Lenssen, Oregon Department of Education, for calling this exercise to my attention. Mr. Lenssen presented it at a workshop at the annual meeting of the American Association of Philosophy Teachers, San Jose State University, July 17, 1991.

13. *Directions for Insiders.* As you will soon see, this is an exercise in hasty generalization. The point is to show students how easy it is to make mistakes about different groups and cultures by demonstrating how the means of communication affects what is communicated.

    Accordingly, you, the Insiders, will not design a new culture at all, even though the Outsiders expect you to do so. Instead, answer all their questions according to the following rules: 1. Answer only those questions that come from Outsiders who are of the same sex as you; that is, males will answer males, and females will answer females. Simply ignore questions from members of the opposite sex. 2. If an Outsider smiles when he asks a question, answer it "Yes." If the Outsider does not smile when she asks a question, answer it "No." The content of the question does not matter. Play it straight. That's all.

    If, by some chance, you are an Outsider reading these directions, quietly make yourself an Insider in order to protect the efficacy of this exercise.

14. This exercise appeared in my inductive logic textbook: Kathleen Dean Moore, *A Field Guide to Inductive Arguments* (Dubuque, Iowa: Kendall/Hunt, 1986), pp. 111–113. Copyright © 1986. Adapted with permission of Kendall/Hunt, Publisher. I have since learned of other textbooks that suggest similar lab exercises.

15. The idea and the facts for this example come from Martin and Inge Goldstein, *How We Know: An Exploration of the Scientific Process* (New York: Plenum Press, 1978), p. 212, a fascinating book.

16. Robert Sheaffer, "Psychic Vibrations," *The Skeptical Inquirer* (Spring 1983), p. 19. Copyright © 1983, The Skeptical Inquirer. Reprinted with permission.

17. Robert Sheaffer, "Psychic Vibrations," *The Skeptical Inquirer* (Spring 1983), p. 22. Copyright © 1983, The Skeptical Inquirer. Reprinted with permission.

18. Robert Scheaffer, "Psychic Vibrations," *The Skeptical Inquirer* (Fall 1987), pp. 33–34. Copyright © 1987, The Skeptical Inquirer. Reprinted with permission.

19. Robert Scheaffer, "Psychic Vibrations," *The Skeptical Inquirer* (Summer 1991), p. 360. Copyright © 1991, The Skeptical Inquirer. Reprinted with permission.

20. Robert Scheaffer, "Psychic Vibrations," *The Skeptical Inquirer* (Spring 1990), pp. 251–252. Copyright © 1990, The Skeptical Inquirer. Reprinted with permission.

21. *The Life and Letters of Charles Darwin*, ed. F. Darwin (London: John Murray, 1888), Vol. 1, pp. 103–104. Quoted in E. Peter Volpe, "The Shame of Science Education," *American Zoologist*, Vol. 24, No. 2 (1984), p. 437.

22. After *A Field Guide to Inductive Arguments*, p. 99. Copyright © 1989, Kendall/Hunt. Reprinted by permission.

23. Stephen P. Maran, "What Struck Tunguska?" *Natural History* (February 1984), pp. 26–27. Reprinted with permission from *Natural History* February 1984; Copyright The American Museum of Natural History, 1984.

24. Sonya Duch, then a student at Heidelberg College, Tiffin, Ohio.

25. George D. Newton and Franklin E. Zimring, *Firearms and Violence in American Life: A Staff Report Submitted to the National Commission on the Causes and Prevention of Violence* (Washington, DC: National Commission on the Causes and Prevention of Violence, 1969), Figure 11–1, p. 70.

26. George D. Newton and Franklin E. Zimring, *Firearms and Violence in American Life: A Staff Report Submitted to the National Commission on the Causes and Prevention of Violence* (Washington, DC: National Commission on the Causes and Prevention of Violence, 1969), Figure 11–6, p. 74.

27. Ronald Giere, *Understanding Scientific Reasoning* (New York: Holt, Rinehart and Winston, 1984).

28. The facts in this example come from Cecie Starr and Ralph Taggart, *Biology: The Unity and Diversity of Life* (Belmont, Calif.: Wadsworth Publishing Co., 1984), but the disorganized format is supplied by the author.

29. From BIOLOGY: THE UNITY AND DIVERSITY OF LIFE 3/E by Cecie Starr and Ralph Taggart © 1984 by Wadsworth, Inc. Reprinted by permission of the publisher.

PART III

PUTTING ARGUMENTS TO WORK

SUMMARY OF PART THREE

In the workaday world of argumentation, in the world of solving problems, writing memorandums, reaching conclusions, making decisions, changing people's minds, and influencing people's actions, the two central virtues are intellectual honesty and clarity. Intellectual honesty is a commitment to be influenced, and to influence others, solely by evidence that is relevant and reliable. Chapter 7 catalogs a set of reasons, called fallacious, that are inherently suspect and notoriously unreliable. Clarity is a quality of thought and prose that illuminates the relationships between ideas and minimizes the chances of making mistakes. Chapter 8 analyzes various kinds of muddleheadedness and deceitfulness that block clear thinking.

All the skills of reasoning and writing—identifying, analyzing, evaluating, writing, and revising arguments—come together at the end. They come together in the art of refutation, through which people come to know not only what is false but what must therefore be true. This is the subject of Chapter 9.

CHAPTER 7

· · · · · · · · · · · · · · · · · · · ·

Honor in Argument

Most human activities could not take place unless participants felt themselves honor-bound to observe a minimal set of standards. Golfers could not play golf if they did not at least pretend to play the ball where it lies. Weddings would not be worth the champagne, if husbands and wives did not feel the smallest obligation to monogamy. Even soldiers engaged in the most hellish, chaotic battles honor strong commitments to their comrades. Trading, teaching, driving, eating, banking, making love—each of these depends on an often unstated, usually vague, continually changing, and frequently violated code of conduct. So it is with the human activity called reasoning.

When one person reasons with another, that is to say, when a person presents reasons in an attempt to influence another's beliefs or behaviors, both people presuppose that the other will generally "follow the rules." Imagine "reasoning" with someone who would lie as readily as speak the truth, who had no consistent view of what constitutes a good reason or, worse yet, had no use for consistency at all, who connected ideas in unpredictable ways, and who perversely misconstrued everything you said. This would not be reasoning. This would be absurdity, something out of *Alice in Wonderland*:

> *"We called him Tortoise because he taught us," said the Mock Turtle angrily. "Really, you are very dull."*[1]

Moreover, individuals generally hold themselves to certain standards when they reach conclusions on the basis of evidence. Without this implicit allegiance to standards, there would be no distinction between reasoning and gut reaction, clearheadedness and self-deception.

This chapter looks carefully at honor in argumentation—the effort to follow the unstated principles that make reasoning possible and productive. It looks also at dishonor and deception—the fallacies that occur when those principles are violated.

·········· Four Principles of Argumentation ··········

A Scout aspires to be trustworthy, loyal, helpful, friendly, courteous, kind, obedient, cheerful, thrifty, brave, clean, and reverent. What constitutes a similar list of the virtues of reasons offered in argument? A good reason is true, relevant, fair, and clear.

1. A good reason is true. It does not make a false claim or deceive by omission.
2. A good reason is relevant to the truth of the conclusion.
3. To the extent that an argument is a contest between disputants, a good reason is fair in the fight; it does not take undeserved advantages or resort to trickery.
4. A good reason is clearly stated so that it does not invite misunderstanding.

In infinitely many ways, arguments can fail to live up to these standards. Many of the failures follow recognizable patterns that occur again and again. Noticing these patterns, logicians have isolated, defined, and labeled a variety of the different ways an argument can go wrong. These are the *fallacies.*

····················· Fallacies ·····················

A *fallacy* is a pattern of argumentation that seems to provide strong support for a claim but that does not. It is a flaw in reasoning that can occur inadvertently, as when a person falls into error from carelessness or ignorance. But, often, fallacies occur by design, as part of an effort to mislead or deceive.

Fallacious reasoning is thus a logical failing, the failure to construct arguments in which the reasons strongly support the conclusion. And, when poor reasoning is part of a plan to deceive, fallacious reasoning is a moral failing. It is a kind of lying or cheating, a violation of the implicit agreement between disputants to hold themselves to a set of standards.

Fallacies fall into rough categories according to the nature of the error they exhibit. The *fallacies of relevance* are arguments that fail to meet the second of the principles of argumentation listed in the preceding section: In a fallacy of relevance, the reasons are not relevant to the conclusion. *Sophistries* are arguments that fail to meet the third principle: They are tricky argumentative moves. These two kinds of fallacies are the subject of this chapter. *Fallacies of ambiguity,* errors that result from ambiguities and obscurities in language and that thus violate the fourth principle, are the subject of Chapter 8. Arguments that lie, in violation of the first principle of argumentation, are not fallacies, strictly speaking, because the mistake is not in how the argument is constructed. The ability to detect errors of fact will come from learning about a wide variety of subjects but not from logic.

A study of fallacies will alert careful thinkers to risky patterns of reasoning so that they can take pains to avoid these errors in their own thinking and writing. Just as important, a study of fallacies will help critical thinkers avoid being duped.

· ·

7.1 ARGUMENT AND ETHICS

This textbook talks of fallacious reasoning in strongly moralistic terms: Arguing fallaciously is a kind of lying or cheating. Yet it could be argued that fallacies are tools, like knives or shovels, that are morally neutral and become right or wrong only when they are used for good or ill. Winning assent is often a very good thing. Democracies could not reach decisions without it, nor could universities teach; generals could not move their armies, and manufacturers could not sell their products. If fallacies are used to win assent in a good cause, one might argue, then fallacies are themselves a good thing.

As an example, one might cite propaganda efforts by the Allies during World War II, blatantly fallacious arguments in what most Americans thought was a good cause. See the following propaganda piece.[2]

In discussion groups, try to reach consensus on at least three situations in which fallacious reasoning is morally appropriate. Then, brainstorm a list of the unintended and perhaps often unnoticed negative consequences of using fallacious arguments in a good cause. Report your decisions to the class.

. . . .

7.2 THE JUNK COLLECTOR, PART I

As you begin to study this chapter, start a collection of the fallacies of relevance and the sophistries that you encounter in your everyday life. You may find them during casual conversation, in lectures, in advertisements, on TV, in the newspaper, and many other places. In fact, once you have the search image in your mind, you will find them everywhere you look. Put together a collection of the "best" examples you find, carefully and accurately labeled and explained. The collection could take the form of a portfolio, an unbound notebook containing photocopies, transcripts, ads, and so forth. Or you could put together a bulletin board display, a videotape, an audiotape, or some other presentation of the results of your search. Find a way to share your collection with the class.

Alternatively, your professor may ask you or your study group to specialize, putting together a collection of fallacies of a particular kind.

. . . .

················· Fallacies of Relevance ···············

In a good argument, the premises support the conclusion as columns support a roof. In a fallacy of relevance, the columns are all in place, standing strong against the sky; but the roof is off somewhere on another hilltop, utterly unsupported. The premises, although true, are logically disconnected from the conclusion. As a result, their truth has little or no effect on whether the conclusion is credible or not. At the same time, the premises *seem* to be connected to the conclusion through some sort of psychological linking or sleight of hand.

The great Greek rhetorician Aristotle believed that when people are trying to persuade each other, they make use of three categories of appeals. They appeal to reason (*logos*) when they offer information and evidence to support their case. This is the kind of appeal logic students know and respect. But even a logically perfect argument may not be persuasive if it does not have any effect on the audience. So, persuasive writers also appeal to the emotions (*pathos*) of the audience, trying to enlist in their own cause the audience's emotional energy, or formulating reasons that resonate with the audience's hopes and fears. And persuasive writers try to develop credibility (*ethos*) with the audience, in hopes that arguments will be better received in an atmosphere of trust.

An argument is most persuasive when it is cogent, when it engages an issue you care about, and when it comes from someone you trust, that is when an argument successfully appeals to logos, pathos, and ethos. This emphatically does not mean that the appeal to emotion or the appeal to the credibility of the speaker can alone support the weight of a conclusion. For feeling good about a claim does not make it true, as feeling hatred toward an idea does not make it false. Nor is the truth or falsehood of a claim affected by who utters it. Mistakes on this issue account for fallacious appeals to emotion and fallacious appeals to credibility.

···

7.3 NEGOTIATING[3]

In this exercise, you and a partner will negotiate the purchase price of a car. As in real negotiations, each of you will have information the other does not have. Decide who will be the seller and who will be the buyer. Sellers will find their instructions in note 4 at the end of this chapter. Buyers will find their instructions in the last endnote in this chapter, note 29. *Read only your own instructions.*

Take ten minutes to negotiate and agree on a price. Then, discuss and prepare answers to these questions:

1.   What price did you decide on?
2.   What kinds of information did you each offer to the other as you negotiated? What information did you withhold? Did either of you lie?
3.   What role did emotions play in your negotiations? Did either of you try to influence the other by making the other feel sorry for you? by evoking any other emotions? How did you feel during negotiations?
4.   What role did personal credibility play in your negotiations? Did you trust your partner to tell you the truth? Why or why not? Did your trust pay off in the end?

• •

Fallacious Appeals to Emotion

People are strongly influenced by their emotions—by pity, fear, loneliness and pride. Thus, an effective way to make a claim more convincing is to link it to an emotion. For example, if a writer arouses strong feelings of fear and then connects that fear to a particular claim, the readers are likely to recoil in horror from the claim, even though they have not weighed reasons for or against the claim and, indeed, none have been offered. Likewise, if a writer arouses strongly positive feelings—feelings of belonging or of satisfaction or pleasure— and casts the warmth of these feelings on a claim, the claim glows with the reflected heat and is more likely to be accepted, once again without the benefit of rational reflection. Writers commit the *fallacy of emotional appeal* when they lead readers to accept or reject a claim by manipulating readers' emotions rather than by appealing to good reasons.

Here is the rationale of the appeal to emotions, given voice by a master of the technique:

> [Since the task of propaganda] consists in catching the masses' attention,] its effect has always to be directed more and more towards the feeling, and only to a certain extent to so-called reason. All propaganda has to be popular and has to adapt its spiritual level to the perception of the least intelligent of those towards whom it intends to direct itself. . . . The more modest, then, its scientific ballast is, and the more it exclusively considers the feelings of the masses, the more striking will be its success. . . .

> *The people, in an overwhelming majority, are so feminine in their nature and attitude that their activities and thoughts are motivated less by sober consideration than by feeling—* . . . *positive or negative; love or hate, right or wrong, truth or lie. . . .*
>
> . . . *[The fundamental principle of propaganda is] to confine itself to little and to repeat this eternally.*[5]

Thus does Adolf Hitler explain the appeal to emotions. Such a rationale gives rise to efforts to convince by linking claims to pity, fear, loneliness, pride, and popular passions.

Appeals to Pity

Writers fallaciously appeal to pity when they arouse feelings of heartfelt sorrow at their own condition or someone else's and use those feelings to persuade readers to accept a conclusion. For example, at the end of a long, televised argument defending himself against charges of financial impropriety, ex-President Nixon volunteered, "It is not easy to come before a nationwide audience and bare your soul as I have done." No doubt true, but utterly irrelevant to the issue of whether Nixon was a crook.

An argument is not fallacious whenever it brings tears to the readers' eyes. But it is fallacious when tears, not reasons, induce the reader to accept a claim. In the following argument, although the facts will break your heart, the facts do support the conclusion and, therefore, the argument is a good one:

> *In Bangladesh, a cyclone kills at least 125,000 people and leaves millions more prey to starvation and plague. In the Middle East, civil war drives an estimated 1.5 million Kurds from their homes, causing countless thousands to die of hunger, cold, and sickness. In South America, a cholera epidemic claims at least 1,300 lives before the onset of the southern winter. And beyond those disasters looms the specter of mass famine in Africa, which, relief experts say, could kill between 20 million and 30 million people. Taken together, the underdeveloped world currently presents a picture of natural and man-assisted catastrophe rarely equaled in the 20th century.*[6]

Appeals to Fear

Fear is certainly one of humankind's most powerful motivators. Fear moves people and moves them fast. Thus, a feeling of disquiet, when attached to a particular claim, can motivate readers to believe that claim, even without good reason. One of President Reagan's re-election advertisements made effective use of fear. The ad began with a deep, rapid thumping, an accelerated heartbeat. Then came a man's voice: "There is a bear in the woods. Some people say it's tame. Some people say it's vicious. Since we can't be sure, wouldn't it be safer to be stronger than the bear?" The bear? The Soviet Union. The implicit message? Vote for the candidate who will build up a stronger nuclear force than that of the Soviet Union, not because the Soviet Union is dangerous (the ad acknowledges that it may not be) but because . . . well, because everybody is afraid of bears in the woods.

A controversial advertisement for Benetton-brand clothes shows a photograph of a bearded man a few hours before his death from AIDS. He lies in a hospital bed, ashen-faced and emaciated, while his anguished father cradles his head, and his mother and sister look on in horror. The only words on the page are the company's brand name: UNITED COLORS OF BENETTON.™ Whether this is an appeal to fear or an appeal to pity is difficult to determine, but the company is clearly trying to link its name with the strongest kinds of emotions.

Bandwagon Appeals

When it comes to fears, most people are terrified of being left out, of being excluded or ostracized. Being basically social creatures, they have a deep need to be part of the in-crowd. This explains the particular effectiveness of *bandwagon appeals,* arguments that lead readers to accept a claim or buy a product by promising membership in a group or threatening exclusion rather than by giving information about the grounds for the claim or the merits of the product.

Advertisers use bandwagon appeals when they cite the thousands of people who are already using their product ("America loves Burger King") or invite membership in a group ("Join the Pepsi generation" or "Join the people who have joined the Army"). Local politicians commonly use bandwagon appeals in print advertisements that list columns and columns of names of prominent local people who support the candidate. The unstated, alarming question: Why isn't *your* name on this list?

Appeals to Pride

Another strongly motivating emotion is pride. Many advertisers take advantage of this fact by flattering the consumer.

Exceptional people deserve exceptional opportunities. (Photocopy machine)

You deserve a break today. (Hamburgers)

The luxury car for those who refuse to relax their standards. (Automobile)

The implicit argument in appeals to pride rests on an unstated, flattering premise that the consumer is happy to provide. "This luxury car is for those who refuse to relax their standards." What consumer would deny the truth of the missing premise, "I am among those with high standards"? The conclusion is inevitable: "This luxury car is for me."

Appeals to pride are also quick and dirty ways to secure assent to a premise. Attach one of these phrases to the beginning of a premise, and you transform the premise into a statement that cannot be disputed by any self-respecting listener: "All right-thinking Americans will agree that . . ." "Anyone who has studied the issues carefully knows that . . ." "Real men understand that . . ." By accepting the claim, the listeners flatter themselves that they are members of this exclusive group of people with rare insight. Deny the claim, and they admit something negative about themselves.

Ad populum Appeals

Ad populum appeals are appeals to emotion stripped down to their barest essentials. An advertiser or a politician or someone else with a claim to sell identifies something about which people feel strongly. Then they simply attach their product or claim to that thing. These kinds of appeals are sometimes called "hookers," a particularly apt name for a variety of reasons, one of which is that the claim is simply hooked to something that evokes a strong emotional response. The Latin phrase *argumentum ad populum* translates "argument to the people"; it is an argument in which a link between a claim and an emotion-laden concept is used to influence the readers' opinions or actions.

Some *ad populum* appeals create a link between a claim and something people love. What do people care about the most? Toward what do people have the strongest positive feelings? Attach these things to the product or opinion or candidate that is up for sale, and you have an *ad populum* appeal.

Marketing agencies invest considerable time and money into finding answers to these questions. Then they design advertising campaigns that attach their product to those things consumers value the most. People care about financial success, so advertisers link liquor and cigarettes to a high-flying life-style. People care about family ties, so advertising campaigns for telephones, for example, are shamelessly sentimental. Sex is big, as always, judging from advertisements for liquor, perfume, cosmetics, cars—even computers, of all things. And then there is always pleasure, particularly in relation to cigarettes (a particularly ironic connection). Glowing good health and environmental themes seem to be coming on strong. The point is that none of these values is connected in any essential way with the products they are used to sell. That doesn't seem to bother advertisers, but it should give pause to consumers.

Because advertisers are understandably skittish about having their *ad populum* appeals dissected by logic students, you will not find particular examples in this book. But you will find them in most other publications you open, particularly magazines targeted to people in your age and economic groups.

Politicians send out their pollsters to find out what counts for voters in a given election year. In the presidential election of 1992, pollsters' advice was to concentrate on change and reform, financial security, and traditional family values. Thus, 1992 saw President Bush giving a speech in which he mentioned "reform" and "change" no fewer than 22 times. Vice President Dan Quayle made a career out of defending the nuclear family. And the Democratic convention of 1992 promised change, reform, *and* a "balance between national security and family security."

The aim of these appeals, like the aim of an argument, is to influence another person's actions or beliefs. But they offer only an imitation of a reason and not a suggestion of evidence or information.

Ad populum appeals do not have to be positive. Historically, some of the most effective *ad populum* appeals have linked a claim with objects of loathing. The hatred rubs off on the claim. For example, a 1984 issue of the Soviet magazine *Military Knowledge* linked U.S. soldiers with monsters:

> *One can boldly and without exaggeration call these cutthroats in the U.S. uniforms monsters. And what, in fact, is human in these frenzied, teethbaring physiognomies, in these eyes, the eyes of killers and rapists? What can be sacred for such fellows?*[7]

The membership drive for the National Socialist White Peoples' Party included this pitch to fear and loathing in America:

NO TROOPS FOR ISRAEL!
AMERICANS WILL NOT DIE
FOR THE JEWS

Are you tired of the Establishment's nauseating slavery to the Jews? Are you weary of seeing America support a gang of vicious murderers in the Middle East? Are you sick of political hacks spending your tax dollars on genocide for Arabs abroad and genocide for White people at home? Are you fed up with integration, pollution, treason in the streets, forced busing, nigger crime, and Watergate-style corruption in high places? Are you ready for a new kind of politics, for a political party which stands up for the interests of the White majority in America?[8]

No argument is made. In its place, the party simply offers a list of subjects likely to raise the blood pressure of the people to whom their advertisement is directed. Since the goal of the ad is to move people to action, to take out their checkbooks, and to find a stamp, getting people's blood moving may, in some cases, be an effective strategy, however dishonorable.

The Appropriate Use of Emotion

Does this catalog of the nefarious ways emotion is misused mean that emotion has no place in argumentation? In the purely formal sciences—in symbolic logic, for instance, and mathematics—reasoning may proceed bloodlessly, in supreme isolation from emotion. But most people take the trouble to make arguments because they want to influence the way other people think or act. Since people are moved by their feelings as well as by reasons, feelings will often be a part of a successful argument. Moreover, arguments have results in the real, emotion-laden world: people go to jail or to the theater, businesses invest in new equipment or they do not, parents send money, politicians become presidents and start wars or make peace. An honest argument will acknowledge that accepting or rejecting the claims it offers may have sad or happy consequences.

The point is not to avoid emotion in argument. The point is to avoid using emotions as unacknowledged substitutes for argument. When emotional appeals pretend to be arguments, they traffic in deception. But emotional appeals can be used honestly in at least two ways to make a sound argument more effective.

First, effective speakers will want to learn about the feelings their audiences bring to the discussion. That information might help guide the speaker to select the most effective reasons from among an array of sound reasons available to support the conclusion. For example, a neighborhood improvement group could encourage people to paint their houses because it will make the neighborhood more beautiful or because it will increase the resale value of the homes; these are both good reasons. A speaker might emphasize one over the other, based on what kind of reason is most likely to make a difference to the audience.

Second (and this gets trickier), sometimes, in some contexts, emotional responses are good reasons. The distinction between motivation to act and reason to act may be convenient for academics, but it is a distinction that sometimes breaks down in real life. Terror may be a very good reason for running away. Love may be the only justification needed for forgiving. Pity may be the very best reason for sharing. In cases like these, the fallacy would be in denying that emotions count as good reasons.

7.4 WRITING ADS

People who make their living writing advertisements for cigarettes face a particularly forbidding challenge: there is no good reason to smoke and many good reasons not to. The same problem faces those who write ads for vodka, with the additional problem that all vodkas are chemically indistinguishable, and thus virtually indistinguishable in taste and smell.

1. Make a study of cigarette advertising or vodka advertising. Compare the ads that appear in different kinds of magazines: magazines directed to young people vs. magazines for the middle-aged or elderly, magazines directed to the rich vs. magazines for middle- and lower-income people, magazines directed to the well-educated vs. magazines directed to the not-so-well-educated. What appeals do you find? How do they differ? What seems to be the general strategy?

2. Design an advertisement to appeal to an unusual audience—royalists in eighteenth-century France, oil well firefighters in Kuwait, Cro-Magnon people, philosophy professors, pot-bellied pigs. Let your classmates speculate about who the intended audience is.

7.5 TIRED OF WHINING

Carefully examine each of the following passages for fallacies of relevance. For each:

a. Write the conclusion of the argument; if the conclusion is not explicitly stated, write the implied conclusion.

b. If the passage seems to offer a good argument, write "Good argument."

c. If the passage is fallacious, name the fallacy (or fallacies) and carefully explain where each fallacy occurs.

1.   TIRED OF WHINING

I'm tired of all those people whining about plans to build a prison outside of town. Prison overcrowding is a terrible problem right now, and criminals are being released onto the streets. Without a new prison, more people will be murdered, raped, robbed, wounded, maimed, and molested. When criminals cannot be locked in jails, children will have to be kept locked in their homes. Is this what the people want?

2.   From a paid political announcement:

. . . [T]he unborn baby is a . . . human being worthy of life. . . . At 9 weeks in the womb, the baby can bend its little fingers around an object placed in its hand. He or she . . . can suck its thumb and react to pain. The entire body is sensitive to touch, and the tiny baby can turn its head, curl its toes and fingers. The mouth can open and close, and might even smile. Since the vocal cords are completed, we are told that the baby would even cry if he could.

3.   An ad paid for by the Government of Puerto Rico:

Rum and Tonic. It's What's Happening
All across America, people are switching to Puerto Rican white rum because it's smoother than vodka or gin. [The rest of the ad shows pictures of people drinking rum and tonic in various pleasure-filled settings.]

4.   From a crudely printed "American Front" poster:

Whites Must Arm!

. . . [T]he American front recommends that white people in full compliance with all federal, state, & local laws governing purchase, carriage, and use of firearms obtain such weaponry as they deem may be necessary to their self-defense should anti-white hate speech and resultant violence occur in their neighborhoods, as it has recently occured [sic] in Los Angeles and other metropolitan areas . . .

IT'S A JUNGLE OUT THERE

Protect Yourselves! Protect Your Wives! Protect Your Children!

5. From the *New Scientist:*[9]

> . . . *[M]any American school children are encouraged by their teachers, by textbooks, . . . to conduct horrifying experiments on captive laboratory animals. . . . Small animals are whirled around in centrifuges until they either become paralyzed—or die. Others are launched, dangling precariously below home-made rockets to simulate space-flight conditions . . . At the high school of Our Lady of Good Counsel. . . , mice were starved in vitamin deficiency experiments. Elsewhere, goldfish were bathed in detergents and, for some inexplicable reason, rats poisoned with vodka. Splenectomies are being conducted by 15-year old school children in New York.*

6. Conversation reported by a student:

    He: Dad, let's go fishing down in the creek.
    Dad: We can't because I think it's illegal to fish above the bridge.
    He: Well, Dad, there are already a lot of people fishing the creek above the bridge, so it must be legal, right?

7. In the case of *Rochin v. California,*[10] police pumped a man's stomach against his will and over his objections. When they found drugs in the stomach contents, they used the drugs as evidence that he had broken the law. The California Supreme Court threw out the evidence (and thus the conviction) on the grounds that the police acted wrongly. Their reasoning:

The actions of the police are wrong because they "offend those canons of decency and fairness which express the notions of justice of English-speaking peoples." In other words, the actions were wrong because most English-speaking people think they are wrong.

8. From Shakespeare's *Julius Caesar*. Mark Antony, speaking over the bloody corpse of Julius Caesar, purportedly addresses the issue of whether or not Brutus killed Caesar for the good of Rome:

    > If you have tears, prepare to shed them now.
    > You all do know this mantle: , . . .
    > Through this the well-beloved Brutus stabb'd;
    > And as he pluck'd his cursed steel away,
    > Mark how the blood of Caesar follow'd it; . . .
    > This was the most unkindest cut of all;
    > For when the noble Caesar saw him stab,
    > Ingratitude, more strong than traitor's arms,
    > Quite vanquish'd him: then burst his mighty heart;
    > And . . . great Caesar fell. . . .
    > I come not, friends, to steal away your hearts:
    > I am no orator, as Brutus is;
    > But, as you know me all, a plain blunt man,
    > That love my friend . . .
    > For I have neither wit, not words, nor worth,
    > Action, nor utterance, nor the power of speech,
    > To stir men's blood: I only speak right on; . . .[11]

9. From "How to Defuse the Population Bomb," *Time*:[12]

    > *Except for thermonuclear war, population growth is the gravest issue the world faces over the decades immediately ahead. In many ways it is an even more dangerous and subtle threat than war, for it is less subject to rational safeguards, and less amenable to organized control. It is not in the exclusive control of a few governments, but rather in the hands of hundreds of millions of individual parents. The population threat must be faced—like the nuclear threat—for what it inevitably is: a central determinant of mankind's future, one requiring far more attention than it is presently receiving.*

10.   As anyone who knows anything about Central Europe will tell you, Central Europe in 1992 is a powder keg, potentially more explosive than it has been at any time since the days immediately preceding World War I.

● ●

Fallacious Appeals to the Credibility of the Writer

The credibility of a writer, the extent to which the writer deserves to be believed, is a second problematic element of persuasive argument. Suppose you stop a person on the street to ask about a train. The person responds to your question by saying: "This train stops in Berkeley." When is that statement true? "This train stops in Berkeley" is a true statement when this train stops in Berkeley. It is a true statement because truth depends on a matching, or correspondence, between a statement and the state of affairs that the statement describes. Given this *correspondence theory of truth,* whether a statement is true or false is completely independent of who makes the statement.

It follows that any argument that purports to prove that a claim is true or that it is false by reasons referring exclusively to the person making the statement runs some risk of committing a fallacy of relevance. An argument that purports to prove that a claim is *true* solely on the basis of the *credibility* of the person making the claim risks a fallacy called the fallacious *appeal to authority.* An argument that purports to prove that a claim is *false* solely on the basis of the *mendacity* of the person making the claim risks a fallacy called the *ad hominem* argument.

This is a matter for careful judgment, however. While a statement is true or false regardless of who gives it voice, in the absence of other information, the degree of confidence you should have in its truth may well depend on who uttered it—the train's ticket taker, for example, or a tourist from Atlanta. The important issue is how likely it is that the person is speaking the truth. And that is a function of the person's competence—how much he knows—and the person's trustworthiness—how likely he is to speak the truth as he knows it.

Fallacious Appeals to Authority

An authority is an expert, a person who has acquired considerable training or experience in a given field and is thus especially competent in that area. It is a fair guess that much of what you believe is based on the testimony of authorities. That $E = mc^2$, that Pluto is beyond Neptune, that Thomas Aquinas debated how many angels can dance on the head of a pin, that excessive alcohol destroys the liver—you do not believe these claims on the basis of your own observations. You believe them because the information came to you from authorities, people whose business it is to know these things. Authorities are necessary, and often reliable, sources of information.

The appeal to authority becomes problematic only when the "authority" is not authoritative for either of two reasons: because she is speaking outside her field of expertise or because he has reasons for not telling the truth. In cases like these, the appeal to authority is fallacious.

First is the issue of competence. The appeal to authority is fallacious when the expert is cited as an authority outside of his field: Lee Iacocca, the head of Chrysler Corporation and the honorary chair of the Statue of Liberty celebration, speaking on immigration policy; Frederick Forsyth, author of *The Day of the Jackal,* testifying to the mechanical excellence of his Rolex watch; Albert Einstein, physicist extraordinaire, speaking about theology. The specialization of knowledge that makes it necessary to rely on expert opinion also narrows the field in which a person can be expert, increasing the risk of a fallacious appeal to authority.

Second is the issue of trustworthiness. Why would an authority ever lie or misrepresent facts? Money, maybe. Experts have discovered that their credibility is a valuable commodity, and they are known to sell out to the highest bidder. Industries, for their part, are willing to pay top dollar to a person who can convince Congress or the public or the insurance company or a jury of the truth of claims favorable to that company. One management expert put it this way:

> *Regulatory policy is increasingly made with participation of experts, especially academics. A regulated firm or industry should be prepared, whenever possible, to co-opt these experts. This is most effectively done by identifying the leading experts in each relevant field and hiring them as consultants or advisors, or giving them research grants and the like. This activity requires a modicum of finesse; it must not be too blatant, for the experts themselves must not recognize that they have lost their objectivity and freedom of action.* [13]

Thus, an expert on radiation biology, for example, can supplement his pitiful professorial salary by signing on with Eco-Destruct Chemical Company to assure the public that there are no health problems associated with the nuclear waste dump next to the middle school. But that very act compromises his credibility and invites a fallacious appeal to authority.

Twenty years ago, critical thinking textbooks took pains to alert students to the dangers of assuming that a person was lying just because she had a special (often financial) interest in making people believe what she was saying. This was called an *ad hominem circumstantial* fallacy and, indeed, it is a fallacious argument. But such is progress that it is now more important to alert students to the dangers of automatically believing the testimony of an expert-for-hire.

• •

7.6 DISAGREEMENT AMONG EXPERTS

Here is a pair of articles about Philippine healers who claim to remove tumors without surgery.

1. For each article, identify the person or persons cited as experts. How inclined are you to trust each of those people? What information in the article affects their credibility?

2. Which article contains the most claims you are least inclined to believe? Rewrite that article, omitting and adding details to make it more credible.

PHILIPPINE HEALERS: FAMILY TELLS OF MIRACLES

If it hadn't been for the "miracle" work of Philippine healers, Henry Beier said he doubts he would be alive today.

Beier has had emphysema for many years and says the healers have suppressed that ailment.

"I owe my life to those boys in the Philippines," he said.

Henry and his wife Leona, daughter-in-law Linda Beier and grandson Tony are convinced that the Philippine healers perform miracle cures.

Sitting around the kitchen table of their North Salem home recently, the Beiers explained.

They told of traveling to the islands and having several physical problems corrected or vastly improved at the hands of Philippine "healers." . . .

The healers plunge their fingers into a person's body and remove tumors or other problem growths, they said.

They offered color photos and vivid testimonials as evidence of their healing. . . .

[In return for the treatments, patients are charged a] $150 "suggested donation" for each person treated by the healers. They do not charge a fee, Leona said. . . .[14]

PHYSICIAN SAYS HEALERS ARE QUACKS, ROBBERS

A Salem surgeon dismisses the work of Philippine healers as "quackery, fakery and robbery."

Dr. Slate Wilson said treatment by the healers can be detrimental, particularly for cancer victims who delay effective treatment while seeking a "miracle cure."

He spoke for the Marion–Polk Medical Society.

"There are a lot of things we can't cure, and that is where these [healers] come in.

"These people don't do anything. It's robbery. A lot of time, people get all their stuff (medical care) done here and off they go over there, and they get better.

"To my knowledge, there have been no faith healers since Christ." . . .

Wilson said he personally knew Steve McQueen, who died of cancer, and cited his case as an example. . . .[15]

• •

Ad hominem Arguments

The fallacy called *argumentum ad hominem* urges that a claim is false because it came from the lips of a scoundrel. This is exactly the opposite of the fallacious appeal to authority, which urges that a claim is true because it came from the lips of a person of high credibility. Psychologically, the disdain that readers feel for writers rubs off on the claims that writers make, so that readers can sometimes be lured into hating an idea by the hatred they feel toward the person who utters it. Such an argument is fallacious since a claim's truth is logically independent of the person who makes it. If grass is green, then "grass is green" is equally true when uttered by cannibal/murderer Jeffrey Dahmer and by Mother Theresa.

The Latin phrase for this fallacy, *argumentum ad hominem,* translates, "argument to the man." The argument addresses the character of the person making the claim rather than the quality of the argument. When you suspect that an argument has slipped into *ad hominem,* look closely to see what the subject of the dispute has become. Do the reasons give information about the issue or about the person making the argument? If the reasons focus on the arguer, chances are good that they are not relevant to the truth of the conclusion.

Historically, some of the fiercest *ad hominem* arguments have been directed against women. The following example is an excerpt from a newspaper article written in 1853. It ostensibly argues against women's suffrage, but the author admits in the first paragraph that he never will engage the issue; instead, he turns the readers against the idea, by turning them against the women who gave it voice:

> We saw, in broad daylight, in a public hall in the city of New York, a gathering of unsexed women . . . publicly propounding the doctrine that they should be allowed to step out of their appropriate sphere, and mingle in the busy walks of every-day life, to the neglect of those duties which both human and divine law have assigned to them. We do not stop to argue against so ridiculous a set of ideas. . . .
>
> It is almost needless for us to say that these women are entirely devoid of personal attractions. They are generally thin maiden ladies, or women who perhaps have . . . found it utterly impossible to induce any young or old man into the matrimonial noose . . . and are now endeavoring to revenge themselves upon the sex who have slighted them. . . . [Some of them,] having been dethroned from their empire over the hearts of their husbands, for reasons which may easily be imagined, go vagabondizing all over the country, boring unfortunate audiences with long essays lacking point or meaning and amusing only from the impudence displayed by the speakers in putting them forth in a civilized society. They violate the rules of decency and taste by attiring themselves in eccentric habiliments, which hang loosely and inelegantly upon their forms, making that which we have been educated to respect, to love, and to admire, only an object of aversion and disgust.[16]

In this diatribe, the author claims that the women have no credibility because they lack two of a woman's greatest assets—attractiveness and a man.

If anyone should think that such *ad hominem* arguments are relics of a distant Neanderthal past, here is the same basic *ad hominem* abuse, this time from a talk show host in 1991:[17]

> "Femi-Nazis" argue for equal rights on the job because "they can't get a man and their rage is one long PMS attack." . . .
>
> All these femi-Nazis out there, demanding their right to abortion as the most important thing in their life, never ever having to worry about having one anyway. Because who'd want to have sex with them?

Two subspecies of *ad hominem* arguments deserve special attention. The first is simple abuse, the degeneration of argument into name-calling and innuendo. The second is the *you're another* fallacy, a specialized kind of name-calling.

Abusive ad hominem *Arguments*

The everyday use of the word *argument,* meaning "a fight or angry dispute," differs fundamentally from the specialized use of *argument* to mean "give reasons to support a conclusion." In the case of abusive *ad hominem* arguments, the distinction blurs. In abusive *ad hominem* arguments, angry insults substitute for reasons.

Both disputants resort to *ad hominem* abuse in this exchange between Malcolm X and Gordon Hall, an "expert on extremist organizations."[18]

Malcolm:	Don't ever accuse a black man [who is] voicing his resentment and dissatisfaction over the criminal condition of his people [of inciting violence.] You have to indict the society that allows these things to exist. And this is where I differ with Dr. Hall.
Hall:	We differ in many places, Malcolm.
Malcolm:	This is another one of the many places where we differ, Dr. Hall.
Hall:	Well, in a sense, didn't Hitler also talk about different points of view, didn't he say that conditions existed, and didn't he also incite?
Malcolm:	I don't know anything about Hitler, I wasn't in Germany. I'm in America. . . . You spend too much of your time, Doctor, trying to investigate —
Hall:	I rarely ever mention you, Malcolm, you're hardly worth mentioning . . . I lectured all over the state of Alabama, when you had nothing to do with the Muslims or anybody else.
Malcolm:	Did you have on a white sheet? Did you have on a white sheet?

The dispute does not shed much light on the important issues raised, even though sparks are flying.

Tu quoque ad hominem *Arguments*

Another frequently heard *ad hominem* argument is a variation on the same theme. Instead of generic your-type-makes-me-puke abuse, the abuser focuses on one particular aspect of the person making the argument: He has the exact fault or shortcoming that he is accusing another of having. Here is an example of a *tu quoque ad hominem* argument:

> Many political commentators consider the 1989 presidential campaigns to be among the most negative ever. When asked how the nastiness of his campaign tactics could be reconciled with his vision of a "kinder, gentler nation," President Bush responded, "I think both sides got into that sort of thing somewhat. They started it."[19]

Here is the pattern of argument: A says to B, you are guilty of C. Instead of responding to the charge directly, B says to A, you also are guilty of C. The response is entirely irrelevant. Whether the charge is true of one person is logically independent of whether it is true of the accuser. This fallacy is called, in Latin, *tu quoque;* in English, "you're another." Like other *ad hominem* arguments, it avoids the real issue and focuses negative attention on the person making the argument. Instead of the general attack in *ad hominem* arguments, it returns the same charge. "I'm one? Well, you're another."

When the U.S. Senate was reviewing the nomination of Judge Clarence Thomas to the Supreme Court, members of the Senate Judicial Committee, including Senators Edward Kennedy, Joseph Biden, and Alan Cranston, closely questioned Judge Thomas, probing deeply for any flaws in his character or record. Right-wing supporters of Judge Thomas did not respond directly to any charges against the judge. Instead, they broadcast a TV commercial showing photos of Kennedy, Biden, and Cranston over the caption, "WHO WILL JUDGE THE JUDGE? How many of these liberal Democrats could themselves pass ethical scrutiny?" All three senators have been deeply scarred by scandals—Chappaquiddick, plagiarized speeches, and the Keating Five banking scandal, respectively. Judge Thomas called the ads "vicious," but there is no doubt that they were effective.

Like other fallacies of relevance, the "you're another" fallacy is psychologically persuasive. People who are open to criticism themselves may not have the moral standing to criticize others. But this does not mean that their claims are false. Who makes a claim is irrelevant to the truth or falsehood of that claim.

• •

7.7 A FAMILY AFFAIR[20]

Families and other close social units (friends, roommates, co-workers, prison inmates, etc.) are notorious contexts for fallacious reasoning and personal attack. Who better to use your sleaziest personal rhetoric on than those near and dear? Even a casual look at a typical family in action will yield a variety of fallacious arguments, particularly *ad hominem* arguments.

For the period of this unit, stay alert for *ad hominem* and related fallacies in use by your family or those closest to you. Keep a notebook of these chintzy moves and, with each entry, describe the context of the fallacy, the effectiveness of the fallacy, and the response elicited by the fallacy. Provide some analysis to substantiate your claim that an actual fallacy was committed. Discuss the difference you see between the logical defectiveness and the psychological effectiveness in the fallacy. Finally, in discussing the response that was actually made, speculate on an effective and logically sound response that might be made in that case.

7.8 *AD HOMINEM* ARGUMENTS ON TRIAL

The relevance of a person's character to that person's trustworthiness is a central, problematic issue in trials for rape. As legislators and courts struggle to decide whether information about the victim's past is relevant to the trial, more and more women charge that unscrupulous defense attorneys are destroying them on the witness stand, turning the trial into a persecution of the victim rather than a prosecution of the accused.

Here are excerpts from the sections of a Proposed Federal Criminal Code (1971) dealing with rape. Write a one-page argument for or against including section 3 in the final draft of the legislation. Make use in your argument of the concepts of abusive and *tu quoque ad hominem* arguments.

§ 1641. Rape

(1) Offense. A male who has sexual intercourse with a female not his wife is guilty of rape if:

(a) he compels her to submit by force, or by threat of imminent death, serious bodily injury, or kidnapping, to be inflicted on any human being; . . .

§ 1645. Corruption of Minors

(1) Offense. A male who has sexual intercourse with a female not his wife or any person who engages in deviate sexual intercourse is guilty of an offense if the other person is less than sixteen years old and the actor is at least five years older than the other person. . . .

(3) Sexually Promiscuous Complainants. It is an affirmative defense to prosecution under sections 1645 . . . that the alleged victim had, prior to the time of the offense charged, engaged promiscuously in sexual relations with others.

The Appropriate Role of Credibility in Argumentation[21]

It is very difficult to separate one's feelings about the writer from one's feelings about the writer's ideas. This may be why, to write an effective argument that succeeds in influencing readers' beliefs and actions, a writer must earn the reader's trust.

One kind of credibility, sometimes called *external credibility,* has to do with the prestige or credentials that writers bring with them to the page. In our culture, advanced education, a prestigious job, publications, and a public reputation generally give writers an aura of respectability and trustworthiness that encourages readers to believe what they have to say.

The other kind of credibility, *internal credibility,* has to do with the trust that is built up between writers and readers. The writers who are most successful at establishing this kind of rapport generally have these characteristics: (1) they know the people who make up their audiences—their backgrounds, their values, their hopes and fears—and they write to that audience. (2) They are scrupulously honorable in their arguments, avoiding fallacies conscientiously and acknowledging their own biases and unresolved doubts. (3) They know what they are talking about and construct their arguments carefully so that each argument demonstrates their competence. (4) They present their arguments clearly and directly so that the readers have no reason to suspect that the writers are trying to mislead them. A careless argument will leave readers confused as to whether a writer is incompetent or corrupt; either one quickly destroys credibility.

• •

7.9 THE COWBOY AND HIS COW

In "Free Speech: The Cowboy and his Cow," Edward Abbey argues that cattle should not be grazed on public land.* Abbey has some fun with his subject; his essay is a gold mine of *ad hominem* arguments.

1. Circle and label every instance of *ad hominem* arguments you can find.

2. Then have some fun yourself. Imagine yourself to be a cowboy who heard Abbey's speech. Write a one-paragraph response, using the

* From ONE LIFE AT A TIME PLEASE by Edward Abbey. Copyright © 1978, 1983, 1984, 1985, 1986, 1988 by Edward Abbey. Reprinted by permission of Henry Holt and Company, Inc.

same "argumentative" techniques that Abbey uses. Then, write a well-reasoned response.

> *You may have guessed by now that I'm thinking of criticizing the livestock industry. And you are correct. Western cattlemen are nothing more than welfare parasites. They've been getting a free ride on the public lands for over a century, and I think it's time we phased it out. . . .*
>
> *Anyone who goes beyond the city limits of almost any Western town can see for himself that the land is overgrazed. . . . Of course, cattlemen would never publicly confess to overgrazing, any more than Dracula would publicly confess to a fondness for blood. Cattlemen are interested parties. Many of them will not give reliable testimony. Some have too much at stake: their Cadillacs and their airplanes, their ranch resale profits and their capital gains. . . .*
>
> *I've suggested that the beef industry's abuse of our Western lands is based on the old mythology of the cowboy as natural nobleman. I'd like to conclude this diatribe with a few remarks about this most cherished and fanciful of American fairy tales. . . . The rancher (with a few honorable exceptions) is a man who strings barbed wire all over the range; drills wells and bulldozes stockponds; drives off elk and antelope and bighorn sheep; poisons coyotes and prairie dogs; shoots eagles, bears, and cougars on sight; supplants the native grasses with tumbleweed, snakeweed, povertyweed, cowshit, anthills, mud, dust, and flies. And then leans back and grins at the TV camera and talks about how much he loves the American West. Cowboys also are greatly overrated. Consider the nature of their work. Suppose you had to spend most of your working hours sitting on a horse, contemplating the hind end of a cow. How would that affect your imagination? Think what it does to the relatively simple mind of the average peasant boy, raised amid the bawling of calves and cows in the splatter of mud and the stink of shit. . . .*
>
> *Especially critical of my attitude will be the Easterners and Midwesterners newly arrived here from their Upper West Side apartments, their rustic lodges in upper Michigan. Our nouveau Westerners with their toy ranches, their pickup trucks with the gun racks, their pointy-toed boots with the undershot heels, their gigantic hats. And, of course, their pet horses. The instant rednecks. . . .*
>
> *I love the legend too, but keep your sacred cows and your dead horses out of my elk pastures.*[22]

•••••••••••••••••••• Sophistries ••••••••••••••••••••

In ancient Greece, the Sophists were itinerant teachers of argumentation and oratory. Although many Sophists were truly "men of wisdom," they taught a dangerous and addictive craft. As time went on, some Sophists began to specialize in teaching students not how to argue well and truly but how to dazzle their opponents and win arguments by, in Plato's words, "making the worse appear the better reason." The profession fell into deep disrespect as some Sophists became the personal and well-paid trainers for the lawyers, politicians, and other shady operators who lived in ancient Athens. Soon the word *sophist* came to mean a dishonest persuader, and *sophistries* came to refer to the dirty tricks of the trade. A *sophistry* is an argumentative move that is unfair, that cheats, that takes unearned advantage, and thus deceives, quite intentionally.

Sophistries take place during debate or some other argumentative exchange. The sophistries themselves are located in the transition from one debater to the other, in the relation between their arguments. Thus, sophistries are moving, hidden targets, difficult to detect and thus often effective. Four sophistries are explained here: straw arguments, red herrings, shifts in the burden of proof, and proof substitutes.

Straw Arguments

An argument built out of straw is insubstantial and weak. Like a scarecrow that looks like a farmer but is only a shirt stuffed with straw with a hat on top, a straw argument is less than it appears to be, and so it is easy to knock down. Just as it would be easier to win a fight with a scarecrow than with a farmer, it is easier to destroy a straw argument than the real argument offered by an opponent.

This is how the straw argument works. A *straw argument* intentionally misinterprets an opponent's argument and replaces it with a weaker one. Then it proceeds to destroy the weaker argument and concludes that the real argument has been demolished. Thus, it involves this sequence of argumentative moves:

A makes an argument.

B recasts A's argument, substituting a weaker argument.

B refutes the weaker argument.

B claims that A's argument has been refuted.

Consider, as an example, this quarrel. Wife: "I would like to take my vacation this spring in Greece." Husband: "I don't know why you want to go around the world spending millions of dollars. We aren't rich people. Forget Greece." This is not fair. The wife never said that she wanted to go around the world or that she wanted to spend millions of dollars and, in fact, she knows perfectly well that she couldn't afford to do so. The husband constructs and then refutes the silly argument, and then dismisses the real argument as if it had itself been refuted.

Although straw arguments are often subtle and thus difficult to detect, there are two giveaways. A straw argument always starts with some sort of restatement of the claim defended in the original argument, and the restated claim is usually more extreme, less qualified than the original.

A: I don't believe in executing murderers. When you execute a person for having committed a murder, there is no way that person can be rehabilitated. His life is simply wasted.

B: It would be a dangerous world if society just let its murderers go free, as you advocate . . .

But in fact, that is not what A advocated. So, when B proceeds to justify the conclusion that murderers should not go free, he will not have touched A's argument in any way; at the same time, he will convey the strong impression of having destroyed it utterly.

• •

7.10 BUILDING ARGUMENTS OF STRAW

Here is a dialogue from which certain parts have been omitted. You supply the missing parts, writing a piece of dialogue to match the logical description that you find inside brackets. Your professor may ask you to read your dialogue to the class.

A: I have been listening to the words of rap music and, frankly, I am appalled and disgusted. I think that local governments should forbid the sale of rap music that incites violence against women.

B: [Insert a straw argument here.]

A: I think we need to worry about the effect that this music has on impressionable people. [In this space, back up that claim with a fallacious appeal to pity.]

B: Freedom of speech is an important issue here.

A: [Respond with an abusive *ad hominem;* insert it here.] I would also point out that some of the so-called lyrics in these rap songs are truly racist, using racist epithets and putting down people because of their race.

B: [Respond with a *tu quoque ad hominem*; insert it here.] You should be careful about censoring music because the censorship may increase sales rather than decrease them. After all, the news stories would be great publicity.

A: [Add an appeal to fear.]

B: [Add a fallacious appeal to authority.]

Red Herrings

When the tide of an argument has turned against a debater and all her best arguments are washouts, when she is really at sea, an unscrupulous debater will sometimes make use of a *red herring*: She will simply change the subject. A red herring is a sophistical argumentative move in which a debater diverts the attention of an opponent by addressing related but irrelevant issues.

> Heavyweight boxer Mike Tyson was indicted on one count of rape, two counts of "deviate sexual conduct" and one count of confinement for actions that allegedly occurred during the 1991 Miss Black America Pageant. Tyson denied the charges, saying, "I love women . . . My mother is a woman."

Of course, Tyson's mother is a woman. Everyone's mother is a woman. But did Tyson rape a contestant?

Everyone knows the advantages of changing the subject when the conversation threatens to lead in a dangerous direction: "So, how's the weather?" The red herring is a sophisticated variation on this theme. In contrast to the clumsy reference to the weather, a sophistical red herring will have three characteristics. First, it will divert attention to a subject that is closely related to the issue at hand. The diversion needs to be so subtle that the opponent does not realize that the subject has been changed. Second, the most effective red herrings are phrased as questions. When the opponent responds to the question—as is only polite—she will be cooperating in her own distraction. Third, the most effective red herrings presume that the conclusion has already been established. Here is an example:

> The House Banking Committee grilled Clark Clifford, president of First American Bank, on his involvement with the corrupt Bank of Credit and Commerce International (BCCI). They asked him how he could have been unaware that he was involved with a criminal enterprise. Clifford's response: "The BCCI fooled the Bank of England, didn't it?"

The shift in subject is subtle, the question draws the opponent into the new subject, and a conclusion is subtly assumed though never stated: "There is nothing surprising or unlikely about being duped by a corrupt agency."

The odd name of this sophistry is said to come from old English hunting traditions. In order to train a hunting dog to follow a scent faithfully, undistracted by other enticing smells, the English dragged a gunny sack of ripe red herring across the trail the hounds were following. Any dogs that yielded to the temptation to follow the red herring were beaten with sticks. That taught them.

Shifting the Burden of Proof

A third kind of sophistry abuses the rules by which the burden of proof is assigned.

The Burden of Proof

It is very difficult to prove that a claim is true or false. This is why the legal system pays such close attention to who bears the burden of proof. The *burden of proof* is the obligation to make a case for your own claim. In the criminal law, the state has the burden of proof. Before it can impose a punishment, the state must prove that the accused is guilty as charged; if it cannot make the case successfully, the defendant goes free. Again, an employee who believes she has been unfairly discriminated against bears the burden of proving the discrimination; the employer does not have to prove that his acts were justifiable.

But, while judges and legislators struggle mightily to assign burden of proof exactly and predictably, rules about the burden of proof in ordinary discourse are somewhat muddled and are thus often abused. Generally, the burden of proof works this way:

1. The person who makes a claim bears the burden of providing evidence that it is true.

2. The person upon whom a claim is urged does not have the burden of showing that it is false.

Shifting the Burden of Proof

The sophistry called *shifting the burden of proof* violates the protocol explained in the list above. The arguer states a claim and then assumes that the claim will be taken as true unless the opponent can prove that it is false. "There is life after death, and I challenge anyone to prove to me that there is not." That no one comes forth with evidence to refute the claim is emphatically not evidence that the claim is true (especially given the difficulty of communicating with the dead).

Here is another example, this one from the *Bulletin of the Atomic Scientists*:

> By mid-November . . . domestic support for Operation Desert Shield was slipping. A November 20 CBS/New York Times *poll concluded that a majority of Americans would not go to war in the Gulf to protect access to Middle East oil, but would support a military effort to prevent Iraq from getting the bomb. A few days later President Bush asserted that Iraq might be [only] months away from nuclear weapons.*
>
> *[After the war, serious questions were raised about how immediate the threat of nuclear capacity really was.]*
>
> *In testimony before the Senate Armed Services Committee . . . William R. Graham, a defense consultant, turned the tables on those who would challenge Gulf hawks to show evidence that Iraq was close to possessing nuclear weapons. "Instead of asking for proof beyond a shadow of a doubt that Iraq has [nuclear weapons]," Graham said, "we should ask ourselves this question: Why wouldn't Iraq, under Saddam Hussein, have done these things?"*[23]

No fair. President Bush claimed that Iraq was perilously close to having nuclear weapons; he bears the burden of giving evidence that the claim is true. It is not the responsibility of his opponents to show that it is false.

The Fallacious Appeal to Ignorance

In a very limited number of situations, the *absence of information* can serve as evidence for a claim. You have already seen one such setting: In criminal courts, the absence of information establishing guilt is decisive evidence that the defendant is innocent. Are there others? Perhaps the medical laboratory. If blood tests show no evidence of the HIV virus, the patient is judged to be uninfected. Usually.

But in most situations, you cannot win an argument by default; the absence of information cannot provide grounds for believing that a claim is true. Consider the Shroud of Turin, the blood-stained strip of linen that some believers claimed was the actual shroud that wrapped the crucified Christ. "The shroud is Christ's shroud," believers argued, "because it has a set of stains on it from the oils used to annoint Jesus' face. We know the stains are from Jesus' face because scientists have not been able to explain how else they might have got there."

This is an example of a fallacious appeal to ignorance. A *fallacious appeal to ignorance* is an argument in which some kind of ignorance—the absence of counterevidence or the lack of an explanation—is cited as evidence for a claim. In the case of the Shroud of Turin, those who claim the shroud is Christ's bear the burden of proving that it is. Disbelievers do not bear the burden of proving that it is not.

If you are a faithful reader of supermarket tabloids, you will have read articles like this:

TATTOOED WOMAN KIDNAPPED BY SPACE ALIENS

A woman found wandering dazed in Dallas last Thursday was most likely the victim of a bizarre kidnapping by space aliens, experts say. She had no memory at all of the events of the previous day, and she was marked by a strange tattoo.

"I was just walking to work, minding my own business," said the victim, Mrs. Josephine Markess, "and the next thing I know, it's today and I've got this tattoo on my biceps. I can't figure it out. Must have been spacemen. But why choose me?"

Extensive psychological tests, including hypnosis, failed to turn up any ordinary explanation of her memory loss. Family and friends report that Mrs. Markess was missing for an entire 24-hour period.

Dr. Robert Kinos, head of the UFO Research Institute, said, "We can't substantiate any other explanation. All the signs point to an intergalactic kidnapping."

The tattoo, medical examiners say, was made by a substance and process that doctors cannot identify. The tattoo is a circle with a line across it. "It looks a lot like Saturn," said a local tattoo artist, who would not give his name.

This is a classic example of an appeal to ignorance, because the only evidence that the woman was kidnapped by aliens is that nobody can figure out what happened. Is it the experts' job to figure out why Mrs. Markess couldn't remember Wednesday? No, it is the obligation of those who make extraordinary claims to come up with extraordinary evidence to back them up.

• •

7.11 CONCLUSIONS BASED ON NO INFORMATION
What conclusions can safely be drawn from each of the following statements?

1. From an argument against removing violent toys from the market: "There is absolutely no evidence, academic or, most important, practical, that playing with soldiers has any bad influence on later behavior."

2. A doctor's 1988 testimony in favor of proposed legislation to put warning labels on alcohol bottles: "No study has of yet been done to suggest . . . that a safe amount of alcohol exists for all pregnant women."

3. In the unending debate about whether or not Shakespeare really wrote Shakespeare's plays, members of the anti-Shakespeare camp question "not merely whether Shakespeare had enough education to be the author of the plays but whether he had any education at all. [One researcher] was the first to discover that there is no record of Shakespeare's having attended the Stratford grammar school."[24]

4. In Ecuador, an amateur archeologist found pieces of pottery, exactly matching Japanese pottery dating back 5,000 years. The find convinced Smithsonian Museum archaeologists that "someone from Japan sailed to South America five millennia ago. . . . [But skeptics believe that Japanese did not reach the New World before Columbus did]. They note the absence of other evidence pointing to a Japanese presence in prehistoric Ecuador."[25]

5. *On the Senate floor in 1950, Joe McCarthy announced that he had . . . 81 case histories of persons whom he considered to be Communists in the State Department. Of case [number] 40, he said, "I do not have much information on this except the general statement of the agency that there is nothing in the files to disprove his Communist connections."[26]*

• •

7.12 REAGANESQUE SOPHISTRIES

During presidential debates, soon-to-be president Ronald Reagan was asked this question: Do unborn children have a right to life? Here is his response.

I believe that until and unless someone can establish that the unborn child is not a living human being, then that child is already protected by the Constitution, which guarantees life, liberty, and the pursuit of happiness to all of us. And I think that this is what we should concentrate on, is trying — I know there were weeks of testimony before a Senate committee, there were medical authorities, there were religious — there were clerics there, everyone talking about this matter of pro-life. And at the end of all that, not one shred of evidence was introduced that the unborn child was not alive.

Discuss to what extent this response does and does not illustrate the straw argument, the appeal to ignorance, and the fallacious appeal to authority.

Proof Substitutes

The fourth kind of sophistry, the last in this list of the subtle tricks of the rhetorical trade, is the proof substitute. A *proof substitute* is a phrase that suggests that the arguer is in possession of evidence for a claim, even though that evidence is not actually cited. "Recent studies have shown . . ." "No one denies that . . ." "Informed sources say . . ." Some people refer to such phrases as *assurances*, pledges inspiring confidence that the evidence is available. These are all shorthand ways of saying, "The evidence is right here in my back pocket, but you might as well just trust me since it would be a lot of trouble to pull it out." Here are some more proof substitutes:

It is obvious that . . .

Doctors tell us that . . .

Research reveals that . . .

There is no question that . . .

Each of these phrases substitutes for the evidence.

When these phrases are used, they are probably used for a reason. A good reason is to save time and simplify discussion; when there really is decisive, familiar evidence for a claim, dragging it all out again is boring. But it is deceptive to use proof substitutes when there is, in fact, no such proof. Honorable authors use proof substitutes honestly and sparingly.

7.13 A ONE-ACT PLAY

Working as a group, your assignment is to write a short one-act play (two to four pages) in which the characters commit as many different fallacies as you can fit in. Even if you are not a playwright, this is not as difficult as it seems. All you need to do is to reflect on some experience you have had in which some drama and lots of (attempted) persuasion occurred. You may use one of the scenarios described below, or you may decide on your own subject matter.

1. Your group is throwing a Roaring Twenties party. One of the guests shows up in a glorious, full-length raccoon coat. Another guest thinks the coat is immoral and disgusting and does not hesitate to say so. What discussion ensues?

2. The university president holds an open meeting with students every Friday afternoon. This afternoon, he has just announced that tuition costs for most students will double, starting the following year. The students are deeply unhappy and go to the open forum to confront the president with their arguments that tuition should not be increased. What happens then?

3. The school board of a small California town is meeting to consider a new program to make the elementary school curriculum fully bilingual so that students can choose to learn in English or in Spanish. The new program is highly controversial. What happens at the school board meeting?

4. A dorm meeting has been called to discuss the issue of whether smoking (or other-sex overnight visitors or alcohol) should be allowed in the dorm. What is said?

Perform your play in front of the class. Then, lead a class discussion during which you call on the students to identify and explain the faulty logic, and the good logic, displayed in your play. Be ready to do an instant replay of a piece of dialogue so that its logic can be more closely scrutinized.

Drawing Conclusions from Dishonorable Arguments

This chapter has cataloged many of the things that can go wrong when a writer disregards or distorts the implicit principles of argumentation. There are lessons in this list for both writers and readers.

As a writer, resist mightily the temptation to fall back on these shortcuts. Using a quick and dirty argument may conserve a little time and thought but, at the same time, it will damage the credibility you are trying to build with your audience. Fallacious arguments display disrespect for readers, who are assumed to be too stupid to know the difference between an argument and a cheap substitute; and they display disrespect for the truth. Neither one is a foundation for a good relationship with readers.

If you do find yourself falling back on trickery and fallacious arguments to defend a claim, one of two things has happened. It is possible that the claim cannot be defended on any legitimate grounds. Fallacious arguments are most useful to people who are in the business of defending indefensible claims. If you cannot think of any good reasons why others should believe your claims, then maybe you should abandon the beliefs yourself. On the other hand, it is possible that the claim can be defended legitimately but you have not figured out how. If this is the case, it is best to go back to the library and get the information you need to do the job right.

As a reader, you are in a better position to defend yourself against being duped by deceitful arguments if you are acquainted with the variety of fallacies at large in the world and can call them by name. When you recognize that the arguments offered in support of a claim are fallacious, you realize that you have, literally, no reason to believe that claim. By the same token, you have no reason to disbelieve it, since even shabbily or dishonorably supported claims can be true. Often, the best response to fallacious reasoning is suspended judgment.

• •

7.14 DISCOVERY[27]

The realm of informal fallacies is a living one; the ways of bad reasoning and duplicitous persuasion are limitless. Thus, the opportunity remains for individuals to discover and catalog new fallacies.

Look critically into an area in which you have some expertise (your major, profession, hobby, interest, etc.), and find a form of argument that is psychologically persuasive but logically defective. Explain it fully in a short report (approximately 250 words), giving examples, analysis, and possible responses. Give your new fallacy a good title.

• •

7.15 TURKEYS

Carefully examine each of the following passages for fallacies of relevance and sophistical argumentative moves. For each:

a. Write down the conclusion of the argument; if the conclusion is not explicitly stated, write the implied conclusion.

 b. If the passage seems to offer a good argument, write "Good argument."

 c. If the passage is fallacious and/or sophistical, name the fallacy or sophistry, and carefully explain where each occurs.

1. Okay, so I'll tell you why I think that the arguments of Animal Rights protesters are ridiculous. This is a true story. A passenger car ran into a truck carrying turkeys and seventy-eight turkeys got loose on the highway. People rounded them up and took them to the Humane Society. The Humane Society decided to donate the turkeys to homeless people, so they could have a nice meal on Thanksgiving. But no; the Animal Rights freaks said this was cruel to the turkeys. So they took the turkeys and found them all foster homes, and they promised they would cook a nice Thanksgiving dinner for the homeless people. What do you think the Animal Rights people served? You got it—turkey.

2. Mother: When I ask my son to pick up his toys, he says, "I love you, Mom." I ask him again and he says, "My leg hurts Mom. I need a Band-Aid." He still hasn't picked up his toys![28]

3. Kid: Who ate all my candy?

 Other kid: I didn't have any.

 Kid: Well you must have, because if you didn't, who did?

4. College student: I was playing basketball with friends, and one of my friends told another that he didn't do a lay-up right. He told him that Michael Jordan does his lay-ups the other way, so he should too.

5. The Iranscam scandal centered on accusations that then-President Ronald Reagan or the members of his administration had sold arms to Iran in order to finance an illegal war in Nicaragua.

 During the investigation, President Reagan was asked whether he had approved of a shipment of arms to Iran on August 8, 1985. He claimed he simply did not remember whether he had given approval or not. "I think it's possible to forget," Reagan told his audience. "I'd like to ask one question of everybody. Everybody who can remember what they were doing on August 8, 1985, raise your hand."

 No one did.

6. Kid: I want to go to the movies because all my friends are going.

 Parent: If all your friends jumped off a bridge, would you go do that too?

7. Parent: I'm sorry, you can't go to the dance tomorrow night because we have a family dinner.

   Offspring: How come you never let me go anywhere?! I hate it when you do that to me. You are ruining my life.

8. One friend [referring to the Indian women in the film *Dances with Wolves*]: Women do most of the work in the Indian villages.

   Other friend: So, you are saying that men don't do any work. Well, I'll have you know that the men are the ones who kill the buffalo and other sources of meat. So, HA!

9. Sociologist and father: I have no problem letting my kids play with toy guns and G.I. Joe. There just isn't any evidence that playing with soldiers causes violent behavior or influences future behavior in any way. There isn't any evidence reported in the academic journals, and I haven't seen any problems in my own children. So I think it's good for my kids to enact war adventures with their toys.

10. TV doctor: I'm not a real doctor, but I play Dr. _____ on TV. When I get a headache, I use _____ .

Notes

1. Lewis Carroll, *Alice's Adventures in Wonderland* (1895).
2. Illustration by Ann Page from FACES OF THE ENEMY by Sam Keen. Illustration copyright © 1986 by Anne Page. Reprinted by permission of HarperCollins Publishers Inc.
3. The exercise was developed by David Acklin, Oregon State University. Used with permission.
4. *Instructions for sellers in Exercise 7.3*: You have listed a car for sale and have had a few inquiries, but no offer has been high enough yet. An acquaintance of yours has contacted one of his friends who is interested in the car. The interested party, in turn, has apparently asked your acquaintance to act as a buyer. The acquaintance also mentioned something about $4,000 as a price limit but was not sure. The book value of the car is $1,800. This is your first meeting.
5. Adolf Hitler, *Mein Kampf*, ed. John Chamberlain et al. (New York: Reynal and Hitchcock, 1939), pp. 232–233, 237–238.
6. John Bierman, "Competing for Charity," *World Press Review* magazine (July 1991), p. 9. Excerpted from *Maclean's* newsmagazine of Toronto.
7. Press Reports on Soviet Affairs (May 18, 1984). Advanced International Studies Institute, Suite 1122 East–West Towers, 4330 East–West Highway, Washington, DC 20014.

8. Quoted in S. Morris Engel, *Analyzing Informal Fallacies* (Englewood Cliffs, N.J.: Prentice-Hall, Inc., 1980), p. 142.

9. John Hillaby, "Sanctified Torture," *New Scientist* (January 9, 1969), pp. 69–70.

10. *Rochin* v. *California,* 342 U.S. 165 (1952).

11. William Shakespeare, *Julius Caesar*, Act III, Sc. II.

12. "How to Defuse the Population Bomb," *Time* (October 24, 1977), p. 93.

13. See Chapter 13: "Beyond the Dreams of Avarice: The Sciences," in Charles T. Sykes, *Profscam* (New York: St. Martin's Press, 1988), p. 229.

14. Lewis H. Arends, Jr. "Philippine healers: Family tells of miracles," *Statesman-Journal* (Salem, Oreg.), (November 23, 1981), p. 7C. Copyright © 1981 Statesman-Journal. Used by permission.

15. "Physician says healers are quacks, robbers," *Statesman-Journal* (Salem, Oreg.), (November 23, 1981), p. 7C. Copyright © 1981 Statesman-Journal. Used by permission.

16. *New York Herald* (September 7, 1853); reprinted in Judith Papachristou, *Women Together* (New York: Alfred A. Knopf, 1976), p. 45.

17. From radio talk-show host Rush Limbaugh, quoted in Richard Corliss, "A Man. A Legend. A What?!" *Time* (September 23, 1991), pp. 65–66.

18. Malcolm X, *Malcolm X Speaks: Selected Speeches and Statements,* ed. George Breitman (New York: Pathfinder, 1965), pp. 191–192. Reprinted by permission of Pathfinder Press. Copyright © 1989 by Pathfinder Press and Betty Shabazz. Used with permission.

19. Thanks to Jon Dorbolo for this example.

20. Thanks to Jon Dorbolo for this exercise.

21. Karyn C. Rybacki and Donald J. Rybacki, *Advocacy and Opposition* (Englewood Cliffs, N.J.: Prentice-Hall, 1991), pp. 200–202.

22. Edward Abbey, *One Life at a Time, Please* (New York: Henry Holt, 1988), pp. 12–19. Copyright © 1988, Henry Holt. Used with permission.

23. David Albright and Mark Hibbs, "Hyping the Iraqi Bomb," *The Bulletin of the Atomic Scientists* (March 1991), p. 27. From the BULLETIN OF THE ATOMIC SCIENTISTS. Copyright © 1991 by the Educational Foundation for Nuclear Science, 6042 South Kimbark, Chicago, Ill. 60637, USA. A one-year subscription is $30. Used with permission.

24. Tom Bethell and Irvin Matus, "Looking for Shakespeare," *The Atlantic* (October 1991), p. 66.

25. Donald Dale Jackson, "Who the heck *did* "discover" the New World?" *Smithsonian* (September 1991), p. 78.

26. From a news report quoted in S. Morris Engel, *Analyzing Informal Fallacies* (Englewood Cliffs, N.J.: Prentice-Hall, Inc., 1980), p. 157.

27. Thanks to my creative colleague, Dr. Jon Dorbolo, for this exercise idea.

28. Thanks to student Micky Shields.

29. *Instructions for buyers in Exercise 7.3:* One of your co-workers has listed a car for sale. A friend of yours has asked you to approach the seller and act as his buyer. He wants this car very much and has saved $4,000, which he has given you to purchase the vehicle. The best part is that you get to keep the extra money that you don't spend on the car. Try to get the best price you can for the car. You have already called the seller, and this is your first meeting.

CHAPTER 8

Clarity in Argument

The philosopher Ludwig Wittgenstein claimed that "everything that can be thought at all can be thought clearly. Everything that can be said can be said clearly." This may be so, but the fact remains that much of what is thought is not thought clearly, and much of what is said is perfectly opaque. Some obscurity can be accounted for by carelessness or lack of art. However, much obscurity (perhaps some of Wittgenstein's) is the result of great care and considerable skill, for obscurity has its uses. Some of its uses are benign, as when a writer uses the suppleness of language to weave poetry that is rich in possible meanings. Some of its uses are dangerous, as when a demagogue twists the meaning of words to make people believe what is not true.

This chapter focuses on the deception and misunderstanding that can result from obscurity. It explains two sorts of fallacies built on the shifting shadows and smoke screens that conceal the truth. The first are the *fallacies of ambiguity,* which arise when words are used in imprecise or shifting ways. The second are *fallacies of presumption,* which occur when a conclusion is presumed to be true and no evidence is offered. In fallacies of presumption, conclusions are the hidden, ghostly companions that arrive uninvited and unrecognized, quietly slipping in through the back door. To help you avoid both kinds of fallacies, the chapter ends with suggestions for how to increase the clarity of the sentences and arguments you write.

• •

8.1 THE JUNK COLLECTOR, PART II

As you begin to study this chapter, start a collection of fallacies of ambiguity that you encounter in your everyday life. Put together a collection of the "best" examples you find, carefully and accurately labeled and explained. The collection could take the form of a portfolio—an unbound notebook containing photocopies, transcripts, ads, and so forth; a bulletin board display; a videotape; an audiotape; or some other presentation of the results of your search. Find a way to share your collection with the class.

• •

• • • • • • • • • • • • • • Fallacies of Ambiguity • • • • • • • • • • • • • •

Language is a complex, imprecise means of communication. Words shift in meaning. Meanings shade off into confusion. Sentences start in one direction, then drift off in another, or fade away entirely. Interpretations pile up in woven layers of significance that change depending on who is listening and how closely and under what circumstances. For writers and readers, this is a fact of life.

Some writers take advantage of the richness of meaning in words to weave poetry or prose that is effective because it is ambiguous. Consider the Bible:

> *The Lord is my shepherd, I shall not want. He maketh me to lie down in green pastures: he leadeth me beside the still waters.* [1]

Or consider Luci Tapahonso's poem about the birth of her daughter:

> *The first born of dawn woman*
> *slid out amid crimson fluid streaked with stratus clouds*
> > *her body glistening August sunset pink*
> *light steam rising from her like rain on warm*
> > *rocks* [2]

Some writers struggle to tame language, to make language serve their need to communicate ideas clearly and unambiguously.

> This limited warranty does not extend to any products which have been damaged as a result of accident, misuse, abuse, or as a result of service or modification by anyone other than the manufacturer or an authorized dealer.

On the other hand, some writers exploit the suppleness of language in order to confuse or mislead readers with prose that is essentially empty. For example, when asked to comment on Congressmen who wrote bad checks, Rep. Robert Michael said, "There frankly are members who I agonize over . . . who find themselves today in the kind of situation where they have to explain why their accounts show they were overdrawn."

In this section, you will see how language that is vague or ambiguous or equivocal can be used in the service of deception.

Vagueness

Like a vagrant who wanders aimlessly from place to place, mindlessly humming no particular tune, *vague* language is imprecise, indefinite, having no particular meaning. Most vagrants are harmless, as is much vague language. But vagueness can become deceptive when people are misled by a vague account into thinking that they have actually heard something meaningful and are thus led to draw a conclusion that is unsupported.

Vagueness is rooted in either of two kinds of failure. One is the failure to be precise. The other is the failure to be complete.

Imprecision

Vagueness can result from using words that have no precise or definite meaning. It can result from addressing issues that are general and indefinite. And it can result from giving information that is less specific than the situation calls for.

There is safety in vagueness. Vague claims are seldom false because they say so little. So, vagueness is a tool used by people who would like to give the appearance of saying something but who would also like to avoid the risk that goes along with making and defending claims. There is also deception in vagueness. Vague claims do not correct misconceptions, and they can occasionally give false impressions.

Children know how to hide the truth behind vagueness. *Where were you? Out. What did you do? Stuff. Where did you go? Around. Who were you with? Friends.* This is vagueness with a vengeance. The parents hear nothing alarming; should they conclude that they need not be alarmed? Politicians know the usefulness of vagueness. Here is President George Bush expressing his view on the place of women in the military:

> *Part of the great success was the fact we have an all volunteer army, and part of the all—the military. And part of the rationale is people will have more say in what they*

want to do. So a mother—I want to be a part of this. I can respect that and understand it.[3]

Here is President Bush, again, responding to a reporter's question about whether the 1990 budget agreement was a mistake:

Total mistake—policy, political, everything else. . . . Policy because it simply did not do what I thought—hoped it would do: control this—control—get this economy moving. There were some good things about it, so I can't say—shouldn't say—total mistake. But it was—spending caps is good, getting the spending caps is good, keeping the government going as opposed to shutting down for whatever number of days it would have taken—that was good. But when you have to weigh a decision, in retrospect—have the benefit of hindsight—I would say both policy and politically, I think we can all agree that it's drawn a lot of fire.[4]

Is there anything here that anyone would be disposed to argue with? Not really, because there is not much of anything here at all. The deception comes when listeners are led to believe that they have actually heard the President's views on women in the military or have actually been informed about the 1990 budget agreement.

And advertisers have learned to use vagueness to mislead with impunity. Consumers are wrong if they think they have learned the source of Crater Lake Pure Spring Water, after they have read this "explanation":

Not far from the icy depths of Crater Lake located in the southern Oregon Cascades stands our bottling facility which we believe produces the purest and most refreshing water available. From this unspoiled beauty, we have captured the best nature offers. If you are visiting Crater Lake, please stop in and visit our plant.[5]

Argument analysis is the greatest enemy of vagueness because, when a reader comes up empty in a search for a vague argument's central claim and the reasons to back it up, the essential hollowness of the "argument" is exposed.

Incomplete Comparative Claims

Vagueness results also from unfinished comparative claims. A comparison is usually between two things: *This* is bigger/smaller/louder/coarser than *that.* So, unless both *this* and *that* are specified, a comparison is incomplete. Because they

..ake incomplete comparisons, many advertising campaigns are based on claims that are empty. A bank offers ten percent more interest. A cake mix is richer. The pleasure lasts longer. A butter-like substance is better. A car is 700 percent quieter (on the outside than on the inside, federal investigators discovered). One-third more. One-third less. More flavor. Less cholesterol. Half the calories. Less tar.

For very good reason, no savvy corporation will allow its fallacious advertisements to appear in a logic textbook. But students do not need to be hit over the head with specific examples, to know that any conclusions a consumer draws on the basis of incomplete comparisons like these will be based on no information at all.

8.2 VAGUENESS IN THE LAW

For better or for worse, vagueness is an important element in legal decision making. In small groups, answer these questions:

1. After a traffic accident, the plaintiff was transferred to a hospital by ambulance. The hospital gave her several blood transfusions that saved her life. One of the transfusions contained AIDS-contaminated blood. This plaintiff contracted AIDS. She sued the hospital. According to the laws in her state, she will win the suit if she was injured by a "product," but she will lose if she was injured by a "service."[6]
   a. Decide the case, and justify your decision with an argument. Be sure your argument specifies the meaning of "service" and "product."
   b. How did you decide what those words mean? Where did you go for information? Did your definitions determine the outcome of the case, or did your intuitions about the fairest decision determine your definitions?

2. In a 1931 case, *McBoyle v. United States,* a man named McBoyle was convicted of transporting a stolen airplane across state lines in violation of the National Motor Vehicle Theft Act. That act states that the words *motor vehicle* "shall include an automobile, automobile truck, automobile wagon, motor cycle, or any other self-propelled vehicle not designed for running on rails." Boyle appealed his conviction, arguing that an airplane is not a vehicle.
   a. Is an airplane a vehicle? How do you know?
   b. Rewrite the National Motor Vehicle Theft Act so that it defines *motor vehicle* so clearly that cases like this will never arise again.

c.   From the point of view of the prosecutor, list three major disadvantages to vagueness in laws. List three major advantages to vagueness in laws. Do the same from the point of view of the defendant.

3.   Common law holds that a person is responsible for the "reasonably foreseeable" consequences of his or her negligent acts.

a.   In which of these cases do you think the defendant should be held responsible, because the damage that resulted from his acts was "reasonably foreseeable"?

Wood v. *Pennsylvania RR.* A train traveling around 60 miles per hour, with a negligent failure to give any warning, struck a woman standing in the railroad right of way. She was hurled about 195 feet and struck the plaintiff, injuring him. The plaintiff was a prospective passenger standing at the station platform. The defendant is the railroad company.

St. Louis-San Francisco RR v. *Ginn.* An engine of the railroad negligently started a fire on the right of way adjacent to Ginn's property. Ginn, upon discovering it, took his tractor and plowed a furrow along his property line to prevent the spreading of the fire. He had just completed the furrow and was driving the tractor to a safe place so he could return and help put out the fire when he struck either a root or a limb with the tractor. It flew up, striking him in the face and injuring him.

b.   What does "reasonably foreseeable" mean? How do you know?

• •

Ambiguity

A word or statement is ambiguous when it has more than one meaning. Ambiguity results in a kind of obscurity that presents risks and problems somewhat different from those posed by vagueness. Language is *vague* when it is blurry and ill-defined like a photo taken by a photographer who forgets to focus the camera. Language is *ambiguous* when it has two or more meanings like a double exposure taken by a photographer who forgets to advance the film.

A *fallacy of ambiguity* is committed when the double meaning of a word or statement in an argument misleads the reader. There are two sorts of fallacies of ambiguity, corresponding to the two general causes of ambiguous prose. A sentence might be ambiguous because the sentence itself is awkwardly or incorrectly constructed. Ambiguity from this source is called *amphibole*. Alternatively, a sentence might be ambiguous because its meaning turns on a word that has more than one meaning. Ambiguity from this source is called *equivocation.*

Amphibole

When a picture can be "seen" more than one way, it is visually confusing:

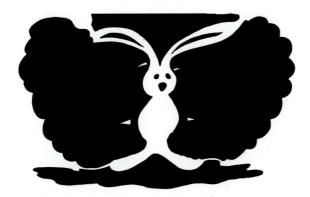

This could be a picture of a rabbit, or, if you turn the page 180 degrees, a picture of two women's faces; it all depends on how you look at it.[7] An *amphibole* is a sentence that is verbally confusing because it can be understood in more than one way. Because of awkwardness or grammatical error in the way the sentence is written, an amphibole shifts from one meaning to another depending on how the reader "looks" at it. All these sentences are amphibolous:

> For Sale: Desk for lady with curved legs and large drawers.
>
> The researchers brought in thirty-five salamanders to do an experiment in the lab.
>
> Come in today for your inoculation against measles which the clinic will give you free of charge.
>
> Wagging his tail, the little boy was enthusiastically greeted by his dog.

Is it the desk or the lady who has the curved legs? Will the salamanders don tiny white coats and do the experiment, or will they be on the receiving end of this research? Who wants to get the measles? How can the little boy wag his tail? The sentences do not answer these questions. The resulting confusion can lead to error; people may decide against an inoculation on the grounds that they do not want measles, even for free.

Equivocation

Many words have more than one meaning. They speak, one might say, with two equal (*equi-*) voices (*vocation*). For example, *buckle* can mean "fasten together" or "fall apart." *Dust* can mean "to sprinkle with powdery dirt" or "remove powdery dirt."[8] *Mad* can mean "angry" or "insane." *Right* can mean "correct" or "a protected liberty."

The *fallacy of equivocation* occurs during argument when an equivocal word shifts meaning on its way from premises to conclusion. Since the meaning has changed but the words have not, the shift in meaning is disguised and is therefore potentially misleading.

> The street people shouting and demonstrating in front of the mayor's house are really *mad.* So, they should be institutionalized.
>
> I have a *right* to believe anything I want. So, anything I believe is *right.*

When the central concept of an argument shifts meaning, the argument splits up the center and falls in two pieces. Look closely at the above argument about rights. (See also the diagram at the bottom of this page.) The premise is entirely plausible; freedom of conscience, the liberty to believe anything one chooses to believe, is an important natural right. Preserving that meaning of *right,* it would follow that anything a person believes is his right. But it does not follow that all one's beliefs are right, when *right* is taken to mean "correct." People have a right, after all, to believe perfect inanities.

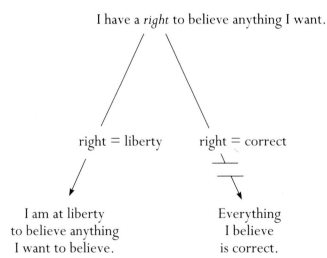

I have a *right* to believe anything I want.

right = liberty   right = correct

I am at liberty
to believe anything
I want to believe.

Everything
I believe
is correct.

8.3 ADVERTISING EQUIVOCATIONS

1. For each of the following ads, identify the equivocal word and summarize the implied argument, making clear how the equivocal word changes meaning from premises to conclusion.

a. To believe our blades can shave below your skin,
you need a clear-cut explanation.

b. UNITED [Van Lines] . . . even our name
begins with YOU.

c. What separates the champions from everyone else
is the ability to duplicate their achievements.
XEROX

d. NO ONE CAN MATCH OUR FARE
TO ANCHORAGE
The food served on Alaska Airlines is anything but "airline food."

e. [Picture of a Subaru in traffic,
stopped at the top of a very steep hill.]
SUBARU. WHAT YOU'VE ALWAYS NEEDED
IN THE CLUTCH.

f. GENERAL ELECTRIC
We bring good things to life.

g. [Ad for ALL detergent]
Lifts out tough stains
to get clothes "all clean."

h. The following ad is reprinted with permission of Martlet Importing Company.

The best Canadian on ice.
Molson *is* Canadian beer.

i. Why every kid should have an Apple after school. . . .
To learn more about it, visit any authorized

> Apple dealer. Or talk to your own computer experts.
> As soon as they get home from school.

j.   The new HP Paint Jet XL300 lets you make
a splash without getting soaked.

2.   Design and write an advertisement for some product. Make your advertisement's effectiveness turn on an equivocation. Your professor may ask you to post your ad on the classroom wall.

• •

8.4 AMBIGUITIES IN THE DAILY NEWS

1.   These are real headlines from real newspapers.[9] Name and precisely explain the source of the confusion in each (vagueness, amphibole, or equivocation, or all of the above). Then, rewrite the headline to avoid the ambiguity (and spoil the fun). The first one is done for you as an example.

a.   "EPA Moves to Slow Ruin" (*Knoxville News Sentinel*)

> Equivocation: The headline authors probably intended the word *slow* to be read as a verb meaning "reduce the speed of." But it could be read as an adjective meaning "not fast."

> Clearer: "EPA Moves to Delay Ruin"

b.   "Hemorrhoid Victim Turns to Ice" (*Milwaukee Sentinel*)

c.   "Owners Responsible for Biting Canines" (New Albany, Indiana, *Tribune*)

d.   "Lebanese Chief Limits Access to Private Parts" (*The Daily Iowan*)

e.   "Condom Faults Could Lead to Dating Policy" (*Courier News*, Charleston, North Carolina)

f.   "Hundreds Vaccinated After Death" (Wayahachie, Texas, *Daily Light*)

g.   "Arafat Appeals to Bush" (*Charlotte Observer*)

h.   "Large Part of North Carolina Fit for Disposal" (*The Raleigh Times*)

i.   "Acid Rain Linked to U.S. Emissions by Reagan's Aide" (*The New York Times*)

j.   "Vatican Unveils Procreation Position" (Corsland, New York, *Standard*)

    k.   "Lower Age for Elderly Opposed" (Norwalk, *Connecticut Hour*)

    l.   "Navy Finds Dead Pilots Flying with Hangovers" (*The Washington Post*)

2.   The following sentences are actual statements that people made on the accident reports for their insurance claims.[10] Rewrite each to make its meaning clear.

    a.   I had been driving my car for 40 years when I fell asleep at the wheel and had an accident.

    b.   I was on my way to the doctor with rear end trouble when my universal joint gave way, causing me to have an accident.

    c.   I collided with a stationary truck coming the other way.

    d.   I pulled away from the side of the road, glanced at my mother-in-law and headed over the embankment.

    e.   The driver and the passengers then left immediately for a vacation with injuries.

8.5 HE OR SHE

The impersonal *he* in English was used for centuries to mean "he or she." For example, in the sentence, "When a judge decides to overturn a precedent, he must justify his decision with a cogent argument," the word *he* may as well refer to Sandra Day O'Connor as to Clarence Thomas. The authoritative stylist E.B. White, coauthor of *The Elements of Style,* wrote in 1979:

No one need fear to use "he" if common sense supports it. The furor recently raised about "he" would be more impressive if there was a handy substitute for the word. Unfortunately, there isn't.

1.   Do you agree with E.B. White that using *he* to refer to both men and women is not something to lose sleep over? Or do you believe the double usage is an invitation to equivocate in ways that have unfortunate results? Explain in a carefully written paragraph.

2.   Conduct an experiment on your friends or family, and summarize the results in a short (250-word) essay. The experiment is designed to test this hypothesis: For the majority of people, the word *he* means "a male person," not "a male or female person." The prediction is that the research subjects will write about a male person when asked to "describe what the lawyer was wearing when he argued the case in the state Supreme Court" more frequently than the subjects will write

about a male person when the request is phrased in a gender-neutral way: "Describe what the lawyers were wearing when they argued the case in the municipal court." What results did you find? What conclusion do you draw? What does that tell you about the wisdom of using *he* as a neutral pronoun?

Fallacies of Presumption

The logical way to convince a person that a claim is true is to offer good reasons for believing that it is true. The fallacies of presumption offer a cheap imitation of a logical argument. In a fallacy of presumption, no reasons are offered at all. The conclusion is simply smuggled in. This can be achieved by carefully selecting words to evoke an emotion that would lead a person to accept a claim without evidence, as is done by *emotive language;* by selecting words that hide the emotional content of a concept, as in *double speak;* or by selecting facts to give a false or misleading impression, as in *slanting.* Or it can be done by simply presuming that the conclusion is true, as in *complex questions* and *circular reasoning.*

The Fallacy of Emotive Language

People use language to do many different jobs. One thing people do with language is convey information. "The house is next to the street" communicates the news that the house is next to the street. This function is called the *cognitive function* of language, referring to "cognition," coming to know or understand. But people do much more with words than this; people use words to ask questions, to lie, to flirt, to guess, to warn, to sing, to goad, and to evoke emotions. In the context of a Western, for instance, "This town ain't big enough for the both of us" may convey information (this is a small town), but it is more likely to evoke emotion (fear), express aggression (I'm a tough character), and encourage action (take the next stagecoach out of town). Consider the multiple functions of a sentence like "I'll still respect you in the morning."

The *emotive function* of language is the power that language has to change people's feelings. Words that convey a positive feeling along with the information they impart are called *eulogistic.* Words that carry along a negative feeling are called *dyslogistic*. For example, about an intoxicated person, one could say eulogistically, "He is certainly jolly tonight," or one could say dyslogistically, "She is falling down drunk." About an abortionist: "She is a doctor who facilitates free choice," or "He is a murderer." About people who keep their money to themselves: "He is careful with his money," or "She is stingy." Congress substituted eulogistic for dyslogistic language in 1947 when it changed the name of the War Department to the Department of Defense.

This double functioning of words, this piggybacking of emotion on meaning, offers temptations to a person who wishes to accomplish the goals of argument—to influence a person's actions or beliefs—without the use of reasons. A fallacy called *the fallacy of emotive language* occurs when the emotive content of words is used surreptitiously to establish a claim without the use of evidence.

Advocating the death penalty for convicted multiple murderer Jeffrey Dahmer, a letter writer's primary tool was emotive language:

> The insanity plea is nuts; psychotic murderers should lose this easy way out. The only response that a civilized nation can make to the rape, murder, and cannibalism perpetrated by that insect, Jeffrey Dahmer, is immediate pesticide.

The fallacy consists of using language carefully selected to make readers respond negatively to the insanity plea and to Dahmer instead of giving relevant reasons why readers should believe that the insanity plea should be abolished. *Easy way out.* Is life confined in an insane asylum an easier way out than immediate and painless death? *Insect.* Can any human being be drummed out of the human race? What rights do convicted murderers have that insects do not? *Pesticide.* Is spraying a cockroach with poison the same as executing a criminal? All these arguable points are drowned in the rich stew of emotion created by the choice of words. The writer may or may not be correct, but he has not provided any reasons that would help a discerning reader make that judgment.

• •

8.6 ADDING EMOTION

Below is a list of sentences written in language that is as neutral as could be managed. For each underlined word, substitute another word or phrase, so that the revised sentence carries a strongly positive or negative emotional load. The first one is done for you as an example.

1. Does that flag still fly over the United States?

    Positive: Does that star-spangled banner yet wave o'er the land of the free and the home of the brave?

    Negative: Is that old rag still flapping over the capitalist empire?

2. The justices of the United States Supreme Court announced today their decision that arresting officers must advise suspects of their rights.

3. The actress's home was featured on the television show, "Lifestyles of the Rich and Famous."

4. The senatorial candidate is a Harvard graduate, the parent of three children, and a consistent opponent of increased taxes.

5. The student received an average grade on the multiple-choice examination, and therefore was not admitted to medical school.

6. Two people died in the nuclear accident, and 176 were hospitalized with injuries.

7. The dog bit the mail carrier and, so, its owner had to have the dog killed.

8. The woman complained to the waiter that there was a fly in her soup.

Doublespeak

The fallacy called *doublespeak*[11] is the exact opposite of the fallacy of emotive language. Emotive language *adds* an emotion to a relatively neutral concept. Doublespeak *hides* the very real emotional content of a concept by using a word that is shorn of its emotional load. Doublespeak uses *euphemisms,* inoffensive words that substitute for words that are indelicate or painful: *terminate* instead of *kill, unconsenting intercourse* instead of *rape, demonstration* instead of *riot.* In an article about the Pentagon's use of doublespeak, the fallacy is described this way:

Doublespeak—whether jargon, euphemisms, or bureaucratese—is not a slip of the tongue but a conscious use of language as both a tool and a weapon. It is language that conceals or manipulates thought. It makes the bad seem [not so bad], the unpleasant appear . . . at least tolerable.[12]

The end result is deception, deception brought about by the careful selection of words that hide the truth.

● ●

8.7 CIVIL DEFENSE DRILL

1. Below is a vocabulary list from the lexicon of the Pentagon and a list of ordinary language translations. Match each doublespeak word with its translation. The answers are in note 13 at the end of this chapter.

Doublespeak:

_____ 1. Service the target
_____ 2. Vertically deployed antipersonnel device
_____ 3. Revenue enhancement
_____ 4. Universal obscurant
_____ 5. Impacted on the ground prematurely
_____ 6. Forcible ejection of the internal bomb components
_____ 7. Unplanned rapid ignition of solid fuel
_____ 8. Hard landing
_____ 9. Target-rich environment
_____ 10. Ambient noncombatant personnel
_____ 11. Interdictional nonsuccumbers
_____ 12. Resources control program
_____ 13. Predawn vertical insertion
_____ 14. Peacemaker
_____ 15. Radiation enhancement device
_____ 16. Incontinent ordinance

Translations:
   a. To malfunction and blow up, as a bomb
   b. Neutron bomb
   c. Kill
   d. Enemy troops who survive bombing
   e. Bomb
   f. First stage of Pershing missile ignited on the ground, killing three soldiers and injuring sixteen

g.   1983 invasion of Grenada
h.   New taxes
i.   Refugees
j.   MX missile, built to deliver nuclear warheads
k.   Soviet Union
l.   Poisoning vegetation with Agent Orange
m.   Smoke used in smoke bombs
n.   Flew out of control and crashed into three pieces
o.   Fatal crash, as of a helicopter
p.   Bombs that accidentally fall on civilians

2.   Write a paragraph in which you describe a wartime event, using at least five terms of Pentagon doublespeak.

Slanting

Doublespeak and the misuse of emotive language are often two parts of a larger form of persuasion that goes by the name of *slanting*. Slanting is the effort to influence the beliefs of an audience, not by presenting them with cogent reasons but by the careful selection of facts and choice of words. Without resorting to an out-and-out lie, a clever author can alter an audience's attitude toward an event by carefully choosing descriptive words, by including details that "slant" or distort the picture in the desired direction, and by excluding details that would tell a different story.

Contrast two accounts of the assassination of Malcolm X,[14] both published in *Newsweek* magazine, one immediately after the assassination in 1965, and the other in 1990. Both appear to be neutral accounts, just the facts. But the first presents a decidedly negative picture of Malcolm X, and the second presents a more laudatory view.

DEATH OF A DESPERADO

He was born Malcolm Little, an Omaha Negro preacher's son. Before he was out of his teens, he was Big Red, a Harlem hipster trafficking in numbers, narcotics, sex, and petty crime. He was buried as Al Hajj Shabazz, a spiritual desperado. . . .

Death came moments after Malcolm stepped up to a flimsy plywood lectern in Manhattan's Audubon Ballroom, just north of Harlem, to address 400 of the faithful and the curious. . . . The extermination plot was clever in conception, swift and smooth in execution. Two men popped to their feet in the front rows of wooden folding chairs, one yelling at the other: "Get your hands off my pockets, don't be messing with my pockets." . . . Heads swiveled, and as they did, a dark, muscular man moved toward the lectern in a crouch, a sawed-off shotgun wrapped in his coat. *Blam-blam!* A double-barreled charge ripped up through the lectern and into Malcolm's chest.[15]

REDISCOVERING MALCOLM X

He strode across the stage, tall and strong, with the bearing, as a friend would say later, of a shining black prince. It was a Sunday in Harlem and the faithful had gathered. He wore his conservative dark suit, the sort favored by accountants and be-bop men, and saluted the crowd with a greeting born of hope. "As-salaam alei-kum," "Peace be unto you." And the crowd answered "Wa-alei-kum salaam," "And unto you be peace." It was not to be. There was a disturbance in the rear of the Audubon Ballroom. . . . Three men came forward and, with a sawed-off shotgun and pistols, they killed Malcolm X.[16]

Can these two writers be describing the same murder? The same man? Is this a "Harlem hipster" or a "shining black prince"? Compare references to Malcolm's personal appearance: "Big Red" in the first article, "a conservative dark suit" in the second article. Compare the descriptions of the location: "a flimsy plywood lectern" in the first article, "Sunday in Harlem" in the second. Compare the words selected for quotation: "Get your hands off my pockets, don't be messing with my pockets" in the first article, "Peace be unto you. And unto you be peace" in the second. Compare "exterminate" to "kill." Both authors selected details and used words that tipped—slanted—the description toward the general emotional effect they were trying to achieve.

Slanting is partly a matter of what details are included. But it is equally a matter of what details are not included. So, slanting is often subtle and difficult to detect. Critical readers have to pay attention to what is not there, a difficult task under any circumstance.

• •

8.8 SLANTED DESCRIPTIONS

1. At the library, in two magazines or newspapers that might be expected to have different points of view, find descriptions of the 1991 videotaped beating of Rodney King by Los Angeles police officers. What slanting techniques do you find in those articles?

2. Find a pair of articles that describe another event from two different points of view. Write your own description of that same event, doing your best to write a perfectly neutral account.

• •

8.9 THE WAR PRAYER[17]

Choose two speech or drama majors to read these two prayers to the class.

Father of us all . . . watch over our noble young soldiers and aid, comfort, and encourage them in their patriotic work; bless them, shield them in the day of battle and the hour of peril, bear them in His mighty hand, make them strong and confident, invincible in the bloody onset; help them to crush the foe, grant to them and to their flag and country imperishable honor and glory —

Bless our arms, grant us the victory, O Lord our God, Father and Protector of our land and flag! AMEN.

* * *

O Lord our Father, our young patriots, idols of our hearts, go forth to battle — be Thou near them! With them, in spirit, we also go forth from the sweet peace of our beloved firesides to smite the foe.

O Lord our God, help us to tear their soldiers to bloody shreds with our shells; help us to cover their smiling fields with the pale forms of their patriot dead; help us to drown the thunder of the guns with the shrieks of their wounded, writhing in pain; help us to lay waste their humble homes with a hurricane of fire; help us to wring the hearts of their unoffending widows with unavailing grief; help us to turn them out roofless with their little children to wander unfriended the wastes of their desolated land in rags and hunger and thirst, sports of the sun flames of summer and the icy winds of winter, broken in spirit, worn with travail, imploring Thee for the refuge of the grave and denied it —

For our sakes who adore Thee, Lord, blast their hopes, blight their lives, protract their bitter pilgrimage, make heavy their steps, water their way with their tears, stain the white snow with the blood of their wounded feet!

We ask it, in the spirit of love, of Him Who is the Source of Love, and Who is the ever-faithful refuge and friend of all that are sore beset and seek His aid with humble and contrite hearts. AMEN.

Mark Twain wrote both prayers. When he was asked if he would publish them, he said, "No. I have told the whole truth in that, and only dead men can tell the truth in this world. It can be published after I am dead."

What do you think Twain was trying to accomplish with the contrasting prayers? What truth has he told? How can it be that slanting, a tool of deception, is here an expression of the truth? Explain the various ways in which Twain "puts a new slant" on the traditional prayer.

• •

Complex Questions

The complex question is another method by which people smuggle in conclusions without arguing for them. A *complex question* is a question phrased in such a way that the respondent, by simply answering the question, must accept a hidden assumption for which no reasons are given. This is the old "Have you stopped beating your horse" fallacy. Either answer ("Yes, I have stopped beating my horse," or "No, I have not stopped beating my horse") admits the truth of the hidden assumption ("I beat my horse") even though no evidence of horse beating has been offered. Complex questions are often called *loaded questions* because the question carries a conclusion along in its saddlebags.

Parents use complex questions as weapons against their children. "When are you going to grow up?" is impossible to answer unless the child admits she is not now grown up. Any answer to the question "Will you stop lying to me?" implies that the child has been lying. "Why don't you have any sense?" "What are you going to do when you get in a wreck?" "How could you do this to me?" Children often give as good as they get: "Why don't you ever trust me?" "Why do you always have to be so old-fashioned?" "Why do you hate me so much?"

But parents and children are not alone in asking complex questions. Critics: "Isn't it about time that reporters get back to basics and dig out a story instead of merely being mouthpieces for lobbyists?"[18] Presidential candidates: "Do we want a constitutional amendment of the kind that gets local politicians into the business of selecting prayers that our children must either recite in school or be embarrassed by, so that they have to ask to be excused?" Retail clerks: "Can I charge this to your account?"

In all these cases, a claim, usually an important claim, is presumed to be true. "Reporters are mere mouthpieces for lobbyists." "The proposed amendment lets local politicians force kids to pray their way." "You have a charge account, or need one." In each case, no evidence whatsoever is offered.

• •

8.10 A COMPLEX QUESTIONNAIRE

1. Locate and explain each fallacy of presumption in the following "Official Claim Certificate." Although this certificate is fictitious, its techniques are all too real.

NATIONAL OPINION SURVEY ON PUBLIC MORALITY

To claim your sweepstakes prize, all questions must be answered.

1. Were you included in the mail-in survey that reported 84% of all Americans think bearing a child out of wedlock is immoral?

    _____ YES   _____ NO

2. Do you want welfare mothers to be rewarded for having more children?

    _____ YES   _____ NO

3. What do you think is the cause of America's moral decline?

    _____ Lower church attendance

    _____ The collapse of the American family due to divorce and unwed mothers

    _____ Immoral behavior on TV and in the movies

    _____ Other

4. Would you support a candidate who did not believe in the family?

    _____ YES   _____ NO   _____ UNDECIDED

5. Will you make a tax-deductible contribution to the Save American Families Foundation (SAFF)?

    _____ YES, I'd like to help preserve basic American morality through SAFF's advertising campaign.

    _____ NO, I don't really care about American morality.

6.   If your answer is YES to question #5, how large a check have you enclosed?
     _____ $15 _____ $25 _____ $50 _____ $100 _____Other
     OFFICIAL CLAIM NUMBER 03045117

_____

2.   Design a fake opinion poll in which every single item is a complex question. It might, for example, pretend to ask opinions about Supreme Court issues: Should state governments be allowed to infringe citizens' constitutional rights by outlawing handguns? Should the Supreme Court allow American morals to deteriorate further by continuing to ban prayer in the public schools? Should a woman's constitutional right to control the use of her own body be curtailed by anti-abortion legislation?

Find a public place on campus and ask passing students to participate in your poll. Observe and report on their responses. How many students simply answered the questions and went on? How many objected to the questions? Of those who objected, what was the nature of their objection?

• •

Circular Reasoning

In 1861, the greatest natural philosophers of the time squared off to debate the hottest issues in anthropology, the relation between brain size and intelligence and the related question of which kinds of people are better than others. Anthropologist Paul Broca believed that brain size correlates directly with intelligence. He cited as evidence his observations that men have larger brains than women: Since men are smarter than women and since men have larger brains than women, he argued, the connection between IQ and cranial capacity is clear. How does Professor Broca know that men are smarter than women? That is easy: Men must be smarter than women because their heads are bigger and (a premise unstated but presumed) brain size correlates directly with intelligence.[19]

This is *circular reasoning,* a fallacy of presumption that occurs when the conclusion of an argument is presumed to be true and is used as a premise in an argument justifying that very conclusion. In other words, the conclusion does double duty, as conclusion and as premise. The conclusion is true because the premise is true, and the premise is true because the conclusion is true. In a diagram of the argument, the arrows would go in a circle, the circle of circular reasoning:

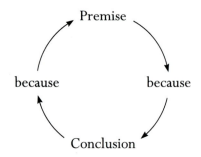

Beyond a doubt, Professor Broca's argument is valid, as are all circular arguments. Circular arguments are valid because their conclusions follow necessarily from their premises (since the conclusion is one of the premises). But circular arguments do not enlighten and do not provide good evidence for any claim. Anthropologists would do better to continue to study the brains of brilliant men and women, going first to Kansas City, where Einstein's brain rests in a jar on a shelf.

Circular arguments come in various degrees of sophistication and complexity. The most blatant circular arguments simply state the conclusion twice, disguising the repetition by gussying up the language the second time around.

> Polygamy should be against the law, since no state should allow women to share a husband.

> Capital punishment for the crimes of murder and kidnapping is justified because it is both legitimate and appropriate to put a person to death for having committed such hateful and inhuman acts.

> A is true because A is true.

In more complex instances of circular reasoning, like Broca's brain argument, the conclusion operates as an implied, unstated premise. The conclusion follows from the stated premises only if one also assumes that the conclusion is true.

Consider this dialogue between one person who believes that all people are basically selfish and another who believes that people often act out of love.

> In my opinion, all humans are basically selfish. The only motivation for any human act whatsoever is the expectation that the act will bring the actor pleasure.

Not so. Humans can be motivated by love. Think of the mother who sits all night by the bedside of a nauseated child. That cannot be explained as a selfish search for self-gratification.

On the contrary, the mother appears to be acting selflessly, but really she expects that, in the long run, she will be better off if she puts in a bad night with the child. If the mother didn't think that, she wouldn't do it, because people only act to benefit themselves.

If you tried to analyze the argument behind the claim that all acts are selfish, you would discover that the conclusion only follows from the premises if you assume that the conclusion is true. Here is the full circle: Since even a mother who appears to be acting out of love is acting selfishly, all human acts are motivated by self-interest; it is clear that the apparently selfless mother is really selfish because all human acts are motivated by self-interest.

Here is the argument in standard form:

All acts are motivated by self-interest.

Therefore, even a mother who appears to be acting selflessly is motivated by self-interest.

Therefore, all acts are motivated by self-interest.

· ·

8.11 THE END OF THE WORLD

Illustrate the circularity of the following passages by diagramming the argument implicit in each. Since major portions of the arguments are suppressed, you will need to supply many missing premises.

1. Don't believe her when she says she hates you. People don't tell the truth to someone they hate.

2. A group in Wisconsin became convinced that the world would come to an end at midnight on March 13, and a new world would come into existence. They sold their worldly goods and waited beside Lake Michigan. At twelve o'clock sharp, they raised their arms in exultation, welcoming in the new world. Skeptics pointed out to them that nothing had changed; the faithful were still standing there and the waves were still lapping at the shore and the stars were still moving in the heavens, just as they had done before midnight. The new world was an exact replica of the old, the faithful said; the old world has come to an end.

3. "Those who believe in God shall not perish, but shall have eternal life," said the preacher. "But preacher," a doubter said, "the members of your parish die at the same rate as the sinners outside your church." "That is because," the preacher replied, "the dead members of my parish are not true believers."

4. The fortune in a fortune cookie: Fortune cookies never lie.

5. Even though many people do not act in racist ways, everybody is really a racist. It's just that some people are better at hiding it than others are.

· ·

Obscurity in argument allows or encourages all these minor misunderstandings and serious deceptions, as well as many more uncataloged inconveniences. Just as pilots proceed cautiously and use all their instrumentation when the night gets foggy, critical thinkers should slow down and take advantage of their analytical skills when the prose starts to cloud up. Some pilots, it is worth noting, refuse to fly when visibility approaches zero.

· · · · · · · · · · · · · How to Write Clearly · · · · · · · · · · · · · · · ·

Writing is clear when a reader can easily follow the line of thought without mistaking the meaning intended by the author. There is no formula for clear writing. But a writer is more likely to write clearly when she knows what she wants to say, when she wants to say it clearly, and when she has mastered some of the basic principles of clear writing.

Remove the Blocks to Clear Writing

The murkiest writing seems to show up under one of two conditions: when the writer does not know what she is trying to say or when the writer knows exactly what he is trying to say but does not really want to say it, either because it is not entirely true or because it is entirely true and the truth hurts. In cases like these, writer's block is impenetrable and self-imposed because the writer actively interferes with his own best efforts. When writers first remove these sorts of blocks, they can write more clearly.

Know What You Want to Say

"Have something to say, and say it as clearly as you can. That is the only secret of style," said Matthew Arnold, a nineteenth-century British poet and critic. If you find that you are not writing clearly, look to see if you really know what you want to say. If you do not, then go back and pay closer attention to the preliminary stages of writing.

Life is short and the temptation is powerful to skip over the time-consuming planning stages of writing. But sketching out an argument is a time investment that almost always pays off in the end. Mozart could hold an entire concerto in his head. When he composed, all he had to do was copy down what was written in his brain. Lincoln was reportedly able to dash off the Gettysburg Address on the back of an envelope and not miss his trainstop. But ordinary people need to know what they will say before they decide how they will say it. Save time and trouble: Before you begin to write a draft, decide what points you will raise and how they are connected. Draw a diagram of your argument, laying out the central claims and connecting them with arrows. If you need to, go back to Chapter 3 and review the techniques for planning an argument.

Be Sure You Want to Say It

The murkiest, most muddled prose almost always comes from a person who is "of two minds," the person who has to say something but doesn't want to say anything. Advertisers often find themselves in this spot; they have to make claims about their products, but they can't say too much without lying. In the novel *Blandings' Way,* Mr. Blandings, a professional advertising copywriter, ruminates on "the minute insanities that were his daily tasks." One such insanity is to write in praise of Old Supine, a blended whiskey:

> *Mr. Blandings' task on this account was to find ten thousand different ways of evading the true issue. Old Supine, unlike some other products, had a true, definite function, which it would unfailingly perform. This function was to get the consumer into a hyper-normal state: buzzed, crocked, looping, fried, boiled, plastered, or stinko, according to the amount ingested. . . . Could this delightful truth be as much as hinted? Even if there were no Federal Trade Commission, the American mores would revolt at the slightest suggestion. In "building" ads for Old Supine, it was Mr. Blandings' task to take such notions as aroma, flavor, body, color, bouquet, mildness, more mildness, more body, less body, and play with them like an eighteen-month infant in a playpen until some combination satisfying to the client emerged. . . . But the joys of getting more or less drunk? No.*

> *Then there was the Hair Removal Institute of America. . . .*
> *One of Mr. Blandings' problems, this very day, . . . was to begin drafting a whole set of [commercials] for Queeze, the new modern luncheon Spread. . . .*
> *A coarse tremor swept Mr. Blandings.*[20]

Some people say that professors, like advertisers, write unclearly in order to hide a shameful fact—that they have nothing new or important to say.[21] The author of this textbook passes no judgment on this issue but does offer an example of academic prose and asks students to decide what could possibly motivate a person to write this way:

> *The male group is ubiquitous in colonizing the conventional sphere of interpersonal activity as a self-sufficient autonomous unit.*[22]

The lesson that advertising copywriters, and perhaps professors, teach to would-be writers is this: If you are having trouble communicating clearly, check to make sure that you are trying to communicate clearly. Writers can—and do—sabotage their own best efforts.

●●

8.12 PROFESSORIAL PROSE

Okay, so what *does* motivate professors to write prose that is difficult to understand? Or, in the words of Charles Sykes, "How is it that normally intelligent, occasionally articulate, sometimes even eloquent men and women become pompous, opaque, and incomprehensible the moment they enter academe? What could possibly seduce them into such rhetorical buffoonery?"[23]

Go to the library and find some of the scholarly arguments produced by your professors, or ask some of your professors to give you reprints of their articles. Review their arguments, using the Reader-based Evaluation questions under "Peer and Group Evaluation" in Chapter 3. Your professor may invite several of these author/professors to come to class to discuss the quest for clarity in academic prose.

●●

Follow Three Principles to Write Clear Sentences[24]

Once the logical and psychological barriers to clear writing are removed, what is left is craft. Like any craft, clear writing can be learned. Writers can dramatically improve the clarity of their sentences by following a few simple guidelines, according to Joseph Williams, a University of Chicago composition professor who wrote *Style: Toward Clarity and Grace*,[25] and Gregory Colomb of the Georgia Institute of Technology. Here is some of the advice they offer.

Express Crucial Actions in Verbs, Not in Nouns

The simplest way to express an action is with a verb: "Spot *ran* to Jane." Every third grader knows this. But once people get past third grade, they often try to fancy up their writing by expressing actions as nouns: "*Spot's running* was in the direction of Jane." Soon they are writing sentences in which verbs have virtually disappeared; their sentences fill up instead with *nominalizations*— abstract, polysyllabic "noun-verbs" like *commitment, overestimation, specification, enhancement, nauseant.* "The committee *decided* to *eliminate* the campaign" becomes "The committee *made a decision* in favor of the *elimination* of the campaign." The prose that results is thick and confusing.

Go back to real verbs, Williams and Colomb recommend, and the payoff is immediate and impressive. Examine, for example, the differences between these two sentences:

1. Actions expressed as nouns: The president's decision in favor of the selection of Miami resulted from Gainesville's failure to submit a proposal.

2. Actions expressed as verbs: The president selected Miami because Gainesville failed to submit a proposal.

What makes the second sentence so much easier to follow than the first? The subject of the sentence is shorter. The sentence itself is shorter. The second sentence is more specific and concrete. It lacks the tangled prepositional phrases that make the first sentence unwieldy. The logical relations are clearer. All these virtues, Williams and Colomb believe, follow directly when a writer uses verbs, not nouns, to express actions.

When you use a verb to express an action, you are forced to identify the agent or actor, the person or thing that is doing the action. Because all the actions in the following sentence are described by nouns, the agent of these actions is invisible.

> His abandonment of the Soviet empire in Eastern Europe was accompanied by repeated affirmations of communism.[26]

When the nominalizations are replaced by verbs, the actor emerges:

> As Gorbachev abandoned the Soviet empire in Eastern Europe, he repeatedly affirmed his faith in communism.

The revised sentence is easier to follow. At the very least, the reader knows who did what.

• •

8.13 THE ENHANCEMENT AND REDUCTION OF NOMINALIZATIONS

In the following sentences, change the verbs to nominalizations, to demonstrate to yourself how complicated the sentences become. The first one is done for you.

1. Sally challenged the parking ticket because she thought it was unfair. (Sally's challenge of the parking ticket was based on her belief in its unfairness.)

2. Work progressed rapidly as the workers completed the brickwork and began to lay concrete.

3. We hold these truths to be self-evident: that all men are created equal.

4. Violence is as American as apple pie. (Rap Brown)

5. Man is born free and is everywhere in chains. (Rousseau)

Clarify these sentences by changing the nominalizations to verbs. Again, the first one is done for you.

1. Blushing is peculiar to human beings, as is the need to blush. (Man is the only animal that blushes, or needs to. —Mark Twain)

2. The commencement of the ceremony came with the striking of the gong.

3. The delay in the production of the report resulted from the insistence of the committee on the correctness of their position.

4. With the inauguration of economic reforms, the reduction of the Soviet Union's influence in world affairs had its beginning.

5. The origin of my journey is Alabama, the position of my banjo being on my knee. My destination is Louisiana, my goal being the viewing of my true love.

• •

Keep the Agent-Action Core of the Sentence Intact

Once you have provided your sentence with an agent and an action, Williams and Colomb say, do not muddy up the sentence by separating the agent from its action. The clearest sentences are those in which the agent (the person or thing doing the action) and the action (what the person or thing is doing) are close together. All the clauses and modifiers and extra pieces of information go either at the beginning of the sentence or at the end of a sentence.

This sentence is hard to follow because the agent, "a small percentage," is separated by fourteen words from the action, "reported."

> Only a small percentage of the 359 senior administrators who responded to a questionnaire sent by the group reported controversy . . .[27]

The sentence is clearer when the extra material is pulled to the front of the sentence:

> Of the 359 senior administrators who responded to a questionnaire sent by the group, only a small percentage reported controversy.

8.14 PLAIN TALK ABOUT LEGAL ETHICS

In 1973, a young woman named Susan Petz disappeared on a camping trip in New York. Her distraught family had no idea where she was, or whether she was alive or dead. At about the same time, Robert Garrow, a 38-year-old mechanic, was accused of murdering a young man who was camping in upstate New York. In confidence, he confessed to his court-appointed attorney, Frank Armani, that he had raped and killed Susan Petz and hidden her body in a mine shaft. Armani never revealed the information, even when Susan's father came to him and begged him for help. The case caused considerable comment, including the following commentary by law professor Kenneth Kipnis.

> "It is difficult to exaggerate the concern that communities can have to solve grisly crimes and to apprehend and punish dangerous criminals. And the interest that a parent can have in learning the fate of a missing son or daughter must be accorded great weight in ethical deliberations. Thus arguments from security, justice, and compassion can all support the conclusion that [the attorneys] should have disclosed what their client had told them. . . . Indeed there was considerable public outrage after Garrow confessed and it became apparent that Armani . . . had withheld the truth. . . .
>
> "The suggestion that Armani . . . be punished for a criminal offense merits first consideration, for in the Anglo-American legal system citizens have no general legal obligation to report to the authorities what they know about criminal conduct. Indeed, what would it be like if everyone—every neighbor, friend, relative—were a deputized agent of the prosecutor, legally obligated to pass along evidence of wrongdoing? . . .

If a public choice is made to let citizens use their own discretion in deciding when to contact the authorities, there may be some loss of efficiency in apprehending criminals, but there may well be a net gain in the quality of social life."[28]

Revise and rewrite Kipnis's prose, following these two guidelines:

1. Express crucial actions in verbs, not in nouns.
2. Keep the agent-action core of the sentence intact.

• •

Put New Information at the End of the Sentence

"Generally, use the beginning of your sentences to refer to what you have already mentioned or knowledge that you can assume you and your reader readily share," Williams advises.[29] Use the end of your sentences to introduce new, important information, the material that you want to be sure sticks in the readers' minds.

Consider the simplest of examples. "Dick's dog is named Spot." The readers know that Dick has a dog, so "Dick's dog" is old stuff. What the writer wants to tell the reader, the new information that the writer is introducing, is the name of Dick's dog. So, that goes at the end of the sentence. It is possible to say, "Spot is the name of Dick's dog," of course. But then the readers get the information "Spot" before they know what to do with it, which makes the sentence harder to follow.

Consider a more complex example, one that conforms to Williams' third rule, in that the old information is at the beginning of each sentence and the new is at the end.

> Another example of how the endangered species act hurts animals is the outrageous story of the alligator. The alligator has never been a truly endangered species. It was first listed as an endangered species by the Department of the Interior under the old law in 1966 when the species was declining rapidly because of habitat loss.[30]

Think of the brain as a rapidly branching set of paths. The job of the first part of a sentence is to get the mind on the right path so that the new information can quickly be routed to its proper position. Here is the same example, annotated with comments that a brain might make, if it could talk.

> Another example of how the endangered species act hurts animals [The next information that comes will be an example] is the outrageous story of

the alligator [Alligators are speeding down the examples path]. The alligator [Yes, I know about alligators] has never been a truly endangered species [that's a new one on me]. It [Yes, still talking about alligators] was first listed by the Department of the Interior under the old law in 1966 when the species was declining rapidly because of habitat loss [Okay, that new information is now stored under "Examples, alligators"].

What if the sentences had been written in a way contrary to Williams' advice?

The outrageous story of the alligator [Have I heard this story?] is another example of how the endangered species act hurts animals. [Now I know what to do with the outrageous story: it will be an example]. Under the old law in 1966 [What old law?], the Department of the Interior [Aren't we still talking about alligators? Switch to "Department of the Interior"] listed alligators [Oh, rats, I *am* supposed to be on the alligator path] . . .

You can make your prose easier to follow if you give your reader a starting point. Old, expected information provides the starting point from which a reader can be easily led on to new, unexpected information.

These three guidelines provide a beginning in the effort to write clear sentences. They are rules of thumb, not rigid laws. So, they should be taken seriously but not slavishly. If nothing else, they can provide you with the kind of attention to language and the degree of compassion for the reader that will, in time, help you write more clearly.

. . . .

8.15 WALKING FAMILIAR PATHS

1. Write a paragraph in which you give the reader a guided tour of your living space — your dorm room or a room in your apartment or house. Make sure that your final version follows all three guidelines. This will probably take several drafts.

2. Now, write a paragraph in which you try to convince your landlord that the rent for that space is too high. Again, make sure your final revision follows all three guidelines.

3. Exchange papers with a classmate. Read your classmate's paragraphs. Underline all nominalizations; should they be edited out, or are they legitimate exceptions to the rule? Circle the agent in every sentence. Circle the action in every sentence. Bracket the new, unexpected information in each sentence. Return the paper to your classmate.

Spend some time explaining just exactly how you feel about this process.

. . . .

"Clear" is wonderful praise. In its early usage, *clear* meant "lustrous" or "shining." When a medieval student observed that the night sky was clear, he meant that it was glowing with light, as from a thousand stars. Since starlight will not glow through sky that is opaque, a night sky that is clear in the old sense will also be clear in the modern sense—transparent, unclouded. An argument that is perfectly clear will be clear in both ways; it will shed light, and the light will not be obscured.

. . . .

8.16 SEX, LIES, AND SO FORTH
Carefully examine each of the following passages for fallacies. For each:

  a. Write down the conclusion of the argument; if the conclusion is not explicitly stated, write down the implied conclusion.
  b. If the passage seems to offer a good argument, write "good argument."
  c. If the passage is fallacious, name the fallacy (or fallacies), and carefully explain where each fallacy occurs.

  1. What you read in the newspaper is untrue because newspapers never print the truth.

  2. From an American Survivalist Front pamphlet:

      George Orwell outlined thought control through language manipulation in his "fiction" novel Nineteen Eighty-Four. *Here it is, Nineteen Ninety-Two and the Liberal/Polilitically [sic] Correct movement has started its own type of brainwashing Newspeak. Wake up America! Get wise to the politically correct Marxists and their doublethink mind control tactics!*

  3. When reporters asked Presidential candidate Bill Clinton if he had used drugs, Clinton responded, "I have not broken the laws of any state." What he neglected to say was that he had smoked marijuana twice in England (but never inhaled).

4. The reasoning in the 1803 case of *Marbury* v. *Madison,*[31] written by the great Supreme Court Justice John Marshall:

> *The Constitution is the superior paramount law in the United States. This is so because the particular phraseology of the Constitution of the United States confirms and strengthens that principle, that a law repugnant to the Constitution is void.*

5. **THE SIEGE OF LA**

"We've got shooting all over the city."

"They're destroying their own neighborhoods—it's as bad as an earthquake."

"Let's bang the mother f—."

Like bulletins from a war zone, the words and images came flying out of a city going up in flames. In Los Angeles last week, it was full-metal-jacket time—lock and load. Downtown, a mob of blacks, whites, and Hispanics torched the guardhouse outside police headquarters, lit a fire in city hall, then trashed the criminal courts building. Across town, hammers banged down storefront security gates. Flames shot 100 feet into the night. Giddy looters lurched off with carts of groceries and cases of beer, armloads of clothes, bundles of everything from running shoes to guns. . . .

After years of neglecting the pent-up misery of the inner cities, the country shuddered at the bloody wake-up call.[32]

6. Said a border guard to a citizen returning to the United States from Mexico: "Are your handguns registered in California?"

7. Advertisement for Bohemia beer (reprinted with permission of Wisdom Import Sales): If you had to name the three finest beers in the world, what would the other two be?

8. The women's rights movement would like us to believe that discrimination against women in hiring is wrong. But an employer must discriminate; she discriminates between those who are college-educated and those who are not, between those who score well on the qualifying test and those who do not, and so forth. So, it is contrary to all reason and practice to say that discrimination against women is wrong.

9.   Aristotle's definition of the good:

The good is that of which the good man approves; a good man is he who approves of what is truly good.

10.   John Stuart Mill's definition of the good:

The utilitarian doctrine is, that happiness is desirable, and the only thing desirable, as an end; all other things being only desirable as means to that end. What ought to be required of this doctrine to make good its claim to be believed? The only proof capable of being given that an object is visible, is that people actually see it; the only proof that a sound is audible, is that people hear it . . . In like manner, the sole evidence it is possible to produce that any thing is desirable, is that people actually desire it.

11.   From a letter Representative Denny Smith sent to his constituents:

[I have] the best voting record in Congress of any member of the Oregon delegation—having voted 97% of the time.

12.   From a survey sent by "Americans to Limit Congressional Terms":

Dear [Ms] Moore,

— Do you think Congessmen should make $129,000 a year and have $2 million pensions?
— Do you think Congressmen should be able to rig election rules in an effort to guarantee their re-election?
— Do you think the "check kiting" scandal, in which members of Congress wrote $25 million in bad personal checks, suggests there is massive corruption in Congress?
— Do you think members of Congress should be able to treat themselves like kings and queens at taxpayer expense?

Ms. Moore, will you help represent Corvallis, Oregon in this national 1992 ELECTION BALLOT and CONGRESSIONAL REFORM SURVEY? . . .

13. "No, you cannot have that dog," said the parent. "The ad says it is a dog who will eat anything, and especially loves little boys. We do not want a dog like that around the house."

14. The following excerpt is from *Newsweek.* Copyright © 1991, Newsweek, Inc. All rights reserved. Reprinted by permission.

> *Columbus Day, never on Native America's list of favorite holidays, became somewhat tolerable as its significance diminished to little more than a good shopping day. But this next long year of Columbus hoopla will be tough to take amid the spending sprees and horn blowing to tout a five-century feeding frenzy that has left Native people and this red quarter of Mother Earth in a state of emergency. For Native people, this half millennium of land grabs and one-cent treaty sales has been no bargain.*[33]

Notes

1. Psalms 23.
2. Luci Tapahonso, "A Breeze Swept Through," *A Breeze Swept Through* (Albuquerque, N.M.: West End Press, 1987). © 1987, West End Press. Reprinted with permission.
3. George Bush, January 3, 1992, in an interview with David Frost. Quoted in "Notebook," *The New Republic* (January 27, 1992), p. 8.
4. George Bush, March 11, 1992. Quoted in "Notebook," *The New Republic* (April 6, 1992), p. 8.
5. Reprinted with permission of Source, Inc.
6. The example comes from Lief H. Carter, *Reason in Law* (Boston: Scott, Foresman and Co., 1988), p. 26n.
7. Women-rabbit figure by Stanley Coren, "Brightness Contrast as a Function of Figure-Ground Relations," *Journal of Experimental Psychology,* Vol. 80, pp. 517–24. Copyright © 1980, by the American Psychological Association. Reprinted by permission.
8. For these and other words with opposite senses, see John Train, "Antilogies," *Harvard Magazine* (November–December 1985), p. 18.
9. Headlines a through j are from the "Lower Case" feature of the *Columbia Journalism Review.*
10. These quotes originally appeared in *Nationwide Claims* magazine. They were quoted in *Buckeye Farm News* magazine. A.R. Sicuro, the author of a newspaper column "Along the Way," passed them along to his readers. The newspaper column was sent to the author years ago by her father, who neglected to jot down the name of the newspaper. The author trusts that no one will object to her passing them along in turn.
11. Students of doublespeak will be delighted to learn of the existence of a journal that reviews the most egregious Orwellian phrases of the day. It is *The Quarterly Review of Doublespeak.* Look for it in a library near you.

12. William Lutz, "No Ordinary Nut," *Common Cause Magazine* (January/February 1990), p. 34. Excerpt from *Doublespeak,* William Lutz. Copyright © 1990. Reprinted by permission of HarperCollins Publishers, Inc.

13. All this information comes from William Lutz, "No Ordinary Nut," *Common Cause Magazine* (January/February 1990), pp. 34–35. Answers to the Civil Defense Drill: 1. c, 2. e, 3. h, 4. m, 5. n, 6. a, 7. f, 8. o, 9. k, 10. i, 11. d, 12. l, 13. g, 14. j, 15. b, 16. p.

14. John Chaffee suggested contrasting news accounts of the death of Malcolm X when Prof. Chaffee spoke at a workshop at the Sixth International Conference on Critical Thinking and Moral Critique, Sonoma State University, Rohnert Park, Calif., August 3, 1987.

15. "Death of a Desperado," *Newsweek* (March 8, 1965), p. 24. Copyright © Newsweek. Reprinted with permission.

16. Vern E. Smith, "Rediscovering Malcolm X," *Newsweek* (February 26, 1990), p. 68. Copyright © Newsweek. Reprinted with permission.

17. Mark Twain, *The War Prayer* (New York: HarperCollins Publishers, Inc., 1951). Reprinted with permission of HarperCollins Publishers.

18. *Dishonoring America,* ed. Lillian Baker (Medford, Oreg.: Americans for Historical Accuracy, 1988), p. 26.

19. See Stephen Jay Gould, "This View of Life: Wide Hats and Narrow Minds," *Natural History,* Vol. 88, No. 2 (February 1979), p. 34.

20. Eric Hodgins, *Blandings' Way* (New York: Simon and Schuster, 1950), pp. 26–27. Copyright © 1950, Simon and Schuster. Reprinted by permission.

21. Charles Sykes, *Profscam* (New York: St. Martin's Press, 1988), p. 109.

22. "Articulating the People's Politics: Manhood and Right-Wing Populism in *The A-Team,*" *Communication,* 1987, Vol. 9; quoted in *Profscam,* p. 112. Professor Sykes offers this translation: ". . . the show is about a bunch of macho guys who hang around together doing macho things."

23. *Profscam,* p. 109.

24. The author wishes to acknowledge the deep influence of the ideas and pedagogical philosophies of Gregory Colomb, Department of English, Georgia Institute of Technology, and Joseph Williams, Department of English, University of Chicago. Their presentations at the University of Chicago conference "From Theory to Practice: Liberal Learning and Its Pedagogical Challenge" (November 16–18, 1990) were inspiring and informative.

25. Joseph M. Williams, *Style: Toward Clarity and Grace* (Chicago: University of Chicago Press, 1990).

26. "The Russian Resolution," *The New Republic* (September 9, 1991), p. 8.

27. "Notebook," *The New Republic* (September 9, 1991), p. 9.

28. Kenneth Kipnis, *Legal Ethics* (Englewood Cliffs, N.J.: Prentice-Hall, 1986), pp. 63–64. Copyright © 1986, Prentice-Hall. Reprinted by permission.

29. *Style: Toward Clarity and Grace,* p. 64.

30. Material adapted from Richard Starnes, "The Sham of Endangered Species," *Outdoor Life* (August 1980).

31. *Marbury* v. *Madison,* 1 Cranch 137, 2 L. Ed. 60 (1803).

32. Tom Mathews, "The Siege of LA," *Newsweek* (May 11, 1992), p. 30.

33. Susan Shown Harjo, "I Won't Be Celebrating Columbus Day," *Newsweek* (Fall 1991), p. 32. Copyright © 1991, Newsweek, Inc. All rights reserved. Reprinted by permission.

••••••••••••••••••••••

CHAPTER 9

Refutation Strategies

The word *refute* comes from the Latin words meaning "to beat back with clubs." And, indeed, refutation conjures up an image of argumentation as an aggressive and Neanderthal activity, an effort to vanquish opponents, to destroy their arguments, to win the field. This is an unjustifiably limited view of the role of refutation in argumentation. The word *refute* has come to mean "to overthrow with argument or evidence." As such, refutation has an important constructive place in the process of justifying beliefs. And refutation skills are important social skills in civil discourse since they allow a person to destroy a claim with arguments rather than with force or insults.

• •

9.1 REFUTATION AND CONFRONTATION

What do ordinary people do with false claims? Do they politely ignore the blunder, the way they ignore egg stains on a person's tie? Do they point out the error by making insulting references to the quality of the blunderer's mind or parentage? Do they effectively refute the claim? Observe your own behavior very closely. How do you respond when someone tells you something you don't believe is true? Do you refute the claim? Do you insult the speaker? Carefully observe the behavior of other people—your friends, your family, your professors, politicians on TV. How do they respond when someone tells them something they don't believe is true?

Now, write a 250-word response to this claim: Most people will do anything to avoid taking the trouble to actually refute a claim, "to overthrow it with argument or evidence."

• •

A person with skills of refutation is far more likely to be effective in argumentation. Arguments are directed toward an audience. The members of the audience are not like empty bottles, sitting there open-mouthed, waiting to be filled with the truth. The members of the audience probably already have a set of beliefs. When their beliefs are contrary to what you want to convince them of, you need to use refutation strategies to raise doubts, to point out mistakes, to clear away misunderstandings, before their minds will find room for the claim you wish to defend.

Moreover, those who know how to use reasons to show that a claim is false are far more likely to avoid errors in their own thinking. Consider those people whose mental exercise is confined to building up evidence for what they already believe. Soon their beliefs are strongly buttressed on all sides with evidence of all sorts; they are irreparably ignorant. Contrast them with people who consider evidence for and against their beliefs, who know when evidence counts against a claim and can show when evidence is faulty and arguments are inconclusive. These people may have fewer strong beliefs, but their beliefs, having been weighed and sorted, are more likely to be correct.

There are two basic approaches to refutation, corresponding to the two requirements of a good argument. A good argument must be correct in form and in content. An argument is correct in form when the parts of the argument are put together in such a way that the evidence really does support the claim. An argument is correct in content when the evidence itself is correct. If both requirements are met, the conclusion is likely to be true. It follows that to refute a claim, you can find fault with the *form* of the argument supporting it; you can show that the evidence does not lead to the conclusion. Or you can find fault with the *content* of the argument; you can show that the evidence gathered in support of a claim is dubious or false.

How to Show That an Argument Is Unreliable

Problems with the Form of an Argument

A conclusion may be suspect because the form of the argument supporting it is unreliable. If an argument is not correctly put together, the premises do not lead to the conclusion. Consider this proof of the existence of Sasquatch, the legendary "Bigfoot" of the northwestern United States, from humorist Patrick McManus:

> *I don't know if Sasquatches exist or not . . . I understand that they smell terrible. If Sasquatches didn't exist, how could anyone know what they smelled like? . . . If something smells bad, it must exist, right? I rest my case for the existence of the Sasquatch.* [1]

You can look at this argument and know, as Mr. McManus did, that something is wrong. But then what? How do you go about showing—demonstrating—that an argument is fatally weak? By definition, a weak argument is one in which the conclusion may well be false, even when the premises are true. But it will not do to say so directly, because whether the conclusion is true or false is precisely the issue in question. [2] In this example, it is not possible to demonstrate the weakness of the argument by stating that even if Sasquatches *do* stink, they still might not exist, because that is exactly what is at issue.

The solution is to construct an example of an argument that has the same form as the argument in question but that has obviously true premises and an obviously false conclusion. That example will demonstrate that an argument of that form can lead a person into error. As with all analogies, the tighter the fit, the closer the comparison, the better the argument.

For example, you could say to Mr. McManus, "That's just like arguing that Martians must exist because Martians, by definition, are the inhabitants of Mars, and if Martians live on Mars, they must exist." If reasoning this way can lead to a conclusion that is patently false even though all the premises are true, it must be an unreliable way to reason.

Refutation by Logical Analogy

An example like this is called a *logical analogue* because the new argument is analogous to the argument in question: It has the same logical form. Using it to demonstrate that other arguments of that form are unreliable is called *refutation by logical analogy.* To formulate a refutation by logical analogy, you need to think up an argument that has two characteristics:

1. The logical analogue is identical in logical form to the argument in question.

2.   The logical analogue has premises that any reasonably well informed person would realize immediately are true. And it has a conclusion that is just as obviously false.

Phrases like "That's just like arguing . . ." "Well, by the same reasoning . . ." "You could as well argue that . . ." introduce the logical analogy.

Here is a straightforward example. A critic once accused Malcolm X of being a Communist on the grounds that he had given a speech in the assembly room of a Communist association. Malcolm X demonstrated the illogic of the charge by saying, "I once preached in a Methodist church. Does that make me a Methodist?" The second argument has the same form as the first; that form leads straight from a true premise to a false conclusion. So, that way of arguing cannot be trusted.

The refutation by logical analogy is a powerful, indeed, decisive, means of refuting *deductive* arguments. Deductive arguments have rigid, readily identifiable forms, so that matching the pattern is a straightforward task. More important, deductive arguments are constructed in such a way that it is logically impossible—literally inconceivable—that the premises are true and the conclusion false. So, one logical analogue with true premises and a false conclusion demonstrates the invalidity of all arguments with that form. On the other hand, using refutation by logical analogy to refute *inductive* arguments is problematic because it is logically possible that even very, very strong inductive arguments will have true premises and a false conclusion. If, for example, you have sampled 99 out of 100 jelly beans in a jar, and each of the 99 was red, it is reasonable to conclude that all the jelly beans are red; but if the last turns out to be green, the argument was still a good argument. So, when it comes to inductive arguments, it is wise to use logical analogies merely to raise questions about the reliability of that way of reasoning.

● ●

9.2 "BUT THAT'S JUST LIKE ARGUING . . ."

1.   Find a partner. Your professor will assign you and your partner one of the following invalid or weak argument forms:

a.   All A is C.
      All B is C.
      _____
      Therefore, all A is B.

b.   If A, then B.
      B.
      _____
      Therefore, A.

c.   If A, then B.
    Not A._____
    Therefore, not B.

d.   B comes after A._____
    Therefore, A causes B.

e.   A or B.
    A._____
    Therefore, not B.

Each of these argument forms is faulty, and each can be refuted by the method of logical analogy. Following your argument form exactly, write an argument that has obviously true premises and an obviously false conclusion. Make sure that their truth value is obvious to a person other than yourself; claims like "It is a dog," "Trevor is a horse," and "My name is Joanne" are not obviously true or false to another person.

Your professor may ask you to get together with other pairs of students who have refuted that same argument form. Make sure each refutation has the same form as the arguments to be refuted, has obviously true premises, and has an obviously false conclusion. Choose the most forceful refutation, and share it with the class.

2.   Refute the following arguments by the method of logical analogy. That requires two steps, as you know: first, determine the form of the argument; second, construct another argument of exactly that form, with obviously true premises and an obviously false conclusion.

a.   I've decided to sit in the front of the class this term because I really need an A. I've noticed that the people who sit in the front row are the ones who get A's at the end of the term, and the people who sit at the back of the classroom end up with the C's and D's.

b.   Jessica is really tall. The center on the basketball team is really tall. So, Jessica must be the center on the team.

c.   Darned environmentalists are all communists, I tell you. Environmentalists all think that the government should tell us what we can and can't do with our own land. All communists think exactly the same thing. Communists, that's what they are!

d.   All welfare mothers are deadbeats. I saw some women at the grocery yesterday, buying steaks and imported mushrooms with food stamps.

e.   If you don't work hard, you can't get good grades. So, if you work really hard, you will get good grades.

Your professor may ask you to compare your work with the work of others in a small-group setting. For each argument, choose the most effective refutation from among those written by your group members. What makes it most effective? Read the best refutations to the class.

• •

Mark Twain was a subtle and masterful practitioner of the art of refutation by logical analogy. In *Letters from the Earth,* Twain considered a question enthusiastically debated during his lifetime: Was the world created for the sake of humankind? He begins his essay by reviewing the history of all evolution, from pterodactyls to birds to kangaroos to mastodons to sloths, leading up to the evolution of human beings. Then he says,

> Such is the history of it. Man has been here 32,000 years. That it took a hundred million years to prepare the world for him is proof that that is what it was done for. I suppose it is. I dunno. If the Eiffel tower were now representing the world's age, the skin of paint on the pinnacle-knob at its summit would represent man's share of that age; and anybody would perceive that that skin was what the tower was built for. I reckon they would; I dunno.[3]

Many of Twain's contemporaries believed that humans were the last species to evolve. This, they thought, was evidence that the evolution of humankind was the purpose of the whole process. Well, said Twain, that's like arguing that the fact that the paint at the top of the Eiffel Tower came last is evidence that the paint is the purpose of the Eiffel Tower. However, no reasonable person would really think that the Eiffel Tower was built solely in order to support the topmost layer of paint. So, that kind of reasoning can lead a person to error, as the analogy demonstrates.

• •

9.3 THE MAN ON MARS

1.   Photographs taken from satellites show a rock formation on Mars that, under certain light conditions, looks exactly like the smiley faces on earthlings' lapel buttons. Be assured that the photograph is real and unaltered; the rock formation does exist. The existence of this rock formation is clear evidence, some believe, of the existence of intelligent beings on Mars, beings with incredible rock-moving capabilities. Are you convinced? If not, refute the argument, using a logical analogy.

2. And while you're thinking of extraterrestrial phenomena, consider the moon effect. In 1972[4] and again in 1978,[5] a Miami psychiatrist published studies showing that violent crimes such as murder and rape occur most frequently when the moon is full. He concluded that the increased pull of the full moon directly affected human behavior, causing the increase in violence. Cast doubt on this conclusion by demonstrating the unreliability of that way of reasoning, using a logical analogy.

Notice that the logical analogy does not prove that a conclusion is false. Rather, by showing that an argument's form is unreliable, that it is the kind of argument that can lead from true premises to a false conclusion, the logical analogy shows that a conclusion is unsupported. In other words, the logical analogy shows that the argument does not give good reason to believe that the conclusion is true or false.

How to Show That a Statement Is False

A conclusion may also be suspect if it rests on an argument with a false premise. An argument with even one false premise is like a table with a broken leg. The argument cannot support its conclusion any more than the table can support any weight. Thus, if you can show that a premise is false, you have essentially refuted the argument.

To show that a statement is false, it helps to be aware of just what kind of statement it is. This is because different kinds of statements are vulnerable to different kinds of counterevidence.

Refuting Universal Generalizations

The easiest of all statements to refute are the statements that make unqualified blanket claims. Statements like "No word processing program is as easy to use as a pencil and paper," or "We Germans fear God but nothing else in the world"[6] are called *universal generalizations* because they make a general statement that is intended to apply universally to all members of a given set. Statements containing *never, always, all, no,* and similar universal words are usually universal generalizations.

It takes only one example that goes against the generalization to do the job of refutation. An example that goes against the generalization is called a *counterexample.* One user-friendly word processing program or one German who is afraid of snakes is enough to refute the generalizations above.

For many years, people believed the universal generalization that no human being can run a mile in fewer than four minutes. Dr. Roger Gilbert Bannister provided the counterexample that disproved the generalization when he ran a mile in 3 minutes 59.4 seconds on the Iffley Road Track, Oxford, at 6:10 P.M. on May 6, 1954.

Here is another instance of refutation by counterexample, from an essay on the dominance of the English language around the world:

> *Evelyn Waugh [asserted] that no man who knew more than one language could express himself in any. (Take that, Nabokov!* Et tu, Samuel Beckett!*).*[7]

Simply naming two exceptions, Vladimir Nabokov, who expresses himself beautifully in both English and Russian, and Samuel Beckett, who wrote in English and French, utterly destroys Waugh's generalization.

• •

9.4 COUNTEREXAMPLES

Here is an exercise on counterexamples that requires some esoteric knowledge of the world. Match the counterexamples with the universal generalizations they refute, if you can. If you can't, the answers are in endnote 8.

1. All the best chess players are Russians.
2. No one can escape from the prison on Alcatraz Island.
3. No mammals lay eggs.
4. All humans need some sleep.
5. No one can make a fortune as a concert pianist.
6. You can't make a silk purse out of a sow's ear.
7. No pilot can exceed the speed of sound and live.
8. All popes are Italian.
9. Man is the only animal that blushes, or needs to.
10. No king was ever crowned in the United States.

a. Chuck Yeager
b. Bobby Fischer
c. John Chase

    d.   Karol Wojtyla

    e.   Jan Paderewski, Prime Minister of Poland

    f.   Arthur D. Little

    g.   The platypus

    h.   Jesus de Frutos

    i.   James Jesse Strang

    j.   Stickleback fish

9.5 AN AMERICAN CHILDHOOD

In her autobiography, *An American Childhood*, Annie Dillard wrote about her mother's efforts to find a counterexample to refute Annie's universal generalizations about nuns.

> One afternoon the following spring, I was sitting stilled on the side-yard swing; . . .
>
>   . . . St. Bede's was, as the expression had it, letting out; . . . I kept an eye out for the nuns. . . .
>
>   In the leafy distance up Edgerton I could see a black phalanx. It blocked the sidewalk; it rolled footlessly forward like a tank. The nuns were coming. They had no bodies, and imitation faces. I quitted the swing and banged through the back door and ran in to Mother in the kitchen.
>
>   I didn't know the nuns taught the children; the Catholic children certainly avoided them on the streets, almost as much as I did. The nuns seemed to be kept in St. Bede's as in a prison, where their faces had rotted away—or they lived eyeless in the dark by choice, like bats. Parts of them were manufactured. Other parts were made of mushrooms.
>
>   In the kitchen, Mother said it was time I got over this. She took me by the hand and hauled me back outside; we crossed the street and caught up with the nuns. "Excuse me," Mother said to the black phalanx. It wheeled around. "Would you just please say hello to my daughter here? If you could just let her see your faces."
>
>   I saw the white, conical billboards they had as mock-up heads; I couldn't avoid seeing them, those white boards like pillories with circles cut out and some bunched human flesh pressed like raw pie crust into the holes. Like mushrooms and engines, they didn't have hands. There was only that disconnected saucerful of whitened human flesh at their tops. The rest, concealed by a chassis of soft cloth over hard cloth, was cylinders, drive shafts, clean wiring, and wheels.
>
>   "Why, hello," some of the top parts said distinctly. They teetered toward me. I was delivered to my enemies, and had no place to hide; I could only wail for my young life so unpityingly snuffed.[9]

In a one- to two-page narrative essay, tell about a false generalization you once believed, and explain the counterexample that made you realize your mistake.

• •

The counterexample is a specialized form of refutation, useful only for demonstrating that universal generalizations are false. Another form of refutation has a far wider applicability. These are the *reductio* arguments.

The **Reductio** *Refutations*

The statements that make up arguments can generally be classified in three groups. These are *claims of fact,* explanations or statements that purport to describe what is the case; *value claims,* statements about what ought to be; and *policy statements,* recommendations for a course of action. With some important variations, each type of statement can be refuted by a strategy called *reductio refutations.* This refutation technique rests on a kind of flanking strategy: the attack is made not against a claim directly, but against consequences of the claim.

A *reductio* argument is defined as an argument that shows that a claim is false by showing that a false claim follows from it. In other words, given any claim (call it A), if another claim (call it B) follows from A and if B is false, then A must be false as well. This kind of argument probably sounds familiar because the *reductio* arguments are identical in form to the conditional syllogism called *denying the consequent,* explained in Chapter 4. You have encountered it, too, in Chapter 6, as a way to test scientific explanations.

If A, then B.
B is false.
Therefore, A is false.

One example: A southern historian has written a new book claiming that President Zachary Taylor was murdered—poisoned, in fact, with arsenic. She arranged to have his body exhumed and tested for traces of poison, reasoning that if he was poisoned, it follows that traces of the poison would remain in his hair and other tissues. But there were no traces of arsenic to be found. Thus, Zachary Taylor is unlikely to have been poisoned by arsenic. The historian's new book is unlikely to be a big success.

This one argument form can be adapted to refute claims of all three types—claims of fact, value claims, and policy claims. To refute a *claim of fact,* you show that a logical consequence of that claim is false or impossible. To show that a *value claim* is mistaken, you show that a logical consequence of that claim is inconsistent with other values or moral beliefs held by the person making the questionable value claim. To show that a *policy claim* is mistaken, you show that a practical consequence of adopting that policy is unacceptable. These are all *reductio* arguments because they proceed by showing that the claim in question can be "reduced" to a claim that is clearly unacceptable.

Refuting Claims of Fact

In the 1972 case of *Furman v. Georgia,* the Supreme Court ruled that capital punishment, as it was then practiced, was unconstitutional. Justice Thurgood Marshall concurred in this opinion because he believed that, as a matter of fact, capital punishment does not deter murderers. He wrote, in part:

> *The most hotly contested issue regarding capital punishment is whether it is better than life imprisonment as a deterrent to crime . . . [O]ne of the leading authorities on capital punishment has urged that if the death penalty deters prospective murderers, the following hypotheses should be true:*
>
> *(a) Murders should be less frequent in states that have the death penalty than in those that have abolished it, other factors being equal. . . .*
>
> *(b) Murders should increase when the death penalty is abolished and should decline when it is restored.*
>
> *(c) The deterrent effect should be greatest and should therefore affect murder rates most powerfully in those communities where the crime occurred and its consequences are most strongly brought home to the population.*
>
> *(d) Law enforcement officers would be safer from murderous attacks in states that have the death penalty than in those without it.*
>
> *. . . [E]vidence indicates that not one of these propositions is true.*[10]

Justice Marshall has provided a complex example of a *reductio* refutation of a claim of fact. At issue is the truth of the factual claim that capital punishment deters. Justice Marshall lists four further claims that must be true if it is true that capital punishment deters murder. All four claims are false. So, the claim at issue is probably false: capital punishment does not deter murder.

This kind of argument may be called a *reductio ad impossibile* because the refutation proceeds by demonstrating that the claim at issue can be "reduced" to claims that are "impossible," or not true in the real world. The refutation strategy works because of a very useful logical fact: *Any claim that has false logical consequences is itself false.* To construct a *reductio ad impossibile* refutation, follow these steps:

1. State the original claim, the claim that is to be refuted.
2. State another claim that follows as a logical consequence of the primary claim.
3. Show that the consequence is false.
4. Draw the conclusion that the original claim is probably false as well.

Here is another example. About a hundred years ago, in the time before people believed that germs caused disease, people commonly suspected that cholera was spread by "effluvia," dangerously foul air wafting from the bodies of the dead and the lungs of the mortally afflicted. But this theory was handily refuted, like this:

> *The low rate of mortality amongst medical men and undertakers is worthy of notice. If cholera were propagated by effluvia given off from the patient, or the dead body, as used to be the opinion of those who believed in its communicability; . . . [then] medical men and undertakers would be peculiarly liable to the disease; but, [these people do not come down with cholera any more than other people do].*[11]

The original claim is that cholera is "propagated by effluvia given off from the patient, or the dead body." The logical consequence is that "medical men and undertakers would be peculiarly liable to the disease." Since the consequence is false, the original claim must also be false.

One last example:[12] In 1987, a young German pilot managed to evade Soviet air defenses and land his small plane in Red Square. *Pravda* recently published a transcript of the discussion among air defense personnel as they tried to decipher the radar signals. In a bizarre exchange, the factual claim that the radar blips were only birds was refuted by an officer's observation that if the signals were birds, they would be moving toward the north.

Major General Aleksandr Gukov: Yes, the Leningraders decided that it was birds. . . . We should go along with the Leningraders' decision and show solidarity. (Laughter.) There's just one thing that fazes me. Birds fly north in the spring. But this is coming *from* the north.

Lt. General Y. Brazhnikov: I still think we will come to the conclusion that it was geese. So, Aleksandr Ivanovich, it will be birds.

Major General Aleksandr Gukov: Yes, sir, let it be that. Yes sir.

● ●

9.6 HE LOVES ME, HE LOVES ME NOT

It is so hard to know whether someone really loves you. Fortunately, it is not so hard to know when someone does not love you. You can do this with a *reductio ad impossibile* refutation strategy.

Suppose that you received the following letter from your steady:

My Darling,

I love you more than words can express. I love the smell of your hair. I love the feel of your legs next to mine. I love the sound of your laugh. I love the taste of your fingertips. Please marry me.

Forever and always,
Chris

You are distressed because Chris has been acting like a stinker. You suspect that the smell Chris really loves is the smell of your money and that the taste Chris really loves is Chivas Regal.

Write back to Chris. Send a devastating refutation of the claim of love. But think carefully about this. "I love you" is one of those claims that cannot be directly refuted. You will have to use a *reductio* refutation strategy. Think along these lines: What are the true tests of love? If a person really loved you, how would that person act? Does that person act that way? Draw freely on your imagination or past experience for any details you need. Make your letter four paragraphs long, each paragraph containing a complete *reductio ad impossibile*.

● ●

9.7 FETUS ABUSE?

In the following passage, Dorothy E. Roberts, associate professor of criminal law at Rutgers, defends her explanation of why prosecutors are bringing criminal charges against mothers who use crack cocaine during pregnancy.

1. Read the passage, and answer the following questions: What explanation of the prosecutors' motivations does Ms. Roberts defend? To do so, she must refute what alternative "official" explanation? What two facts are cited by Ms. Roberts as inconsistent with the official explanation? For each of those facts, write the implied *reductio ad impossibile* argument.

MOTHER AS MARTYR

The debate over the prosecution of mothers who use drugs during pregnancy has been framed as an issue of fetal rights versus women's rights, but the real issue changes when you look at the primary targets of prosecutors. The overwhelming majority of women who have been charged with fetal abuse—approximately 70 percent—are African-American. Most are poor and addicted to crack. What these racially discriminatory prosecutions amount to is punishing poor women of color for having babies.

It is significant that prosecutors have chosen to focus on crack use out of the universe of material conduct that can harm fetuses. Excessive alcohol and marijuana consumption during pregnancy, for example, can also adversely affect the unborn. If fetal protection were the true motivation of prosecutors, wouldn't charges be brought against those women who cause the greatest harm to their unborn children, regardless of race or class? Instead, poor Black women have been made criminals because society is more willing to condone their punishment. . . .

The historical neglect of Black children belies government's sudden "concern" for the welfare of the fetus. Society has always turned its back on the inadequacy of prenatal care available to poor women of color, so its current expression of interest in unborn Black children must be viewed with suspicion. Need proof? Look at the high rate of infant death in the Black community. In 1987 the mortality rate for Black infants was 17.9 deaths per 1,000 live births—more than twice that of white infants. The disparity is even greater between poor inner-city neighborhoods and wealthier communities. Central Harlem, for example, has an infant-morality rate three times higher than those in upper- and middle-income areas in New York City. And the main reason for this high death rate is inadequate prenatal care. If the government were truly concerned about the health of Black infants, why hasn't there been a national commitment to ensuring that pregnant women in poor communities receive high-quality prenatal care? . . . [13]

2.   Do you believe that women who use drugs during pregnancy should be prosecuted for the crime of "fetal abuse"? Defend your view with a practical syllogism. You may need to read ahead to the section "Refuting Policy Statements," where refutation by results is introduced.

Refuting Value Claims

Moral argument is very difficult. One problem is establishing a common ground between disputants. One person might believe that God is the ultimate source of decisions about what is right, important, and valuable. You might believe that what is right has ultimately to do with what makes *you* happiest. Another might make value judgments based on the conviction that happiness is the highest value and all other values are instrumental to that end. But, across all the shifting, unsteady ground of discourse about values, there is one value that remains steady for all people who are committed to reason in argument. That is the value of consistency. Moral judgments and other claims about what is of value cannot be correct unless they are consistent. A person's value judgments are open to criticism as arbitrary and unprincipled if they are contradictory and unpredictable.

So, no matter what the philosophical basis for a person's value judgments, if a person is committed to a rational basis of discourse, his value judgments can be criticized if they undercut each other. So, a generally useful way to refute value claims is to point out inconsistencies in a person's judgments. This is done by yet another form of *reductio* argument: *A value claim is faulty, not to be trusted, if the consequence of that value claim is inconsistent with the beliefs of the person making the argument.* Hypocrisy is wrong in any moral system.

Consider the moral reasoning of Martin Luther King, Jr., during the Montgomery, Alabama, bus boycott of 1955. King's home had been firebombed, and a large crowd had gathered outside. Some of the people in the crowd were armed, and many people were shouting for violent action against those who were presumed to have thrown the firebombs. "If you have weapons, take them home," King told the crowd. "We must meet violence with non-violence. . . . We must love our white brothers no matter what they do to us."

Later, King wrote, "The Negro . . . has grown up politically, culturally and economically. Many white men fear retaliation. The job of the Negro is to show them that they have nothing to fear. . . . He must convince the white man that all he seeks is justice for both himself and the white man."[14]

For all the controversy King's nonviolent philosophy evoked, it can be understood as a *reductio* argument: You say we should react violently to oppression. But if we should react violently, it follows that violence against another human being is sometimes correct. But violence against another human being is precisely what we have been struggling against. So, our response should not be violent.

The logic of this refutation is the logic of denying the consequent: If you wish to defend this claim, then you must defend the claim that follows from it. What? . . . You are unhappy with this second claim? Then you must renounce the first one. If A, then B. Not B? Then not A either!

9.8 ABORTION ABSURDITY

Read the following excerpts from Michael Kinsley's *New Republic* essay on anti-abortion laws:

Louisiana's new anti-abortion law . . . declares, "Life begins at conception and . . . is a continuum until the time of death." . . .

If a fetus is a fully human being with the same moral claims as any other from the moment of conception, it is only reasonable that doctors who kill fetuses by performing abortions should be punished with up to ten years in prison and a $100,000 fine. . . .

If every fetus is a fully human being, a woman who procures an abortion is exactly like someone who hires a gunman to murder her child. . . . Yet when a pro-choice Louisiana legislator introduced an amendment to the abortion bill imposing penalties on the patient as well as the doctor, the pro-life majority saw this—quite accurately—as sabotage and it got only two votes.

In January Utah enacted an antiabortion law almost as restrictive as Louisiana's. After the bill passed, the ACLU discovered that this law, combined with an earlier law . . . could lead to the death penalty (by firing squad) for both doctor and patient. . . . [T]o make absolutely sure the patient would not be punished, . . . the abortion law and the murder statute were both amended. . . .

If the fetus is to be considered a person . . ., then states that punish murder (all states, of course) would have to treat abortion—the purposeful killing of a fetus— exactly like murder. If a state regards people who arrange for a murder to be guilty of murder themselves (as all states do), that state would have to prosecute as murderers women who procure abortions. If a state has the death penalty . . . , that penalty would have to apply equally to murderers of fetuses. . . .

The point, though, is not that women are likely to be punished as criminals for seeking an abortion or using birth control. The point is that even abortion's strongest opponents turn logical somersaults to avoid punishing women abortion customers. What this reveals is that they don't really think abortion is the equivalent of murder. That is, they don't really believe that every fetus from the moment of conception has the same moral claims as a post-birth human being.[15]

1. Discuss answers to the following questions:
   a. What issue is Michael Kinsley addressing?
   b. Is it a factual issue or an issue related to values? Be careful with this one.
   c. What conclusion is he defending?
   d. What morally uncomfortable consequence follows from treating a fetus as a human being from the moment of conception?
   e. How would you paraphrase the central argument to make it a clear example of a *reductio* argument?
   f. Is his argument sound, or does he have a false premise?

2. Consider one of the central issues of the controversy over abortion rights: Is the fetus a person, that is, a human being with all the rights of "a post-birth human being"? If you would answer, "Absolutely yes," take a seat on the right side of the classroom. If you would answer, "Absolutely not," take a seat on the left side of the classroom. If you are not sure, find your appropriate position between the two extremes.

   Joining with three or four like-minded students, prepare several *reductio* arguments in support of your position. The arguments of those on the left side of the classroom will begin, "If a fetus is granted all the rights of a person, . . ." The arguments of those on the right side of the classroom will begin, "If a fetus is not granted all the rights of a person, . . ."

   Take turns giving your arguments. Your goal is (literally) to move students toward your own position. Anyone may shift physical positions at any time in accordance with a shift in philosophical position.

• •

9.9 MORAL DISPUTES

Consider a moral dilemma. Your professor may show a video clip from a popular movie in which actors try to sort out a moral dilemma. Or your professor may ask you to work with this dilemma, a problem that has become familiar through the work of moral psychologists:

In Europe, a woman was near death from a very bad disease, a special kind of cancer. There was one drug that the doctors thought might save her. It was a form of radium that a druggist in the same town had recently discovered. The drug was expensive to make, but the druggist was charging ten times what the drug cost him to make. He paid $200 for the radium and charged $2,000 for a small dose of the drug. The sick woman's husband, Heinz, went to everyone he knew to borrow the money, but he could get together only about $1,000, which was half of what it cost. He told the druggist that his wife was dying and asked him to sell it cheaper or to let him pay later. But the druggist said, "No, I discovered the drug and I'm going to make money from it."[16]

Individually, freewrite about Heinz's situation for several minutes. Then, in small groups, list all the different values that would be affected by a decision about the proper course of action for Heinz to take. Which of these values do you think are probably most important to Heinz? Which are most important to you? Brainstorm all the different courses of action that are open to Heinz. Which of these are unacceptable because they are inconsistent with other values? What do you think Heinz ought to do?

In a letter to Heinz, write a carefully reasoned argument to convince him that your group's advice is correct. Share it with the class.

· ·

Refuting Policy Statements

Many of the claims made in arguments about policy are claims about what should be done. Policy statements can sometimes be refuted by another sort of *reductio* refutation strategy. In this variation, the "consequences" are a prediction of what will happen in the future if the claim is accepted. That is, they are the results expected from a proposed course of action. So, this strategy can be called the *refutation by results.*

If you can show that a course of action will have undesirable results overall, you have given some reason for believing that the course of action itself is undesirable. It may not be a decisive reason since other factors may well outweigh the consequences and since listeners may disagree about the undesirability of the results. But such an argument raises considerations that should be weighed and thus can be persuasive and enlightening.

Take, for example, the claim that teenagers should be required by law to get parental consent for an abortion. The consequences of such a policy could be disastrous in many cases, so that one could argue against the claim this way:

> A parental-consent law would have the effect of forcing teenagers to confide in parents against the teenagers' own best judgment. Teenagers who have decided not to talk to their parents about their pregnancy and abortion usually have a good reason. In some cases, the parents are alcohol- or drug-dependent or abusive. In rare extreme cases, a parent is the father of the teenager's child. Forcing a teenager to confide in such parents forces teenagers to face parental anger and possibly their abuse. To avoid these consequences, the parental-consent law should not be upheld.

This argument states the results to be expected from adopting a suggested course of action, explains why these are undesirable results, and concludes that the course of action should not be followed. It is a variation of the *reductio* refutation strategy and can be represented in standard form this way:

If this suggestion is followed, then these results
   can be expected.
The results are undesirable.

Therefore, the suggestion should not be followed.

The usual name for this form of argument is the *practical syllogism* — "practical" because it has to do with what happens in practice and "syllogism" because, in form, it is a conditional syllogism.

This same form of reasoning is often encountered in law when a judge makes a decision based on the consequences of that decision. If this legal policy is adopted, these consequences can be expected; if those consequences are unacceptable, then the policy should not be adopted. Here is an example: John Moore, a pipeline worker in Alaska, went to a doctor for treatment of leukemia. Without informing Moore or seeking his consent, the doctor removed cells from Moore's spleen and used them to develop a blood protein called GM-CSF. GM-CSF, as it turned out, was a very valuable substance, with potential uses in the treatment of cancer and AIDS. Moore sued for a share of the multimillion dollar profits.

The California Supreme Court ruled against Moore, arguing that if the suit were allowed, it would "destroy the economic incentive to conduct important medical research."[17] Those consequences were so undesirable, the Court decided, that Moore should not be allowed to share the doctor's profits.

9.10 AN OPINION POLL

1. Circle the appropriate number to indicate to what extent you agree or disagree with the following claims.

		Agree				Disagree
a.	Polygamy should be legalized.	1	2	3	4	5
b.	Bicyclists should be legally required to wear helmets.	1	2	3	4	5
c.	Trial marriages—cohabitation for a period of time before a marriage decision—should be more widely practiced.	1	2	3	4	5
d.	Drug testing should be a part of the application process for all jobs.	1	2	3	4	5
e.	Random police blockades to check for drunk driving should be instituted.	1	2	3	4	5
f.	Doctors who help terminally ill patients commit suicide should be prosecuted for murder.	1	2	3	4	5
g.	Capital punishment should be outlawed.	1	2	3	4	5
h.	Condoms should be sold in dormitory school restrooms.	1	2	3	4	5
i.	Student athletes should be paid for the time they spend on intercollegiate athletics.	1	2	3	4	5
j.	State-funded universities should be open to all students, regardless of high school grade-point average.	1	2	3	4	5

2. Find the statements with which you most strongly disagree. Choose one of these, and join in a small group with others who are equally appalled by that particular idea. Your group's assignment is jointly to write a paragraph in which you argue against that idea, using a refutation by results strategy. Here's how you proceed:

    a. Brainstorm undesirable results of the suggestion you oppose. What would happen if condoms were sold in dormitories or if universities had an open-enrollment policy? From the list of probable results, choose one or two results that are most likely to give your classmates pause.

b. As a group, write a paragraph in which you (1) argue against the claim by pointing out the undesirable results it would have ("If condoms were sold in high schools, . . ."), and (2) draw your own conclusion. Write prominently on your paper the number of the claim you refuted.

3. Now, leave the paragraph on the desk, and rearrange yourselves into a different set of groups, like this: Look again at the list of claims. Find the claim you *agree* with most strongly. Then, go to the location of the refutation of that claim. Thus, you and other like-minded people will form a new group around a refutation.

4. As a group, read and consider the argument against the claim you strongly believe in. Then, explain to the class why you do or do not consider it convincing. Some points to consider: Do you think these results really would occur? Do you think those results are all that bad? Are they perhaps outweighed by good consequences? Are they perhaps outweighed by another factor entirely?

Good Uses for Refutations

The attack-and-destroy mentality so often associated with refutation should not mislead anyone into thinking that refutation is a primarily negative activity. In many different ways, refuting false claims leads to stronger arguments and more persuasive prose. Here are three different models for clear and powerful arguments, all of which rest on refutation.

Using Refutations to Clear the Way for Your Own Arguments

Refuting positions contrary to your own leaves the field clear for you to develop your own argument. A very effective essay is one that first addresses the opposite point of view, shows that it is untenable, and then presents and defends the author's own point of view. By anticipating and meeting possible objections, you give your own arguments greater moral and logical credibility: moral credibility because you fairly weigh alternative views; logical credibility because you eliminate all the competition before you even began to develop your own argument.

The medieval philosopher Thomas Aquinas made a practice of beginning his arguments by refuting the contrary conclusion. His example is often useful to follow. Here is the form he used. While it may sound complicated in the abstract, the resulting essay is clear and powerful.

a.   In the title, he stated the question to be addressed.
b.   In a first paragraph, he stated the conclusion contrary to the conclusion he intended to defend and made a brief but fair argument for it.
c.   In a second paragraph, he refuted that argument.
d.   In a third paragraph, he stated and defended his own conclusion.

Aquinas's arguments are generally too arcane to make useful examples, but here is a modern imitation of Aquinas's method:

SHOULD LAWYERS DEFEND GUILTY CRIMINALS?

In the debate over the moral responsibility of lawyers, many critics argue that lawyers should not defend people they know are guilty. For the lawyer's skill, they say, is likely to win an acquittal or lesser sentence for the guilty party. This frustrates the goal of the justice system, which is to punish people for their crimes.

However, the goal of the justice system cannot simply be to guarantee the punishment of every criminal, as these critics argue, for this could be achieved without trials by punishing everyone — guilty or innocent. The claim that lawyers should not defend guilty clients is thus based on a mistaken view of the purpose of the justice system.

The true goal of the justice system is to ensure that only those who deserve punishment are in fact punished and only as much as they deserve. In a trial, the accused has to defend himself against all the power of the government. The aid of a skilled attorney is essential to force the government to prove that the accused is in fact guilty of the crime he is charged with and to ensure that the punishment does not exceed that deserved. Thus, lawyers should defend guilty criminals.

This strategy is honorable, acknowledging that this is a subject about which reasonable people differ, sweeping nothing under the rug, clarifying the basis of disagreement, playing fair and square. And it is an effective strategy, a preemptive strike against the biggest guns of the opposition.

9.11 WRITING LIKE A MEDIEVAL MONK

Rewrite one of the following student essays, using the format that Aquinas put to such effective use. At this point, don't worry if the result is stilted, obvious, or even obnoxious; once you master the format, you can improve it to fit your own style. You may have to add or subtract information in order to make the arguments work. Make any necessary corrections, remembering that the student essays reprinted here are first drafts.

The format:

a. In the title, state the question to be addressed.

b. In a first paragraph, state the conclusion contrary to the original claim to be defended, and make a brief but fair argument for it.

c. In a second paragraph, refute that argument.

d. In a third paragraph, state and defend the original claim.

1. A very controversial issue that has baffled lawmakers and agitated many citizens is a ban on pornography. This is a highly emotional topic and many first reactions are to ban obscenity. However, we must keep in mind our constitutional rights. A ban on pornography would be illegal and against our civil rights.

    The most common and straightforward argument that would ban pornography is that it is obscene and offensive. Here, the opponent[s] state [that] they find the material is offensive. It is also likely that their friends and neighbors find it offensive. From this they conclude that if they and their neighbors find it offense then probably the whole community finds it offensive.[18]

2. With the number of scholarships and grants available to pay for this education, should the college student still work during the school year? I say yes.

    Most people feel that if a student doesn't need to work to pay for college that he shouldn't work during school. They feel that working would take valuable time away from studies. I have found from experience, however, that the extra time one has if he doesn't work is more often wasted than spent studying. [For another] thing, it teaches the student to take responsibility and pride in his work as he prepares to enter his chosen career.[19]

3. Defense spending is one of the biggest controversies in our economy today. The reason for this is that some people feel we should keep

spending on defense and others feel drastic cuts are necessary. Hundreds of thousands of jobs come from defense spending. What would we do if we cut back on spending and thousands of people lost their jobs? Also think about how weak our defense would become if we cut back. Therefore, I feel we should not cut back on defense spending, but if anything increase spending.

There are thousands of people in this country that believe the exact opposite as I. They feel there is no threat of any countries that will attack us and that the money that goes to the defense department should be cut in half. The other half should go to other organizations, such as welfare, the environment, and housing development. I strongly disagree with this view, because those departments don't protect our country and provide nearly as many jobs as the Defense Department.[20]

4. When our fathers founded the constitution, their purpose was outlined in the preamble. One line in the preamble reads: "and secure the blessings of liberty to ourselves." This reflects the idea of freedom. There has been a proposal to enact a mandatory seat belt law for all people. This would be in violation of the first amendment and should not be enacted.

My opponents will argue that seatbelts save so many lives that it's only common sense that it should be a law. It is true that wearing a seatbelt saves many lives; however, there are also the times when they don't save one's life or even cause death. It should be a person's own choice how he wants to live his life and what risks he wants to take.[21]

5. Today's professional athletes are getting paid extraordinary salaries these days. Many people are saying that their salaries are way too much. I believe that these athletes are getting paid the right amount. These athletes are role models for just about everyone who are fans. They are consistently being bugged by the media and have to always be in the spotlight of the community.

The people that are opposed to these athletes getting paid so much, are saying that they are out there just having fun and they don't deserve the big salaries they're getting. They also believe that these athletes didn't work to get where they are. These athletes have been working to make it to the professional level since they were just kids. The more they worked at being a pro the better they get and the more they get paid.[22]

Give your revised version to your professor, who may decide to choose the best rewrite of each passage, photocopy it onto an overhead transparency, and show the class during the next class period. You can then evaluate your own efforts in light of the best efforts of your peers.

· ·

Using a Series of Refutations as Evidence for a Conclusion

There is a further way in which refutations can be a valuable tool in establishing the truth of the view you wish to defend. Sometimes, the only way to learn what is true is by the process of elimination. By showing that claims contrary to yours are false, you provide evidence that your own conclusion is more likely to be true. This might be called the Sitting Duck Theory of Truth: One way to learn which of several competing claims is true is to line them up like sitting ducks. Then, try to shoot them all down. The one left standing, the one that most resisted refutation, is most likely to be true.

The detectives in Agatha Christie's novels often proceed this way: "Well, the facts are very simple," Dr. Calgary said, "Mary Durant went down to the kitchen, leaving her husband alive, at ten minutes to four—at that time there were in the house Leo Argyle and Gwenda Vaughan in the library, Hester Argyle in her bedroom on the first floor, and Kirsten Lindstrom in the kitchen. Just after four o'clock, Micky and Tina drove up. . . . Tina stopped to speak to Hester, then went on to join Miss Lindstrom and together they found Philip dead."[23] The detective's job is to narrow down this long list of suspects. Do any of these people have perfect alibis? The one who is left after this process of elimination must have been the murderer, no matter how unlikely that may seem, *if* the list of suspects was complete in the first place.

Scientific investigations often share the same logic. Given an observation to be explained, scientists try to think of all the likely explanations. Then, using the *reductio ad impossibile* refutation strategy, they try to eliminate as many explanations as possible. The process of elimination gets them closer to understanding the fact to be explained. Scientists looking for an explanation of the demise of the dinosaurs came up with a list of possible causes—an asteroid, a climatic shift, diarrhea-causing plants, competition from mammals—and looked for ways to disprove each explanation.[24]

Socrates, a great Greek philosopher and teacher, often used a similar strategy. First, he cajoled his students into suggesting possible definitions for difficult concepts such as justice or temperance. Then, Socrates refuted each in turn, until only one remained. Here is a drastically abbreviated sample. Socrates is the narrator.

Tell me, I said, what, in your opinion is temperance?

At first he hesitated, and was not very willing to answer. Then he said that he thought temperance was doing all things orderly and quietly.

Temperance is not quietness, I answered, for the life which is temperate is admitted to be good. And very seldom do the quiet actions in life appear to be better than the quick and energetic ones.

I think that you are right, Socrates.

After a moment's pause, in which he made a real manly effort to think, he said, My opinion is, Socrates, that temperance is the same as modesty.

But surely you would agree with Homer when he says, "Modesty is not good for a needy man"?

Yes, he said, I agree.

Then temperance cannot be modesty—if temperance is good, and if modesty is not good.

All that, Socrates, appears to me to be true, but I should like to know what you think about another definition of temperance, "Temperance is doing our own business." . . .[25]

To this day, many professional philosophers use this same method. You have not seen intellectual bloodletting until you have seen several philosophers in the same room trying to arrive at the truth by the process of elimination.

What all these examples offer the contemporary student of writing and reasoning is a powerful model of argumentation that proceeds by a process of elimination. It works this way:

a.   State the issue or question to be addressed.

b.   State the most plausible answers.

c.   Refute all but one of those answers.

d.   Draw the tentative conclusion that the answer remaining is most likely to be correct.

Be aware that this is a tricky strategy, however, since it is never possible to come up with a complete list of plausible answers. Even if only one of the answers you have thought of remains standing, there are always answers you have not thought of yet. So, proceed with caution. Misused, this strategy can lead you seriously astray.

• •

9.12 TROUBLESHOOTING[26]

1.   Divide into groups of three to four. Each group works with one of the following scenarios:

a.   You have agreed to babysit for a neighbor's baby. When you arrive, the parents leave in a rush. The baby is screaming so loudly you can scarcely bear it. Since the baby is too small to tell you what is making her cry, you have to figure it out yourself. The baby is crying because . . .

b. You come home late from work and run to your house through a driving rainstorm. When you switch on the front hall light, nothing happens. The hall light does not work because . . .

c. When you walk up the sidewalk toward your apartment, your usually friendly dog runs out and stands square in front of you, snarling, snapping, and drooling. His ears are flattened against his head and the hair on his back stands straight up. "Hey, Old Man," you say, "It's just me, your faithful master." But the dog does not answer. He just keeps snarling. The dog is acting strangely because . . .

d. You and your friends have just eaten an anchovy pizza. In addition, you and your boyfriend split a chocolate milkshake. Now, twenty minutes later, you have a terrible stomach ache. The stomach ache is caused by . . .

2. Brainstorm possible explanations. On the left-hand column of a piece of paper, list the five explanations that you consider most likely to be true. Notice that none of these can be tested by direct observation.

3. On the right side of the same piece of paper, for each explanation, write a statement that follows from that explanation. Each statement should be one that can be tested by direct observation.

4. Write a paragraph describing how you would proceed by testing each explanation to find out by elimination which explanation is most likely to be correct. Your paragraph will be full of if-then statements like this: "If the light won't go on because there is a general power outage (the hypothesis), then there will be no other lights on in the neighborhood (the prediction)."

• •

Using Refutations as Indirect Proofs

A good way to prove that your own claim is true is to prove that the contrary claim is false. A good way to prove that it is night is to prove that it is not day. A good way to prove that a sore throat is caused by a virus is to prove that it is not caused by a bacterium. A good way to argue that drugs should be legalized is to argue that laws against drugs are not working. This approach is called the *indirect proof.* An indirect proof is an argument that proves that a claim is true because its contrary is false. It is another way the *reductio* refutation strategies can work for you.

Suppose you want to prove the truth of a given statement A. You come at the task indirectly by trying to show that it is not the case that A is false. You do this by a *reductio ad impossibile* argument. Here are the steps. Notice that steps 2 through 4 proceed by denying the consequent in a conditional syllogism.

If you want to demonstrate that A is true:

1. Assume, for the sake of argument, that A is false.   Not A.
2. Deduce a consequence from not-A.   If not-A, then B.
3. Show that the consequence is false.   Not B. _____
4. Draw the conclusion that not-A is false.   Not (not-A).
5. Draw the conclusion that A is true.   Therefore, A.

The author of this letter used an indirect proof to show that affirmative action has given blacks no economic advantage over whites.

INCOME FIGURES SHOW NO GAINS BY BLACKS

To the Editor:

The affirmative action debate associated with Judge Clarence Thomas's nomination hearings . . . [gives the false impression that Judge Thomas's own story shows that affirmative action has given Blacks an advantage over whites. This] confuses person with population. . . . The position of African-Americans relative to whites has eroded since 1975.

Look at the percent change in the ratio of black-to-white median family income from 1975 to 1989. In 1975, the ratio was 62 percent. In 1982, it was 55 percent. For 1989 it was 56 percent, down from 57 percent in 1988. Gains and losses over those 15 years show black median family income dropped 6 percent relative to whites. In the same period, cumulative gross national product increased 19 percent.

If African-Americans are successful and have been taking opportunities from whites, their incomes relative to whites should increase, but they have not.

C.S.[27]

Here are the steps of his indirect proof.

The goal is to demonstrate that A is true: Affirmative action has given blacks no economic advantage over whites.

1. Assume that A is false.

   Affirmative action has allowed African-Americans to take economic opportunities from whites.

2. Deduce a consequence from not-A.

   The incomes of blacks relative to whites will have increased.

3. Show that the consequence is false.

   [Statistics show that] over those 15 years . . . , black median family income dropped 6 percent relative to whites.

4. Draw the conclusion that not-A is false.

   It is not the case that affirmative action has allowed African-Americans to take economic opportunities from whites.

5. Draw the conclusion that A is true.

   Affirmative action has given blacks no economic advantage over whites.

Although indirect proofs seem complicated, the lesson of indirect proofs is simple. If you are having trouble coming up with a good argument to show that some claim is true, try coming at the task from the other direction. Try to show that the denial of the claim is false. Success in the one task is the same as success in the other.

•••••••••••• Refutations Bolster the Truth ••••••••••••

Nine times out of ten, in the arts as in life, there is actually no truth to be discovered; there is only error to be exposed.[28]

There is one final good use to which refutations can be put. That is to help people distinguish between true and false beliefs and thus to reduce the power of superstition, hypocrisy, pseudoscience, and befuddlement in the world.

Those who have been raised to be open-minded and have been weaned on the principle that all people have a right to their own opinions often cringe at refutation. Refuting other people's arguments is seen as morally akin to mugging children in dark alleyways. It is thuggish and un-American, many students think, maybe even unconstitutional.

This view is understandable but mistaken. That all people have an equal right to express their opinions does not mean that all opinions are equally right. Moreover, to the extent that false beliefs harm a person, correcting false beliefs is an act of kindness. The German philosopher Arthur Schopenhauer said it this way:

> To free a man from error is to give, not to take away.

• •

9.13 TRULY GREAT MISTAKES

Each of the following selections (arguably) contains some sort of error. For the argument or claim in each selection, determine what the error is, decide what method of refutation would be most effective, and then write a refutation.

1.   From Thoreau, *Civil Disobedience:*

> *I heartily accept the motto, "That government is best which governs least;" . . . Carried out, it finally amounts to this, which also I believe — "That government is best which governs not at all."[29]*

2.   A proverb:

> What you don't know can't hurt you.

3.   From Ernie Chambers, testifying before the Kerner Commission on the nation's ghettos:

> *A policeman is an object of contempt. A policeman is a paid and hired murderer and you never find the policeman guilty of a crime no matter what violence he commits against a black person.[30]*

4.   From Benjamin Franklin's *Autobiography:*

> *[B]eing becalm'd off Block Island, our people set about catching cod, and hauled up a great many. Hitherto I had stuck to my resolution of not eating animal food, and . . . I considered the taking of every fish as a kind of unprovoked murder. . . . But I had formerly been a great lover of fish, and, when this came hot out of the frying-pan, it smelt admirably well. I balanc'd some time between principle and inclination, till I recollected that,*

when the fish were opened, I saw smaller fish taken out of their stomachs; then thought I, "If you eat one another, I don't see why we mayn't eat you." So I din'd upon cod very heartily. . . . So convenient a thing is it to be a reasonable creature, *since it enables one to find or make a reason for every thing one has a mind to do.*[31]

5. From UFOlogist John Keel's book, *Strange Mutants,*

    Has our nuclear technology unleashed . . . the beast of Revelations? Strange mutants—not for the weak hearted! [A centaur—half man, half horse—was sighted by a witness in Illinois, and] police could not prove [the witness] was lying.[32]

6. Conventional wisdom:

    Homeless people live on handouts and sleep on the street because they prefer that to working.

7. For almost fifty years, the United States and the Soviet Union possessed enough nuclear weapons to destroy one another many times over. And during that time, neither nation used nuclear weapons against the other. This proves that MAD, the strategy of Mutually Assured Destruction, has been an unqualified success. Thus, disarming at this point and dismantling the one thing that has kept the peace would truly be madness, an invitation to nuclear war.

8. From Bertrand Russell's essay, "Why I Am Not a Christian":

    You find as you look around the world that every single bit of progress in humane feeling, every improvement in the criminal law, every step towards the diminution of war, every step towards the better treatment of the coloured races or every mitigation of slavery, every moral progress that there has been in the world, has been consistently opposed by the organized Churches of the world. I say quite deliberately that the Christian religion, as organized in its churches, has been and still is the principal enemy of moral progress in the world.[33]

9. More conventional wisdom:

    The primary cause of wars is overcrowding brought on by overpopulation.

10.   Overheard:

> Of course homosexuals have no place in the Army. I've been an officer for 17 years, and never once have I heard another officer say that the Army could maintain its level of operations if we let in homosexuals.

• •

• • • • • • • • • • • • • • • • • • Notes • • • • • • • • • • • • • • • • • • •

1.   Patrick McManus, *Real Ponies Don't Go Oink!* (New York: Henry Holt and Company, 1991), p. 195.

2.   This approach comes from Robert J. Fogelin and Walter Sinnott-Armstrong, *Understanding Arguments: An Introduction to Informal Logic* (New York: Harcourt Brace Jovanovich, 1991), pp. 129–130.

3.   Mark Twain, "Was the World Made for Man?" *Letters from the Earth,* ed. Bernard DeVoto (New York: Harper and Row Publishers, 1942).

4.   A.L. Lieber and C.R. Sherin, "Homicides and the lunar cycle: Toward a theory of lunar influences on human emotional disturbance," *American Journal of Psychiatry* (129), pp. 101–106.

5.   A.L. Lieber, *The Lunar Effect: Biological Tides and Human Emotions* (Garden City, New York: Anchor Press/Doubleday, 1978).

6.   Otto von Bismarck, Speech in the Reichstag, Feb. 6, 1888.

7.   Pico Iyer, "Excusez moi! Speakez-vous Franglais?" *Time* (July 2, 1990), p. 70.

8.   All this information comes from two sources: Bruce Felton and Mark Fowler, *Felton and Fowler's Best, Worst, and Most Unusual* (New York: Thomas Y. Crowell Co., 1975) and *Guinness Book of World Records,* ed. Donald McFarlan (New York: Sterling, 1989).

> Answers to "Counterexamples": 1. b: The greatest Grandmaster chess player of all time is Bobby Fischer, an American. 2. c: John Chase is the only man to have escaped from Alcatraz Island; he was captured as soon as he reached the mainland. 3. g: The platypus is an Australian mammal that lays eggs. 4. h: Jesus de Frutos of Segovia, Spain, claims that he never sleeps at all. 5. e: Jan Paderewski, the Prime Minister of Poland, was the highest-paid classical concert pianist in history, accumulating a fortune of $5 million. 6. f: Arthur D. Little boiled sows' ears into a milky fluid, reduced the juice to a long strand of synthetic silk, and wove the thread into a purse that is on display in the Smithsonian Institute. 7. a: Although many people believed the human body could not withstand the forces of breaking the sound barrier, supersonic flight was achieved in 1949 by Chuck Yeager. 8. d: The present Pope, the former Karol Wojtyla of Wadowice, Poland, became the first non-Italian pope since 1522. 9. j: Mark Twain was mistaken; the stickleback fish flush pink when they are courting. 10. i: James Jesse Strang was crowned king of Zion, a Mormon colony near Lake Michigan.

9.   Excerpt from AN AMERICAN CHILDHOOD by Annie Dillard. Copyright © 1987 by Annie Dillard. Reprinted by permission of HarperCollins Publishers, Inc.

10. *Furman* v. *Georgia,* 408 U.S. 238 (1972).

11. John Snow, "On the Mode of Communication of Cholera," *Snow on Cholera* (New York: The Commonwealth Fund, 1936), p. 122; quoted in Martin Goldstein and Inge F. Goldstein, *How We Know: An Exploration of the Scientific Process* (New York: Plenum Press, 1979), p. 49.

12. Information comes from "Soviet Airhead Defense," *Newsweek* (July 6, 1992), p. 48.

13. Dorothy E. Roberts, "Mother as Martyr," *Essence* (May 1991), p. 140. Copyright © 1991, Dorothy E. Roberts. Used by permission.

14. See David J. Garrow, *Bearing the Cross* (New York: William Morrow and Co., 1986), pp. 60–61.

15. Michael Kinsley, "Life Terms," *The New Republic* (July 15 and 22, 1991), p. 4. Copyright © 1991, The New Republic. Used by permission.

16. Lawrence Kohlberg, *The Philosophy of Moral Development: Moral Stages and the Idea of Justice* (San Francisco: Harper and Row Publishers, 1981), p. 12. Copyright © 1981, HarperCollins Publishers. Used by permission.

17. "Organ donor loses share of profits," *Corvallis Gazette-Times* (July 10, 1990), p. B7.

18. Trent Began, PHL 101, Oregon State University, Spring 1990. Used with permission.

19. Paula Chambers, "A Working Education?" PHL 101, Oregon State University, Spring 1990. Used with permission.

20. Gerald Gereb, "Defense Spending," PHL 101, Oregon State University, Spring 1990. Used with permission.

21. Christi Groleau, "Final Paper," PHL 101, Oregon State University, Spring 1990. Used with permission.

22. Gabriel Godwin, "The Salaries of Professional Athletes," PHL 101, Oregon State University, Spring 1990. Used with permission.

23. Agatha Christie, *Ordeal by Innocence* (New York: Dodd, Mead and Co., 1959), p. 233.

24. For more information on the way in which science proceeds by refutation, see Karl R. Popper, "Science: Conjectures and Refutations," *Conjectures and Refutations* (New York: Harper and Row, 1968), Chap. 1 and John R. Platt, "Strong Inference," *Science* (October 16, 1964), pp. 347–352.

25. Plato, "Charmides," *Plato: The Collected Dialogues,* eds. Edith Hamilton and Huntington Cairns (Princeton, N.J.: Princeton University Press, 1969), pp. 104–107 (abbreviated).

26. Thanks to Dr. Jon Dorbolo, an especially creative friend and colleague, who created the initial version of this exercise.

27. Courtland Smith, "Letter to the Editor," *The Oregonian* (September 26, 1991), p. C6. Copyright © 1991, by Courtland Smith. Reprinted with permission.

28. H.L. Mencken, *Prejudices, Third Series,* (New York: Knopf, 1921–1927), Chapter 3.

29. Henry David Thoreau, "Civil Disobedience," in *Walden, Civil Disobedience,* ed. Sherman Paul (Boston: Houghton Mifflin Co., 1960), p. 235.

30. Quoted in William Katz, *Eyewitness: The Negro in American History* (New York: Pitman Publishing Co., 1974), p. 539.

31. *Benjamin Franklin: The Autobiography with Sayings of Poor Richard, Hoaxes, Bagatelles, Essays and Letters,* ed. Carl van Doren (New York: Pocket Books, Inc., 1940), pp. 41–42.

32. Quoted in Robert Sheaffer, "Psychic Vibrations," *The Skeptical Inquirer* (Fall 1984), p. 19.

33. Bertrand Russell, "Why I Am Not a Christian," *The Basic Writings of Bertrand Russell, 1903–1959,* eds. Robert Egner and Lester Denonn (New York: Simon and Schuster, 1961), p. 595.

Glossary/Index

345

Appeal to fear: An argument in which a writer arouses fear in the readers in order to persuade them to accept a conclusion.   *243*

Appeal to ignorance: An argument in which some kind of ignorance — the absence of information or the lack of an explanation — is cited as evidence for a claim.   *266*

Appeal to pity: An argument in which the writer arouses sympathy in the readers in order to persuade them to accept a conclusion.   *243*

Appeal to pride: An argument in which the writer arouses pride in the readers in order to persuade them to accept a conclusion.   *244*

Argument: A claim put forward and supported by reasons.   *6*

Argument by analogy: An argument based on the similarity between two things.   *154, 161*

Argument summary: Concise statement of the conclusion and the main supporting points in an argumentative passage.   *35*

Argument surrogate: A form of discourse having the purpose of influencing a person's beliefs or actions but distinguished from an argument by the fact that no reasons are given.   *14*

Audience: The readers of an argument who must be considered during the process of writing.   *70*

Bandwagon appeal: An argument that leads readers to accept a claim or buy a product by promising membership in an exclusive group or by threatening exclusion; an argument that supports its conclusion by claiming that everyone else believes it.   *244*

Brainstorming: A method of generating ideas by spontaneously listing all the ideas one has on a subject or problem.   *65*

Burden of proof: The obligation to make a case for a claim.   *265*

Categorical statement: A claim about the relationship between two categories; "All A is B," or "No A is B."   *111, 132*

Categorical syllogism: A deductive argument made up of three categorical statements.   *133*

Causal argument: A form of hypothetical reasoning in which evidence is used in support of causal claims.   *194*

Causal claim: The claim that one event causes another.   *218*

Causal generalization: A generalization about the causal connection between two events.   *198, 218*

Chain argument: A basic pattern of argumentation in which the conclusion is based on a reason, which is itself based on another reason, which is itself supported by further evidence.   *42*

Denying the consequent: A type of conditional syllogism in which the first premise is a conditional statement and the second premise is the simple statement that the consequent of the conditional statement is false. From this, it follows that the antecedent cannot be true.   *123, 320*

> If A, then B.
> Not B.
> Therefore, not A.

Diagram: A visual representation of the inferences in an argument, using arrows to represent inferences and numbers to represent statements.   *38*

Dialogue writing: A method of generating reasons for and against a claim by creating a dialogue on paper between imaginary characters with opposing opinions.   *83*

Dilemma: A deductive argument form in which the conclusion is the disjunction between the consequents of the two conditional statements in the premises.   *127*

> If A, then B, and if C, then D.
> A or C.
> Therefore B or D.

Disjunctive statement: An either-or statement.   *110, 113*

Disjunctive syllogism: A valid three-statement argument with a disjunctive statement as the first premise.   *110, 113*

> A or B.
> Not A.
> Therefore B.

Doctrine of precedent: In Anglo-American law, the doctrine requiring that a legal case be decided in the same way that similar cases have been decided in the past.   *166*

Doublespeak: Language using inoffensive words to hide the true emotive content of the concepts.   *288*

Dyslogistic words: Words that convey a negative feeling.   *287*

Emotive function: The power that language has to arouse emotions.   *286*

Enthymeme: An argument in which a statement is understood but not stated.   *51*

Ethos: The credibility of the person making the argument.   *58, 241*

Eulogistic words: Words that convey a positive feeling.   *286*

Euphemisms: Inoffensive words that substitute for words that are indelicate or painful.   *288*

Exclusive or: The word *or* when used to indicate that only one of two options can be true.   *116*

Explanation: A statement with the purpose of explaining a claim to an audience that already believes the claim is true.   *12*

External credibility: A writer's prestige or institutional credentials.   *260*

Fallacious: Misleading because based on a faulty argument.   *173*

Fallacy: An argument that seems to provide support for a claim but does not.   *238*

Fallacy of affirming the consequent: The mistake that occurs in forming a conditional syllogism when one assumes that because the consequent is true, the antecedent must also be true.   *126*

Fallacy of ambiguity: The fallacy that occurs when words are used in imprecise or shifting ways to mislead the audience.   *239, 280*

Fallacy of biased sample: An error in generalization that occurs when the sample is not randomly selected.   *204*

Fallacy of bifurcation: A misleading argument that falsely claims that one of two options must be true.   *115*

Fallacy of denying the antecedent: The mistake that occurs in forming a conditional syllogism when one assumes that because the antecedent of a conditional statement is false, the consequent must also be false.   *125*

Fallacy of emotional appeal: When the writer leads the reader to accept or reject a claim by manipulating the reader's emotions rather than by appealing to good reasons.   *242*

Fallacy of emotive language: When the emotive content of words is used surreptitiously to establish a claim without the use of evidence.   *287*

Fallacy of equivocation: An argument that is misleading because a word shifts meaning in an argument between the premises and conclusion.   *282*

Fallacy of presumption: When a conclusion is presumed to be true without evidence.   *275, 286*

Fallacy of relevance: Arguments in which the reasons offered in support of the conclusion are not relevant to the conclusion.   *239*

False analogy: A fallacious argument based on a false claim of a relevant similarity between two things.   *173*

False dichotomy: A false claim that one and only one of two alternatives must be true.   *115*

Flexibility: A tentativeness of belief that allows people to see the issue from another point of view and to change their minds when evidence suggests that they are mistaken. *20*

Freewriting: A method of generating ideas by writing without stopping for a given length of time. *65*

Going between the horns of the dilemma: Refuting a dilemma by pointing out an unrecognized alternative. *131*

Group brainstorming: An idea-generating or problem-solving process whereby all the members of a group spontaneously come up with and record their ideas together. *65*

Hasty generalization: A generalization that is based on a sample that is too small. *204*

Horizontal argument: An argument structure in which at least two independent reasons or lines of argument support a conclusion. *42*

Hypothesis: A general principle or explanation assumed to be true for the purpose of testing its truth against facts that may be observed. *210*

Hypothetical reasoning: A pattern of inductive reasoning in which the results of experimental tests provide evidence for and against explanations and general rules. *194, 206*

Hypothetical statement: A complex statement with the form "If A, then B"; a conditional statement. *118*

Hypothetical syllogism: A deductive argument composed of three hypothetical statements. *120*

> If A, then B.
> If B, then C.
> _____
> Therefore, if A, then C.

Impartiality: The ability to gather and weigh information without bias or blindness imposed by one's own hopes and fears. *20*

Implied analogy: When a word or phrase that applies to one thing is used in reference to another to suggest a likeness between them. *155*

Inclusive or: The word *or* used to claim that two options can be true at the same time. *116*

Indirect proof: Proof that a claim is true because its contrary claim is false. *337*

Indoctrination: Persuading without giving reasons; propagandizing. *4*

Inductive argument: A pattern of reasoning in which the premises provide persuasive (but not conclusive) support for the conclusion.   *193*

Inductive generalization: A pattern of inductive reasoning in which a conclusion about all the members of a given set is based on information about some of the members of that set.   *194, 196*

Inference: The logical relationship between the evidence and the claim in an argument.   *7*

Intellectual honesty: The willingness to change conclusions that conflict with the evidence.   *20*

Invalid: Said of deductive arguments, logically incorrect, so that the conclusion may be false even when the premises are true.   *107*

Issue: The particular controversial point addressed in an argument.   *29, 74, 76*

Listing: A way of generating ideas for arguments by listing possible reasons for and against a claim.   *83*

Loaded question: A question phrased in such a way that the respondent must accept a hidden assumption for which no reasons are given; also called *complex question.*   *293*

Logical: Following correct principles of reasoning; appealing to relevant reasons to support claims.   *18*

Logical analogue: An argument that has the same form as another.   *313*

Logical analysis: The process of understanding and evaluating an argument by identifying its parts.   *28*

Logos: Reasons or evidence for a claim.   *58, 241*

Looping: A variation on freewriting that alternates writing and analysis.   *66*

Metaphor: A figure of speech in which a term is applied to something to which it is not literally applicable in order to suggest a resemblance.   *154*

Mixed argument: Arguments that combine horizontal and vertical argument structures.   *43*

Necessary condition: A statement that must be true in order that another statement may be true.   *119, 123*

Open-mindedness: The ability to see and accept information that may conflict with beliefs already held; intellectual inquisitiveness.   *20*

Parable: An elaborate form of explanatory analogy consisting of a vivid story that helps the audience understand an abstract idea.   *159*

Resolution: In debating, a claim.   *7*

Revise: To change or improve.   *66*

Role-playing: A way of generating reasons for and against a claim by imagining situations in which it is necessary to respond extemporaneously from the point of view of a particular person.   *83*

Sample: The observed cases, used as evidence supporting an inductive generalization.   *198*

Seizing the bull by the horns: Refuting a dilemma by demonstrating that the purported consequent does not really follow from an alternative.   *131*

Shifting the burden of proof: The sophistry that states a claim and then assumes that the claim will be taken as true unless the opponent can prove it false.   *265*

Signpost: A word that has the function of identifying a statement as a premise or conclusion; *therefore* and *since* are examples.   *32, 88*

Simile: A figure of speech explicitly comparing one thing to another.   *154*

Simple dilemma: A dilemma presenting two alternatives, both of which lead to the same result.   *128*

> If A, then B, and if C, then B.
> A or C.
> _____
> Therefore, B.

Simple statement: A statement that does not contain another statement.   *111*

Slanting: The subtle use of emotive language, doublespeak, and selected facts to give a positive or negative impression of events.   *290*

Sophistry: A deceptive move in argumentation.   *239, 262*

Sound argument: A deductive argument that is valid in form and that has true premises.   *107*

Standard form: A method for displaying the logical structure of an argument by stacking the premises above a horizontal line and putting the conclusion below.   *47, 105*

Statement of fact: A statement about what is true, sometimes used as evidence for a claim.   *82*

Statement of value: A statement about what is desirable or undesirable, sometimes used as a reason to believe a claim.   *82*

Stereotype: A standardized image, often arrived at by a hasty generalization.   *204*

Stratified sample: A sample in which members of subpopulations are proportionately represented.   *200*

Straw argument: An argument that intentionally misinterprets an opponent's argument and replaces it with a weaker one.   *262*

Sufficient condition: A statement that, if true, establishes the truth of another statement.   *119*

Syllogism: A valid deductive argument with two premises and a conclusion.   *110*

Thesis statement: In essays or position papers, the claim to be defended.   *7*

Topic: A noun or noun phrase that defines a content area to be addressed.   *30, 74*

Universal categorical statement: A categorical statement that refers to all the members of a set.   *132*

Universal generalization: A general statement that is intended to apply universally to all members of a given group.   *197, 317*

Valid: In deductive logic, said of an argument that is formally perfect, such that the conclusion must be true if the premises are true.   *107*

Value judgment: A belief about something's relative importance, desirability, worth.   *320*

Vertical argument: An argument in which a conclusion is supported by a premise, which is, in turn, supported by a premise.   *42*

Weight of the evidence: The relative strength of supporting arguments.   *79*